MOON

ICELAND

JENNA GOTTLIEB

ICELAND
Denmark Strait
GREENLAND SEA
Bolungarvík
Ísafjörður
Ísafjarðardjúp
Drangajökull
Húnaflói
Skagafjörður
Arnarfjörður
Westfjords
Patreksfjörður
Breiðavík
Skagaströnd
Drangsnes
Blönduós
Sauðárkrókur
Hóp
Varmahlíð
Reykhólar
Hvammstangi
Breiðafjörður
Laugarbakki
Stykkishólmur
Búðardalur
Blöndulón
Hellissandur
Ólafsvík
Grundarfjörður
Snæfellsnes Peninsula
Snæfellsjökull National Park
Hveravellir Nature Reserve
Bifröst
Reykholt
Langjökull
Borgarnes
Hvanneyri
Faxaflói
Akranes
Þingvellir National Park
Laugarvatn
REYKJAVÍK
Þingvallavatn
Mosfellsbær
Reykholt
Sandgerði
Hafnarfjörður
Flúðir
Reykjanesbær
Reykjanes Peninsula
Njarðvík
Hveragerði
Friðland að Fjallabaki
Reykjanesfólkvangur
Selfoss
Grindavík
Stokkseyri
Hella
Hvolsvöllur
NORTH ATLANTIC OCEAN
Myrdalsjökull
Vestmannaeyjar
Skógar
Heimaey

NORWEGIAN SEA
Grímsey
Raufarhöfn
Þistilfjörður
Kópasker
85
Bakkafjörður
Bakkaflói
Siglufjörður
Skjálfandi
Ólafsfjörður
Húsavík
Dalvík
Grenivík
Eyjafjörður
864
Jökulsárgljúfur
Vopnafjörður
87
Vopnafjörður
82
North Iceland
Laugar
917
Bakkagerði
Akureyri
Reykjahlíð
85
Eastfjords
Mývatn
1
94
Seyðisfjörður
Egilsstaðir
93
F26
Neskaupstaður
Hallormsstaður
96
Eskifjörður
The Highlands
Reyðarfjörður
Vatnajökull
Fáskrúðsfjörður
Hálslón
Hofsjökull
National
Djúpivogur
Park
Kvíslavatn
F26
Vatnajökull
Þórisvatn
Höfn
Langisjór
Öraefajökull
0
25 mi
0
25 km
Kirkjubæjarklaustur
204
© MOON.COM

Contents

DISCOVER

Iceland

Scale soaring mountaintops. Dive into some of the clearest water in the world. Explore crystalline ice caves and mineral-rich lava tubes. Hike the rim of a remote volcano that rises from an arctic desert. Witness a rainbow materialize over a thundering waterfall. Iceland is a place not just to see, but to experience.

Iceland is revered for its breathtaking landscapes, unrivaled trekking, and arctic wildlife. Three national parks and a dozen smaller reserves protect these resources. Vatnajökull National Park makes up 13 percent of the country and contains the largest glacier in the world outside the poles. Geothermal pools, like the famous milky waters of the Blue Lagoon and Mývatn Nature Baths, bubble up from beneath the earth and provide a place to soak away your worries.

If city life is more your speed, Reykjavík is waiting for you. Stroll the capital's streets and explore the galleries, coffeehouses, intimate concert venues, and record shops—you can't help but feel the city's creative energy. Handcrafted local beers replace specialty coffees as the drink of choice come evening time, when low-key daytime hangouts morph into pulsing parties that fuel a thriving nightlife scene.

Clockwise from top left: annual Viking Festival in Hafnarfjörður; lupine; Dettifoss; puffins; fireworks over Akranes; road on the Snæfellsnes Peninsula.

In summer, the days seem endless—the sun shines for nearly 24 hours around the solstice—the ideal time to embark on an epic drive around the Ring Road. And winter tourism is increasing, with visitors lured by the chance to see the northern lights, yet another of Iceland's spectacular natural wonders. Watching the lights flicker in the sky, changing colors, disappearing and reappearing stronger and brighter, makes braving the wind and cold worth it.

For scenery and adventure, Iceland is unmatched.

Clockwise from top left: Siglufjörður; Jökulsárlón Glacier Lagoon; Húsavíkurkirkja; Icelandic horses.

9 TOP EXPERIENCES

1 Feeling the spray from wondrous waterfalls like **Goðafoss** (page 211) and **Dettifoss** (page 225).

2 Soaking in one of Iceland's **pools and hot springs,** from the milky blue waters of the Blue Lagoon to less famous pools frequented by locals (page 25).

3 Exploring mountains, volcanoes, lava fields, and valleys on well-maintained **hiking trails,** from the famous four-day **Laugavegurinn Trail** (page 116) to spectacular **day hikes** around the island (page 27).

4 Getting a glimpse of Iceland's rich **wildlife,** from reindeer and puffins to seals and whales (page 28).

<<<

5 Hitting the road on a **scenic drive** to enjoy the country's nature and culture, whether you're touring the entire **Ring Road** (page 276) or the famous **Golden Circle** (page 96).

>>>

6 Strolling through artsy, vibrant **Akureyri,** unofficial capital of the north (page 200).

<<<

^
^
^

7 Getting up close to one of Iceland's mighty glaciers, whether you're trekking the lunar landscape of **Snæfellsjökull** (page 150) or sailing along the gorgeous glacier lagoon **Jökulsárlón** (page 260).

8 Watching the green and white lights of the **northern lights** dance and flicker in the sky (page 19).

9 Immersing yourself in **Reykjavík's legendary nightlife,** from craft beer joints to cool cocktail bars to live music venues (page 65).

Planning Your Trip

Where to Go

Reykjavík

Home to two-thirds of Iceland's population, the **capital city** is the **cultural and social hub** of the country, with an energy distinct from the rest of the island. Here you'll find chic hotels, eclectic restaurants, and top-notch shopping on the main street, **Laugavegur**—not to mention a thriving **art scene** and vibrant **nightlife.** Pay a visit to the distinctive church **Hallgrímskirkja,** the placid pond **Tjörnin** near city hall, and, for a taste of history, the **National Museum of Iceland.** A trip to the **old harbor** is also a must—take in a concert at the striking glass hall **Harpa,** or head out on a **whale-watching** tour.

Reykjanes Peninsula and the South

Outside of Reykjavík, the **Reykjanes Peninsula** and the natural sights in South Iceland get the most traffic on the island. The Reykjanes Peninsula is home to charming fishing villages, **Keflavík** airport, and the **Blue Lagoon,** where you can take a healing dip in the heated water. The **Golden Circle** route encompasses three key sights: the powerful waterfall **Gullfoss,** bubbling geothermal phenomenon **Geysir,** and history-steeped national park **Þingvellir.** Some of the best **hiking** trails in the country are in the south. A favorite is the **Laugavegurinn Trail,** where you'll see towering mountains, vast glaciers, hot springs, roaring rivers, and stunning waterfalls.

view from Hallgrímskirkja

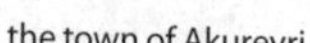

the town of Akureyri

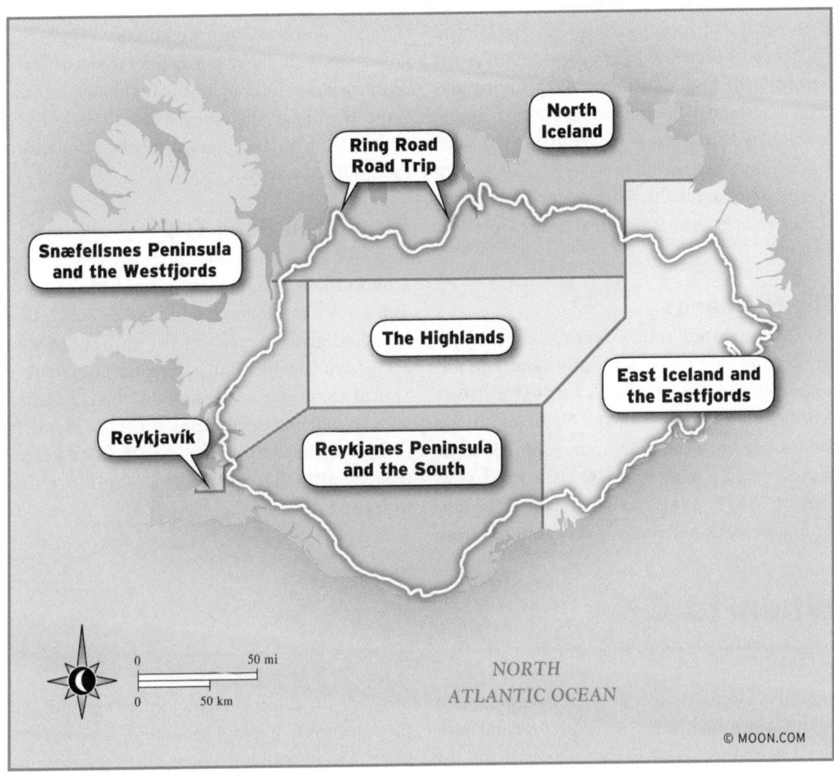

Snæfellsnes Peninsula and the Westfjords

Called "Iceland in miniature" by locals, the **Snæfellsnes Peninsula** has a bit of everything: quaint fishing towns, spectacular mountains, hiking, whale-watching, and even a glacier you can walk on—**Snæfellsjökull,** world famous as the starting point of Jules Verne's *Journey to the Center of the Earth.* Endless coastlines, offbeat museums, and beautiful rocky landscapes await in the **Westfjords.** For outstanding bird-watching, visit the **Látrabjarg cliffs** in summer to check out thousands of nesting puffins.

North Iceland

Iceland's "second city," low-key **Akureyri** offers beautiful botanical gardens, first-rate hotels and restaurants, and a booming art scene. It's the perfect place to base yourself for a visit to the north. The **Mývatn region** lures visitors with its birdlife-rich lake, gorgeous hiking trails, vast lava fields, enormous craters, soaring mountains, and soothing **Mývatn Nature Baths. Jökulsárgljúfur,** part of **Vatnajökull National Park,** offers a number of treasures, including the gigantic canyon **Ásbyrgi** and **Dettifoss,** the largest waterfall in Iceland. **Húsavík** has some of the best **whale-watching** opportunities on the island, with a chance to see as many as 12 species of whales.

East Iceland and the Eastfjords

Looking for the "ice" in Iceland? Head to East Iceland, where the giant white **Vatnajökull glacier** will take your breath away. Drive or hike close to the glacier's edge in **Skaftafell,** home to snowcapped mountains, green fields, and black-sand beaches. Hikers can scale **Mount Snæfell,** the highest mountain (excluding glaciers) in Iceland, with spectacular views spanning the highlands to the sea. Weave through the unspoiled **Eastfjords,** where each fjord has its own charm. The east is the most remote part of the island, and summer is the ideal time to tour this region.

The Highlands

The uninhabited interior draws adventure-seekers and avid hikers with its unique and unforgiving landscape. Iceland's **largest glaciers** (Vatnajökull, Langjökull, and Hofskjökull) are the backdrop to the highlands, with dramatic scenery cut by wind and ice. Hike the rim of **Mount Askja,** a volcano with a lake-filled crater and sensational views. Askja emerges from the eerie, desolate **Ódáðahraun lava field,** the largest desert in Europe. You have to stay abreast of the weather forecast in the highlands—it can snow any day of the year here, and self-guided trips to the highlands should only be planned for the summer months.

Ring Road Road Trip

Iceland's Ring Road **(Route 1)** is a scenic loop around the island, revealing some of the most well-known attractions in Iceland as well as unexpected gems. Traveling the entirety of this 1,332-kilometer (828-mi) paved route in your own **rental car** is one of the best and most popular ways to tour the inhabited parts of the island. It is recommended to have at least **10 full days** on the road to do the trip justice, as there is so much to see and do along the way.

When to Go

Iceland is a **year-round destination,** but when to visit depends on what you want to do and what you'd like to see. For instance, winter is not the time to go hiking, but the lure of lower airfare and hotel prices, as well as the northern lights, draws many people over this season.

While the summer offers the best weather and the freedom to explore the island, it comes at a price. Airfare and hotel rates are highest during these months, and there is a rush of tourists.

Summer (June-August)

The summer is the **high season** and offers the **best weather** to explore all of Iceland's **outdoor activities** such as hiking, diving, whale-watching, glacier-walking, bird-watching, and swimming. Average temperatures in the summer range between 10-25°C (50-76°F). The landscape is green and lush and the days long. The **midnight sun** has to be seen to be believed. June-August is also the best time to embark on a **Ring Road trip,** as the roads are the best this time of year, and the weather is not likely to cause many problems. That said, it's important to closely monitor the weather forecast for wind or heavy rain.

Autumn (September)

Autumn is quite short in Iceland, and attracts travelers who want to **avoid the tourist crush** of summer but still explore some of the countryside and enjoy outdoor activities. There remains plenty of daylight, and **hiking** is viable in the fall, but you must monitor the weather because storms can pop up. It's also possible to see **northern lights** this time of year; check the forecast at www.vedur.is.

September is perfect for a long weekend in **Reykjavík.** This time of year is also known for local festivals in the capital city, such as the Reykjavík International Film Festival. Average temperatures in September and October range between 2-10°C (36-50°F). The winds can make it feel colder.

Chasing the Northern Lights

the northern lights

The biggest winter attraction in Iceland is the northern lights, or the aurora. People travel from around the world to catch a glimpse of the green, white, blue, and red lights dancing in the night sky. The phenomenon is caused by solar winds, which push electrically charged particles to collide with molecules of atmospheric gases, causing an emission of bright light. Seeing the lights comes down to a mix of timing, location, solar conditions, and some luck.

TIPS FOR SEEING THE AURORA

- **Pick the right month:** Timing is essential, since the northern lights are visible from mid-September to mid-March.
- **Monitor the forecast:** To see northern lights, you'll need clear skies and solar activity. Before you head out on a northern lights hunt, check the aurora forecast at **www.vedur.is.**
- **Dress appropriately:** It can get cold out there, so be prepared. Dress in warm layers and carry a hat, scarf, and gloves.
- **Find darkness:** For optimum visibility, get away from bright city or town lights. Tours take you out of town, or if you are self-driving, find a dark place, safely out of the road. Do not park next to the road with your headlights off; find a suitable location.
- **Have a good dose of patience:** It's not like turning a switch. It can take time for the lights to appear even if the forecast is favorable. You may have to wait several hours.
- **Take a tour:** Northern lights tours are offered by companies like **Reykjavík Excursions** (www.re.is).

BEST SPOTS TO SEE IT

Though all you really have to do to see the northern lights when they're on is venture outside a city area and look up, here are some particularly excellent places to see the lights in all their splendor:

- **Grótta Lighthouse:** Grótta is probably the best spot in Reykjavík to catch the lights (page 74).
- **Þingvellir National Park:** The park is lovely in all seasons and is a favorite for local photographers capturing the aurora (page 96).
- **Akranes Lighthouse:** The lighthouse is far from the town lights and is perfect on a dark night (page 137).

Winter (October-April)

Iceland's **low season,** winter, isn't a bad time to visit if you're willing to go with the flow, as the weather can be unpredictable at best and punishing at worst. Pluses are that airfare and hotel prices are the lowest of the year, you won't battle any crowds, and this is the best time to catch a glimpse of the **northern lights.** Popular outdoor activities during the winter include **riding snowmobiles and horses** and **skiing** in the

Visiting Iceland on a Budget

Pulling off a budget trip to Iceland is difficult; the country routinely ranks as the most expensive destination in Europe. However, there are some ways to save money:

- Consider staying in **hostels, apartments,** or **guesthouses** with shared facilities instead of hotels.
- Shop in local **grocery stores** and self-cater instead of dining out every day.
- Plan a **camping trip** in the summer and stay in budget-friendly designated campsites.
- Splurge on a couple of activities like a glacier walk or snorkeling tour, but be sure to take advantage of the **free attractions.**
- Skip the Blue Lagoon and swim like a local in **heated public pools** and **hot tubs.**
- Pack a **reusable water bottle** and never pay for water: Iceland's water is some of the cleanest and best tasting on earth.

north. Temperatures tend to hover around freezing with averages of -3-3°C (26-38°F). The winds make it feel colder.

The downside to winter travel is, unsurprisingly, the **changeable, challenging weather.** You will likely encounter wind, rain, snow, sleet, and everything in between. Travel to the countryside is limited in the winter as **many roads are closed,** and even open roads can have tough conditions. Also, **many establishments outside Reykjavík close** for the winter or have limited hours.

Spring (May)

April and May fall in between the low winter season and high summer season and are good options for **budget-conscious** travelers. You have a crack at **decent weather** without paying the higher summertime prices. That said, the weather is unpredictable, so a visit in April can feel like winter—it's **hit or miss.** But if the weather is pleasant enough, you can enjoy hikes, horse riding, whale-watching, and all that Reykjavík has to offer. The temperatures for April and May range between 0-8°C (32-47°F).

Before You Go

Passports and Visas

Visitors to Iceland must arrive with a valid **passport** that expires no sooner than three months after your intended departure date. Travelers from the **United States, Canada, Australia, New Zealand, South Africa**, the **United Kingdom,** and **Ireland** do not need a visa for trips shorter than 90 days. However, if you would like to stay longer, you need to procure a permit from the **Directorate of Immigration** (www.utl.is), which is very difficult to get. There are different, more lenient rules for residents of European Union and European Economic Area countries.

Reservations

As Iceland is a sparsely populated island with limited accommodations, it's strongly recommended you **book accommodations in advance.** For summer trips, plan to book hotels and guesthouses at least six months in advance to get the best choices at the most favorable prices. For the rest of the year, plan to book rooms at least three months in advance. **Campervans** and

motorhomes, which should only be rented during the summer months for safety reasons, should be booked far in advance as well, at least five months before your arrival date.

The **Blue Lagoon** must be booked in advance through its website, www.bluelagoon.is. Be sure to reserve as soon as possible because time slots frequently sell out, even in the winter. If you're considering any **private or small-group tours,** be sure to book those in advance. It's also recommended to make **dinner reservations during the Christmas season** because there are limited options, and it's necessary to book **New Year's Eve dinner reservations** far in advance (think July/August).

Transportation

GETTING THERE

Flying into Iceland is a pretty seamless experience. The country's main carrier, **Icelandair** (www.icelandair.com), serves more than 30 destinations in the United States, Canada, and Europe. Iceland's accessibility has been the island's main selling point as a travel destination, as the country is just over five hours from New York City and about three hours from London. There are no direct flights from South Africa, Australia, or New Zealand, so expect to connect to Iceland via continental Europe.

For those traveling from mainland Europe, a **ferry** can be a great option, especially if you want to bring a car, camper, or bicycle for the trip. **Smyril Line** (www.smyril-line.fo) runs a ferry to Iceland from Denmark and the Faroe Islands. The ferry drops you off in Seyðisfjörður in East Iceland, which is convenient if you're traveling with a car and want to spend time in the countryside. If you want to stay in the south, where Reykjavík and the Golden Circle attractions are, a ferry may not be the best option.

GETTING AROUND

Having access to a **car** gives you the ultimate freedom in seeing the island on your own schedule (but with insurance, expect to pay dearly). If you plan to stay in Reykjavík for most of your trip, or want to do short day trips in the southern or western parts of the country, it's not necessary to rent a car as you can book **tours.** Public transportation is not ideal for tourists as the buses in the countryside connect towns and villages, and do not travel to tourist attractions.

The Best of Iceland

Even with just a week, it's possible to see many of Iceland's highlights. Keep your home base in Reykjavík, visiting the Golden Circle and South Coast before traveling west to the Snæfellsnes Peninsula. This itinerary is best suited for the summer months.

Days 1-2: Reykjavík

After landing at **Keflavík International Airport,** either pick up your rental car or take the Flybus into Reykjavík. Check into your accommodation and explore the town, including the landmark church **Hallgrímskirkja,** the **Reykjavík Art Museum,** and the **National Gallery of Iceland.** Have a delicious dinner at **Fish Market,** followed by taking in some of the city's **nightlife** at a concert at Harpa concert hall or by having a couple of drinks at Kex Hostel, a favorite among locals and tourists alike.

Spend the next morning wandering Reykjavík's numerous **cafés, galleries,** and **shops.** You can pick up gifts and quality clothing at top-notch stores like 66 North and Farmers Market and take a coffee break at Mokka or Café Babalu. In the afternoon, board a boat in Reykjavík's harbor for a **whale-watching tour,** where you will have the chance to spot numerous whale species as well as dolphins and seabirds.

Day 3: The Golden Circle

From Reykjavík, get in your rental car and kick off your drive of the famous **Golden Circle** route. Make your first stop **Þingvellir National Park,** an ideal introduction to the Icelandic countryside due to its historical and geological significance. Next, drive to the Haukadalur geothermal area for a look at **Geysir,** the original geyser, and its spouting neighbor **Strokkur.** Have lunch at the **Geysir Center** before continuing to **Gullfoss,** the golden waterfall. Next, drive to the small village of **Fluðir** and take a dip in the **Secret Lagoon,** a smaller and more intimate

the interior of Harpa concert hall

Þingvellir National Park

Winter Wonders

Sure, Iceland's winter weather can be challenging. But you'll be rewarded with truly unique experiences that make it all worthwhile.

- **Hunt for northern lights:** The main season to see northern lights is mid-September to mid-March. Book a guided tour or venture out on your own (page 19).
- **Soak in the Blue Lagoon:** This is the most popular tourist attraction in Iceland for a reason, and it is just as special in the winter. It's soothing and beautiful to soak during light snowfalls or while watching northern lights dance above on clear nights (page 92).
- **Tour the Golden Circle:** Iceland's number one tour is available year-round. Book a bus tour or drive the attraction-heavy route yourself. The frozen **Gullfoss** falls and rocky landscape are gorgeous when mantled in winter white (page 96).
- **Take a glacier walk:** Tour operators offer the unique opportunity to hike on a glacier. They supply all the necessary equipment and provide pickups at your hotel or guesthouse. **Icelandic Mountain Guides** (www.mountainguides.is) offers a year-round guided tour walking on a glacier in Skaftafell (page 262).
- **Ride majestic Icelandic horses:** Icelandic horses are hardy creatures that are beautiful to ride along the snowy landscape. Akureyri-based tour company **Saga Travel** (www.sagatravel.is) offers horse-riding day tours from Akureyri and Mývatn (page 205).
- **Go cross-country skiing up north:** Iceland isn't known for its skiing, but it does have a well-maintained ski area in its north, not too far from Akureyri. The **Hlíðarfjall** ski area (www.hlidarfjall.is) has more than a dozen well-kept trails (page 205).

a glacier walk tour

- **Ride snowmobiles:** It's spectacular to glide atop the pristine white snow on crisp, clear winter days. **Arctic Adventures** (https://adventures.is) offers several snowmobile tours, including one on Vatnajökull glacier, the biggest glacier in Europe (page 260).
- **Embark on an art museum crawl in Reykjavík:** If the weather outside is frightful, head indoors to explore Iceland's modern artists, like Erró, and old masters such as Jóhannes Kjarval at the **Reykjavík Art Museum** (page 36).

bathing experience than the Blue Lagoon. After you're refreshed, head back to Reykjavík for dinner at **Grillmarkaðurinn.**

Day 4: Waterfalls of the South

Start your day early with breakfast at **Deig** in Reykjavík before heading south to explore the spectacular South Coast. Be sure to pack some snacks—there won't be many places to stop for food on today's itinerary.

First, head to the delicate **Seljalandsfoss** waterfall. Spend some time walking the area

Djúpalónssandur beach in Snaefellsjökull National Park

around the waterfall for the best view, and climbing the set of steps that offer you the unique chance to walk behind the cascading water. Next, continue to the mighty **Skógafoss** waterfall, which has a drop of 60 meters (196 ft). Drive to nearby town **Hvolsvöllur** for a late lunch at **Valhalla Restaurant** before making the journey back to Reykjavík for dinner at **Sumac.**

Day 5: Snæfellsnes Peninsula

Spend a day in the **Snæfellsnes Peninsula** exploring charming fishing villages and the mighty **Snæfellsjökull glacier,** which appeared in Jules Verne's classic tale *Journey to the Center of the Earth*. Make a stop at **Djúpalónssandur,** a vast black-sand beach on the southern edge of Snæfellsjökull, before continuing to the town of **Grundarfjörður.** Have lunch at **Bjargarsteinn** before going on a whale-watching tour with **Laki Tours.** This region is your best chance to see orca whales off the coast of the island. Drive the 2.5 hours back to Reykjavík and have dinner and drinks at **Mathöll Hlemmur.**

Day 6

Get an early start and head to the Reykjanes Peninsula, where you will explore natural sites like **Seltún** and **Lake Klefarvatn** before checking out the **Bridge Between Continents.** Have lunch at **Salthúsið** before heading to the **Blue Lagoon.** Relax in the healing waters of the lagoon while enjoying a cocktail, an in-water massage, or special access to The Retreat, a private section of the lagoon. Have dinner at **Moss Restaurant** at the Blue Lagoon before calling it a night at the luxurious **Retreat Hotel.**

Day 7

If your flight is in the afternoon, you might be able to fit in an outdoor activity like **hiking** or an **ATV tour,** or just head back to the Blue Lagoon for one final soothing dip. Arrive at the airport at least two hours before your flight and have a great trip back home or on to your next destination.

With More Time

If you have more time in Iceland, the best way to spend it is to drive the entire Ring Road (page 276).

Getting Yourself in Hot Water: Iceland's Hot Springs

Swimming in Iceland is a national pastime; it's a time to relax catch up with friends and family. Every town in Iceland has a swimming pool, and many villages do as well. Every pool is heated and many swimming facilities have hot tubs, so it's a year-round activity. While pools are the most popular swimming locales for Icelanders, they love hot springs as well.

An important note: You must **shower** before entering pools or hot tubs. Icelanders shower, sans bathing suit, in gender-divided locker rooms prior to taking a dip, and you're expected to do the same.

Mývatn Nature Baths

BLUE LAGOON

A trip to Iceland would not be complete without visiting the Blue Lagoon just outside of Grindavík. Against a backdrop of lava fields, the human-made hot spring soothes and exhilarates at the same time. And that goes for any weather conditions—rain, snow, or sunshine. Soaking within the deep mist is a unique and slightly eerie experience, one you will remember—and talk about—for ages (page 92).

MÝVATN NATURE BATHS

Up north, the Mývatn Nature Baths feel secluded in comparison to the Blue Lagoon, with fewer people and more room to wade. The water comes from the National Power Company's borehole in Bjarnaflag, scorching when it arrives at the basin next to the human-made bathing lagoon but cooling significantly before filtering into it. The bottom of the lagoon contains minerals beneficial to the skin. The bathing experience is divine, relaxing every inch of your body (page 213).

SECRET LAGOON

In the south, the Secret Lagoon is a popular stop for tourists driving the Golden Circle. Located in the small village of Fluðir, the Secret Lagoon is small and less touristy than the Blue Lagoon, offering a more intimate experience. Surrounded by a landscape of lush moss and hot springs, the Secret Lagoon is a perfect place to relax after logging some hours on the road (page 106).

GEOSEA BATHS

Just outside the North Iceland town of Húsavík, you will find the GeoSea Baths, which overlook the Arctic Circle to the north. Guests can bathe in the warm geothermal seawater, visit a steam room, and enjoy refreshments from a dining area. The GeoSea Baths are a lovely way to spend some time after whale-watching in Húsavík or exploring Jökulsárgljúfur (page 222).

LOCAL SWIMMING POOLS

Almost every town has its own local pool, and tourists who visit them will quickly see how integral they are to Icelandic culture. It's common to see families, friends, and coworkers relaxing in a hot tub and talking about politics, music, or the latest movies. The pools are also a great option when the weather is particularly bad—which can happen in Iceland at any time, in any season. There are indoor and outdoor pools. You'd be surprised how many people go to outdoor pools in bad weather, but the pools are heated.

Iceland Weekend Getaways

Some of Iceland's best features are its compactness and its accessibility from Europe and North America: If you don't have a lot of time, it's possible to see some of the country's highlights in four short days. Short stopovers are very common, as Iceland is just five hours from the East Coast of the United States and about three hours from London.

Getaway for Outdoor Adventurers

This long weekend getaway is perfect for active travelers, focusing on activities like hiking Mount Esja just outside Reykjavík and scuba diving the Silfra fissure on the Golden Circle. Wildlife lovers can book tours to see puffins and watch whales, both unforgettable Iceland experiences.

DAY 1

After landing at **Keflavík International Airport,** pick up your **rental car** and head into **Reykjavík.** After checking into your hotel, drive to **Esja** for an easy hike. Just outside Reykjavík, the mountain is a great introduction to hiking in Iceland. The hike is 8 kilometers (5 mi) round-trip and relatively easy, and you will be treated to a beautiful view from the top.

DAY 2

From Reykjavík, drive northeast. Stop in **Þingvellir National Park** for the chance to go snorkeling with Dive Iceland (www.dive.is) in the **Silfra ravine** and explore the park after. Next, continue to **Hveragerði** to hike the **Reykjadalur trail** and bathe in the hot river at the top. The hike is about one hour each way. Spend the night in **Selfoss** at Hotel Selfoss.

DAY 3

Get ready to see the Westman Islands today! Board the ferry from **Landeyjahöfn** harbor, with your rental car. Once on the island, you can hike **Eldfell,** go on a puffin-watching boat ride (in the summer) with Viking Tours (www.vikingtours.is), and visit the new beluga whales in the beluga whale sanctuary. Have dinner at **Slippurinn** before heading back to the ferry. Spend another night in **Selfoss.**

DAY 4

On your way back to the airport for your flight home, stop by the **Blue Lagoon** for a rejuvenating soak in the milky geothermal water.

Getaway to Relax and Unwind

For those who actually like to relax on their vacation—as opposed to hiking volcano rims or driving ATVs through the mud—this getaway is for you. Enjoy Iceland's bathing culture at the Blue Lagoon and other local pools, sightsee at natural sites along the Golden Circle, and dine at top restaurants.

DAY 1

After landing at **Keflavík International Airport,** pick up your rental car and drive to the **Blue Lagoon Silica Hotel** near Grindavík, where you will stay for the night. Spend your first day soaking in the milky blue water and have dinner at the Lagoon's **Lava Restaurant.**

DAY 2

After a healthy breakfast, treat yourself to an in-water massage at the **Blue Lagoon** before checking out of your hotel. Spend the rest of the day exploring the **Reykjanes Peninsula,** including the geothermal region of **Krýsuvík** and the **Bridge Between Continents.** Drive to Reykjavík for the evening.

DAY 3

Spend today exploring the main sights of the Golden Circle—**Gullfoss, Geysir,** and **Þingvellir**—before driving to the **Secret Lagoon** for a relaxing swim. Stop by **Friðheimar** to check out the **greenhouses** and enjoy a

Best Day Hikes

Iceland is undeniably a hiker's paradise. The mountainous landscape begs to be climbed, lava fields invite you to explore, and the highlands offer the adventurous a place to conquer.

hiking Mount Hekla

- **Mount Esja** is the picture-perfect backdrop to Reykjavík and a favorite hiking destination for locals and tourists. The hike is 8 kilometers (5 mi) round-trip and relatively easy, but it does get steeper toward the top. Along the way, you'll see a placid stream and gorgeous scenery. The vista from the top is breathtaking, with views of Reykjavík across the bay (page 76).
- Hike to the summit of **Mount Hekla** via a moderately challenging 7-kilometer (4-mi) trail crossing lava fields and you'll be rewarded with gorgeous views, which, on clear days, include Vatnajökull glacier (page 113).
- Looking for a challenging day hike? Consider the **Fimmvörðuháls Trail,** which some tackle over two days but which can also be done in a long day hike of around 8-10 hours. Along the way you'll see gorgeous lava fields, glaciers, and waterfalls (page 121).
- In the West, **Mount Akrafjall** offers moderate hiking, with two paths from which to choose. The shorter climb (about two hours) gains 555 meters (1,855 ft) in elevation and offers a lovely view of the outskirts of Akranes. If you're up for a longer climb (about five hours), the more strenuous path climbs 643 meters (2,110 ft), and on clear days you can see Snæfellsjökull glacier (page 139).
- For those who make it to the highlands, hiking the rim of **Mount Askja** is a must. The approximately two-hour trek is moderate, and the trail is well maintained and sees a bit of traffic from hikers. It offers special views of looming mountains, lava fields, and the spectacular Víti crater (page 269).
- Hiking in Hveradalir, a geothermal area, is a popular option. For those seeking a taste of the highlands without committing to an all- or multi-day hike, a 3-kilometer (1.9-mi) loop trail near **Neðri-Hveradalir** (Lower Hveradalir) takes you through the glacial landscape, juxtaposed with bubbling hot springs and the muted hues of the desert-like earth (page 274).

Local Iceland

Icelandic culture is relaxed yet quirky, with a heavy dose of appreciation for the arts and the outdoors. Below are some ideas on how to **live like a local** while on vacation.

- Enjoy **ice cream** any month of the year, in any weather. Seriously, ice cream is very popular here. Some lovely places in Reykjavík are Valdís and Gæta Gelato.
- Take advantage of the **local swimming pools.** While the Blue Lagoon is great for first-time visitors, swimming pools are where you will find the locals. There's a local pool in almost every town.
- When in Reykjavík, go to a concert at local hotspots like **Mengi, Kex Hostel,** or **Harpa concert hall.**
- **Rent a bike** and ride down to the **Grótta lighthouse** in Reykjavík, one of the locals' favorite ways to spend a Saturday.
- **Chase the sun.** If you are visiting in the summer and camping, base your itinerary on the weather and travel where the sun is shining. Icelanders like to keep things flexible.
- Visit **breweries** here like Ægir Brewery and Bryggjan Brúgghús to sample the beer, or go on an epic **pub crawl** in Reykjavík.

nonalcoholic Bloody Mary before driving back to Reykjavík.

DAY 4

Enjoy an early morning soak at the local pool **Laugardalslaug** before picking up some last-minute souvenirs in downtown Reykjavík and returning to Keflavík International Airport for your flight.

Wildlife-Watching in Iceland

TOP EXPERIENCE

Iceland's animals, found on land, sea, and air, are quite special, starting with everyone's favorite bird, the puffin. These adorable birds are the unofficial mascot of Iceland and there are numerous opportunities for tours (in the summer months). Whales, dolphins, and seals are the main attractions of the sea; on land, you will see plenty of horses and sheep, but it will take a little more effort to catch a glimpse of the arctic fox (in the Westfjords) and reindeer (in the east).

Puffins

From May through August, it's possible to see puffins in several parts of the country.

- **Heimaey:** Thousands of visitors flock to this island off the South Coast to walk along the sea cliffs and spend time with its puffin population (June-Aug.) (page 130).
- **Látrabjarg:** In West Iceland, trails allow you to access the colossal Látrabjarg cliffs, where puffins gather to nest in intricate crevices (May-Aug.) (page 174).
- **Borgarfjörður Eystri:** Get a close-up view of puffins at this fjord in East Iceland, which has an observation platform connected to a small islet that the birds love (mid-Apr.-mid-Aug.) (page 243).

Whales and Dolphins

Several whale-watching tour companies operate around the island. Some head out year-round, while others are restricted to the summer. The main whale-watching destinations are in the south (Reykjavík), west (Grundarfjörður), and north (Dalvík and Húsavík).

- **Reykjavík:** Operating from Reykjavík's harbor, whale-watching tours offer opportunities to see minke, blue, and fin whales as well as dolphins and porpoises (year-round) (page 47).
- **Grundarfjörður:** This western town is your best shot at catching a glimpse of orcas (it's possible to see orcas year-round, but it is more likely during the winter months) (page 156).
- **Dalvík:** You may see humpback whales, minke whales, blue whales, harbor porpoises, and dolphins on tours leaving from the harbor of this small northern fishing town (year-round) (page 191).
- **Húsavík:** The unofficial whale-watching capital of the island has several species off its shores, including minke, humpback, pilot, northern bottlenose, sperm, sei, fin, orca, and blue whales (mid-May-late Oct.) (page 222).
- **Heimaey:** Iceland's beluga whale sanctuary is a lovely place to visit if you are heading to the Westman Islands (page 130).

Seals

Six species of seals have been spotted off the coast of Iceland. Most commonly sighted are **gray seals** and **harbor seals.** The remaining four species (hooded, harp, bearded, and ringed seals) are hit or miss.

- **Vatnsnes Peninsula:** In the summer, you have a good chance of spotting gray seals and harbor seals around this peninsula in the north (page 183).
- **Icelandic Seal Center:** Also on the Vatnsnes Peninsula, the Icelandic Seal Center contains some wonderful exhibits, along with information on the best sites for seal-spotting (page 182).

Arctic Fox

The Arctic fox is the only land animal native to Iceland, and you'll see the largest populations of them where birdlife is most abundant: in the Westfjords.

- **Arctic Fox Center:** At the Arctic Fox Center in the Westfjords, travelers can meet some pups on site (page 165).
- **Hornstrandir Nature Reserve:** Foxes are protected from hunting in this region, and they thrive at this reserve (page 168).

Reindeer

Iceland's reindeer herds live only in **East Iceland.** The best places to view them during the summer are the areas around **Mount Snæfell** (page 242).

puffins

Reykjavík

Reykjavík is having a moment. Relatively affordable airfares are drawing weekenders from both sides of the Atlantic, giving Iceland's capital city a chance to show off its urban appeal and individualistic style.

Reykjavík's history dates back to AD 874, when Ingólfur Arnarson from Norway established the first settlement in Iceland. The city slowly grew over the centuries, and in 1786, Reykjavík was established as an official trading town.

Today, Reykjavík has a lot of people, cars, and trees, in stark contrast to the rest of the country. Roughly 230,000 of Iceland's 370,000 residents live in the capital city. Though it's small, its energy mimics that of bigger cities like Berlin. Reykjavík residents are known to have

Highlights

Look for ★ to find recommended sights, activities, dining, and lodging.

★ **Tjörnin:** Close to Reykjavík City Hall, this pond is a lovely place to take a stroll and enjoy the birdlife (page 37).

★ **National Gallery of Iceland:** The largest collection of Icelandic art on the island has everything from classic portraits to gorgeous landscapes (page 37).

★ **Hallgrímskirkja:** The "Church of Hallgrímur" is a striking national monument dedicated to one of Iceland's most cherished and celebrated poets. Its tower boasts spectacular views of the city (page 40).

★ **Harpa:** This striking concert hall features individual glass panels that light up during the darkness of winter (page 45).

★ ***Sun Voyager* Sculpture (*Sólfar*):** The large boat sculpture by the sea has been delighting photographers and tourists for decades (page 45).

★ **Perlan:** This unique dome-shaped building has one of the best views of Reykjavík from its outdoor deck (page 46).

★ **Reykjavík Nightlife:** Whether you're up for some live music, want to dance, or are interested a classic pub crawl, Reykjavík will not disappoint (page 65).

★ **Hiking Esja:** An easy climb on basalt rock climaxes with gorgeous views out to sea (page 76).

two lives: They work by day, and by night become musicians, artists, novelists, or poets. While strolling on Reykjavík's main street, Laugavegur, you'll see street art among the high-end shops, musicians playing impromptu concerts outside coffeehouses, and small art galleries boasting original "Icelandic Design." It's undeniably a creative city.

While Reykjavík can seem quite urban with its galleries and restaurants, nature is never too far away. The air is unbelievably clean, and whales can be seen passing by the harbor during the summer.

ORIENTATION

Reykjavík is the most compact capital city in all of Europe. Its **downtown** and the **Old Harbor** are situated in the northern half of the city, and the **main bus station** (BSÍ) for intercity and tour buses is in the south. Most of the hotels, museums, shops, and restaurants are also in the northern half. The main street in central Reykjavík is **Laugavegur,** which starts in the east. As you move west, it eventually becomes **Bankastræti,** which ends as **Austurstræti.** The streets tend to have long names, and there isn't a grid system in place, but the city is small enough that you won't get too lost. **Hlemmur bus station** on the east end of Laugavegur is a main depot downtown for Strætó, the city bus company. It can connect you to just about anywhere in central and greater Reykjavík.

Central Reykjavík

Also referred to as downtown Reykjavík, Central Reykjavík is the heart of the city, with a high concentration of fine restaurants, hotels, and tourist attractions like **Hallgrímskirkja, Tjörnin,** and the main street, **Laugavegur.**

Old Harbor

North of the center, the Old Harbor used to be a hub for fishermen and not much else, but the neighborhood has undergone a transformation over the last 10 years. It's where you'll find the **Grandi** area, which is home to **Harpa concert hall** and is filled with shops and restaurants. It's also where **whale-watching tours** depart from.

Outside City Center

Heading east, in the Laugardalur area you'll find the **Reykjavík Zoo** and **Botanical Garden.**

PLANNING YOUR TIME

Reykjavík is small enough that you can get a good sense of it in 1-2 days. Some travelers treat Reykjavík as their starting point, given its proximity to **Keflavík International Airport,** before heading out on the **Ring Road** or booking day trips to the **Golden Circle** or further into the countryside, while others travel to Reykjavík specifically for the **nightlife** and **art scene.**

Previous: colorful downtown Reykjavík; Hallgrímskirkja; Reykjavík harbor and Gunnar Árnason's *Sun Voyager* sculpture.

Itinerary Ideas

THE BEST OF REYKJAVÍK

With quaint museums, cool music venues, and top-notch restaurants, small Reykjavík makes a big impression.

Reykjavík on Day 1

Explore downtown Reykjavík and all the shops, galleries, restaurants, and coffeehouses the city has to offer.

1 Walk down the street Skólavörðustígur to the landmark church **Hallgrímskirkja** to check out the amazing interior, the beautiful organ, and the view from the top.

2 Grab coffee or lunch on Skólavörðustígur at **Café Babalu,** which makes tasty lattes and light meals like crepes and panini.

3 Down the street, you can pick up a traditional Icelandic sweater at the **Handknitting Association of Iceland.**

4 Walk down the main street, **Laugavegur,** and pop into Farmers & Friends for Icelandic design and Eymundsson for books, T-shirts, and other tourist wares.

5 Walk toward City Hall and stroll around the human-made pond **Tjörnin,** where you can check out swans, ducks, and other birds.

6 For dinner, consider trendy **Fiskfelagid** for the freshest catch of the day.

7 Reykjavík nightlife is epic, and **Kiki Queer Bar** is perfect for checking out local DJs or live bands and dancing the night away.

Reykjavík on Day 2

Reykjavík's harbor has a lot to see.

1 Have breakfast at **Deig,** then watch boats enter the harbor.

2 Sign up for a whale-watching or bird-watching excursion with **Elding Whale Watching** for a chance to spot minke whales, dolphins, fin whales, blue whales, and seabirds (depending on the season).

3 Once back on land, walk to the **Saga Museum** to learn about Iceland's history and enjoy a coffee and snack or light meal at the in-house restaurant, Matur og Drykkur.

4 Walk over to **Harpa** concert hall to take in a concert or just to check out the amazing interior and architecturally striking exterior.

5 Walk back downtown and explore **Hafnarhús,** part of the Reykjavík Art Museum.

6 Next have dinner at wildly popular sushi restaurant **Sushi Social.**

7 Stop by **Mengi** to hear some local live music.

Reykjavík Like a Local

While Reykjavík is relatively small, you will need to take a couple of buses or quick cab rides today.

Itinerary Ideas

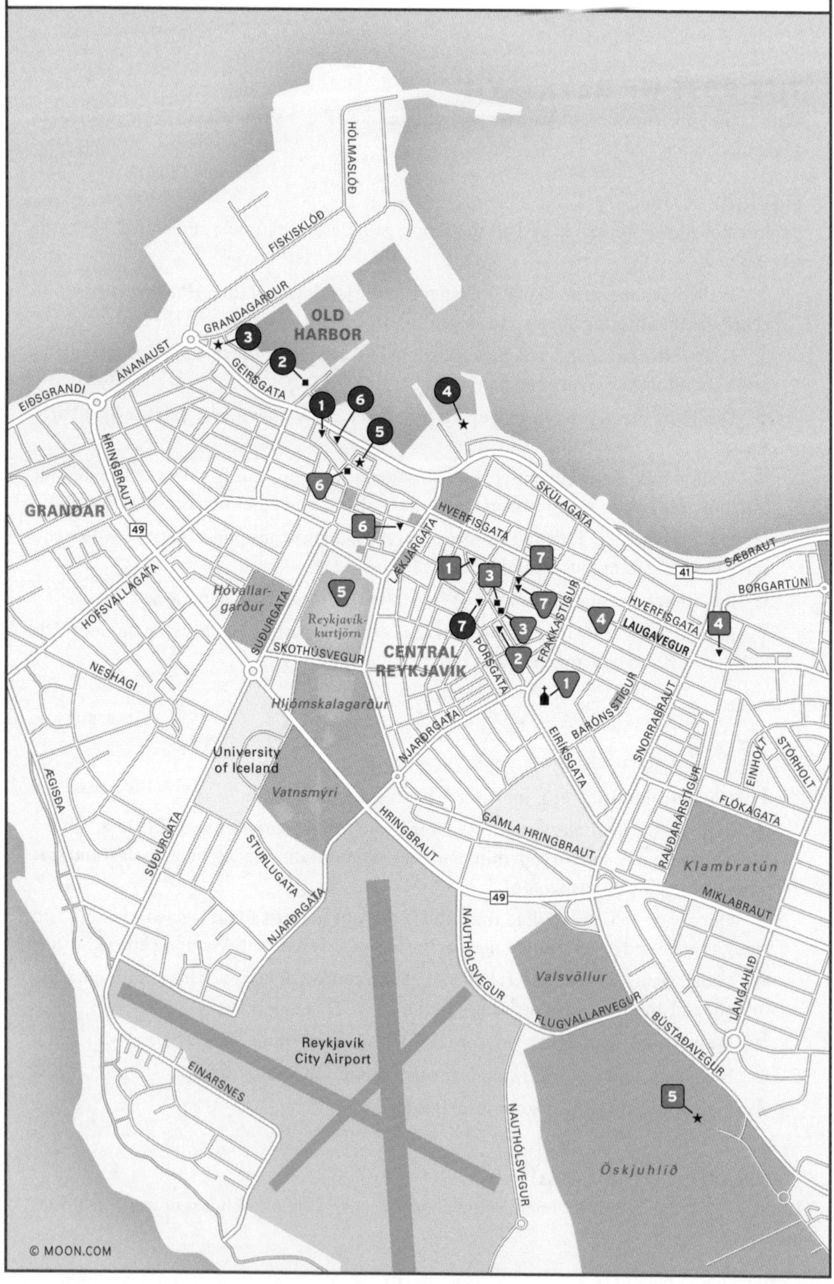

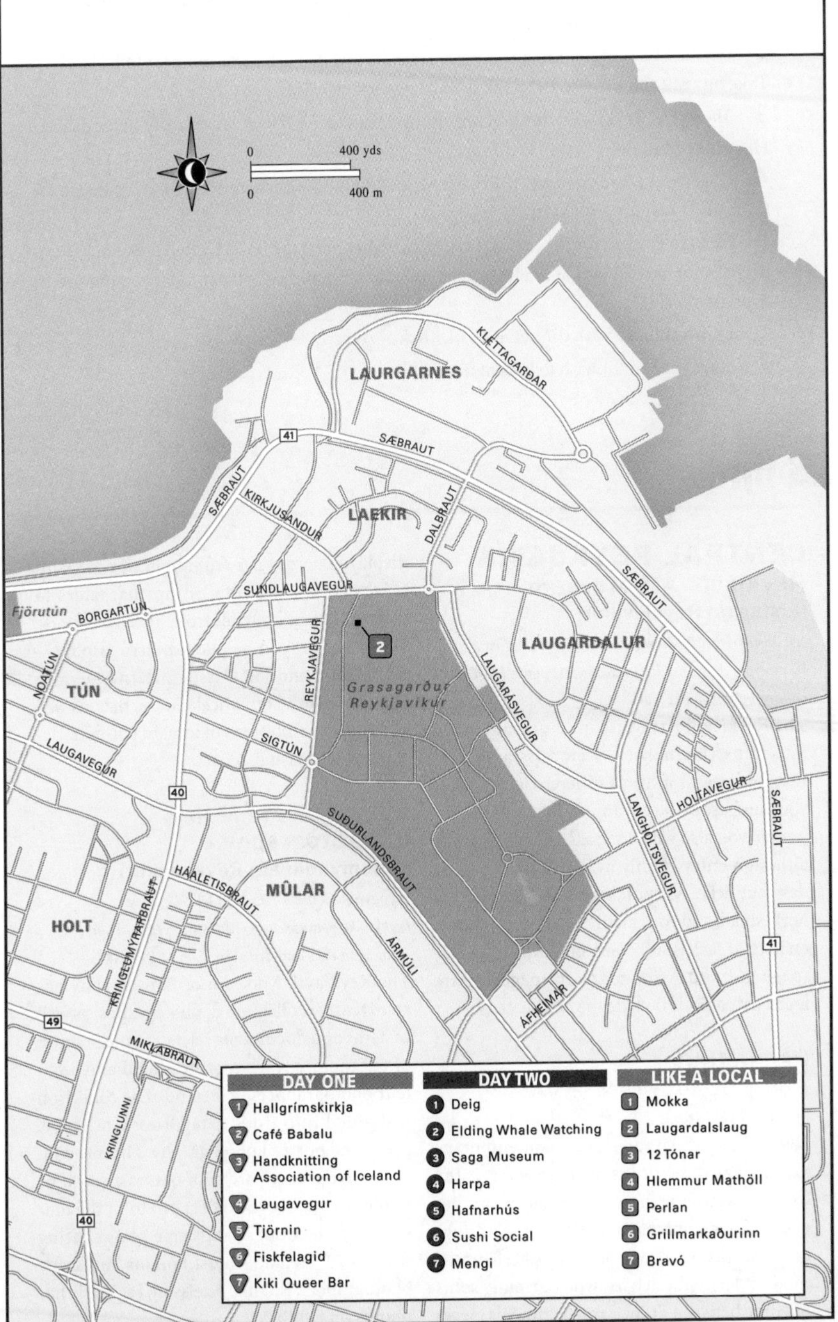
0
400 yds
0
400 m
LAURGARNES
KLETTAGARÐAR
41
SÆBRAUT
SÆBRAUT
KIRKJUSANDUR
LAEKIR
DALBRAUT
SUNDLAUGAVEGUR
SÆBRAUT
Fjörutún
BORGARTÚN
LAUGARDALUR
2
NOATÚN
TÚN
REYKJAVEGUR
Grasagarður Reykjavikur
LAUGARÁSVEGUR
SIGTÚN
LAUGAVEGUR
40
HOUTAVEGUR
SÆBRAUT
SUDURLANDSBRAUT
LANGHOLTSVEGUR
HÁALETISBRAUT
MÚLAR
HOLT
KRINGLUMÝRARBRAUT
ÁRMÚLI
41
ÁFHEIMAR
49
MIKLABRAUT
KRINGLUNNI
40
DAY ONE
1 Hallgrímskirkja
2 Café Babalu
3 Handknitting Association of Iceland
4 Laugavegur
5 Tjörnin
6 Fiskfelagid
7 Kiki Queer Bar
DAY TWO
1 Deig
2 Elding Whale Watching
3 Saga Museum
4 Harpa
5 Hafnarhús
6 Sushi Social
7 Mengi
LIKE A LOCAL
1 Mokka
2 Laugardalslaug
3 12 Tónar
4 Hlemmur Mathöll
5 Perlan
6 Grillmarkaðurinn
7 Bravó

1 Stop by **Mokka** on Skólavörðustígur for breakfast—the waffles with homemade jam and fresh cream are delightful.

2 Go for a relaxing swim at **Laugardalslaug** and soak in a hot tub next to Icelanders. Take bus #12, 14, or 16 to the pool, or take a quick cab ride.

3 Then visit Reykjavík's best record shops: Head to **12 Tónar**, and Lucky Records near Hlemmur Mathöll.

4 Check out **Hlemmur Mathöll**, a new food hall, for lunch and a drink: Try Fuego for tacos and Skál! for a cocktail.

5 Head to **Perlan** for the exhibitions, then walk one of the trails by the museum, a wonderfully forested area that is a favorite among locals. Take bus #1, 3, or 6 to Perlan, or take a quick cab ride.

6 Finish the day with dinner at **Grillmarkaðurinn.**

7 Start your night with drinks at **Bravó.**

Sights

CENTRAL REYKJAVÍK

Reykjavík Art Museum (Listasafn Reykjavíkur)

tel. 354/411-6410; www.listasafnreykjavikur.is; 10am-5pm daily; adults 1,950ISK, students 1,200ISK, children and seniors free

The Reykjavík Art Museum is actually three museums (Hafnarhús, Kjarvalsstaðir, and Ásmundarsafn) in three different locations. If you purchase a ticket to any one of the three museums, you also gain access to the other two—although entry is only available on the same day your ticket was purchased. Each museum is fairly small, and you can hit all three in one day; an hour at each is sufficient. Both Kjarvalsstaðir (page 46) and Ásmundarsafn (page 46) are located a cab ride outside the city center.

HAFNARHÚS

Tryggvagata 17; tel. 354/590-1200; www.listasafnreykjavikur.is

Hafnarhús, which focuses on contemporary art and has three floors of exhibitions, is the crown jewel of the three museums, in part because of its permanent collection of paintings and prints by Erró, one of the most celebrated modern Icelandic artists, who currently splits his time between France and Spain. His pieces displayed here range from light pop art with bright colors and interesting characters to samples of line sketches from his earlier work. While the art can be playful, Erró also tackles political and social issues. Hafnarhús also houses works by other Icelandic artists, as well as rotating exhibitions of foreign painters, designers, and visual artists.

Reykjavík Museum of Photography (Ljósmyndasafn Reykjavíkur)

Tryggvagata 15; tel. 354/563-1790; www.reykjavikcitymuseum.is; 10am-6pm Mon.-Thurs., 11am-5pm Fri., 1pm-5pm Sat.-Sun.; 1,000ISK

The Reykjavík Museum of Photography has an extensive collection of photographs, as well as items and documents related to the practice of photography, from professional and amateur photographers in Iceland. The collection is divided into three categories: landscape, press, and portrait photography. The museum is small, but there are a lot of treasures to be found, including the oldest photo in the museum's collection, a landscape photo dating from 1870. Iceland's most famous landscape photographer, Ragnar Axelsson, regularly has photos on exhibit.

Culture House
(Safnahúsið)

Hverfisgata 15; tel. 354/545-1400; www.culturehouse.is; 10am-5pm daily; adults 2,000ISK, students 1,000ISK, children free

Culture House is a stately white neoclassical building that opened as a museum in 1909. It is home to significant medieval manuscripts, including unique sagas, narratives, and poems from early settlers. Guided tours of exhibitions on Mondays and Fridays at 3pm last about an hour, or you can tour on your own. Rotating exhibitions throughout the year can include paintings, photography, or literary works. The exhibits do an excellent job of placing the manuscripts, literature, and artwork in context, giving visitors a great overview. Be sure to check the website to see what's on view. Culture House also plays host to conferences, gatherings, and readings throughout the year, including Reykjavík's annual design festival, DesignMarch, in the spring. The cafeteria serves light meals, and the traditional meat soup is delicious.

Alþingishúsið

Alþingishúsið, or Parliament House, is the meeting place of the national parliament members of Iceland. Iceland's democracy dates back to the year 930, when parliament members met at Þingvellir; the parliament was moved to Reykjavík in 1844. Situated near Austurvöllur park, the stone building was designed by Danish architect Ferdinand Meldahland and built in 1881. Currently, only the debating chamber and a few small meeting rooms are actually located in the building. Offices of most of Alþingi's members are in other buildings in the area around Austurvöllur, which is actually the address of the building. It's not possible to attend sessions of parliament.

Reykjavík City Hall
(Ráðhús Reykjavíkur)

Tjarnagata 11; tel. 354/411-1111; www.visitreykjavik.is; 8:30am-4:30pm daily

Reykjavík City Hall is more than just a building that houses the mayor and other officials. Built in 1992, the large white structure has a wall of windows overlooking the Pond. On the ground floor, visitors will find a large hall that is often used for art exhibitions and markets; a huge model of Iceland is a favorite among tourists and worth a visit.

★ Tjörnin

next to Reykjavík City Hall

Tjörnin (the Pond) is a small body of water, rich with birdlife, situated next to Reykjavík City Hall. The scenic strip of colorful houses surrounding the Pond begs to be photographed. When the weather is nice, a walk around the Pond, which is about 1.5 kilometers (1 mile) around, is delightful. Sculptures and benches dot the perimeter. Birdlife is plentiful, with arctic terns, ducks, gulls, and swans. Feeding the birds is not allowed, so don't be that tourist who empties a bag of stale bread at the edge. In the winter, the water freezes and it becomes a popular spot for ice-skating.

★ National Gallery of Iceland
(Listasafn Íslands)

Fríkirkjuvergur 7; tel. 354/515-9600; www.listasafn.is; 10am-5pm daily; 2,000ISK

If you have time for only one art museum, make it the National Gallery of Iceland. The National Gallery has a large and varied collection, and houses the country's main Icelandic art. It places particular emphasis on 19th- and 20th-century Icelandic and international art. Here you will see everything from traditional landscape paintings to art depicting the Icelandic Sagas to works by modern Icelandic artists. Works from international artists on display include some from Pablo Picasso and Richard Serra. The stately white building is a stone's throw from Tjörnin (the Pond), so if the weather is fair, taking a leisurely stroll after visiting the museum is quite nice.

Reykjavík

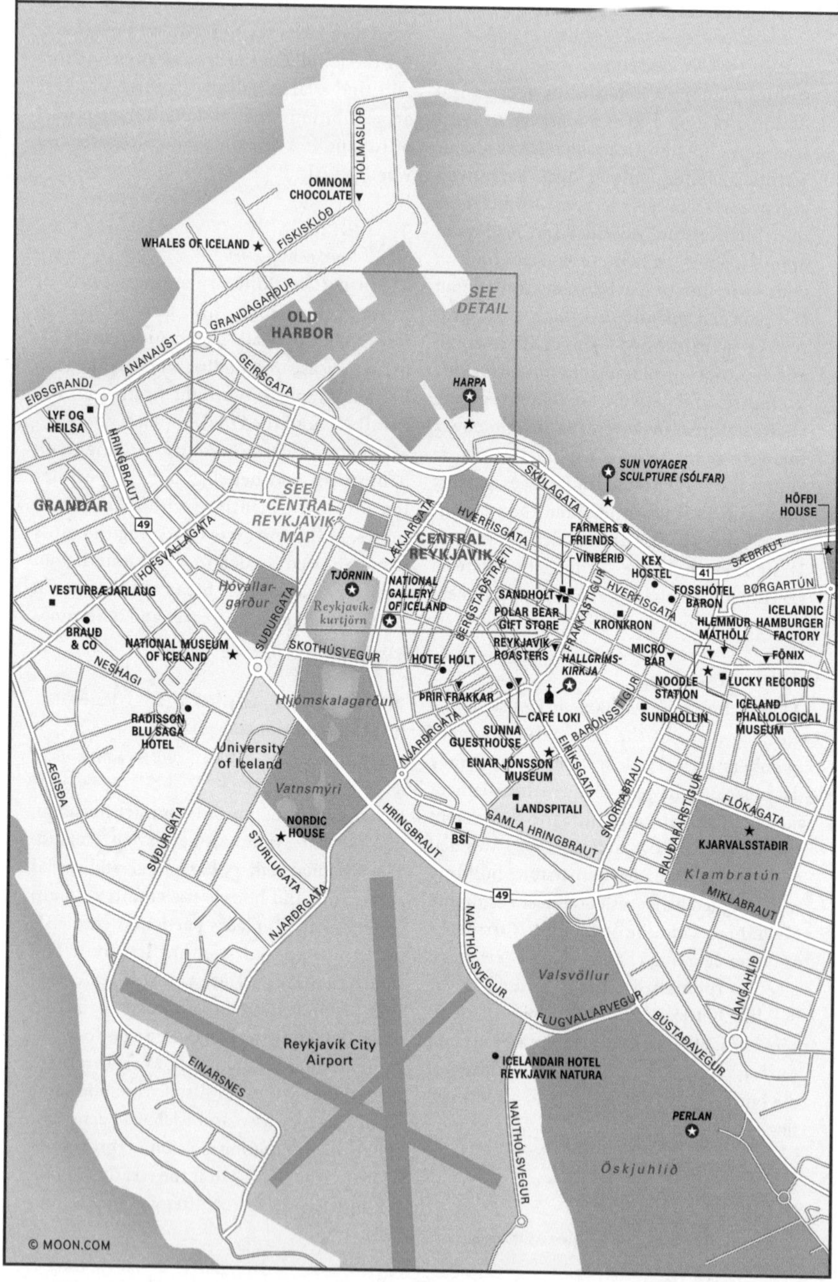
HÓLMASLÓÐ
OMNOM CHOCOLATE
FISKISLÓÐ
WHALES OF ICELAND
GRANDAGARÐUR
OLD HARBOR
SEE DETAIL
ÁNANAUST
GEIRSGATA
EIÐSGRANDI
HARPA
LYF OG HEILSA
HRINGBRAUT
SKÚLAGATA
SUN VOYAGER SCULPTURE (SÓLFAR)
GRANDAR
SEE "CENTRAL REYKJAVÍK" MAP
LÆKJARGATA
HVERFISGATA
HÖFÐI HOUSE
49
HOFSVALLAGATA
CENTRAL REYKJAVÍK
FARMERS & FRIENDS
VÍNBERIÐ
KEX HOSTEL
SÆBRAUT
41
BORGARTÚN
VESTURBÆJARLAUG
Hóvallar-garður
TJÖRNIN
NATIONAL GALLERY OF ICELAND
Reykjavík-kurtjörn
SANDHOLT
POLAR BEAR GIFT STORE
FOSSHÓTEL BARON
ICELANDIC HAMBURGER FACTORY
BRAUÐ & CO
SUÐURGATA
BERGSTAÐASTRÆTI
FRAKKASTÍGUR
KRONKRON
HLEMMUR MATHÖLL
NATIONAL MUSEUM OF ICELAND
SKOTHÚSVEGUR
REYKJAVÍK ROASTERS
MICRO BAR
FÖNIX
NESHAGI
HOTEL HOLT
HALLGRÍMS-KIRKJA
NOODLE STATION
LUCKY RECORDS
Hljómskalagarður
ÞRÍR FRAKKAR
RADISSON BLU SAGA HOTEL
CAFÉ LOKI
BARÓNSSTÍGUR
SUNDHÖLLIN
ICELAND PHALLOLOGICAL MUSEUM
SUNNA GUESTHOUSE
NJARÐARGATA
University of Iceland
EINAR JÓNSSON MUSEUM
EIRÍKSGATA
ÆGISÍÐA
Vatnsmýri
LANDSPÍTALI
SNORRABRAUT
RAUÐARÁRSTÍGUR
FLÓKAGATA
HRINGBRAUT
NORDIC HOUSE
BSÍ
GAMLA HRINGBRAUT
KJARVALSSTAÐIR
SUÐURGATA
STURLUGATA
Klambratún
49
MIKLABRAUT
NJARÐARGATA
NAUTHÓLSVEGUR
LANGAHLÍÐ
Valsvöllur
FLUGVALLARVEGUR
BÚSTAÐAVEGUR
Reykjavík City Airport
ICELANDAIR HOTEL REYKJAVÍK NATURA
EINARSNES
NAUTHÓLSVEGUR
PERLAN
Öskjuhlíð
© MOON.COM

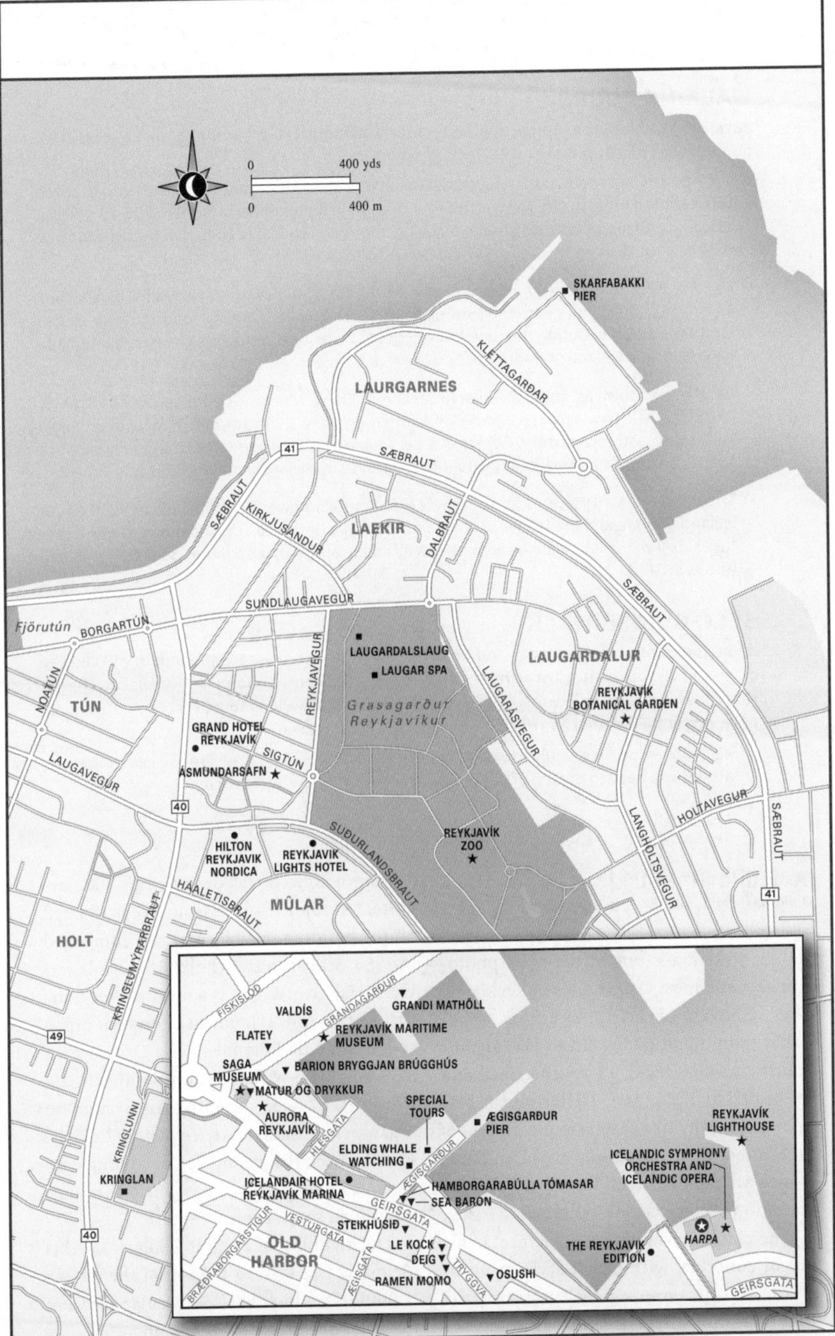

0 400 yds
0 400 m
SKARFABAKKI PIER
KLETTAGARÐAR
LAURGARNES
41
SÆBRAUT
SÆBRAUT
KIRKJUSANDUR
LAEKIR
DALBRAUT
SÆBRAUT
SUNDLAUGAVEGUR
Fjörutún
BORGARTÚN
LAUGARDALSLAUG
LAUGAR SPA
LAUGARDALUR
NOATÚN
TÚN
REYKJAVEGUR
Grasagarður Reykjavíkur
LAUGARÁSVEGUR
REYKJAVÍK BOTANICAL GARDEN
GRAND HOTEL REYKJAVÍK
SIGTÚN
ÁSMUNDARSAFN
LAUGAVEGUR
40
HOLTAVEGUR
SÆBRAUT
SUÐURLANDSBRAUT
REYKJAVÍK ZOO
LANGHOLTSVEGUR
HILTON REYKJAVIK NORDICA
REYKJAVIK LIGHTS HOTEL
HÁALETISBRAUT
MÚLAR
41
HOLT
KRINGLUMÝRARBRAUT
49
KRINGLUNNI
KRINGLAN
40
FISKISLÓÐ
GRANDAGARÐUR
VALDÍS
GRANDI MATHÖLL
FLATEY
REYKJAVÍK MARITIME MUSEUM
SAGA MUSEUM
BARION BRYGGJAN BRÚGGHÚS
MATUR OG DRYKKUR
AURORA REYKJAVÍK
SPECIAL TOURS
ÆGISGARÐUR PIER
HLESGATA
ELDING WHALE WATCHING
ÆGISGARÐUR
REYKJAVÍK LIGHTHOUSE
ICELANDIC SYMPHONY ORCHESTRA AND ICELANDIC OPERA
ICELANDAIR HOTEL REYKJAVÍK MARINA
HAMBORGARABÚLLA TÓMASAR
SEA BARON
GEIRSGATA
BRÆÐRABORGARSTÍGUR
VESTURGATA
STEIKHÚSIÐ
OLD HARBOR
ÆGISGATA
LE KOCK
DEIG
TRYGGVA
RAMEN MOMO
OSUSHI
THE REYKJAVIK EDITION
HARPA
GEIRSGATA

Strolling Reykjavík

WALKING TOURS

Reykjavík is a compact capital city, perfect for walking tours. A number of niche tours have popped up in recent years.

- **The Pub Crawl** (www.citywalk.is; 2,500ISK) is a three-hour tour that takes you to three top watering holes in city center. The tour doesn't include drinks but offers a 20-30 percent discount and happy hour deals on beer, wine, shots, and cocktails. Note that the drinking age is 20 in Iceland.
- Foodies will rejoice over the **Reykjavík Food Walk** (www.thereykjavikfoodwalk.com; 13,900ISK), where you get to see landmarks of the city while sampling food at five or six Icelandic restaurants. During the tour you will get to taste local lamb, fish, cheeses, homemade ice cream, and Iceland's famous hot dogs.
- Local music journalist and radio host Arnar Eggert Thoroddsen runs the popular **Reykjavík Music Walk** (www.reykjavikmusicwalk.arnareggert.is; 5,000ISK), which focuses on Reykjavík's pop and rock history. Guests will get to see music venues, artist hangouts, practice spaces, and other landmarks important to an array of musicians including Björk and Sigur Rós.
- The **Icelandic Mythical Walk** (www.re.is; 4,480ISK) gives you a chance to learn about Icelandic Sagas, and the stories of elves and trolls that have been passed down over the centuries. You will visit two graveyards, see an elf stone, and learn about the 13 Santas of Iceland (the Yule Lads).

SELF-GUIDED WALK

While spending at least one day and taking a tour in Reykjavík is recommended, you can see quite a bit on your own in just an hour, which is approximately how long this walk takes without stops. It's ideal to complete this five-kilometer (three-mile) walking tour in the early afternoon, but monitor the weather and decide when it's best for you to go.

- Start your leisurely self-guided walking tour at **Hallgrímskirkja,** where you can explore the interior and head to the top of the tower for a fantastic view over the city.

★ Hallgrímskirkja

Hallgrímstorgi 1; tel. 354/510-1000; www.hallgrimskirkja.is; 10am-5pm daily; free

Hallgrímskirkja is one of the most photographed, and most visited, sites in Reykjavík. The "Church of Hallgrímur" is a national monument dedicated to Hallgrímur Pétursson (1614-1674), a poet cherished and celebrated by Icelanders. Hallgrímur is best known for 50 hymns that he wrote, *Hymns of the Passion,* about the passion of Christ. These hymns are familiar to all Icelanders, and are read annually on Icelandic radio before Easter.

The church is a modern structure, made out of concrete, with basalt-style columns at the bottom coming to a point at the top. Standing 73 meters (240 ft) high, the Lutheran church was designed by state architect Guðjón Samúelsson. Work started on the building in 1945, and was completed in 1986. Still an active church that holds services, Hallgrímskirkja is a must-see for tourists. The interior is home to a gorgeous organ constructed by Johannes Klais Organworks in Germany, as well as beautiful stained glass windows. Concerts ranging from choirs to organ performances are frequently held; be sure to check the website for upcoming concerts. An annual Christmas concert features traditional songs sung in English.

The highlight of a trip to Hallgrímskirkja for many is a visit to the top of the **tower** (1,000ISK), which has spectacular views of the city. An elevator takes you up.

- Then walk down Skólavörðustígur, the street directly across from the church entrance, to check out some quirky shops and cafés. **Café Babalu** is a nice stop on Skólavörðustígur for a cup of coffee and slice of dynamite carrot cake.
- Continue walking down Skólavörðustígur until you hit **Laugavegur,** the city's main drag and center of life in downtown Reykjavík, and turn left. Proceed until you meet Lækjargata street, where you'll turn left and head to **Tjörnin,** a pretty pond where you can watch ducks and swans.
- Walk clockwise around the perimeter on a pondside path, and loop past **Reykjavík City Hall** at the pond's northwest corner.
- Follow Tjarnargata street from here for one block, turning right on Kirkjustræti to see Iceland's Parliament House, **Alþingishúsið,** near Austurvöllur square.
- Then it's time to head toward the harbor; backtrack slightly the way you came, heading west down Kirkjustræti, and turn right onto Aðalstræti, continuing on it as it becomes Vesturgata. Turn right on Mjóstræti and left onto Tryggvagata, crossing the road here and heading east on Geirsgata. In about 400 meters (1,300 ft) you'll link up with the Sculpture & Shore Walk, a waterfront path that leads to **Harpa** concert hall, a striking architectural gem.
- After some time exploring the building or taking pictures, head 600 meters (2,000 ft) farther southeast along the waterfront walkway to see ***Sólfar,*** a popular sculpture and another excellent photo opportunity.
- Next, cross Sæbraut at the pedestrian crossing east of the sculpture and turn left onto Skúlagata, continuing about 150 meters (500 ft) until you see **Kex Hostel** on the right. Stop for a coffee, beer, snack, or chance to chat with locals and other tourists at this hip and wildly popular spot's bar and lounge area.
- Afterward, exit the hostel to the left and head south on Vitastígur for a couple of blocks, turning right back onto Laugavegur to check out more shops like **Epal** design shop and **Eymundsson** bookshop. You're back in the center of town and will soon connect with the portion of Laugavegur covered earlier in the walk.

Einar Jónsson Museum

Hallgrímstorgi 3; tel. 354/561-3797; www.lej.is; 10am-5pm Tues.-Sun.; adults 1,500ISK, children under 18 free

This museum houses the works of one of Iceland's most celebrated sculptors, Einar Jónsson (1874-1954). Situated across the street from Hallgrímskirkja, the museum features work ranging from Christian-themed sculptures to those depicting Iceland's rich folklore. Einar worked almost entirely with plaster, which was rare for the period. The outdoor sculpture garden is beautiful, whether the sun is shining or if it is under a layer of snow. The garden makes the museum a very special place to visit. Plan to spend about an hour checking out the art inside, and if the weather is nice, spend additional time outside in the garden.

Icelandic Phallological Museum

(Hið Íslenzka Reðasafn)

Hrafnartorg; tel. 354/561-6663; www.phallus.is; 10am-7pm daily; 2,500ISK

The Icelandic Phallological Museum is just as weird as it sounds. Guests can view the penises of 200 animals, including the arctic fox, walrus, seal, and polar bear. After the museum was moved to its current location in Reykjavík (from Húsavík in North Iceland) in 2011, the curator unveiled his latest acquisition—a human member. The museum has members on display in glass cases,

Central Reykjavík

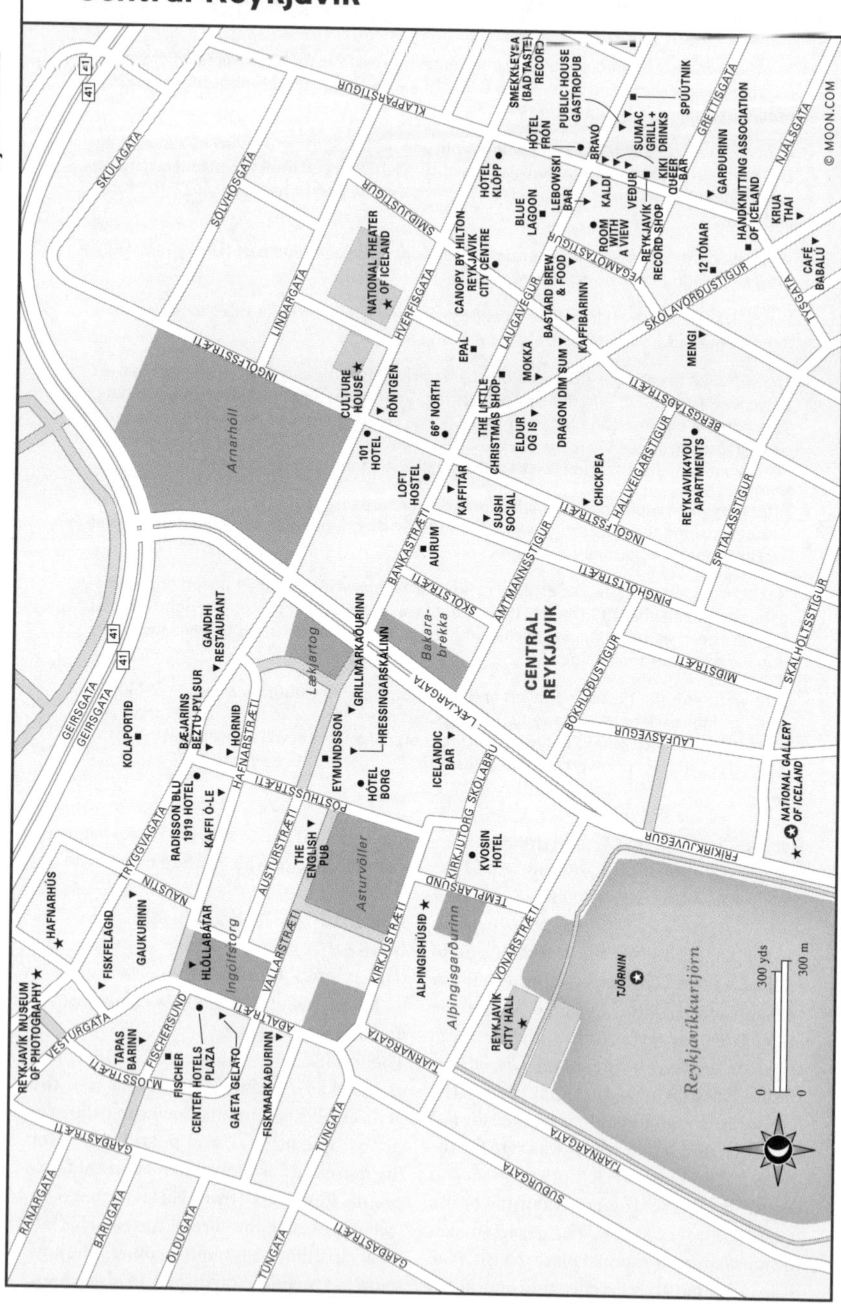

and preserved bones of certain mammals are hanging on the wall. The highlight is also a unique photo op: the huge whale specimen on display. Some people find the museum humorous, while others are a bit freaked out. Looking for unique postcards, T-shirts, and souvenirs? Look no further.

National Museum of Iceland (Þjóðminjasafn Íslands)

Suðurgata 41; tel. 354/530-2200; www.thjodminjasafn.is/english; 10am-5pm daily; 2,500ISK

Reykjavík's main heritage and history museum houses everything from tools and clothing of the settlement era to models of Viking-era ships. This is the best museum in the city to get insight on the history of the Icelandic nation and its people. The artifacts and exhibitions are well presented with clear information in English. Budget about two hours to take in all the exhibits.

Nordic House (Norræna Húsið)

Sturlugata 5; tel. 354/551-7030; www.nordichouse.is; 10am-5pm Tues.-Sun., closed Mon.; free

Nordic House is home to a library, a café, and numerous cultural events during the year. Literary and film festivals are held at the building, as well as fashion and music events. Most tourists visit Nordic House for the structure itself. The building, which was opened in 1968, was designed by noted Finnish architect Alvar Aalto, and several of his signature traits are reflected in the design, including the use of tile, white, and wood throughout the building. The one-story building's exterior features a blue ceramic roof.

OLD HARBOR (GRANDI)

Reykjavík's Old Harbor has been undergoing a transformation over the past few years, and it's become a dynamic place to visit, with shops, museums, new hotels, and the Ólafur Elíasson-designed Harpa concert hall.

Saga Museum

Grandagardi 2; tel. 354/511-1517; www.sagamuseum.is; 10am-5pm daily; 2,500ISK

The Saga Museum has 17 exhibits covering everything from Iceland's first inhabitants to the nation's conversion to Christianity to the Reformation. Special emphasis is placed on important characters in Iceland's history, such as Ingólfur Arnarson, who is believed to have been Iceland's first settler. There are interactive displays and artifacts on view and even a Viking dress-up area that is great for kids. An audio guide in English, German, French, or Swedish is available to accompany your walk around the museum. The in-house restaurant, **Matur og Drykkur,** serves traditional Icelandic food with a modern twist. Budget two hours for this museum.

Aurora Reykjavík

Grandagarður 2; tel. 354/780-4500; www.aurorareykjavik.is; 9am-9pm daily; 2,000ISK

Aurora Reykjavík gives you a chance to check out northern lights in any season. If you can't make it to Iceland in the wintertime, this is the next best thing. The multimedia exhibition gives a history of the aurora borealis, relates stories of northern lights from around the world, and provides an introduction to northern lights photography. The highlight of the center is a 13-minute film that shows some of the most majestic northern lights displays over the island.

Reykjavík Maritime Museum

Grandargarður 8; tel. 354/517-9400; www.reykjavikcitymuseum.is; 10am-5pm daily; 1,950ISK

Reykjavík Maritime Museum is Reykjavík's main museum devoted to the city's fishing history. The exhibitions show the progression from rowboats to modern trawlers and describe the vessels used, trading routes, and the construction of Reykjavík's harbor. There are daily tours of the coastal vessel *Odinn* available at 11am, 1pm, 2pm, and 3pm that last about an hour. The exhibitions cover the city's fishing history from the settlement to the present day. The museum

1
2
3
4

café has great views of the harbor and offers an outdoor eating area when the weather cooperates.

Whales of Iceland

Fiskislóð 23-25; tel. 354/571-0077; www.whalesoficeland.is; 10am-5pm daily; adults 3,400ISK, children 7-15 1,700ISK, children under 7 free

Whales of Iceland is a large museum near the harbor dedicated to Iceland's gentle giants. The museum is home to 23 life-size models of different whale species found off the coasts of Iceland. There are also interactive displays where you can learn about the whales, and a film. There's a small café inside for snacks.

★ Harpa

Austurbakki 2; tel. 354/528-5000; www.harpa.is; 10am-6pm daily

A striking glass structure, Harpa hosts rock concerts, operas, the Icelandic Symphony, and international conferences. Designed by Icelandic-Danish artist Ólafur Elíasson, the hall's exterior features individual glass panels that light up during the darkness of winter, sometimes blinking in a pattern or simply changing colors, and the building's waterside location lends itself to lovely reflections. Since opening its doors in 2011, Harpa has been lauded by design organizations and magazines around the world. It's also just a fun place to explore and take pictures of, even if you're not going to attend a concert or conference. **Hnoss Restaurant** (10am-6pm Mon.-Wed., 10am-midnight Thurs.-Sat., 11:15am-3pm Sun.), a café on the bottom floor, serves coffee, soft drinks, light meals, and cakes, and **La Primavera** (5:30pm-midnight Thurs.-Sat.), a formal restaurant on the 4th floor, has stunning views of the harbor.

Reykjavík Lighthouse

Sæbraut

A small bright yellow lighthouse was built near *Sólfar* in 2019. The lighthouse has become a tourist attraction since opening, but it has an official function to guide sailors coming into the harbor. It sits on a platform that overlooks the water, and it's a lovely spot to take photos.

Höfði House

Borgartún 105

Höfði House (Borgartún) is one of Reykjavík's most historically significant buildings and worth a photo or two. Built in 1909, the stately white building was initially used as the French consulate, and later served as a sort of guesthouse for famous folks passing through, including Winston Churchill, Queen Elizabeth II, and even actress Marlene Dietrich. Perhaps its most famous use was as the backdrop for a 1986 meeting between U.S. president Ronald Reagan and the head of the Soviet Union, Mikhail Gorbachev. Today, Höfði is owned by the city of Reykjavík and is used for official receptions and meetings. Although the house is not open to the public, visitors are welcome to explore the exterior of the building.

★ *Sun Voyager* Sculpture (*Sólfar*)

Sæbraut

Situated near a coastal path popular with cyclists and runners, *Sólfar* (by Sæbraut street) is a huge stainless steel sculpture described as a dreamboat. Before Harpa was built, *Sólfar* was the top spot to take photos near the harbor. It remains a big draw for tourists and is definitely worth a visit. Icelandic sculptor Jón Gunnar Árnason (1931-1989) wanted to convey a sense of undiscovered territory, hope, progress, and freedom, and built the piece as an ode to the sun, hence the name. The sculpture was unveiled in 1990, just months after the artist's death. The view of Mount Esja, the sea, and passing boats is a perfect backdrop for photos. On clear days, you can see the town of Akranes across the bay.

1: Hallgrímskirkja **2:** Tjörnin in wintertime **3:** Reykjavík Lighthouse **4:** view of the Reykjavík harbor from Harpa

OUTSIDE THE CITY CENTER

Reykjavík Zoo (Fjölskyldu- og Húsdýragarðinum)

Laugardalur; tel. 354/575-7800; www.mu.is; 10am-5pm daily; adults and teenagers 900ISK, children 5-12 680ISK, children 4 and under free

The Reykjavík Zoo is more park than zoo. You won't see monkeys or polar bears, but instead horses, pigs, goats, sheep, and other farm animals. The main attraction is a pair of seals. It's a pleasant place to walk around and bring children, but it isn't much of a tourist destination; if you're not on a long trip with small children, you can skip the zoo and not feel bad about it. Inside is a tiny aquarium that houses mainly fish. In the summer months, you'll see Icelandic families taking a stroll, looking at the animals, and visiting a small play area for children. There isn't an official petting zoo, but it's common to see parents holding their children up to pet horses in a penned area.

Reykjavík Botanical Garden (Grasagardur Reykjavíkur)

Laugardalur; tel. 354/411-8650; www.grasagardur.is; 10am-10pm daily May 1-Sept. 30, 10am-3pm daily Oct. 1-Apr. 30; free

The Reykjavík Botanical Garden is a beautiful spot tucked away in a quiet part of the city. East of downtown Reykjavík, the neighborhood is more residential. During the summer months, the garden is chock-full of bright flowers, hardy plants, peaceful ponds, and thriving birdlife. The café within the garden, Café Flora, is a little-known spot among tourists. You will find locals sipping on coffee drinks and enjoying light meals while taking in the view from grand windows. If you're not visiting in the summer, you can skip the garden.

★ Perlan

Öskjuhlíð; tel. 354/562-0200; www.perlan.is; 9am-10pm daily

Perlan, "the Pearl," is the distinctive, dome-shaped structure in Reykjavík's skyline. It offers one of the best views of the city skyline from its **outdoor viewing platform** (9am-10pm daily), where you can walk the perimeter and get a perfect panorama. The interior underwent a significant renovation in 2017, and the public building now hosts exhibits (4,490ISK), kicked off by an installation on glaciers and ice caves. There is also a planetarium and northern lights exhibition in the building, as well as a café that serves coffee and light meals, and a souvenir shop.

Kjarvalsstaðir

Flókagata 24; tel. 354/517-1290; www.listasafnreykjavikur.is

Kjarvalsstaðir explores the works of Icelandic painter Jóhannes Kjarval (1885-1972), best known for his dark and moody paintings of Iceland's landscapes. Kjarval was a master of capturing the country's raw nature in the winter light. The majority of Kjarval's collection was left to the city of Reykjavík after his death. The other wing of the museum features various Icelandic artists, ranging from well-known modern artists to some of the country's best and brightest art students. The museum is one level with a coffeehouse in the middle of the two wings, and the high ceilings and wall of windows here add to the visual interest of the space. A large field behind the museum sometimes serves as a spot for sculpture exhibitions.

Ásmundarsafn

Sigtún 105; tel. 354/553-2155; www.listasafnreykjavikur.is

Ásmundarsafn is an impressive sculpture museum exclusively featuring the works of Ásmundur Sveinsson (1893-1982), who worked with materials including wood, copper, and iron. Ásmundur's work is housed in a gorgeous stark-white domed building. An exhibit features a replica of his workshop and contains renderings of projects, as well as his masterpiece, a chair carved out of wood; the level of detail in the craftsmanship of the chair is spectacular. An outdoor sculpture garden features intriguing works of human forms among trees, shrubs, and flowers.

Sports and Recreation

WHALE-WATCHING, BIRD-WATCHING, AND FISHING

ELDING WHALE WATCHING

Ægisgarður 5; tel. 354/519-5000; www.elding.is; year-round; tours adults 12,000ISK, children 7-15 5,995ISK, children 6 and under free

Whale-watching is in some ways the best part of natural Reykjavík, in that you get to see a slice of nature just minutes from shore. Elding Whale Watching, which has 12 boats in Reykjavík, offers tours year-round and boasts a 95 percent chance of seeing whales in the summer, and an 80 percent chance in the winter. Guides are enthusiastic, and the business is one of the oldest at the harbor. Tourists relish the sightings of minke and humpback whales, dolphins, porpoises, and various seabirds, including puffins and arctic terns. Make sure you dress warmly, even in the summer, as it can get quite cold on the open waters. Tours are about three hours, and the company has environmentally responsible whale-watching policies.

For sea angling tours, Elding Whale Watching offers a tour with a "gourmet" twist, where you can cook and eat your catch on board the boat. The tour is available May 1-September 20. The tour is about three hours, departs daily from Reykjavík harbor, and costs 14,900ISK.

SPECIAL TOURS

Ægisgarður 13; tel. 354/560-8800; www.specialtours.is; year-round; 11,990ISK per person

Special Tours has a fleet of five boats of different speeds and sizes and runs year-round tours from Reykjavík harbor, with five daily departures May-August and 1-2 daily departures the remainder of the year. Tours are about three hours, and the company also has environmentally responsible whale-watching policies.

For bird-watchers, the "Puffin Express" tour, which leaves from Reykjavík harbor May through mid-August, is operated by Special Tours. The owners have been running bird-watching tours since 1996; they provide binoculars on board, and the company says they have a 100 percent sighting success rate. The guides have a soft spot for the funny black-and-white birds with the brilliant beaks and take great pride in telling you all about them.

POOLS AND HOT SPRINGS

Swimming is a central part of Icelandic culture, and if you don't visit a pool or two during your stay in Iceland, you're missing out. Icelanders treat the pools as places for social gatherings. You'll see friends and families in the pools and relaxing in hot tubs, chatting, laughing, and catching up. Each pool has its own character and local flavor, and some pools are more child-friendly than others, with slides and bigger areas designated for children. And, for roughly $5, it's a great way to spend a few leisurely hours. The pools listed here are recommended. Pools are open year-round.

LAUGARDALSLAUG

Sundlaugavegur 30; tel. 354/411-5100; 6:30am-10pm Mon.-Fri., 8am-10pm Sat.-Sun.; 1,060ISK

Laugardalslaug is the biggest pool facility in Reykjavík, and the one that gets the most tourists. The heated 50-meter (164-ft) outdoor pool is a big draw, along with the hot tubs, steam bath, and sauna. It's very crowded in the summer months (June-August) and can be loud because the giant waterslide in the children's pool is a favorite among local kids.

SUNDHÖLLIN

Barónstígur; tel. 354/551-4059; 6:30am-10pm Mon.-Fri., 8am-10pm Sat.-Sun.; 1,060ISK

The only indoor pool in Reykjavík is popular among locals and tourists alike. The outdoor sundeck overlooking Hallgrímskirkja is a great spot to spend a couple of hours when the sun is shining. Sundhöllin also has a steam room and two hot tubs. Given its proximity to the city center, the pool gets a lot of traffic.

VESTURBÆJARLAUG

Hofsvallagata 104; tel. 354/566-6879; 6:30am-10pm Mon.-Fri., 8am-10pm Sat.-Sun.; 1,060ISK

Vesturbæjarlaug is situated in a quiet neighborhood west of the city center. If you're looking to beat the crowds and experience the pool culture among locals, this is the spot. Facilities include a 25-meter (82-ft) pool, a few hot tubs, and a sauna.

SPAS

If you're after something more luxurious than a local swimming pool, there are a couple of spas in Reykjavík where you can relax and get treatments. Many tourists opt to spend an afternoon at the **Blue Lagoon** near Grindavík, and several buses depart from the bus station BSÍ (www.bsi.is). But if you want to beat the crowds, a local spa is a great option.

LAUGAR SPA

Sundlaugavegur 30A; tel. 354/553-0000; www.laugarspa.is; 6am-11pm Mon.-Fri., 8am-9:30pm Sat.-Sun.; 6,500ISK

Laugar Spa is Reykjavík's largest private spa, offering an extensive menu of treatments including facials, body massage and scrub, tanning treatments, waxing and nail services, and clay wrap treatments. The spa is marketed as an "aquatic heaven," and it's as good as it sounds. The entrance to the spa is reminiscent of a cave, with the soothing sound of water drops falling from a six-meter-wide (20-foot-wide) waterfall. Inside, six sauna rooms are kept at different temperatures, each with its own unique theme. The treatment rooms feature muted hues and calming music. There is an on-site gym, as well as a café serving fresh, healthy meals.

Entertainment and Events

PERFORMING ARTS

ICELANDIC OPERA (Íslenska Óperan)

Ingólfsstræti 2A; tel. 354/511-6400; www.opera.is

The Icelandic Opera has been thriving since productions moved in 2011 to the exquisite Harpa concert hall by the harbor. Productions have become more elaborate, and entire runs have been selling out. If you are an opera fan, check the website to see the current and upcoming shows. Past performances include *Carmen, Il Trovatore, La Boheme,* and *The Magic Flute.*

ICELANDIC SYMPHONY ORCHESTRA (Sinfóníuhljómsveit Íslands)

Austurbakki 2; tel. 354/545-2500; www.sinfonia.is

The Icelandic Symphony Orchestra consists of 90 full-time members and performs about 60 concerts each season, including subscription concerts in Reykjavík, family concerts, school concerts, and recordings, as well as local and international tours. Based in the Harpa concert hall, the symphony has performed works by Igor Stravinsky, Sergei Rachmaninoff, and Pyotr Tchaikovsky.

NATIONAL THEATER OF ICELAND (Þjóðleikhúsið)

Hverfisgata 19; tel. 354/551-1200; www.leikhusid.is

The National Theater of Iceland has been a Reykjavík mainstay since its opening in 1950. The emphasis is on Nordic and Scandinavian plays and musicals, but some foreign works are translated into Icelandic. In 2019, the theater put on productions of *The Great*

1: rainbow road for Reykjavík Pride **2:** Winter Lights Festival **3:** Reykjavík Culture Night

1

2

3

Dictator and *A Midsummer Night's Dream* in the 500-seat main stage. The exterior is a cold, concrete-gray building, but inside is a different story. The interior is modern, the theater is comfortable, and there's a lovely lounge area with plush seats and small tables where you can have a drink and wait for the show to begin.

FESTIVALS AND EVENTS

Spring

DESIGNMARCH

(HönnunarMars)

www.designmarch.is

Coinciding with the Reykjavík Fashion Festival is DesignMarch, a broader event that covers everything from product design to graphic design. With pop-up stores around the city and exhibitions held in museums and open-air spaces, the festival attracts people from around the world to check out the latest and greatest in Icelandic design.

EVE FANFEST

www.fanfest.eveonline.com

Gamers rejoice! The EVE Fanfest takes over the city every April or May, celebrating the beloved video game *EVE*, which is the creation of local company CCP. Thousands of gamers and curious locals gather, attend roundtable discussions, play live tournaments, and indulge in a pub crawl.

REYKJAVÍK INTERNATIONAL LITERARY FESTIVAL

www.bokmenntahatid.is/en

Every April, Reykjavík celebrates local and international authors during this five-day festival. The program includes discussions, readings, workshops, meet and greets, and lectures. Past participants have included Maja Lunde, Ian Reid, Yoko Tawada, and Hallgrímur Helgason.

Summer

REYKJAVÍK ARTS FESTIVAL

(Listahátíð í Reykjavík)

www.listahatid.is/en

Delighting locals and tourists since 1970, the Reykjavík Arts Festival manages to keep the program fresh, showcasing visual and performance artists from around the globe. The festival spans two weeks over late May and early June and holds events in different cultural venues as well as outdoor exhibitions.

REYKJAVÍK PRIDE

(Hinsegin Dagar)

www.hinsegindagar.is/en

Reykjavík Pride is a citywide celebration of human rights, diversity, and culture. It garners a huge turnout every year. Each August, the city hosts rainbow-themed events ranging from concerts to guest speakers. It's known as the highest-profile event for Iceland's gay, lesbian, bisexual, and transgender community. Hundreds of volunteers organize the event, and people from around the country congregate to celebrate their fellow citizens.

REYKJAVÍK JAZZ FESTIVAL

(Jazzhátíð Reykjavíkur)

www.reykjavikjazz.is

Since 1990, the Reykjavík Jazz Festival has been delighting horn section enthusiasts. International artists like Aaron Parks and Chris Speed are invited to put on concerts and jam with locals over five days in mid-August. There are off-venue free events throughout the city for this popular festival. Headline concerts take place at the concert hall Harpa.

REYKJAVÍK DANCE FESTIVAL

www.reykjavikdancefestival.com

Independent choreographers launched the Reykjavík Dance Festival in 2002, and the annual event is still going strong today. The focus is on bringing contemporary dance closer to the people. The weeklong event held every August showcases local talent as well as international dancers.

REYKJAVÍK CULTURE NIGHT (Menningarnótt)

www.culturenight.is

Reykjavík Culture Night has the darling slogan "Come on in," which is a reference to the island's old-fashioned customs of hospitality. Culture Night actually starts during the day, with select residents opening up their properties to offer waffles and coffee to their neighbors and visitors. Hundreds of events around the city range from cultural performances to free museum events. The festival culminates with a huge outdoor concert that features some of the biggest names in Icelandic rock and pop music. It's held at the end of August.

Fall

REYKJAVÍK INTERNATIONAL FILM FESTIVAL

www.riff.is

Beginning at the end of September, the Reykjavík International Film Festival takes place over 11 days, during which films from more than 40 countries are screened. They range from short films to full-length features and documentaries, and the festival is a great venue to discover new talent. Invited special guests have included American director Jim Jarmusch, English director Mike Leigh, and American actor John Hawkes.

ICELAND AIRWAVES

www.icelandairwaves.is

Iceland Airwaves has been delighting music lovers since 1999. The five-day festival, held in late October/early November, has hosted an impressive list of performers, including Sigur Rós, Björk, and Of Monsters and Men, as well as international artists including Robyn, Kraftwerk, and The Flaming Lips. There are also off-venue performances held for free in bars, bookstores, record shops, and coffeehouses—so if you don't score tickets to the festival, you can still check out some amazing music. A detailed off-venue schedule is published along with on-venue appearances.

Winter

WINTER LIGHTS FESTIVAL

www.winterlightsfestival.is

Reykjavík is lit up during the dark winter days and nights of February with outdoor light exhibits as well as concerts, art exhibitions, workshops, and discussions.

Shopping

Reykjavík may not strike you as a shopping destination, but there are quite a few local brands, like clothing labels 66 North and Cintamanti, that are quite popular. If you're up for some shopping, be sure to take a stroll on **Laugavegur.** The street is chock-full of design shops, jewelers, boutiques, and bookstores.

CENTRAL REYKJAVÍK

Art/Design

AURUM

Bankstræti 4; tel. 354/551-2770; www.aurum.is; 10am-5pm daily

Aurum is the place to go for unique Icelandic jewelry. Shoppers are treated to an impressive display of rings, necklaces, and earrings made from silver, gold, or lava stones. Aurum's jewelry is distinctively Icelandic, with pieces inspired by the raw nature of the island. An adjoining section is dedicated to modern toys, knitwear, accessories, and home goods.

EPAL

Laugavegur 7; tel. 354/551-3555; www.epal.is; 10am-6pm Mon.-Sat., 11am-5pm Sun.

The original design store in Iceland, Epal stocks everything from furniture to light fixtures to bedding and small goods. At Epal, which was founded in 1975, you'll find Icelandic designers as well as international brands, including Fritz Hansen, Georg Jensen,

Marimekko, OK Design, and Tin Tin. Other than the downtown Reykjavík store, Epal has three other stores at Skeifan, Keflavík International Airport, and Harpa concert hall.

FISCHER

Fischersund 3; tel. 354/860-6662; www.fischersund.com; noon-6pm Mon.-Fri., noon-4pm Sat.

Fischer is a small shop located in a black house owned by Sigur Rós frontman Jón Þór "Jónsi" Birgisson and run by his sister. The shop features unique products that can't be found in other shops in Reykjavík, including shampoo bars with activated charcoal, natural deodorant, loose Icelandic tea, special edition vinyl records, art prints, and candles. This is a niche shop to satisfy those looking for something other than a stuffed puffin doll to take home.

Bookstores

Reykjavík was named a UNESCO City of Literature in 2012, and locals like to boast that 1 in 10 Icelanders will publish a book in their lifetime. Iceland has the highest number of Nobel Prize winners for literature per capita. That would be one winner—Halldór Laxness for *Independent People.* Due to the importance of literature to the city and the exceptionally high literacy rate of its citizens, Reykjavík boasts an unusually large number of bookstores.

EYMUNDSSON

Austurstræti 18; tel. 354/540-2000; www.eymundsson.is; 10am-8pm daily

Eymundsson is the oldest and largest bookstore chain in Reykjavík, dating back to 1872. The main shop on Austurstræti has four levels, with an impressive magazine section, tourist books on Iceland, and a large English-language book section.

Music

Icelandic music is more than Björk and Sigur Rós, and a few choice music shops will help you discover local favorites as well as up-and-coming Icelandic artists.

12 TÓNAR

Skólavörðustígur 15; tel. 354/511-5656; www.12tonar.is; 10am-6pm Mon.-Wed., 10am-8pm Thurs., 10am-11pm Fri.-Sat., noon-6pm Sun.

A lot more than a record shop, 12 Tónar is a place to mingle with other music lovers. The shop was founded in 1998 and is an integral part of Reykjavík's music culture; the owner also runs an independent music label, and the shop is often used as a music venue during Reykjavík's annual autumn music festival, Iceland Airwaves. This is a landmark, a cultural institution. The shop also serves coffee, snacks, and alcoholic beverages.

SMEKKLEYSA (BAD TASTE) RECORDS

Hverfisgata 32; tel. 354/551-3730; www.smekkleysa.net; noon-6pm Mon.-Sat., closed Sun.

Smekkleysa (Bad Taste) Records was born from the legendary Smekkleysa record label that has released albums from the Sugarcubes (Björk's former band), Sigur Rós, and scores of other Icelandic artists. Its record shop, while small, has a great collection of Icelandic music on CD and vinyl, as well as a DVD section, box sets, and classical music on CD.

REYKJAVÍK RECORD SHOP

Klapparstígur 35; tel. 354/561-2299; noon-6pm Mon.-Sat., closed Sun.

Reykjavík Record Shop is a small shop specializing in vinyl that has an impressive selection of local music as well as international artists. You can browse new and used records, as well as CDs, books, and T-shirts.

LUCKY RECORDS

Rauðarárstígur 10; tel. 354/551-1195; www.luckyrecords.is; noon-6pm Mon.-Fri., noon-5pm Sat., closed Sun.

If you like vinyl, Lucky Records is the place for you. The shop has the largest collection of new and used vinyl in the city, with an extensive Icelandic selection as well as

---

1: downtown Reykjavík 2: 12 Tónar 3: the Handknitting Association of Iceland

1

2

3

foreign rock, pop, hip-hop, jazz, soul, and everything else you could imagine. Bands and DJs frequently play free concerts at the shop, and it's a fun place to spend a couple of hours. There's a turntable and headphones, with which you're welcome to sample used records.

Clothing and Knitwear

66° NORTH

Bankastræti 5; tel. 354/535-6600; www.66north.com; 10am-6pm daily

Perhaps Iceland's best-known and oldest brand, 66° North has been keeping Icelanders warm since 1926. You will find hats, rainwear, gloves, fleeces, vests, and parkas in colors ranging from basic black (a favorite among Icelanders) to lava orange. Heavy parkas cost an arm and a leg (around 50,000ISK), but you pay for the Thermolite insulation and design details. If you're not looking to make a fashion investment, you can grab a hat for about 3,000ISK.

FARMERS & FRIENDS

Laugavegur 37; tel. 354/552-1960; www.farmersmarket.is; 10am-6pm Mon.-Fri., 11am-6pm Sat.-Sun.

Farmers & Friends is the flagship store of the wildly popular Farmers Market clothing label. If you are looking for sweaters other than the traditional garb available at Handprjónasamband Íslands (Handknitting Association of Iceland), Farmers Market offers everything from cardigans to capes in stylish colors and patterns. The label, which was launched in 2005, is focused on combining classic Nordic design elements with a modern aesthetic.

SPÚÚTNIK

Laugavegur 28; tel. 354/533-2023; 10am-6pm Mon.-Fri., noon-6pm Sat.-Sun.

A trendy secondhand store, Spúútnik is perfect to dig through for that perfect vintage 1980s or '90s item. You will find everything from denim to leather bags to military jackets and faux fur coats.

HANDKNITTING ASSOCIATION OF ICELAND

Skólavörðustígur 19; tel. 354/552-1890; www.handknitted.is; 10am-6pm daily

Handknitting Association of Iceland (Handprjónasamband Íslands) is a collective of Icelanders that knit and sell sweaters, scarves, shawls, hats, mittens, and other woolen goods. If you are looking for an authentic, traditional Icelandic sweater, and are willing to pay top dollar, this is your place. There are a lot of colors and patterns to choose from in an array of sizes.

KOLAPORTIÐ

Tryggvagata 19; tel. 354/562-5030; www.kolaportid.is; 11am-5pm Sat.-Sun.

Kolaportið is Reykjavík's only flea market, and boy, do they go all out in this space. You can find everything from secondhand traditional Icelandic sweaters to used CDs and vinyl records to books and even fresh and frozen fish. A very popular place, it's usually packed, regardless of the weather or season.

KRONKRON

Laugavegur 63b; tel. 354/562-8388; www.kronkron.com; 10am-6pm Mon.-Sat., closed Sun.

KronKron is a hip shop that focuses on up-and-coming designers. Fashions for men and women range from fun and flirty to chic and modern. You can find elegant dresses, fashion-forward sweaters, and unique accessories. The clientele ranges from teens to young professionals, which shows the variety of duds available.

Gifts and Souvenirs

BLUE LAGOON

Laugavegur 15; tel. 354/420-8849; www.bluelagoon.com; 10am-6pm Mon.-Sat., 1pm-5pm Sun.

Blue Lagoon is a tiny shop on the main street that carries all of the Blue Lagoon's skin-care line. If you can't make it to the actual Blue Lagoon near Grindavík, don't fret, because you can take home some of the essence that makes the site so special. The shop is decked out in cool blue hues and lots of lava stones, and the shelves are filled with everything from a nourishing algae mask to mineral bath salts.

THE LITTLE CHRISTMAS SHOP

Laugavegur 8; tel. 354/552-2412; 9am-6pm Mon.-Fri., 10am-5pm Sat., 11am-5pm Sun.

The Little Christmas Shop is a small shop where it's Christmas all year round. A pair of stone Santa shoes outside the store draws you into a world of Christmas tree ornaments, ceramic Yule Lads figurines, soft toys, dishes, and just about everything with a Christmas theme. No matter what the season, it's a joyous shop to visit and will get you buying Christmas ornaments in July.

POLAR BEAR GIFT STORE

Laugavegur 38; tel. 354/578-6020; www.isbjorninn.is; 10am-10pm daily

Polar Bear Gift Store is bound to catch your attention with its huge toy polar bear models outside the store. While polar bears are not indigenous to Iceland, don't let that fact stop you from checking out the cute wares inside. You can pick up T-shirts, hats, magnets, keychains, and other souvenirs.

VÍNBERIÐ

Laugavegur 43; tel. 354/551-2475; 10am-7pm Mon.-Sat., noon-5pm Sun.

This sweets shop is stocked with everything from chocolates to rhubarb toffee. There's a good mix of local and foreign brands, and it would be almost impossible to not find something you like. Gift options include treats wrapped in pretty packaging. In the back there are spices and baking products, and in the summer there is frequently a mini outdoor fruit market just outside the shop. One sweet that is wildly popular among Icelanders is black licorice. You can find a selection of licorice candies with or without a chocolate coating.

OUTSIDE THE CITY CENTER

Shopping Malls

KRINGLAN

Kringlunni 4-12; tel. 354/568-9200; www.kringlan.is; 10am-6:30pm daily

Kringlan resembles just about any mall in America. There are clothing stores, a bank, a movie theater, and a food court packed with teenagers and shoppers. If the weather is particularly bad and you want to get some shopping done, it's a good destination. There's a 66 North shop in Kringlan, as well as some other Icelandic brands. Kringlan is a five-minute drive east from downtown Reykjavík, and it can be reached by Strætó bus numbers 1, 2, 3, 4, 6, 13, and 14. One-way bus fare is 470ISK, and it takes about 10 minutes from downtown Reykjavík.

Food

Reykjavík's culinary charm may be surprising to some. While there are traditional Icelandic restaurants serving up fresh fish and tender lamb fillets, there are also fantastic eateries specializing in food you may not expect to see in Iceland. For instance, there's an impressive collection of Asian and Mediterranean restaurants, which have authentic menus that incorporate the great ingredients found in Iceland. If you're in the mood for tapas, there's a place to have an exquisite meal. Craving sushi? You will not be disappointed. As for Icelandic cuisine, there are upmarket restaurants catering to foodies as well as fast-food joints offering quick, affordable bites.

CENTRAL REYKJAVÍK

Icelandic

CAFÉ LOKI

Lokastígur 28; tel. 354/466-2828; www.loki.is; 10am-10pm daily; entrées from 2,200ISK

Located across the road from the landmark church Hallgrímskirkja, Café Loki is the ideal place to indulge in classic Icelandic fare after some time sightseeing in the city. Here you will find rye bread slices with mashed fish, smoked trout, dried fish with butter, meat soup, and rye ice cream for dessert.

ICELANDIC BAR

Ingólfsstræti 1; tel. 354/517-6767; www.islenskibarinn.is; 11:30am-1am Sun.-Thurs., 11:30am-3am Fri.-Sat.; entrées from 2,600ISK

Icelandic Bar (Íslenski Barinn) takes classic Icelandic ingredients like lamb, whale, and puffin and puts a creative spin on the dishes with interesting flavor combinations. For example, the restaurant serves a sweet and savory dish of grilled puffin with blueberries, pickled red onions, skyr, and herbs. Guests can also order items like local salmon, traditional lamb meat soup, and the famous Icelandic hot dog. The reindeer burger is highly recommended.

ÞRÍR FRAKKAR

Baldursgata 14; tel. 354/552-3939; www.3frakkar.is; 6pm-10pm daily; entrées from 3,950ISK

Þrír Frakkar (Three Coats) is a Reykjavík institution that has been serving up classic Icelandic food for more than three decades. The menu is heavy on seafood; you will find options like creamy fish soup, fried cod cheeks, grilled halibut, and pan-fried salted cod. This restaurant also offers a taste of "rotten shark" if you dare.

Seafood

FISKFELAGID

Vesturgata 2a; tel. 354/552-5300; www.fiskfelagid.is; 11:30am-10:30pm Mon.-Thurs., 11:30am-11:30pm Fri., 5pm-11:30pm Sat.-Sun.; entrées from 4,900ISK

Fiskfelagid (Fish Company) has a striking, chic interior with modern wooden tables and chairs, candleholders throughout the space, and personal notes and photos adorning the walls. There are comfortable couches in the lounge, where you're welcome to sip a cocktail while waiting for a table. The food is flawless, ranging from pan-fried prime lamb and oxtail with artichoke puree to blackened monkfish and fried langoustine with lobster spring rolls.

★ FISKMARKAÐURINN

Aðlstræti 12; tel. 354/578-8877; www.fiskmarkadurinn.is; 5:30pm-10:30pm daily; entrées from 4,900ISK

Fiskmarkaðurinn, or Fish Market, stands out among a number of fantastic seafood restaurants in Reykjavík. What makes Fish Market special is the way the chef combines ingredients. The grilled monkfish comes with crispy bacon, cottage cheese, tomato yuzu pesto, and crunchy enoki mushrooms. It's a vision, as is the salted cod with lime zest and potato puree, dried cranberries, and celery salad.

Asian

★ DRAGON DIM SUM

Bergstaðastræti 4; tel. 354/766-1400; www.dragondimsum.is; noon-9pm daily; from 1,390ISK

Dragon Dim Sum is not authentic, but it is delicious. The tiny eatery with a painted exterior is a lovely spot for a quick bite. You will find on the menu bao buns, shao mai, and meat and vegan dumplings. This place is kitschy, adorable, and worth a stop.

NOODLE STATION

Laugavegur 103; tel. 354/551-3198; 11am-9pm daily; dishes from 1,820ISK

Noodle Station is a popular spot for Reykjavík natives, students, and tourists. People flock to the tiny shop for one of the tastiest and cheapest meals you can find in downtown. Noodle soup is available with chicken or beef or as a vegetarian option. The smell of spices wafting down Laugavegur will draw you in.

1: Dragon Dim Sum 2: Ramen Momo 3: Bæjarins Beztu Pylsur

DRAGON DIM SUM
點心
1
RAMEN MOMO
ラーメン
2
3
Bæjarins beztu pylsur
Vinsamlegast hjálpið okkur að halda borðunum hreinum

KRUA THAI

Skólavörðustígur 21; tel. 354/551-0833; www.kruathai.is; 11:30am-9pm Mon.-Fri., noon-9pm Sat., 5pm-9pm Sun.; dishes from 2,500ISK

Krua Thai has all your favorite Thai classics, ranging from chicken pad thai to spring rolls and noodle soups.

FÖNIX

Bíldshöfði 12; tel. 354/567-7888; www.fonixveitingahus.is; 11am-2pm and 5pm-9pm Mon.-Fri., 4:30pm-9pm Sat.-Sun.; dishes from 2,500ISK

It was hard to find good Chinese food in Reykjavík until Fönix opened. You can sample all the classics here, including wonton soup, lo mein, egg rolls, sweet and sour pork, and dumplings. There are vegan entrées on the menu as well as a kids' menu.

GANDHI RESTAURANT

Bergstaðastræti 13; tel. 354/511-1691; www.gandhi.is; 5:30pm-10pm daily; entrées from 3,800ISK

Gandhi Restaurant features the creations of two chefs from southwest India. Combining local Icelandic ingredients with traditional Indian spices, the menu offers authentic dishes like chicken vindaloo and fish masala as well as vegetarian options. The food is fresh and perfectly spiced. The butter chicken is gorgeous, rivaling that of the top Indian restaurants in London.

SUMAC GRILL + DRINKS

Laugavegur 28; tel. 354/537-9900; www.sumac.is; 5:30pm-10pm Tues.-Thurs., 5pm-11pm Fri.-Sat.; dishes from 3,990ISK

Sumac Grill + Drinks is a stylish addition to the restaurant scene in downtown Reykjavík. Opened in 2017, the menu is a fusion of Lebanese and Moroccan dishes created from seasonal Icelandic ingredients, resulting in some surprising yet delicious courses. On the menu you will find tahini-glazed cod; lamb ribs with lentils, grapes, and almonds; shawarma chicken thighs; and an array of vegan dishes. There is also a seven-course menu to share with the entire table for 8,990ISK per person.

SUSHI SOCIAL

Þingholtsstræti 5; tel. 354/568-6600; www.sushisocial.is; 5pm-11pm Sun.-Thurs., 5pm-midnight Fri.-Sat.; entrées from 4,990ISK

Sushi Social combines Japanese and South American elements to create inventive and delicious sushi rolls and entrées. You'll find traditional fresh seafood like tuna, salmon, crab, lobster, and shrimp, along with South American influences like spicy salsa, jalapeño mayo, and chimichurri. Main entrées include baked vanilla-infused cod and grilled beef tenderloin with mushroom sauce, jalapeño, and coriander.

Mediterranean

HORNIÐ

Hafnartsræti 15; tel. 354/551-3340; www.hornid.is; 11am-midnight daily; large pizzas from 2,190ISK

Hornið, with its yellow and blue walls, looks like a bistro from the outside, and the interior reveals a relaxed atmosphere with friendly service and yummy pizzas. Classic pizzas include pepperoni, four cheese, and vegetable, but there are also adventurous creations like the Pizza Pescatore, which has shrimp, mussels, and scallops on top. If you're not up for pizza, entrées include salted cod with risotto and fillet of lamb with vegetables.

TAPAS BARINN

Vesturgata 3b; tel. 354/551-2344; www.tapas.is; 5pm-10pm Sun.-Thurs., 5pm-11pm Fri.-Sat.; entrées from 4,990ISK

Tapas Barinn has many delightful choices, but if you'd like to taste its best Icelandic dishes, go for the "gourmet feast" in which the chef prepares dishes with smoked puffin, Icelandic sea trout, lobster tails, grilled Icelandic lamb, minke whale with cranberry sauce, and pan-fried blue ling with lobster sauce. The seven plates, along with a shot of the famous Icelandic spirit Brennivin and a chocolate skyr mousse dessert, will only set

Food Trucks Arrive in Reykjavík

Street food is pretty new to Reykjavík, but the number of trucks grows each month. Be sure to check the trucks' Facebook pages or websites to see where they are parked when you are visiting, as the trucks move around the city.

- **Fish and Chips Vagninn** (tel. 354/840-4100; www.fishandchipsvagninn.is; 11am-9pm daily) serves up delicately battered codfish and chips (1,890ISK).
- **Lobster Hut** (tel. 354/691-3007; 11:30am-8pm daily; from 1,600ISK) specializes in all things lobster. There's lobster soup, lobster sandwiches, lobster salads, and lobster hot dogs.
- **Tacoson** (tel. 354/777-5855) serves pork, chicken, chili con carne, and vegan tacos for the unbeatable price of 650ISK per taco. Quick eats at a cheap price.
- **Fish & Co.** (tel. 354/823-1667; noon-9pm daily) offers delicious, fresh pan-fried cod with a side of tomatoes for 1,000ISK, a price that's hard to beat.

Lobster Hut

- **Vöffluvagninn** (tel. 354/626-2882; 11am-7pm daily; 950ISK) is for those with a sweet tooth—and craving waffles. You can choose from classic waffles to cinnamon with cream, caramel, chocolate and cream, and a number of syrups including rhubarb, blueberry, and even licorice syrup (for the brave).

you back 8,990ISK. If you would like more traditional tapas, there are lots of options, including salmon and bacon-wrapped scallop bites.

Steak Houses

★ GRILLMARKAÐURINN

Lækjargata 2a; tel. 354/571-7777; www.grillmarkadurinn.is; 6pm-10pm daily; entrées from 4,990ISK

Grillmarkaðurinn (Grill Market) is an upscale restaurant specializing in all things meat. Expect dishes like grilled rack of lamb, dry-aged rib eye steaks, and beef tenderloin. But the restaurant also offers spectacular fish courses like salmon, cod, and fresh langoustine tails. The decor is modern yet rustic with Scandinavian design and a lot of wood. If you are after a top-notch carnivore's dinner, this is your place.

Vegetarian

CHICKPEA

Hallveigarstigur 1; tel. 354/776-5757; 10am-8pm daily; entrées from 1,690ISK

Chickpea splashed onto the Reykjavík scene in 2020, and quickly became a favorite for vegetarians. The menu isn't extensive, but there's something for everyone. The restaurant offers sourdough sandwiches with either classic falafel, beetroot falafel, or spicy falafel. There are also salads with fresh-baked sourdough flatbread and soups.

GARÐURINN

Klapparstigur 37; tel. 354/561-2345; 11am-6pm Mon.-Fri., noon-5pm Sat.; entrées from 2,500ISK

Garðurinn is a lovely café inhabiting a quiet corner downtown. It has an eclectic rotating menu of vegetarian meals including items like curry, vegetable chili, and lentil patties, all at affordable prices. You can also expect soups, sandwiches, cakes, teas, and coffee.

Fast Food

★ BÆJARINS BEZTU PYLSUR

Tryggvatagata 1; tel. 354/511-1566; www.bbp.is; 10am-1am Sun.-Thurs., 10am-4:30am Fri.-Sat., 450ISK

You have to visit Bæjarins Beztu Pylsur (The Town's Best Hot Dog). Even if you don't eat hot dogs, you should get a look at the tiny shack that has long been delighting tourists, locals, food critics, and even U.S. president Bill Clinton. Located close to the harbor, the hot dog stand serves up lamb meat hot dogs, with fresh buns and an array of toppings. If you're out for a late-night bar crawl and get hungry, the stand is open until 4:30am on weekends.

HLÖLLABÁTAR

Ingólfstorg; tel. 354/511-3500; www.hlollabatar.is; 10am-10pm daily; sandwiches from 1,690ISK

Hlöllabátar has hot and cold hero/hoagie sandwiches on offer, including barbecue, curry, ham and cheese, and veggie boats. It's a great place to get something quick and fuel up before you continue exploring the city.

ICELANDIC HAMBURGER FACTORY

Höfðatún 2; tel. 354/575-7575; www.fabrikkan.is; 11:30am-9pm daily; burgers from 2,799ISK

Icelandic Hamburger Factory (Islenska Hamborgarafabrikkan) is a wildly popular hamburger joint. It has the look and feel of a casual eatery, but the hamburgers are pretty special. They range from classic hamburgers with lettuce, cheese, and tomatoes to more creative concoctions like the surf-and-turf, which combines a beef patty with tiger prawns, garlic, Japanese seaweed, cheese, lettuce, tomatoes, red onions, and garlic cheese sauce. Other options include chicken and lamb, as well as a whale meat burger.

Gastropubs and Breweries

PUBLIC HOUSE GASTROPUB

Laugavegur 24; tel. 354/555-7333; www.publichouse.is; 11:30am-1am daily

Public House has 10 beers on tap, a number of flavorful cocktails, and a menu with a touch of an Asian flair. You will find small plates like bacon-wrapped dates with chili jam, tuna tacos with wasabi and guacamole, and crispy duck breast with jalapeño teriyaki. On weekends you can enjoy a bottomless brunch with bottomless drinks for 4,990ISK a person.

BASTARD BREW & FOOD

Vegamótastígur 4; tel. 354/558-0800; www.bastard.is; 11:30am-1am Sun.-Thurs., 11:30am-4am Fri.-Sat.

Bastard offers fast food kicked up a notch. Some favorites on the menu are duck confit flatbread, the Fat Bastard burger with beef brisket, and pulled pork tacos. The food is good, but locals tend to come for the drinks. You can enjoy a beer tasting of four brews for 2,900ISK. Bastard brews an IPA and an amber ale, and serves beers from Tuborg, Guinness, Brió, and Borg. They also have an extensive gin menu and impressive cocktails.

Cafés

SANDHOLT

Laugavegur 36; tel. 354/551-3524; www.sandholt.is; 7:30am-6pm daily

Sandholt is a lovely place to have a coffee and fresh-baked pastry, sandwich, or panini. The bakery also has fine chocolates and other packaged goodies, like jams and cookies, which make good souvenirs.

MOKKA

Skólavörðustígur 3A; tel. 354/552-1174; www.mokka.is; 9am-6pm daily

The oldest coffeehouse in Reykjavík, Mokka retains a faithful following. It's busy all day, with tourists as well as artists, writers, and other folks stopping by for a cup of coffee and Mokka's famous waffles with fresh cream and homemade jam. Art and photography exhibitions are frequently held at the coffeehouse, so stop by and have a look at the walls.

1: Café Babalu 2: Brauð & Co

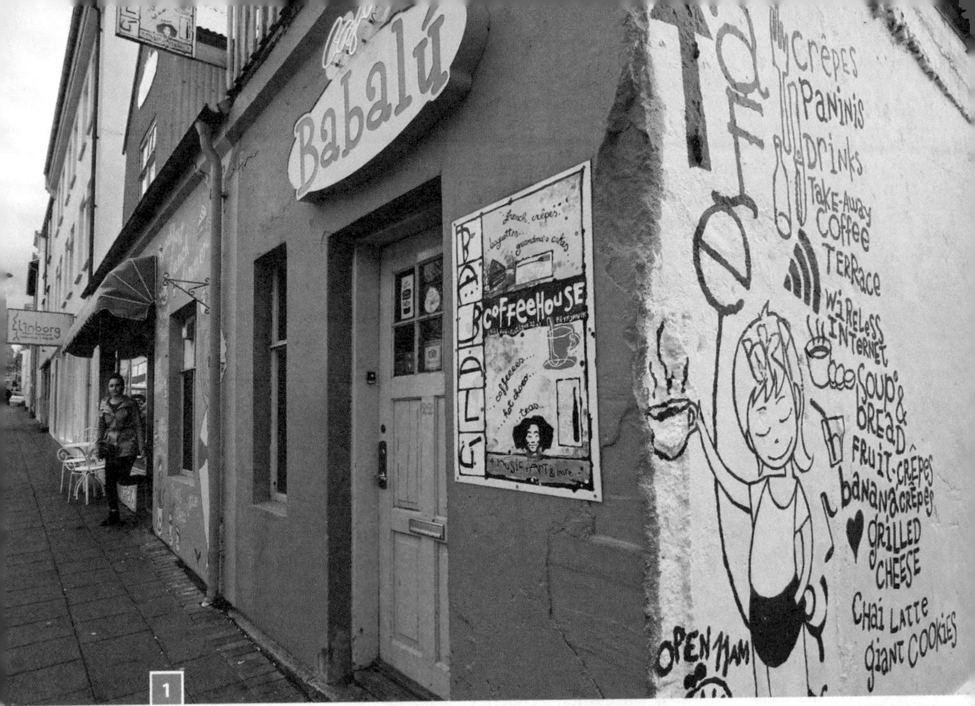

Babalú
Elinborg
Crêpes
Paninis
Drinks
Take-Away Coffee
Terrace
Wireless Internet
Soup & Bread
Fruit-crêpes
banana crêpes
grilled cheese
Chaí Latte
giant Cookies
Open 11am
French crêpes
Coffeehouse
music, art & more...

1

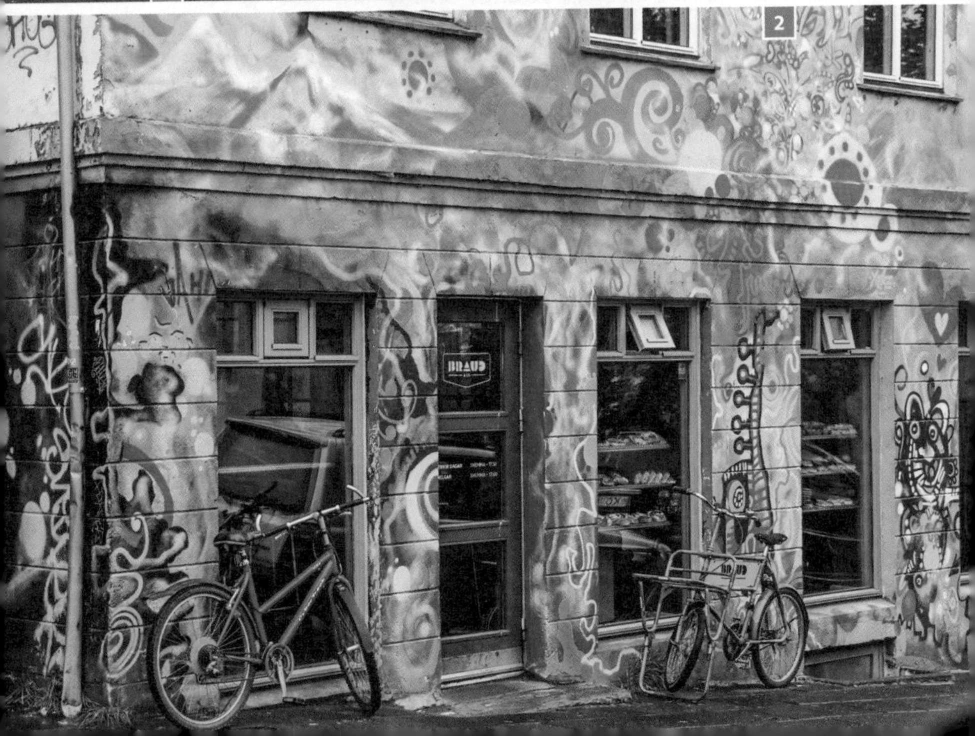

BRAUÐ

2

★ KAFFI Ó-LE

Hafnarstræti 11; tel. 354/888-2688; 8am-5pm Mon.-Fri., 10am-5pm Sat.-Sun.

Kaffi Ó-le opened its doors in 2021 and quickly became the best place in town for a coffee. Locals love the spot and coffee-loving tourists shouldn't skip it. The interior is Scandinavian chic with light wood and clean lines, and the coffee is divine, served by trained baristas using top quality coffee beans by local roastery Kaffibrugghúsið. The café sells sandwiches, soup, skyr, and small snacks to accompany your latte.

REYKJAVÍK ROASTERS

Karastigur 1; tel. 354/517-5535; www.reykjavikroasters.is; 7:30am-6pm Mon.-Fri., 8am-5pm Sat.-Sun.

Reykjavík Roasters is a charming corner coffeehouse situated in a great part of town. Just a stone's throw from Hallgrímskirkja, Reykjavík Roasters is a wonderful spot to sit down for a coffee to break up a busy day of sightseeing. Decorated with vintage couches and chairs and wood tables with delicate tablecloths, the coffeehouse is packed with tourists and locals chilling out, drinking lattes, and taking advantage of the free Wi-Fi. During the summer months, when the weather is cooperating, there's an outside sitting area where guests can enjoy their drinks while soaking in the sun.

KAFFITÁR

Bankastræti 8; tel. 354/511-4540; www.kaffitar.is; 7am-5pm daily

Kaffitár is the closest thing Iceland has to a coffee chain like Starbucks. There are locations in the city center, Keflavík airport, and a smattering of other sites. They also sell coffee beans and ground coffee in supermarkets and takeout coffee at gas stations. The city-center location is bright, colorful, and usually crowded. The coffee is fresh and the cakes and other sweets are delicious. You can't go wrong at Kaffitár.

CAFÉ BABALU

Skólavörðustígur 22; tel. 354/555-8845; www.babalu.is; 11am-10pm daily

This charming coffeehouse is decorated with vintage wood furnishings and kitschy knick-knacks. Other than coffee drinks, the two-floor café serves light meals including soup, panini, and crepes. This is a favorite among tourists, and in the summer months there's an outdoor eating area on the 2nd floor.

BRAUÐ & CO

Frakkastígur 16; tel. 354/456-7777; 7am-5pm daily

Brauð & Co is the hippest bakery in Reykjavík. You can get great pastries, breads, and cookies, as well as a delicious cup of coffee, plus do some fun people-watching in the heart of downtown. The owners and many of the employees are connected to the music industry.

Ice Cream

GAETA GELATO

Aðalstræti 6; www.gelato.is; noon-10pm daily; 490ISK

Gaeta Gelato serves authentic Italian gelato, something new for Reykjavík. You can enjoy gelato sorbets, frappé shakes, affogato coffee drinks, hot chocolate, and cinnamon rolls filled with creamy gelato. Flavors include lemon, strawberry, pistachio, mint chocolate chip, and salted caramel. For something Icelandic, try the licorice sorbet.

ELDUR OG IS

Skólavörðustígur 2; tel. 354/571-2480; noon-10pm Mon.-Tues., noon-11pm Thurs.-Sat., noon-6pm Sun.; 600ISK

Eldur og Is offers soft-serve and Italian-style ice cream with flavors including the basics—vanilla, chocolate, and strawberry—as well as coffee, pistachio, and several others. A crepe bar inside has delicious combinations, including the Nutella and nut special crepe. This place has a central location and a good reputation, so it can be a bit crowded. The sofas and armchairs inside make it very comfortable.

Food Halls

Indoor food halls (mathölls) have opened in Reykjavík in the past few years as Reykjavík's appetite for street food grows. The food halls, which are upscale food courts, have seating areas to enjoy your food and drinks.

HLEMMUR MATHÖLL

Laugavegur 107; tel. 354/577-6200; www.hlemmurmatholl.is; 10am-11pm daily

Hlemmur Mathöll is housed in the building that used to be the main bus station in Reykjavík. It's now home to Los Angeles-style taco masters **Fuego,** experimental bar and restaurant **Skál!, Flatey** pizza, and Vietnamese street food eatery **Bánh Mí.**

OLD HARBOR (GRANDI)

Icelandic

MATUR OG DRYKKUR

Grandagarður 2; tel. 354/571-8877; www.maturogdrykkur.is; 6pm-10pm Thurs.-Sun.; seasonal six-course menu 11,900ISK per person

Matur og Drykkur has an eclectic menu that includes items such as double-smoked lamb with buttermilk and nutmeg, a whole cod's head cooked in chicken stock with dulse (a type of seaweed), and rutabaga soup with red beet caviar and sunflower seeds. The restaurant, which is housed in the Saga Museum, has a casual atmosphere with reminders of the fishing industry—appropriate, because the building used to be a saltfish factory.

Seafood

★ SEA BARON

Geirsgata 8; tel. 354/553-1500; www.saegreifinn.is; 11:30am-10pm daily; entrées from 2,000ISK

Sea Baron (Sægreifinn) has been a Reykjavík institution for years. With its prime location by the harbor, the Sea Baron is known for its perfectly spiced, fresh lobster soup, which comes with a side of bread and butter. Fish kebabs on offer include scallops, monkfish, and cod. Whale meat is also available if you're so inclined. Inside, visitors will find a hut-like atmosphere with fishing relics, photos, and equipment. A net hangs from the ceiling, and charming knickknacks are displayed.

Asian

OSUSHI

Tryggvagata 13; tel. 354/561-0562; www.osushi.is; 11:30am-9pm daily; bites 250-480ISK

Osushi is a sushi train with bites snaking their way around the restaurant on a conveyor belt. Diners are treated to everything from deep-fried shrimp tempura rolls to tuna sashimi and grilled eel bites. For kids, there are chicken teriyaki kebabs, spring rolls, and even a chocolate mousse for dessert.

RAMEN MOMO

Tryggvagata 16; tel. 354/571-0646; www.ramenmomo.is; 11:30am-9pm Mon.-Fri., noon-9:30pm Sat., noon-4pm Sun.; 2,090ISK

Ramen Momo is an adorable hidden restaurant not too far from the harbor. Owned and operated by a Tibetan immigrant, Ramen Momo serves up glorious chicken, beef, and vegetarian ramen soup and dumplings. The nondescript eatery has an authentic feel to it, and your taste buds will thank you.

Mediterranean

★ FLATEY

Grandagarður 11; tel. 354/588-2666; www.flateypizza.is; 11am-9pm Mon.-Wed., 11am-10pm Thurs.-Fri., noon-10pm Sat.-Sun.; pizzas from 1,790ISK

Located in the hip Grandi neighborhood, Flatey serves up delicious Neapolitan pizzas with fresh ingredients and eclectic combinations. You can try the Padrino pie with San Marzano tomatoes, fresh mozzarella, pepperoni, pickled chili peppers, honey, fresh basil, and olive oil. Other pies include margheritas, parmas, a vegan pizza, and even a dessert pizza with Nutella, almond flakes, and powdered sugar.

Steak Houses

STEIKHÚSIÐ

Tryggvagata 4; tel. 354/561-1111; www.steik.is; 5pm-10pm Tues.-Sun.; steaks from 4,680ISK

Steikhúsið offers beef rib eye, porterhouse, and T-bone cuts or lamb fillets, with tasty sauces including béarnaise, creamy pepper, and blue cheese. There are also fish entrées on offer, as well as a dynamite hamburger with brie, pickled vegetables, mango chutney, chipotle, and bacon. For the adventurous, the surf-and-turf features minke whale and horse meat grilled in a coal oven.

Fast Food

HAMBORGARABÚLLAN TÓMASAR

Geirsgata 1; tel. 354/511-1888; www.bullan.is; 11am-9pm daily; burgers from 1,490ISK

Hamborgarabúllan Tómasar (Tommi's burger joint) is situated in the Old Harbor district, close to where the whale-watching tours depart. The food is tasty, the service quick, and the decor a little kitschy, making this a great spot to grab a quick bite to eat. A special includes a hamburger or veggie burger, fries, and soda for 2,690ISK, which is pretty cheap for a meal in downtown Reykjavík.

★ LE KOCK

Tryggvagata 14; tel. 354/571-1555; www.lekock.is; 11:30am-10pm daily; 2,100ISK

Le Kock is part dive, part foodie paradise. The chefs are creative, constantly playing with flavors. Their Nacho Lambre consists of nachos, braised lamb, grilled lamb hearts, chipotle sauce, cheddar cheese, red onions, and pickled chili peppers. There's also beer-battered cod, burgers, and fried buffalo wings on the menu, and beer on tap in the bar.

Gastropubs and Breweries

BARION BRYGGJAN BRÚGGHÚS

Grandagarður 8; tel. 354/456-4040; www.bryggjanbrugghus.is; 11:30am-11pm daily

This brewery has a retro feel to it with a dash of fishing culture. The menu is simple, with the fish of the day, fish and chips, burgers, and duck legs. Their beers are brewed on-site, and they have fun cocktails, like the Jude Law, with pear cognac and lemon soda.

Cafés

★ DEIG

Tryggvagata 18; tel. 354/555-0434; www.lekock.is/deigworkshop; 7am-7pm daily

Reykjavík was a bagel desert before Deig opened in 2018. Now, locals and travelers can enjoy freshly baked bagels in the heart of Reykjavík. They bake plain, sesame, and everything bagels, as well as sourdough bread and some of the tastiest donuts on the island.

Ice Cream

VALDÍS

Grandagarður 21; tel. 354/586-8088; www.valdis.is; noon-11pm daily; from 600ISK

Valdís draws a crowd during sun-soaked summer days and the dim, windy dog days of winter. It's always busy here, and for good reason. The harbor location and its creative and delicious ice cream flavors make this a favorite among locals and tourists. Flavors include coconut, white chocolate, vanilla coffee, Oreo, and local favorites black licorice and rhubarb. During the summer, there are tables and chairs outside the shop, where scores of people enjoy their cones.

OMNOM CHOCOLATE

Hólmaslóð 4; tel. 354/519-5959; www.omnom.is; 1pm-10pm daily; 1,090ISK

OMNOM Chocolate in Grandi is an actual chocolate factory, with an ice cream shop too. The chocolate brand is a favorite in Iceland and can be found in candy shops around the world. Stop by for a tour of the chocolate-making facilities and grab a couple of scoops of their delicious ice cream.

Food Halls

GRANDI MATHÖLL

Grandagarður 16; tel. 354/787-6200; www.grandimatholl.is/en; 11am-8pm daily

Grandi Mathöll is the perfect place to grab something to eat when exploring the harbor area. Here you will find Korean fusion restaurant **Kore; Gastro Truck,** which has a dynamite chicken burger; Italian food purveyors **Pastagerðin;** and pizza place **Eatlan Pizza.**

★ Bars and Nightlife

TOP EXPERIENCE

Reykjavík may be small, but its nightlife is epic. The main drag, **Laugavegur**, is ground zero for the hottest clubs and bars in town. If you are up for dancing, **Kiki Queer Bar** is your spot. If you fancy a whiskey bar, **Dillon** is the place. If you want to catch a hot Reykjavík band performing live, **Húrra** is your best bet.

Be prepared for it to be a late night and for your wallet to take a hit. Locals don't venture out until around midnight, and drinks are expensive—expect to pay upward of 1,200ISK for a pint of beer and 2,500ISK for a cocktail. Because mixed drinks are so expensive, cocktail bars are scarce, and beer is the favored beverage. But, for such a small city, you can't help but be impressed by the number of hot spots catering to different genres. Your biggest challenge will be narrowing down your options!

CENTRAL REYKJAVÍK

Bars

HRESSINGARSKÁLINN

Austurstræti 22; tel. 354/561-2240; www.hresso.is; 8am-10pm daily

Hressingarskálinn, simply known as Hresso, is a casual restaurant by day, serving up hamburgers and sandwiches. Free Wi-Fi attracts writers, tourists, and locals, who are known to spend hours sipping endless cups of coffee. By night, Hresso transforms into a dance club, with hot DJs and live bands. Expect trendy dance music.

KALDI

Laugavegur 20b; tel. 354/581-2200; noon-1am Sun.-Thurs., noon-3am Fri.-Sat.

Kaldi has a very warm, relaxed atmosphere with cozy seating and four types of Kaldi beer on tap (Kaldi is a brewery). There is a piano on-site and sometimes there is live music. If you are looking for a quiet place for a beer or two, stop by here before 10pm.

RÖNTGEN

Hverfisgata 12; www.rontgenbar.is; 4pm-1am daily

Röntgen opened at the end of 2019 and quickly became a favorite hangout among the locals. In fact, the magazine *Reykjavík Grapevine* named it the "best goddamn bar" in 2021. They have a good selection of beer and wine, as well as cocktails, and hold pub quizzes, karaoke nights, and concerts.

LEBOWSKI BAR

Laugavegur 20; tel. 354/552-2300; www.lebowski.is; 11:30am-1am Sun.-Thurs., 11:30am-4am Fri.-Sat.

Lebowski Bar pays not-so-subtle homage to the Coen brothers movie *The Big Lebowski*. Inside, there is bowling paraphernalia, posters from the film, and even a hanging rug by the bar that brings the room together. It's a casual eatery during the day, like many of Reykjavík's bars, but at night it transforms into a pretty wild scene, playing the latest dance music. There's a dance floor in the back of the room. A White Russian, the cocktail famously featured in the film, costs 1,850ISK.

THE ENGLISH PUB

Austurstræti 12b; tel. 354/578-0400; www.enskibarinn.is; noon-1am Mon.-Fri., noon-4:30am Sat.-Sun.

The English Pub is part English pub, part sports bar. There's a nice selection of Icelandic and foreign beer, and Guinness is on tap. If there's a soccer game being played anywhere in the world, it will likely be shown on one of the many screens in the bar. If there's a Premier League game on, expect a crowd of expats, tourists, and locals.

KAFFIBARINN

Bergstaðastræti 1; tel. 354/551-1588; 5pm-1am Sun.-Thurs., 3pm-3am Fri.-Sat.

Kaffibarinn has been a Reykjavík institution since scenes from the indie film *101 Reykjavík* were filmed here. Damon Albarn, the Blur and Gorillaz front man, used to own a stake in the bar. It's a tiny space with a rich red exterior, and it gets jam-packed during the weekends, but it's one of those places that it's cool to say you were there. Expect trendy dance music to be blaring as you enter.

VEÐUR

Klapparstígur 33; www.vedurbarinn.is; 2pm-1am daily

Veður, which means "weather" in Icelandic, is a chic bar popular for happy hour and a casual drink with friends. On nice days there are tables and chairs outside so patrons can enjoy the sun. In addition to beer, wine, and cocktails, Veður serves charcuterie plates, cheese, and olives, as well as coffee drinks and pastries.

BRAVÓ

Laugavegur 22; tel. 354/580-8020; 11am-1am Sun.-Thurs., 11am-4:30am Fri.-Sat.

Located downstairs from Kiki Queer Bar, Bravó is a place to chill, have a cold beer, and meet with friends. There is a casual vibe, and at night local DJs routinely play, attracting a younger crowd.

MICRO BAR

Laugavegur 86; tel. 354/893-5960; 3pm-midnight Sun.-Thurs., 3pm-1am Fri.-Sat.

Micro Bar is a beer lover's paradise. The bar carries about 80 different beers from countries including Belgium, Germany, Denmark, and the United States. The big draws are the wide selection of Icelandic beers on tap and the number of Icelandic craft beers available. Stop by and try a local stout, pale ale, or lager. The atmosphere is relaxed and relatively quiet, with dim lighting and a large wood bar. You'll find locals at the tables enjoying a beer and conversation with friends.

Gay and Lesbian

KIKI QUEER BAR

Laugavegur 22; tel. 354/571-0194; www.kiki.is; 8pm-1am Thurs., 8pm-4:30am Fri.-Sat.

Kiki Queer Bar is Reykjavík's only LGBTQ+ bar and is a welcome addition to the scene. Many locals will tell you this is *the* place to go to dance because it attracts some of the best local and visiting DJs. You can expect music ranging from Lady Gaga to the latest Icelandic pop music.

Live Music

LOFT HOSTEL

Bankastræti 7; tel. 354/553-8140; www.lofthostel.is

Loft Hostel has earned a reputation as a place to see and be seen. The 4th-floor bar/café hosts up-and-coming bands, established live acts, and DJs. An outdoor deck overlooks Bankastræti and is packed with locals and tourists alike when the sun is shining during the day, and filled with mingling concertgoers at night. Since this is a hostel, it's open 24 hours, so check listings at www.grapevine.is for concert and event times.

MENGI

Óðinsgata 2; tel. 354/588-3644; www.mengi.net; 11am-5pm Tues.-Wed., noon-11pm Thurs.-Fri., 1pm-11pm Sat.

Mengi is an exciting music and art space that showcases up-and-coming and established artists. The room holds no more than 100, so performances are intimate, making this a unique space in Reykjavík. You can see experimental musicians like Ben Frost and dj. flugvél og geimskip, or Icelandic favorites like Ólafur Arnalds and Högni Egilsson. There is also a small shop inside where you can pick up CDs, vinyl records, and art prints during opening hours.

GAUKURINN

Tryggvagata 22; www.gaukurinn.is; 4pm-1am Sun.-Thurs., 4pm-3am Fri.-Sat.

Gaukurinn is the place to go for live events—concerts, karaoke, drag shows, it's all here. Expect high energy, cold drinks, loud music, and a lot of fun.

1: Lebowski Bar **2:** Kiki Queer Bar **3:** Gaukurinn **4:** Hótel Borg

OPEN
WELCOME
OPEN
1
2
BRAVÓ
Kiki
queer bar
3
OPIÐ
GAUKURINN
4
HÓTEL BORG

KEX HOSTEL

Skúlagata 28; tel. 354/561-6060; www.kexhostel.is

Kex Hostel has become a Reykjavík institution over the past few years. The building, formerly a biscuit factory, is a great space, complete with mid-century furniture, vintage wall maps, and a lot of curiosities. A small stage in the entryway hosts up-and-coming bands while guests drink and hang out at the **bar** (11:30am-11pm daily). A back room serves as a **venue** for more formal concerts. If you're in your twenties and aren't bothered by hipsters, this is your place. Since this is a hostel, it's open 24 hours, so check listings at www.grapevine.is for concert times.

Accommodations

Accommodations in Reykjavík fall into three categories: hotels, guesthouses, and self-catering apartments. The city isn't known for luxurious hotels, but there are a few more upmarket choices; however, they remain "no frills" when compared to other cities in Europe.

By and large, expect to pay a lot during the high season (June-August). While most of the options are downtown, there are a few outside the 101 postal code. However, given how small Reykjavík is, most options are within walking distance or a short bus ride to downtown.

CENTRAL REYKJAVÍK

Under 25,000ISK

SUNNA GUESTHOUSE

Thórsgata 26; tel. 354/511-5570; www.sunna.is; rooms from 20,800ISK

Sunna Guesthouse offers several types of accommodations: one- and two-bedroom apartments, studios, rooms with private bathrooms, and rooms with shared bathroom facilities. All rooms are decorated in a light, minimalist style with muted colors and wood furniture. The location is key, as it's right across the street from Hallgrímskirkja in downtown Reykjavík. Guests have access to a shared kitchen to prepare meals, and a breakfast buffet is included in the price. The breakfast accommodates vegetarians as well as those with gluten allergies.

CENTER HOTELS PLAZA

Aðalstræti 4; tel. 354/595-8500; www.centerhotels.is; rooms from 21,000ISK

Center Hotels Plaza is in the heart of Reykjavík. Many of the 180 rooms have spectacular views of the city, but with that comes quite a bit of noise during the weekends. The rooms are cozy and sparsely decorated but clean and bright. The bathrooms are small, with a shower, and each room has a flat-screen TV and free Wi-Fi. The clientele is a mix of business and leisure travelers. A lounge downstairs tends to be sleepy because of the proximity to popular bars downtown.

LOFT HOSTEL

Bankastræti 7; tel. 354/553-8140; www.lofthostel.is; private rooms from 22,000ISK

Loft Hostel has a reputation as a place to see and be seen. Rooms range from dorm accommodation to privates, but the big draw is the 4th-floor bar/café that hosts up-and-coming bands, established live acts, and DJs. An outdoor deck overlooks Bankastræti in downtown Reykjavík, and it's packed with locals and tourists alike when the sun is shining.

HÓTEL KLÖPP

Klapparstígur 26; tel. 354/595-8520; www.centerhotels.is; rooms from 23,000ISK

Hótel Klöpp offers fresh rooms on a quiet corner in the city center. Some rooms feature warm, bright hues including red walls, while others are stark white, clean, and cool. All rooms have hardwood floors and small private bathrooms. Guests have access to free Wi-Fi, assistance with booking tours is provided, and the friendly staff even offers a northern lights wake-up service in the winter when the aurora borealis is visible.

★ KEX HOSTEL

Skúlagata 28; tel. 354/561-6060; www.kexhostel.is; private rooms from 24,000ISK

Kex Hostel is a lot more than a hostel; it's where music lovers, hipsters, and the beautiful people of downtown Reykjavík congregate, meeting for drinks and live music. The hostel offers options ranging from dorm accommodations to private rooms, all with shared bathroom facilities. That said, most people don't stay for the style or comfort of the rooms, but for the Kex experience. The front lounge houses vintage wall maps, mid-century furniture, and a small stage for live bands to plug in and play. The back room is a converted gym that hosts concerts, fashion and vinyl markets, and even food festivals.

FOSSHÓTEL BARON

Baronsstígur 2-4; tel. 354/562-3204; www.islandhotel.is; rooms from 24,000ISK

Fosshótel Baron may not be pretty from the exterior, but it's clean, convenient, and in a good location in downtown Reykjavík. The 120 rooms range from standard singles and doubles to apartment-style accommodations that have kitchenettes and mini refrigerators. The lobby looks a little depressing, but the accommodating staff and the location make up for it. Guests have access to free Wi-Fi, free and plentiful parking, and an adequate included breakfast.

REYKJAVÍK4YOU APARTMENTS

Laugavegur 85; www.reykjavik4you.com; rooms from 24,000ISK

The Reykjavík4You Apartments offer great spaces in a central location. Studios and one- and two-bedroom apartments are available, and all are stocked with well-equipped kitchens, spacious bathrooms, and bright decor. Apartments are clean and comfortable, with lots of light in the summer months.

ROOM WITH A VIEW

Laugavegur 18; tel. 354/552-7262; www.roomwithaview.is; rooms from 25,000ISK

Room with a View is near all the great bars downtown. Rooms range from small singles to three-bedroom apartments for groups. Rooms are clean and modern, some with private bathroom facilities. Guests have access to two hot tubs as well as a common kitchen area. Be advised that because of the proximity to bars and restaurants, it can be quite noisy on Friday and Saturday nights. If you're looking for a quiet room on a sleepy street, this isn't it.

★ HÓTEL FRÓN

Laugavegur 22A; tel. 354/511-4666; www.hotelfron.is; rooms from 25,000ISK

Hótel Frón couldn't have picked a better location if it tried. Located on the high street Laugavegur, the hotel has single, double, and apartment-style studios that are clean, bright, and comfortable. The apartments come with small kitchens, and a couple of them feature Jacuzzi bathtubs. It's also conveniently close to the bars on Laugavegur—though this means it can be quite noisy on Friday and Saturday nights.

RADISSON BLU SAGA HOTEL

Hagatorg; tel. 354/525-9900; www.radissonhotels.com; rooms from 25,000ISK

Radisson Blu Saga Hotel has a dynamite location in the city center, close to the Reykjavík Art Museum and the famous Bæjarins Beztu Plysur hot dog stand. Rooms are larger than average, many with a maritime theme that's charming. Beds are lush, and the 209 rooms are stocked with bath products from Anne Semonin. Amenities include free Wi-Fi, access to the spa and health center, and two in-house restaurants: Grillið for fine dining and Restaurant Skrudur for more casual meals.

Over 25,000ISK

HOTEL HOLT

Bergstaðastæti 37; tel. 354/552-5700; www.holt.is; rooms from 30,000ISK

Hotel Holt offers spacious, tastefully decorated rooms, some with balconies. Holt is one of the few hotels in downtown Reykjavík that offers room service, and its service and amenities are comparable to upscale hotels in large European cities. Guests also have access to free parking, free Wi-Fi, and a staff eager to assist with tour bookings and recommendations for sights and restaurants.

RADISSON BLU 1919 HOTEL

Posthússtræti 2; tel. 354/599-1000; www.radissonblu.com; rooms from 33,000ISK

Radisson Blu 1919 Hotel is an 88-room hotel that occupies a central location in the capital. Built in 1919, the hotel has undergone a couple of renovations, but it has maintained a lot of its charm. The rooms are large, with hardwood floors, sizable bathrooms, comfortable beds, and free high-speed Wi-Fi. Guests who reserve a suite are treated to a king-size bed, Jacuzzi bathtub, and bathrobe with slippers. Guests also have access to a fitness center with some basic machines. The in-house restaurant is dynamite, with a menu ranging from fresh fish caught off of Iceland's shores to lamb fillets and duck breast entrées.

★ HÓTEL BORG

Posthússtræti 9-11; tel. 354/551-1440; www.keahotels.is; rooms from 40,000ISK

Hótel Borg is a popular choice for celebrities and politicians passing through Reykjavík. Why? Built in 1930, the 56-room four-star downtown hotel is at once elegant, modern, and steeped in old-time charm. Hótel Borg's rooms have custom-made furniture, flat-screen satellite TVs, and very comfortable beds. The in-house restaurant, Silfur, is a favorite, and a café/bar serves light meals.

101 HOTEL

Hverfisgata 10; tel. 354/580-0101; www.101hotel.is; rooms from 40,000ISK

Award-winning 101 Hotel is quite posh for Reykjavík. Rooms are cozy and stylish with a black-and-white color palette, wood floors, and in-room fireplaces. And while the rooms are pricey, the amenities are pretty great. Each room has a large walk-in shower, flat-screen TV with satellite channels, free high-speed Wi-Fi, a CD/DVD player with a Bose sound dock, and bathrobes and slippers. The restaurant offers an eclectic menu with creations ranging from mussels and pommes frites to Icelandic cod with saffron risotto.

KVOSIN HOTEL

Kirkutorg 4; tel. 354/571-4460; www.kvosinhotel.is; rooms from 41,000ISK

Kvosin Hotel is a gorgeous modern boutique hotel situated close to the Pond and parliament in downtown Reykjavík. Rooms come in four adorably described sizes: normal, bigger, biggest, and larger than life. All rooms feature a mini refrigerator, a Nespresso machine, a Samsung Smart TV, and skin-care amenities from Aveda. The rooms are sleek and Scandinavian cool with accents from local Icelandic designers. A delicious breakfast is included and served downstairs at the Bergsson restaurant.

CANOPY BY HILTON REYKJAVÍK CITY CENTRE

Smiðjustígur 4; tel. 354/528-7000; www.canopyreykjavik.com; rooms from 51,000ISK

Canopy by Hilton is modern, full of art and interesting architecture with a funky lobby and spacious rooms. The room decor features soft muted colors, hardwood floors, and exquisite linens. Each room has a Nespresso coffee maker, a 48-inch HDTV, memory-foam beds, and an included breakfast.

OLD HARBOR (GRANDI)

Over 25,000ISK

★ ICELANDAIR HÓTEL REYKJAVÍK MARINA

Myrargata 2; tel. 354/560-8000; www.icelandairhotels.com; rooms from 32,000ISK

Icelandair Hótel Reykjavík Marina is in a

great location by the harbor district, close to the whale-watching tours, restaurants, and museums. One of the most design conscious of the Icelandair Hótels chain, Reykjavík Marina displays art throughout the lobby, restaurant, and rooms, featuring everything from murals by local Icelandic artists to impressive wood sculptures. Rooms are minimalist and modern, the staff is warm, and the hotel is home to one of the hippest hotel bars in the city, **Slipp Bar.**

OUTSIDE THE CITY CENTER

Under 25,000ISK

REYKJAVÍK LIGHTS HOTEL

Suðurlandsbraut 16; tel. 354/513-9000; www.keahotels.is; rooms from 22,000ISK

Reykjavík Lights Hotel is a concept design hotel with 105 rooms, including singles, doubles, triples, and group rooms. Just past the reception area is an airy lobby that houses a bar and the common eating area. Rooms are large, featuring Nordic-style decor and luxurious beds. The bathrooms are modern and stark white with showers. Located outside of the city center, it's about a 10-minute walk to downtown.

Over 25,000ISK

ICELANDAIR HÓTEL REYKJAVÍK NATURA

Hlídarfótur; tel. 354/444-4500; www.icelandairhotels.com; rooms from 26,400ISK

Icelandair Hótel Reykjavík Natura pays homage to Reykjavík's rich art culture with murals and sculptures throughout the building. Built in 1964, the hotel has been a favorite among business travelers due to its proximity to the Reykjavík City Airport and conference facilities. The in-house restaurant Satt offers a delicious breakfast buffet and meals throughout the day. The main attractions, for many, are the indoor swimming pool and Soley Natura Spa, where guests can get massages, manicures, pedicures, and facial treatments. The hotel is a 20-minute walk to downtown Reykjavík, but guests are given free passes for the city bus, which stops just outside the hotel.

GRAND HOTEL REYKJAVÍK

Sigtún 38; tel. 354/514-8000; www.grand.is; rooms from 33,000ISK

Grand Hotel Reykjavík is a huge 311-room high-rise hotel just a few minutes from downtown Reykjavík. This is a favorite among business travelers and conference attendees because the hotel has meeting rooms and conference facilities. The rooms are large, with hardwood floors and comfortable yet uninspiring furnishings. The **restaurant** (lunch noon-2pm, dinner 6pm-10pm) offers dishes ranging from lamb fillets with mushrooms to duck breast with parsnip.

HILTON REYKJAVÍK NORDICA

Suðurlandsbraut 2; tel. 354/444-5000; www.hiltonreykjavik.com; rooms from 35,000ISK

Hilton Reykjavík Nordica is a 252-room four-star hotel situated in the financial district, about a 10-minute walk from downtown Reykjavík. It attracts business travelers as well as families and individuals thanks to its comfortable rooms, top-notch service, luxurious spa, and memorable in-house restaurant, Vox.

THE REYKJAVÍK EDITION

Austurbakki 2; tel. 354/582-0000; www.editionhotels.com; rooms from 101,000ISK

The Reykjavík Edition opened in late 2021, becoming the capital city's first five-star hotel. Located right next to Harpa concert hall, it's close to everything and has stunning ocean and mountain views. Rooms feature design elements curated by the world-renowned hotelier Ian Schrager, with bespoke furniture, faux fur rugs, and local artwork. There's an in-house restaurant and bar as well as a spa and fitness center. If you want a luxury hotel experience in Reykjavík, this is it.

Information and Services

VISITORS CENTERS

There are currently no tourist information centers in Reykjavík.

MEDIA

The **Reykjavík Grapevine** (www.grapevine.is) is Iceland's only English-language newspaper, and it's geared toward tourists, hipsters, and music-loving locals. There are listings for bands and DJ club dates, information about what's on at museums and art galleries, and articles ranging from humorous to informative to sarcastic on what's going on in Reykjavík. To get the pulse of the city, pick up a copy in bookstores, museums, and shops, or check it out online. In summertime, the newspaper comes out every other week, and in the winter it's monthly.

EMERGENCY SERVICES

The telephone number for emergencies is **112.** If you are having a medical emergency, are stranded by car trouble, or are experiencing a safety issue or any other pressing, dire emergency, dial this number.

MEDICAL SERVICES

LANDSPITALI

Norðurmýri; tel. 354/543-1000; www.landspitali.is

Landspitali is the national hospital of Iceland. It houses day-patient units, an emergency room, and clinical services. If you are experiencing a medical emergency, dial 112 for an ambulance.

LYF OG HEILSA

Haaleitisbraut 68; tel. 354/581-2101; 8am-midnight Mon.-Fri., 10am-midnight Sat.-Sun.

For a pharmacy, visit Lyf og Heilsa. Keep in mind that over-the-counter medication and aspirin are only available at a pharmacy, not in supermarkets or convenience stores like in other countries.

Getting There and Around

GETTING THERE

By Plane

KEFLAVÍK INTERNATIONAL AIRPORT

Reykjanesbær; www.isavia.is

Keflavík International Airport (KEF) is just 50 minutes east of Reykjavík. The **Flybus** (tel. 354/580-5400; www.flybus.is) runs regularly from Keflavík International Airport to **BSÍ,** Reykjavík's main bus station, where you can get a shuttle to the downtown hotels. It takes about 50 minutes to get from Keflavík to BSÍ bus station, and buses depart about 40 minutes after flights land. One-way tickets cost 3,499ISK. (BSÍ is also the main departure site for day-tour bus trips with various companies, including Reykjavík Excursions.) **Taxis** are also available at Keflavík; the fare from the airport to Reykjavík is upward of 15,000ISK.

There is no shortage of companies in Iceland eager to rent you a car, and many of them make it quite easy, with offices at Keflavík International Airport. They include the following: **Avis** (Knarrarvogur 2; tel. 354/591-4000; www.avis.is), **Budget** (Vatsmýrarvegur 10; tel. 354/562-6060; www.budget.is), **Europcar** (Hjallahrauni 9; tel. 354/565-3800; www.europcar.is), and **Hertz** (Reykjavík City Airport; tel. 354/505-0600; www.hertz.is).

REYKJAVÍK CITY AIRPORT

Þorragata 10; tel. 354/569-4100; www.isavia.is

Reykjavík City Airport is the city's domestic airport, with regional connections to towns throughout the country, including Akureyi and the Westfjords. The only international flights are to the Faroe Islands and Greenland. **Strætó** (www.straeto.is) bus numbers 15 and 19 stop at the Reykjavík City Airport near the Air Iceland and Eagle Air terminals, respectively. Taxis are also available on-site.

Several airlines have offices in Reykjavík, including **Eagle Air** (Reykjavíkurflugvöllur; tel. 354/562-4200; www.eagleair.is) and **Icelandair** (Reykjavíkurflugvöllur; tel. 354/505-0100; www.icelandair.is).

By Car

In addition to rental car centers at Keflavík, there are convenient outposts at BSÍ bus stations, and around the city. If you are planning to stay in Reykjavík for the duration of your trip, a rental car will not be necessary.

GETTING AROUND

By Bus

BSÍ

Vatnsmýrarvegur 10; tel. 354/562-1011; www.bsi.is

Reykjavík's bus system is a convenient, reliable, and affordable way to get around the city. The bus system, called **Strætó** (www.straeto.is), which means "street" in Icelandic, runs about 30 bus lines within the city center as well as to outlying areas like Kópavogur and Hafnarfjörður. The bright yellow buses cost 490ISK per ride within the city limits, and you can ask for a free bus transfer if you need to switch buses to get to your destination. You must pay with exact change; bus drivers don't make change. Buses run daily 7am-11pm. Be sure to check the website for information on holiday schedules and delays due to weather.

If you plan to use the bus a fair amount, a great option is the **Reykjavík Welcome Card,** which grants you free access to the city's swimming pools, almost all the city's museums, and unlimited city bus rides. You can purchase a card for one, two, or three days for 4,200ISK, 5,850ISK, and 7,200ISK, respectively. If you will be spending a lot of time in Reykjavík, this is a great option to save a lot of money. Cards can be purchased online and at select hotels and bus stations. You can also buy individual tickets through the Strætó app.

Strætó's blue long-distance buses depart from **Mjodd station** (tel. 354/557-7854), 8 kilometers (5 mi) southeast of the city center, traveling to several regions around the country.

By Taxi

The two things you need to know about taxis in Reykjavík is that they are expensive, and you have to call ahead for one (for instance, a ride from the BSÍ bus station to Harpa takes about eight minutes and costs roughly 2,000ISK). **Hreyfill** (tel. 354/588-5522; www.hreyfill.is) and **BSR** (tel. 354/561-0000; www.taxireykjavik.is) are two popular taxi companies in the city. You can also reserve taxis with Hreyfill through an app. Taxis arrive 5-10 minutes after you call, and the price on the meter is inclusive—you don't tip in Iceland. Cab prices rival those in New York City: It's rare to spend less than 2,000ISK on a taxi ride, even for short distances. There are a couple of cab stations downtown where you don't have to call ahead—just outside **Hlemmur bus station** and near **Lækjartorg,** a square in downtown Reykjavík where Lækjargata, Bankastræti, and Austurstræti streets meet. The taxi stands are hard to miss, as the cabs can be lined up 10 deep.

By Car

If your entire stay is in Reykjavík, it is not necessary to rent a car as the city is walkable, and buses are widely available. However, if you are getting out of the city and do not want to take tours, a car rental is necessary.

Be advised that **parking** isn't easy in Reykjavík. Most locals have cars, and street parking can take some time. However, there are several parking garages and lots around the city, and parking at a garage will cost less than 200ISK per hour.

On Foot

Reykjavík is a very walkable city—depending on the weather, of course. Because of its small size, it's a perfect place to roam, pop into quaint shops, visit museums, and photograph the city's many statues.

Around Reykjavík

VIÐEY ISLAND

Viðey is a little gem of an island accessible by ferry. Historically, the island was inhabited by an Augustinian monastery from 1225 to 1539 and was a pilgrimage destination in the Middle Ages. It's also home to Viðeyjarstofa, one of the oldest buildings in Iceland. The island, which is just 1.6 square kilometers (0.6 sq mi) in size, hosts unspoiled nature with vast stretches of grassy plains and rich birdlife, as well as the Imagine Peace Tower, an installation created by Yoko Ono.

Sights

VIÐEYJARSTOFA

www.visitreykjavik.is

One of the oldest buildings in the country, Viðeyjarstofa dates back to 1755. Over generations, it has served as a home to many of Iceland's most powerful men. The building, made from white stone with a black roof, is open to the public.

IMAGINE PEACE TOWER

www.imaginepeacetower.com

This outdoor installation was created by artist Yoko Ono in memory of her late husband, John Lennon. Ono chose Iceland because it's one of the most peaceful countries in the world. The base of the tower is 10 meters (33 ft) wide, and the words "imagine peace" are inscribed on the structure in 24 languages. A vertical beam of light shines from the structure 4,000 meters (13,123 ft) into the sky and is visible from miles away. It was unveiled on October 9, 2007, Lennon's 67th birthday. It's lit every year from October 9 to December 8, the latter of which is the anniversary of Lennon's death.

Getting There and Around

In the summer, **Elding** (tel. 354/533-5055; www.elding.is) operates a ferry with eight daily departures mid-May through September from **Skarfabakki pier, Harpa,** and **Ægisgarður pier.** Ferries run in the afternoon. During the rest of the year the ferry runs three departures on Saturdays and Sundays from Skarfabakki to Viðey. The round-trip ferry ride costs 1,700ISK for adults and 850ISK for children 7-15, and takes about 10 minutes.

SELTJARNARNES

Grótta Lighthouse

www.visitreykjavik.is

Northwest of Reykjavík sits Grótta, a lovely lighthouse you can walk to during low tide. The lighthouse is located in Seltjarnarnes, which is technically outside of Reykjavík, and has stood since 1947. In the summer, Grótta is a great spot to visit to bask in the sun and observe the rich birdlife in the area. In the winter, locals and travelers drive to the car park on clear nights and hope to catch a glimpse of the northern lights.

Getting There

To reach Grótta Lighthouse, you can take a taxi from downtown Reykjavík, which will cost about 2,500ISK, or you can take bus 11 to the lighthouse. It's about a 10-minute drive along Eiðsgrandi, which runs along the peninsula northwest of Reykjavík where Seltjarnarnes sits. Better yet, it's an easy cycle.

MOSFELLSBÆR

Just 15 minutes from downtown Reykjavík, Mosfellsbær is a quaint, placid town with a picturesque bay, beautiful mountains, and clean streams and rivers. About 10,000 people live in Mosfellsbær, and despite its proximity to downtown, it feels remote enough to make it seem like you're in the countryside.

Around Reykjavík

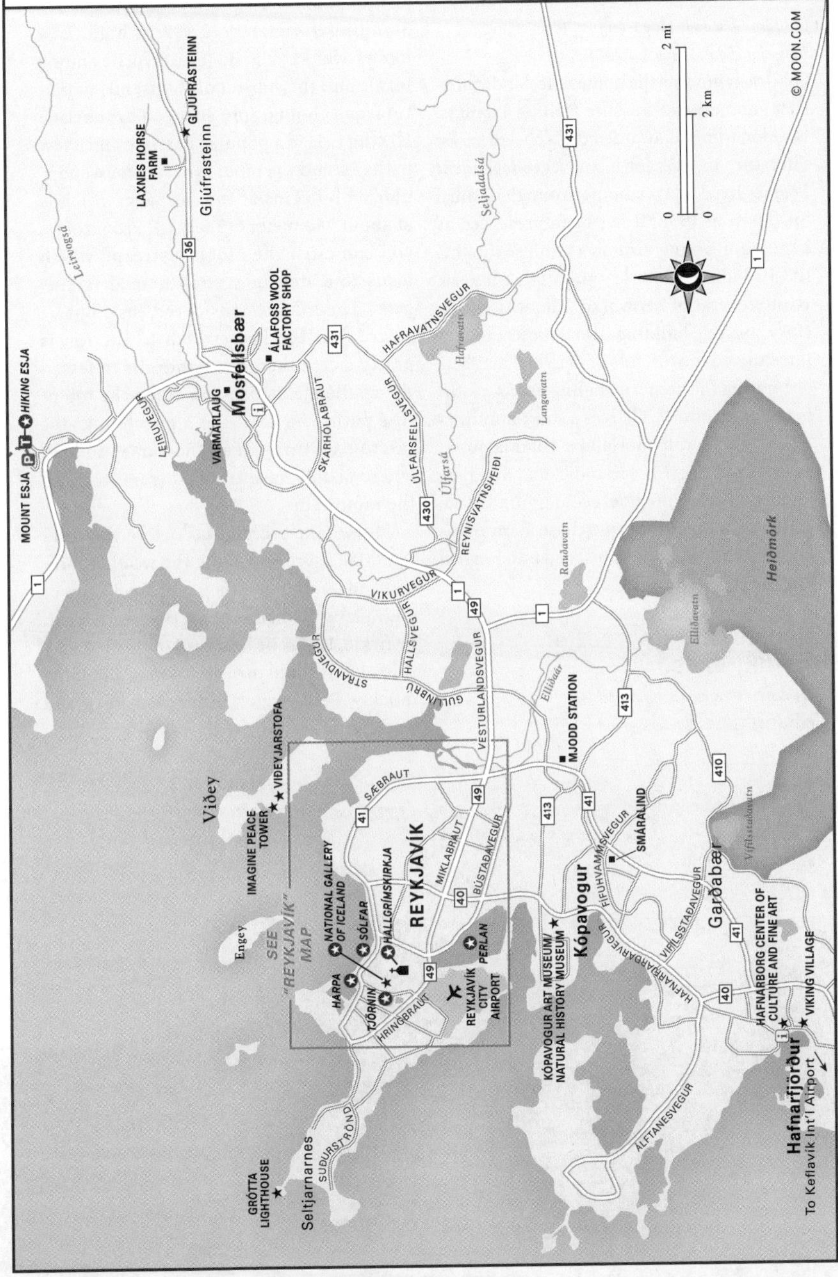
MOUNT ESJA
HIKING ESJA
LAXNES HORSE FARM
GLJÚFRASTEINN
Gljúfrasteinn
Leirvogsá
Mosfellsbær
ÁLAFOSS WOOL FACTORY SHOP
VARMÁRLAUG
LEIRUVEGUR
SKARHÓLABRAUT
HAFRAVATNSVEGUR
Hafravatn
ÚLFARSFELLSVEGUR
Úlfarsá
Langavatn
Seljadalsá
REYNISVATNSHEIÐI
Rauðavatn
VIKURVEGUR
HALLSVEGUR
STRANDVEGUR
GULLINBRÚ
VESTURLANDSVEGUR
Elliðavatn
Heiðmörk
Elliðaár
MJODD STATION
Viðey
VIÐEYJARSTOFA
IMAGINE PEACE TOWER
Engey
SEE "REYKJAVÍK" MAP
NATIONAL GALLERY OF ICELAND
SÓLFAR
HALLGRÍMSKIRKJA
HARPA
TJÖRNIN
REYKJAVÍK
SÆBRAUT
MIKLABRAUT
BÚSTAÐAVEGUR
HRINGBRAUT
REYKJAVÍK CITY AIRPORT
PERLAN
KÓPAVOGUR ART MUSEUM/ NATURAL HISTORY MUSEUM
Kópavogur
FÍFUHVAMMSVEGUR
SMÁRALIND
VÍFILSSTAÐAVEGUR
Vífilsstaðavatn
Garðabær
HAFNARFJARÐARVEGUR
HAFNARBORG CENTER OF CULTURE AND FINE ART
VIKING VILLAGE
Hafnarfjörður
To Keflavík Int'l Airport
ÁLFTANESVEGUR
Seltjarnarnes
SUÐURSTRÖND
GRÓTTA LIGHTHOUSE
1
36
431
430
49
413
410
41
40
0
2 mi
2 km
© MOON.COM

Sights

GLJÚFRASTEINN

Pósthólf 250; tel. 354/568-8066; www.gljufrasteinn.is; 10am-5pm daily May 1-Aug. 31, 10am-4pm Tues.-Sun. Sept. 1-Nov. 1; 1,200ISK

Gljúfrasteinn was the home of Icelandic novelist and national treasure Halldór Laxness. Halldór, who was awarded the Nobel Prize for Literature in 1955 for his novel *Independent People*, lived at this home from 1945 until his death in 1998. It has been preserved as a museum, giving visitors a glimpse into his life, including the library and study where he wrote several of his works. The white two-story concrete building is well preserved, but it feels lived in with lots of personal artifacts decorating the home, including books, clothing, and furniture. There is a short multimedia presentation about Halldór's life and work, available in English, Icelandic, and Swedish. Guided tours of the house and grounds take about an hour. You can purchase many of his books at the museum, translated into English and German.

Sports and Recreation

★ HIKING ESJA

Distance: *8 km (5 mi) round-trip*
Hiking time: *2 hours round-trip*
Information and Maps: *www.visitreykjavik.is*
Trailhead: *Car park just off the Ring Road, signed for Esja*

Standing 914 meters (2,999 ft) high, Esja looms over Reykjavík. It's a favorite among locals and the subject of thousands of picturesque photographs snapped by tourists. Hiking Esja is a popular pastime and a few paths ascend the mountain. The most popular path begins at the car park, which is at about 780 meters (2,559 ft). From there, you can cross the Mógilsa stream, which leads to a steeper stretch named "steinnin." The hike is considered easy, but be aware that the last stretch to the top is pretty steep; there are handrails to lessen the challenge. When you reach the top of this path, you can sign a guestbook. It's fun to read through all the names and see where people have traveled from to climb the mountain.

Please take precautions before you head out. Make sure you check the weather forecast and let your guesthouse or hotel know of your plans. Remember that the weather can be fickle. It may be beautiful out with sunny skies, but it could turn very windy and rainy quickly. Bring water, proper footwear, and waterproof clothing with you.

Mount Esja

Getting to Esja is pretty easy, even if you don't have access to a car. It's 11 kilometers (6.8 mi) north of Mosfellsbær, about 20 minutes and accessible from Route 1. Drive through Mosfellsbær and you'll see signs pointing to the car park. You can also take the **Strætó** 57 bus (www.straeto.is) from the bus station Mjodd in Reykjavík. The bus fare is 980ISK and the bus departs 12 times a day. It's a 30-minute ride. Let the bus driver know that you are heading to the base of Esja (the bus stop is Esjumelar) and you will get dropped off at the car park.

LAXNES FARM

off Route 36; tel. 354/566-6179; www.laxnes.is

If you're staying in Reykjavík and want to do some horseback riding, Laxnes Farm is just a 15-minute drive northeast from downtown. Icelandic horses are available to ride year-round for different tour lengths. The staff is warm and friendly and shows a great deal of love and respect for the horses. A popular tour is called the "Laxnes Special"; you will be picked up at your hotel or guesthouse in Reykjavík and taken to the farm, where you will meet your guide and horse. You are given all the gear you need, including helmets, rain clothes, and boots, and are taken on a glorious two-hour tour (12,900ISK) that has spectacular landscape views. The Laxnes Farm is close to Halldór Laxness's home, but they are not related.

VARMÁRLAUG

Þverholt 2; tel. 354/566-6754; 6:30am-9pm Mon.-Fri., 9am-5pm Sat.-Sun.; 850ISK

If you're planning to stay in town for a few hours or more, check out the local swimming pool, called Varmárlaug. The pool isn't as impressive as some of the pools in the Reykjavík city center, but the water is warm and the facilities are clean. You're likely to see locals taking a dip, but not many tourists.

Shopping

ÁLAFOSS WOOL FACTORY SHOP

Álafossvegur 23; tel. 354/822-9100; www.alafoss.is; 10am-6pm daily

The Álafoss Wool Factory Shop is home to the Álafoss wool brand, which was established in 1896 and was for decades the leading manufacturer and exporter of Icelandic wool products. The brand is still manufacturing in Iceland today. The shop is located in the old factory house by the Álafoss waterfall, which was used to drive the mills. The shop sells wool skeins, scarves, hats, sweaters, and blankets, along with some other small goods. You can also purchase a sheep skin as well as other Icelandic design products. The prices are comparable to those in downtown Reykjavík, but the selection is better and bigger. The site also includes an exhibition of old knitting machinery and photographs from the mill's early days.

Food

MOSFELLSBAKARÍ

Háholti 13-15; tel. 354/566-6145; www.mosfellsbakari.is; 7:30am-5:30pm Mon.-Fri., 8am-4pm Sat.-Sun.; pastries from 600ISK

Mosfellsbakarí is a decadent bakery known for its chocolate creations. Located in the center of town, it does a roaring business. In addition to its indulgent cakes and pastries, the bakery offers light meals, including sandwiches and soup.

Information and Services

TOURIST INFORMATION OFFICE

Þverholti 2; tel. 354/525-6700; www.mosfellsbaer.is; 9am-5pm daily

Mosfellsbær's tourist information office is based inside the **Mosfellsbær public library,** which is housed in a shopping area. It's a great place to gather some tourist brochures and maps as well as buy some food at the grocery store inside the shopping center.

Getting There

Mosfellsbær is just a 15-minute drive (14 km/9 mi) from downtown **Reykjavík** via **Route 49. Street parking** is available, and it's easy to find parking spots.

You can take the **15 bus** to the **Haholt stop,** which is in the center of town. Check www.straeto.is for more bus information. Depending on the time of day, buses run every 30 minutes to every hour, and it takes 30 minutes from downtown Reykjavík to Mosfellsbær. A single ride on the bus is 470ISK.

KÓPAVOGUR

Kópavogur is a quiet suburb home to families, young professionals, and immigrants, and it attracts people traveling on business or shoppers headed to the Smáralind mall or the island's only IKEA and Costco. There are a couple of museums worth checking out for local art and history.

Sights

KÓPAVOGUR ART MUSEUM

(Gerðarsafn)

Hamraborg 4; tel. 354/570-0440; www.gerdarsafn.is; 10am-5pm daily; 1,000ISK

The Kópavogur Art Museum is named Gerðarsafn in Icelandic, after sculptor Gerður Helgadóttir, who died in 1975. In 1977, her heirs donated roughly 1,400 of her works to the municipality of Kópavogur on the condition that a museum bearing her name would be opened. The museum opened in 1994. Gerður's black-iron works in the 1950s made her a pioneer of three-dimensional abstract art in Iceland. Around 1970 Gerður returned to working with plaster, terra cotta, and concrete, using simple circles with movement in many variations. Other works on display range from contemporary to landscape art. It's a pretty museum with varied works of art, and it's worth a visit if you're in the neighborhood.

NATURAL HISTORY MUSEUM

(Náttúrúfræðistofa)

Hamraborg 6A; tel. 354/570-0430; www.natkop.is; 8am-6pm Mon.-Fri., 11am-5pm Sat.; free

The Natural History Museum is a great place to bring kids to learn about the animals and geology of Iceland. The exhibits fall into two categories: zoological and geological. The geology section, where you learn about the major rock types and minerals of Iceland, is of more interest to adults. The zoological part focuses on the mammals, fish, birds, and invertebrates of the country. It's educational and entertaining, and kids love the exhibitions on seals, foxes, and cute birds like puffins.

Sports and Recreation

KÓPAVOGUR SWIMMING POOL

Borgarholtsbruat 17; tel. 354/540-0470; 6:30am-10pm Mon.-Fri., 8am-8pm Sat.-Sun.; 900ISK

The Kópavogur Swimming Pool is frequented by locals and their children and has a very family-friendly atmosphere. Amenities include a 50-meter (164-ft) outdoor pool, two smaller indoor pools, three waterslides, seven hot tubs, and a steam bath. You aren't likely to see crowds or tourists, so if you're looking to just swim, this is a good spot.

Food and Shopping

SMÁRALIND

Hagasmara 1; tel. 354/528-8000; www.smaralind.is; 11am-7pm Mon.-Fri., 11am-6pm Sat., noon-5pm Sun.

Smáralind is Iceland's largest shopping mall. You will find everything from Adidas sneakers to Levi's, but for double the price that they would be back home. However, there is a movie theater and an entertainment area with rides for kids. In addition to a food court, there is coffee shop Kaffitár, and Serrano, which serves Mexican-style food.

Information and Services

SERVICE AND ADMINISTRATION CENTER

Fannborg 2; tel. 354/570-1500

The town's service and administration center is open 8am-4pm Monday-Friday.

Getting There

Kópavogur is just a 10-minute ride, 5 kilometers (3 mi) south from downtown **Reykjavík** by car. Take **Route 40** to **Route 49.** Street parking is available and it's easy to find parking spots.

City buses go to Kópavogur, including **buses 1, 2,** and **28.** Buses leave every 30 minutes or so, the fare is 490ISK one-way, and it takes about 20 minutes by bus. Check www.straeto.is for more bus information.

HAFNARFJÖRÐUR

Hafnarfjörður is a picturesque fishing town that about 30,000 people call home. Attractions include a scenic harbor, pretty parks, and the famous Viking Village, a restaurant and hotel that plays host to numerous Viking-related events.

Sights

HAFNARBORG CENTER OF CULTURE AND FINE ART

Strandgata 34; tel. 354/555-0800; www.hafnarborg.is; noon-5pm Wed.-Mon.; free

Hafnarborg Center of Culture and Fine Art consists of two galleries with rotating exhibitions ranging from contemporary art by modern Icelandic artists to works by some of the island's most celebrated artists of years past.

VIKING VILLAGE

(Fjörukráin)

Strandgata 55; tel. 354/565-1213; www.fjorukrain.is

Viking Village is great fun for kids and adults alike. The closest thing Iceland has to a theme park, the Viking Village celebrates the island's history—with a sense of humor. It's kitschy, with lots of Viking horns, reproduced wood huts, and wooden furnishings. Guests can stay at the hotel, visit the gift shop, have a meal at the restaurant, or just check out the decor.

Sports and Recreation

ÍSHESTAR

Sörlaskeið 26; tel. 354/555-7000; www.ishestar.is

This town is a lovely place to ride a horse. With its rolling landscape and picturesque views, it doesn't get much better than this in the greater Reykjavík area. Íshestar is a local company that offers an array of tours year-round. It provides transportation to the riding center from your accommodation and all gear needed to ride. A half-day tour starts at 15,900ISK.

SUÐURBÆJARLAUG

Hringbruat 77; tel. 354/565-3080; 6:30am-10pm Mon.-Thurs., 6:30am-8pm Fri., 8am-6pm Sat., 8am-5pm Sun.; 850ISK

Take a dip with the locals at the Suðurbæjarlaug pool, which has an outdoor pool with a waterslide, a steam bath, and a few hot tubs.

Food

SÚFISTINN

Strandgata 9; tel. 354/565-3740; 11:30am-5:30pm daily; 1,500ISK

Súfistinn is a cozy café that sells stellar coffee drinks, fresh pastries, and light meals. Situated by the central downtown shopping area and performance hall, it's a perfect place to grab a blueberry muffin and latte or a soup or sandwich.

VIKING RESTAURANT

Strandagata 55; tel. 354/565-1213; www.fjorukrain.is; 2,800ISK

Viking Restaurant (Fjörugarðurinn) at the Viking Village is a restaurant that serves traditional Icelandic fare like lamb and fish dishes in a fun, Viking-themed atmosphere. There are lots of wood furnishings and medieval accents displayed throughout the space. You can book a Viking performance in advance for groups of any size for a fee, which

1

2

includes the guests being "kidnapped" from their bus, brought into a "cave" in the restaurant, served mead, escorted to dinner, and entertained with singing and music. The restaurant is open for dinner 6pm-10pm daily.

Accommodations

HÓTEL VIKING

Strandgata 55; tel. 354/565-1213; www.vikingvillage.is; rooms from 26,000ISK

Hótel Viking at the Viking Village has 42 hotel rooms and 14 "Viking cottages" next to the hotel. All rooms and cottages include private bathrooms, comfortable beds, televisions, and stylish Viking accessories. The hotel features artwork from Iceland, Greenland, and the Faroe Islands. Guests have access to free Wi-Fi, free parking, and an on-site hot tub. Breakfast is included in the price.

Information and Services

TOURIST INFORMATION CENTER

Strandgata 6; tel. 354/585-5555; www.hafnarfjordur.is; 10am-5pm Mon.-Fri. year-round, 10am-3pm Sat.-Sun. June-Aug.

The tourist information center is situated in **Hafnarfjörður Town Hall.** You can arrange for transportation, buy tickets to local tours, and peruse brochures about the town's sights.

Getting There

Hafnarfjörður is just a 15-minute drive, 11 kilometers (7 mi) south of downtown **Reykjavík.** Take **Route 40** to get there.

City Bus 1 stops in town. Check www.straeto.is for bus schedules and information.

1: Viðey Island 2: Hafnarfjörður

Reykjanes Peninsula and the South

South Iceland is the country's busiest tourist destination, but in many places it still feels untouched.

Glaciers, mountains, and two active volcanoes (Katla and Hekla) beckon. A wide and diverse region, the south is home to well-known sights like Þingvellir National Park and the Geysir geothermal region, both on the popular Golden Circle tour, and lesser-known gems like Þórsmörk, an area with colorful mountains, waterfalls, canyons, and lava-shaped landscapes.

The terrain is rugged, even desert-like in some areas; elsewhere, heather, moss, and lichen cover lava stones for miles. It's also steeped in history. Þingvellir National Park is commonly referred to as the site of the world's first democracy: It's said that a group of settlers

Highlights

Look for ★ to find recommended sights, activities, dining, and lodging.

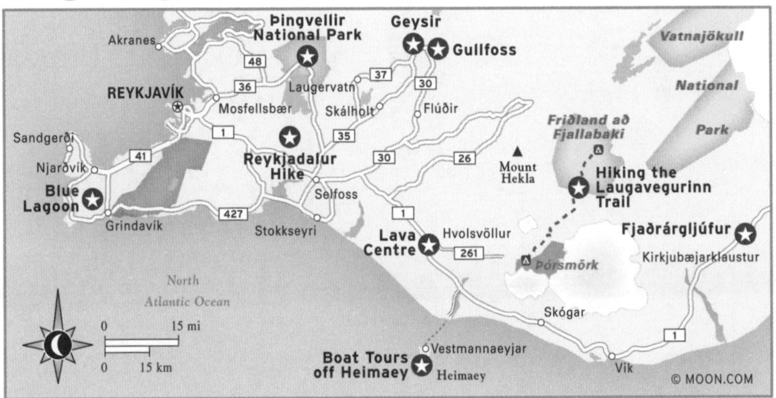

★ **Blue Lagoon:** This gorgeous, geothermally heated spring heals the skin and soothes the body (page 92).

★ **Þingvellir National Park:** Appealing to both geology buffs and history enthusiasts, this park is home to where Europe and North America meet, as well as the site where Iceland's first parliament gathered (page 96).

★ **Geysir:** Make the trip to see the Strokkur geyser shoot steam and boiling water up to 30 meters (98 ft), a natural phenomenon that occurs every 10 minutes or so (page 102).

★ **Gullfoss:** If you have time to see only one waterfall in Iceland, this should be it (page 104).

★ **Reykjadalur Hike:** This increasingly popular, relatively short hike gives you the chance to soak your feet in picturesque hot springs (page 110).

★ **Lava Centre:** Take a deep dive into Iceland's unique geology, from volcanoes to the constant small tremors that parts of the island experience (page 114).

★ **Hiking the Laugavegurinn Trail:** See vast glaciers, bubbling hot springs, and towering mountains on this 55-kilometer (34-mi), four-day hike, one of the most popular trails on the island (page 116).

★ **Fjaðrárgljúfur:** This long, narrow canyon is an extremely picturesque place to hike and take photos (page 127).

★ **Boat Tours off Heimaey:** Whether you choose a tour offered by the new beluga whale sanctuary, or one of the others offering views of rocky coastlines, bird cliffs, and ocean caves, the island of Heimaey is a lovely place to take a boat ride (page 129).

Reykjanes Peninsula and the South

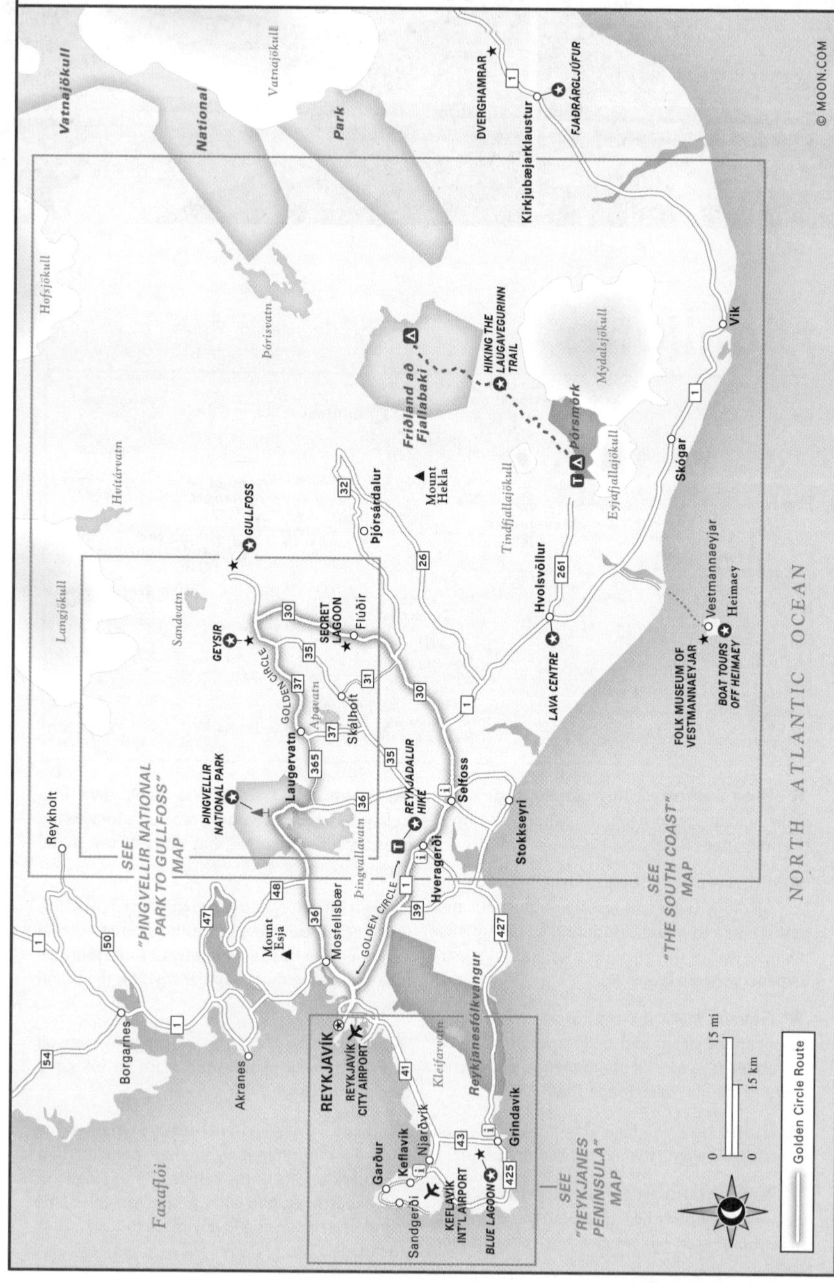

Volcanic Eruption in Geldingadalur Valley

In March 2021, deep in the Reykjanes Peninsula, a large crack opened up in the earth, birthing Iceland's newest volcano. After weeks of earthquakes, the eruption began the evening of March 19. The initial fissure was reported to be 700 meters (2,300 ft) long and was quickly dubbed a "tourist eruption," as there was no immediate danger and it was relatively easy to get to. Lava spewed in fountains for months, filling valleys and drawing tens of thousands of locals and tourists to marvel at the power and beauty of the natural phenomenon.

The enormous lava field is a 15-minue drive (about 11 km/7 mi) from Grindavík. The volcano officially ceased activity on October 16, but it's only a matter of time until the next eruption! This is the land of fire and ice, after all.

met as a democratic legislature here close to a millennium ago. Geology buffs will be thrilled to visit the Mid-Atlantic Ridge, which separates the North American and Eurasian tectonic plates: You can literally plant one foot on Europe's side and the other in North America.

Outside of Reykjavík, Þingvellir is the most visited site in Iceland, but heading further afield, the South Coast is also not to be missed. Here you will find the romantic Seljalandsfoss and Skógafoss waterfalls and the vast black-sand Reynisfjara beach. The Westman Islands make a wonderful day trip, for whale-watching and learning about volcanic history. And to the south, the Reykjanes Peninsula is one part of the country that visitors are sure to see, as it's home to Iceland's only international airport. It's also where you'll find the famous heated waters of the Blue Lagoon, where you can soak away your jet lag.

PLANNING YOUR TIME

The dynamic Reykjanes Peninsula, **Golden Circle,** and southern coast region is defined by its vast lava fields, numerous hot springs, geothermal energy, and rugged terrain. Most tourists plan to visit at least two sites other than **Keflavík airport**—the **Mid-Atlantic Ridge** at **Þingvellir National Park** and the glorious **Blue Lagoon,** where you can soak in geothermally heated water. Plan to spend at least an afternoon on the Reykjanes Peninsula (likely, at the Blue Lagoon), one day for the Golden Circle, and at least one day exploring the South Coast.

If you are planning to spend one night in the Reykjanes Peninsula region, rather than just basing yourself out of nearby Reykjavík, stay in **Keflavík** or **Grindavík,** where there are several guesthouses and hotels, as well as the largest selection of restaurants and shops. From there, you are close to attractions such as the Blue Lagoon, **Garður lighthouses,** and the **Viking World** museum.

The south is also home to the Golden Circle, arguably the most popular route on the island. It takes you to three must-see sites: the towering **Gullfoss waterfall,** Þingvellir National Park, and **Geysir.** The Golden Circle takes about 6-8 hours to drive in full and can be accomplished in one day, either by a bus tour or independently using a rental car. Though it can definitely be done as a day trip out of Reykjavík, you can also base yourself in the towns of **Selfoss** or **Hvolsvöllur** to cut out a bit of driving time.

Meanwhile, the South Coast has black-sand beaches, waterfalls, and quaint villages like **Vík,** a good place to base yourself for extended exploration in the area. The island of **Heimaey,** off the South Coast, is a wonderful place to explore as a day trip.

Previous: Geysir; walking in Þórsmörk; Gullfoss.

Itinerary Ideas

For maximum flexibility on this itinerary, you'll want your own **rental car.** Many people find themselves in the Reykjanes Peninsula on their way to or from Keflavík airport; it would be possible to do Day 1 of this itinerary straight off your flight, but many people opt to head straight to the **Blue Lagoon** en route to Rekjavík, a more relaxed introduction to the island.

DAY 1: BLUE LAGOON AND REYKJANES PENINSULA

1 Start your day at the **Viking World** museum in Njarðvík, which centers around an authentically rebuilt Viking ship.

2 Next, stop at the **Bridge Between Continents,** a 20-minute drive down Route 425, where you can get a close look at the Mid-Atlantic Ridge, a rift between two continental plates.

3 Enjoy a delicious seafood lunch at **Salthúsið,** 20 minutes east on Route 425.

4 Relax after your meal at the world-famous **Blue Lagoon,** just 10 minutes' drive north.

5 Finally, visit the **Krýsuvík** geothermal area, 30 minutes east on Route 427, where you can see bubbling mud pots and hot springs, before driving 40 minutes north on Route 42 to Rekjavík, where you'll stay for the night. (See Reykjavík chapter, page 30, for ideas on where to stay, go, and eat.)

DAY 2: THE GOLDEN CIRCLE

1 From Reykjavík, embark on your Golden Circle tour, starting at **Þingvellir National Park.** Here, you can walk along a well-maintained path in the rift valley between the Eurasian and North American plates.

2 Drive to the Haukadalur geothermal area for a look at **Geysir,** the original geyser, and its spouting neighbor Strokkur.

3 Enjoy a break at the **Geysir Center,** grabbing lunch at their cafeteria.

4 Visit the roaring **Gullfoss** waterfall, watching the water thrash and tumble meters below.

5 Go for a dip at the geothermally heated **Secret Lagoon** in the village of Fluðir.

6 Stop by **Friðheimar** to check out the tomato greenhouses and taste one of the best Bloody Marys on the island.

7 Drive to Hvolsvöllur for the night, staying at **Midgard Base Camp** and having dinner there.

DAY 3: THE SOUTH COAST

1 Begin your morning with a three-hour tour via super Jeep (a huge Jeep with gigantic tires outfitted to handle rough terrain) with **Midgard Adventure** in Hvolsvöllur, crossing rough terrain and seeing waterfalls and volcanoes.

2 Visit the nearby **Lava Centre** to learn about Iceland's unique geology through interactive display, and then have lunch in the café.

Itinerary Ideas

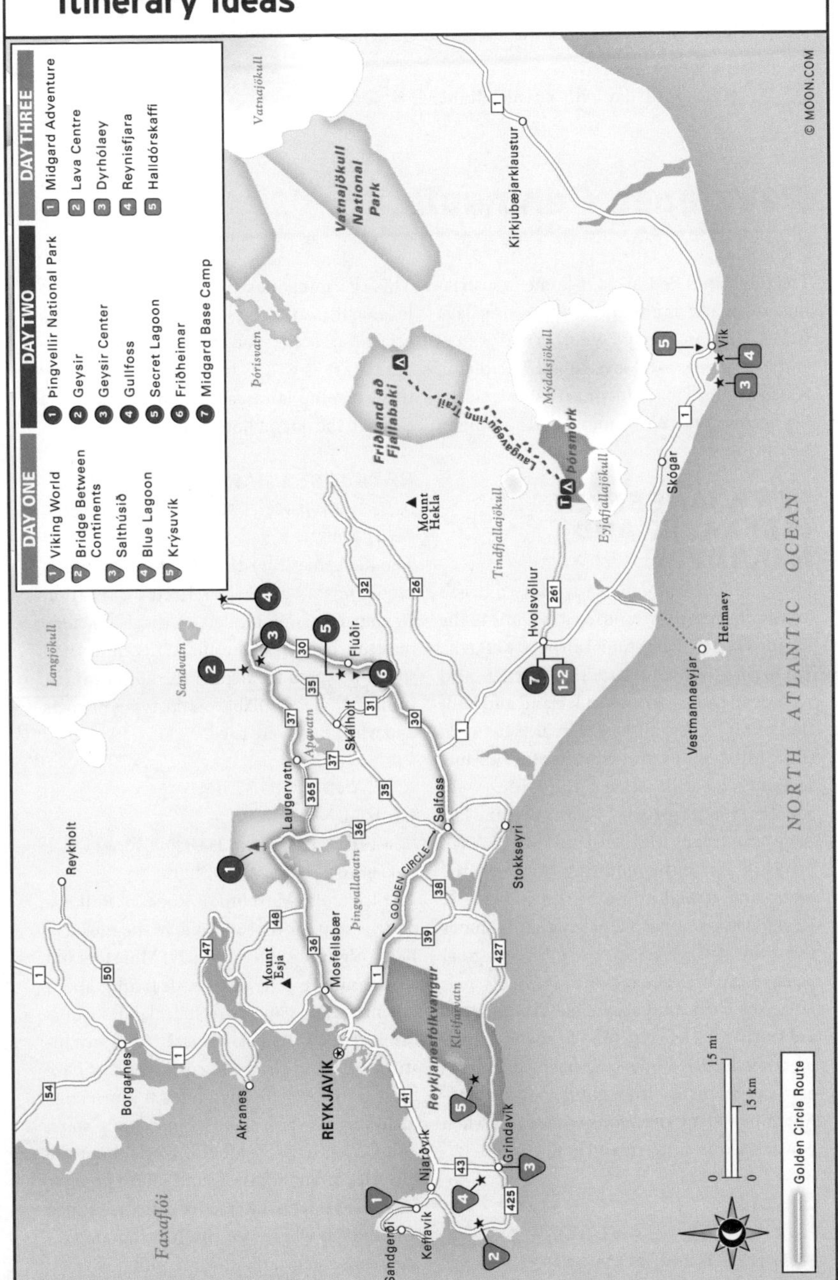

3 Hit the road toward the quaint village of Vík. Stop first at **Dyrhólaey** peninsula, known for its unusual basalt columns.

4 Just a bit to the east are the black-sand beaches of **Reynisfjara**, a scenic place for a bracing walk.

5 Finish a full day with a casual dinner at **Halldórskaffi**.

Reykjanes Peninsula

The Reykjanes Peninsula is home to a striking, dramatic landscape comprising lava fields, volcanic craters, geothermal waters and hot springs, and lava caves. The region is also a hotbed for outdoor activities, including horse riding, ATV riding, and bathing in hot springs.

REYKJANESBÆR (KEFLAVÍK AND NJARÐVÍK)

Reykjanesbær is where nearly every tourist's journey begins in Iceland, as it is home to the country's only international airport, Keflavík.

During World War II, British and American troops arrived in Iceland and built the country's first air base. Situated between the United States and continental Europe, Iceland's location served the Allies well; some may be surprised to learn that the last American troops left the island only in 2006.

While it may be tempting to get off the plane and straight on a bus to Reykjavík, Reykjanesbær, a municipality that includes the towns **Keflavík** and **Njarðvík**, is a great place to explore. The region's lava fields, majestic sea cliffs, and accessible hiking trails are worth a bit of your time to roam. Throw on some hiking boots and have your camera ready. This is also a good spot for birdwatching during the summer months, when you can see arctic terns and gannets.

Sights

REYKJANES ART MUSEUM

Duusgata 2-8, Keflavík; tel. 354/421-6700; www.listasafn.reykjanesbaer.is; noon-5pm daily; 1,000ISK

This charming museum hosts exhibitions of local artists and gives a taste of the region's eclectic art scene. You can check out contemporary art as well as traditional paintings of the sweeping landscape, from its vast lava fields to the quaint houses along the sea.

REYKJANES MARITIME CENTER

Duusgata 2, Keflavík; tel. 354/421-6700; noon-5pm daily; 1,000ISK

The Reykjanes Maritime Center houses 100 model boats built by a retired local sailor, Grímur Karlsson. Models on display include masted schooners of the mid-19th century and steam-powered trawlers of the 20th century. Information is available on the types of boats and when they were used.

ICELANDIC MUSEUM OF ROCK 'N' ROLL

Hjallavegur 2, Keflavík; tel. 354/420-1030; www.rokksafn.is; 11am-6pm daily; 1,500ISK

The Icelandic Museum of Rock 'n' Roll is a perfect stop for those who love the music of Björk, Sigur Rós, Kaleo, and Of Monsters and Men, and are interested in learning about other rock and pop acts from Iceland. Visitors can listen to the music of local artists, see instruments, and check out costumes that have been worn by well-known local musicians, including one of Iceland's biggest pop stars, Páll Óskar. Guests can also learn about the histories of some of the island's most popular bands and singers. Interactive displays include a sound lab where you can have a karaoke-style sing-along or play drums, guitar, or bass. A café and music shop are also on-site.

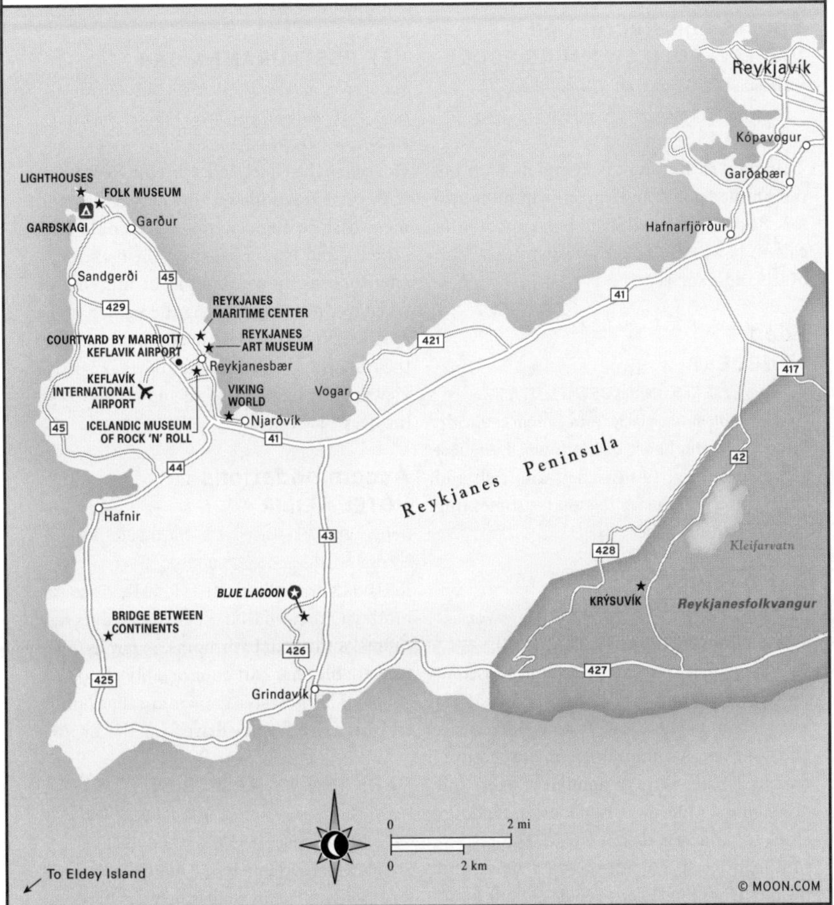

VIKING WORLD
(Vikingaheimar)

Vikingabraut 1, Njarðvík; tel. 354/422-2000; www.vikingworld.is; 10am-4pm Mon.-Sat., 10am-3pm Sun.; 1,500ISK

The Viking World museum is centered on the replica Viking ship *Íslendingur (Icelander),* which was built in 2000 to sail from Iceland to Greenland in commemoration of Leifur Eiríksson's voyage to North America. The ship, which makes for a great photo op, is housed inside a grand building with huge windows overlooking the shore. Lifted slightly above the ground, the ship can be viewed from many angles; tables and chairs below allow you to spend time gazing at the boat with the ocean in the background. A video exhibit shows how Viking ships were constructed. Other exhibitions include information on the settlement of Iceland as well as Norse mythology. When the weather is pleasant, it's great to sit on the large grass field and enjoy a coffee from the café inside. For kids, there's a "settlement zoo" exhibit, which allows children to get up close and personal with baby lambs, calves, and birds.

Sports and Recreation

VATNAVERÖLD SWIMMING POOL

Sunnubraut 31, Keflavík; tel. 354/421-1500; 6:30am-9:30pm Mon.-Fri., 9am-6pm Sat.-Sun.; 900ISK

This pool in Keflavík is complete with hot tubs, heated pools, and a great swimming area for children. It's a wildly popular spot for locals and gives you a peek into an integral part of Icelandic society.

Food

LANGBEST

Keilisbraut 771, Keflavík; tel. 354/421-4777; www.langbest.is; 11am-10pm daily; entrées from 1,900ISK

Situated in the heart of the town, Langbest serves up pizza, sandwiches, and fish and chips. It's a great place to stop for something quick and affordable.

KAFFI DUUS

Duusgata 10, Keflavík; tel. 354/421-7080; www.duus.is; 11am-10pm daily; entrées from 2,850ISK

This lovely café is based in the Duus Museum, Reykjanesbær's arts and culture center. It has a casual atmosphere and attracts both locals and tourists. An impressive menu features creamy lobster soup (a popular starter) and main courses like pan-fried lobster, tandoori chicken, and vegetarian curry. The restaurant features spectacular harbor views, and the quality of food keeps people coming back.

LIBRARY BISTRO/BAR

Hafnargata 57, Keflavík; tel. 354/421-5220; www.librarybistro.is; kitchen 11:30am-10pm daily, bar 11:30am-midnight daily; entrées from 2,990ISK

Library Bistro/Bar is the chic eatery at the Park Inn by Radisson hotel. The decor is modern and casual, and the menu features sandwiches, salads, soups, burgers, and main courses like grilled leg of lamb and fried bacalao. There are also several vegan options as well as a kids' menu for the little ones. On the bar side, they offer an impressive wine list as well as an array of author-inspired cocktails like Stephen King's Bloody Mary and Tolkein's Tanqueray Gimlet.

KEF RESTAURANT & BAR

Vatnsnesvegur, Keflavík; tel. 354/420-7000; www.kef.is; 11:30am-11pm Sun.-Thurs., 11:30am-11:30pm Fri.-Sat.; entrées from 3,500ISK

Housed in the Hótel Keflavík, KEF Restaurant & Bar is known for serving classic fish and meat dishes. Expect to see Icelandic cod, salmon, and lamb recipes on the menu. The chef focuses on sourcing local ingredients whenever possible. During the winter, if the northern lights decide to make an appearance, the restaurant's glass facade allows expansive views of the lights dancing and flickering in the deep black sky.

Accommodations

HÓTEL KEILIR

Hafnargata 37, Keflavík; tel. 354/420-9800; www.hotelkeilir.is; rooms from 25,000ISK

Keflavík's centrally located Hótel Keilir boasts modern, minimalist decor, average-size rooms, and small bathrooms. A family suite is available that can comfortably sleep five people. This hotel is a good mid-range option and just a five-minute drive from the airport.

PARK INN BY RADISSON

Hafnargata 57, Keflavík; tel. 354/421-5222; www.radissonhotels.com; rooms from 27,000ISK

Situated just 5 kilometers (3 mi) from Keflavík airport, Park Inn by Radisson offers 81 rooms ranging from standard doubles to superior rooms to junior suites. Rooms are comfortable but sparsely decorated, with amenities including free Wi-Fi, kettles, and mounted flat-screen TVs. Park Inn has an on-site restaurant, a fitness center, luggage storage, and express check-out, as well as a free shuttle to and from the airport.

HÓTEL BERG

Bakkavegur 17, Keflavík; tel. 354/422-7922; www.hotelberg.is; rooms from 30,000ISK

At Hótel Berg, modernized rooms are

comfortable and have flat-screen televisions and free Wi-Fi. The boutique hotel, renovated in 2018, offers 36 rooms, free drop-off to Keflavík International Airport, a comfortable lounge area with a fireplace, and a rooftop pool. If you get one of the two loft suites during the winter months, you might catch a glimpse of the northern lights from the skylight.

COURTYARD BY MARRIOTT KEFLAVÍK AIRPORT

Adalgata 60, Keflavík; tel. 354/599-6100; www.marriott.com; rooms from 34,000ISK

Courtyard by Marriott is a convenient option for travelers that want a hotel close to the international airport with spacious rooms and numerous amenities. The hotel features an in-house restaurant, a fitness center open 24/7, and a large comfortable lounge with free Wi-Fi. Rooms, which range from twin to deluxe king, are large with crisp linens and blackout curtains, flat-screen TVs, and mini refrigerators.

Information and Services

REYKJANESBÆR TOURIST OFFICE

Duusgata 2-8; tel. 354/420-3246; www.visitreykjanes.is; noon-5pm daily

Reykjanesbær's tourist office offers a booking service for tours and has brochures on activities, restaurants, and sights in the region.

Getting There and Around

Reykjanesbær is 49 kilometers (30 mi) southwest from **Reykjavík.** By car, take **Route 41,** which is paved, to reach the region. It's about a 50-minute drive.

Reykjanes has a **walkable** small downtown area, but a **rental car** is necessary to visit major attractions.

KEFLAVÍK INTERNATIONAL AIRPORT

Reykjanesbær; www.isavia.is

Reykjanesbær is about 3 kilometers (2 mi) from Keflavík International Airport, a 5-minute drive. If you are coming from the airport and staying in Reykjanesbær, and don't have a car, be sure to contact your hotel or guesthouse to see if there is a shuttle to pick you up at the airport. If not, taxis are available at the airport.

GARÐUR

Garður is a placid seaside town on the northwest tip of Reykjanes and a great place to spend a couple of hours. Garður is best known for a pair of lighthouses. On sunny summer days, locals and tourists picnic by the lighthouses, basking in the sun and enjoying the serenity and scenery. The lighthouses are a great spot to catch a glimpse of the northern lights in the winter, as the location is away from the bright lights of downtown.

Sights

LIGHTHOUSES

Route 402

The highlights of Garður are the two lighthouses, each with unique charm. The older, more traditional red-striped lighthouse was built in 1847, while the newer square-designed one was built in 1944 in a more modern Nordic style. This is a popular destination for photos. Fishing boats can often be seen from shore, and there is rich birdlife in the region, ranging from hordes of gulls circling in the summer months to ravens dominating the skies in the winter. It's also common to see arctic terns and gannets in the summer. In the winter, the lighthouses appear against a backdrop of mist and mystery, and if you're lucky, you will see northern lights dancing in the night sky.

FOLK MUSEUM (Byggðasafn Garðskaga)

Skagabraut 100; tel. 354/425-3008; www.sudurnesjabaer.is; 10am-5pm daily May 1-Oct. 15, open by appointment the rest of the year; free

The Folk Museum sits amid a rugged landscape with thriving birdlife. The quaint museum houses items that were essential for the livelihood of residents on both land and sea, including tools, fishing items, and maps. It offers a window into what life was like in past generations, reminding visitors that life in Iceland was not easy for early settlers. The museum also has an extensive collection of 60 functional engines provided by local resident Guðni Ingimundarson.

Food and Accommodations

THE OLD LIGHTHOUSE CAFÉ

Garðskagi; tel. 354/893-8909; noon-8:30pm daily; entrées from 2,100ISK

The Old Lighthouse Café, housed one of Garður's lighthouses, offers cakes, coffee, soft drinks, and light meals. It's a good place to grab a quick bite, and you can also go to the top of the lighthouse for a great view of the Reykjanes Peninsula, the lava fields, and, if you're lucky, maybe a whale in the distance.

GARÐUR APARTMENTS

Skagabraut 62a; tel. 354/779-0707; www.gardurapartments.is; apartments from 19,000ISK

This charming property has seven apartments ranging from studios to two-bedrooms available year-round. Located close to the harbor, the apartments have private kitchens, bathrooms with showers, free Wi-Fi, and satellite TV. The friendly staff can help arrange local tours, including golfing, bird-watching, and fishing. The cozy guesthouse is just a 10-minute drive to Keflavík airport.

GARÐSKAGI CAMPGROUND

Skagabraut; tel. 354/422-7220; open all year; 1,500ISK

The Garðskagi campground is close to the two lighthouses in a quiet stretch of town. Campers have access to running water and toilets. Electricity is available for 1,000ISK per 24 hours.

Getting There

Garður is 55 kilometers (34 mi) west of **Reykjavík.** By car, take **Route 41** to **Route 45.**

BRIDGE BETWEEN CONTINENTS

Route 425, GPS coordinates N 63.8683, W 22.6752

Travelers can visit a spot where the Mid-Atlantic Ridge crosses Iceland, the meeting point of the Eurasian and North American plates. The small footbridge is a symbolic site that connects the two land masses, and it offers visitors an impressive view of the ridge. You can reach the bridge from Route 425, a 20-minute (20-km/12-mi) drive south from Reykjanesbær.

★ BLUE LAGOON

(Bláa Lónið)

Svartsengi; tel. 354/420-8800; www.bluelagoon.com; 9am-9pm daily; adults from 6,500ISK, children 2-13 free, children under 2 not admitted

Built on an 800-year-old lava field, the Blue Lagoon covers an area of 8,700 square meters (93,646 sq ft) and draws visitors from around the world to soak in its gloriously milky-blue waters amid a dreamlike atmosphere. The geothermally heated water, which ranges between 37-39°C (98-102°F), is heavenly any time of year. Enjoying the steamy air while soaking during the summer is lovely, especially on sunny days. And in the winter, a visit here is eerie and wonderful; watching as snow falls from the jet-black December sky or as northern lights dance across it while lounging in the hot water is sublime.

The water isn't deep, about 1.5 meters (5 ft), and the bottom is covered with white silica mud, the result of a natural process of recondensation. It's common to see visitors cover their faces with the mud—it's great for your skin, and all guests receive a free silica mud mask with standard admission. The gift shop sells Blue Lagoon skin products that have ingredients ranging from silica mud to algae found in other parts of Iceland. At the **Lagoon Bar,** a swim-up bar in the main section of the lagoon, you can purchase drinks to be enjoyed while lounging in the waters. There are also two steam baths on the property, as well as a dry sauna and massage area, and spa treatments are available.

Many tours feature a visit to the Blue Lagoon, but if you're traveling independently, it makes sense to visit right after you fly in or before you head home, as it's very close to **Keflavík airport.** A rejuvenating soak is a great way to kick off your trip or end it on a relaxing note.

TICKETS

The **comfort package** fee is 6,5000ISK for those over 14 years of age, and free for children 2-13. Children under the age of 2 are not allowed in the lagoon. Also included in the price of a ticket is a silica mud mask, the use of a towel, and your first drink of choice. The **premium package** (8,200ISK) includes everything the comfort package offers, as well as slippers, a second mask of choice, use of a bathrobe, a table reservation at **Lava Restaurant,** and sparkling wine if dining.

Because of the increase in tourism over the past several years, the Blue Lagoon now requires you to book a time slot ahead of your arrival, which you can do on its website. Reserve your time at least several weeks before your trip. Thousands of people visit the site every day, and it can get quite crowded during summer months. For the best chance of avoiding crowds, try to book early in the morning or late in the evening.

Other Sights

KRÝSUVÍK

www.visitreykjanes.is

The Krýsuvík geothermal area, 35 kilometers (22 mi) south of Reykjavík, is popular among geology buffs and hikers. Gurgling mud pools bubble from the yellow, red, and orange clay-like earth, intertwined with dancing steam and hot springs. Many short walking paths allow you to feel lost in the outer space-like atmosphere. The region gives you a great sense of Iceland's raw, natural geothermal energy, which powers much of the island. Take some time to roam, but be sure to stay within the designated roped-off areas to avoid getting burned by spray and steam. Plan to spend 1-2 hours here.

To get to the region, take **Route 42** south from **Reykjavík,** about a 40-minute drive (36 km/22 mi). From Grindavík and the **Blue Lagoon,** it is 30 kilometers (19 mi), about 27 minutes, on **Route 427.**

the Blue Lagoon

Sports and Recreation

4X4 ADVENTURES ICELAND

Tangasund 1, Grindavík; tel. 354/857-3001; www.4x4adventuresiceland.is; adults 13,900ISK, children 6-12 6,950ISK

For those looking for a little adventure, 4x4 Adventures Iceland offers a number of ATV/quad bike tours that let you get off the beaten track. Its one-hour Panorama tour takes travelers around the Reykjanes Peninsula and near rocky lava formations, mountains, and even to a view over the Blue Lagoon. No experience is necessary for this year-round tour.

GRINDAVÍK SWIMMING POOL

Austurvegi 1; tel. 354/426-7555; www.grindavik.is; 6am-9pm Mon.-Fri., 9am-6pm Sat.-Sun.; 980ISK

The Grindavík Swimming Pool is one of the best pools in South Iceland with its 25-meter (82-ft) pool, hot tubs, tanning beds, water-slide, children's pool, and fitness center.

Food

HJA HOLLU

Víkurbraut 62; tel. 354/896-5316; www.hjahollu.is; 11am-5pm daily; entrées from 2,790ISK

This modern and casual eatery with a friendly atmosphere has a menu chock-full of healthy options like salads and vegan dishes. Guests can also choose from local cod, lobster pizza, steak sandwiches, and vegetable soup.

★ SALTHÚSIÐ

Stamphólsvegur 9; tel. 354/426-9700; www.salthusid.is; noon-9pm daily; entrées from 3,300ISK

Salthúsið, or "the Salt House," is a favorite among local fishermen, residents, and tourists. A lot of saltfish is on the quiet eatery's menu, but guests can also choose from lamb and chicken dishes, as well as burgers, sandwiches, and fish and chips. The garlic-roasted lobster with salad and garlic bread is delicious. If you have room, be sure to check out the decadent dessert menu, which includes items such as deep-fried bananas with vanilla ice cream and caramel sauce, and French chocolate cake with fresh cream.

MAX'S RESTAURANT

Grindavíkurvegi 1; tel. 354/426-8650; www.nli.is/maxs; lunch noon-3pm daily, dinner 5:30pm-9:30pm daily; entrées from 3,900ISK

Max's Restaurant is the in-house restaurant at the Northern Light Inn. The atmosphere is very much that of a hotel restaurant, with good service and not many surprises, but it charms with huge windows overlooking mountains and lava fields. The menu consists of classic Icelandic food like lamb fillet and fresh fish dishes. There is also a vegan section to the menu that includes dishes like falafel and fries, Moroccan stew, and pumpkin risotto.

★ BLUE LAGOON LAVA RESTAURANT

Svartsengi; tel. 354/420-8800; www.bluelagoon.com; lunch 11:30am-2pm daily, dinner 5pm-9pm daily; dinner entrées from 5,400ISK

The Blue Lagoon Lava Restaurant is the epitome of a spa restaurant: Ingredients are local, and the recipes are healthy. You will find fresh vegetables and fish as well as lean meats. The menu accommodates a host of dietary requirements. The restaurant also offers a tasting menu and a kids' menu. The atmosphere is minimalist chic with cool hues and modern accents. Casual clothing is allowed.

BLUE LAGOON MOSS RESTAURANT

Norðurljósavegur 11; tel. 354/420-8700; www.bluelagoon.com; 6pm-11pm daily; meals from 14,000ISK

Moss Restaurant opened as part of the Retreat extension to the Blue Lagoon. The restaurant is elegant fine dining at its best, with unbeatable views of the volcanic landscape. The restaurant offers two five- and seven-course set menus from 14,000ISK a person. The first set menu includes fish and meat in the dishes, while the second is customized for vegan guests. The menus are seasonal and change often; contact the restaurant to find out what will be served. In addition to the two set menus, the restaurant also offers a chef's table, where the chef will create a seven-course meal (from 19,000ISK) based on the day's fresh catch and seasonal produce.

Accommodations

GEO HOTEL GRINDAVÍK

Víkurbraut 58; tel. 354/421-4000; www.geohotel.is; rooms from 21,850ISK

Geo Hotel Grindavík has double, single, and family rooms, all with private bathroom facilities. The hotel's design includes a spacious social area for guests to relax in cozy surroundings. Room walls are painted in muted colors, and there are wood floors and minimalist furniture. Shops and conveniences are nearby in the town center.

NORTHERN LIGHT INN

Grindavíkurvegi 1; tel. 354/426-8650; www.nli.is; doubles from 36,000ISK

The 32-room guesthouse Northern Light Inn offers cozy, bright rooms with free Wi-Fi, satellite TV, and sweeping views. An in-house restaurant serves classic Icelandic fare with plenty of fish and lamb dishes, as well as a couple of vegetarian options. Its proximity to the Blue Lagoon is a big draw for tourists: It's just a 0.7-kilometer (0.4-mi) walk from the lagoon.

★ BLUE LAGOON SILICA HOTEL

Svartsengi; tel. 354/420-8806; www.bluelagoon.com; rooms from 72,000ISK

The Blue Lagoon Silica Hotel is a luxurious hotel connected to the Blue Lagoon. It has 35 bright and airy double rooms, each with private bathroom and a terrace overlooking the surrounding lava fields. Silica offers luxury beds, modern decor, and beautiful views of the lagoon. Guests have access to a private lagoon open daily 9am-10pm.

Also at the Blue Lagoon, **The Retreat** (Norðurljósavegur 11; tel. 354/420-8700; www.bluelagoon.com; suites from 165,000ISK) opened in 2018 to target luxury travelers; suites start at a whopping 165,000ISK per night all the way up to 312,000ISK. The suites overlook the Retreat Lagoon, a body of water that has the same geothermally heated seawater as the Blue Lagoon, but for the Retreat guests only. Guests have access to private changing rooms, spa treatments at a hidden spa, and reservations for Moss Restaurant.

GRINDAVÍK CAMPSITE

Austurvegur 26; tel. 354/660-7323; mid-May-mid-Sept.; 2,000ISK

The popular Grindavík Campsite by the harbor accommodates tents, RVs, and campers, with access to hookups (electricity costs an extra 1,200ISK per night) and a dump station. There's a paved entrance and a large parking area, and the grassy field has beautiful mountain views. The campsite offers laundry facilities, a common eating area, and a playground with swings and a spider net. Showers are included in the price, and washing machines and dryers are available for 700ISK per load.

Information and Services

The gas station **N1** and grocery chain **Netto** are situated downtown, on Víkurbraut.

- **Grindavík Tourist Information Center:** Duusgata 2-8; tel. 354/420-3246; 10am-5pm daily

Getting There

The Blue Lagoon is located in the placid fishing town of **Grindavík,** where you can see fishers hauling their daily bounty of cod out of the harbor by day and dine on the local catch at night.

Driving from **Reykjavík,** the Blue Lagoon is about 48 kilometers (30 mi), roughly 45 minutes, away on paved roads; head southwest on Route 41 and turn left onto Route 43. From **Keflavík International Airport,** the Blue Lagoon is about 23 kilometers (14 mi) away; take Route 41 and turn right onto Route 43, and you'll arrive in approximately 20 minutes. If you're making your way to or from the airport, note that the Blue Lagoon offers luggage storage.

Bus transfers via **Reykjavík Excursions** (tel. 354/580-5400; www.re.is) can be booked in conjunction with Blue Lagoon entrance tickets; the buses run between both Reykjavík and the Blue Lagoon and Keflavík International Airport and the Blue Lagoon. Buses are available from Reykjavík to the Blue Lagoon, every hour 7am-7pm year-round, with additional services seasonally (round-trip 6,000ISK). From KEF to the Blue Lagoon, there are seven daily departures year-round and added service during the high season.

The Golden Circle

TOP EXPERIENCE

If you ask an Icelander which tour you should take if you want a taste of Iceland outside of Reykjavík, he or she will most likely recommend the Golden Circle. Encompassing the three most visited sights in South Iceland, the Golden Circle gives you a slice of Icelandic history at Þingvellir, a view of Iceland's bubbling geothermal activity at Geysir, and a peek at a roaring, powerful waterfall at Gullfoss. The sights are classically Icelandic, and postcard-perfect in summer or winter. Because of the popularity of the sights, it's pretty easy to get there.

Tours

You can pre-book a tour through many tourism companies: **Troll Expeditions** (Fiskislóð 45G; tel. 354/519-5544; www.troll.is) offers a Golden Circle small group day tour from Reykjavík for 10,700ISK, including Gullfoss, Geysir, and Þingvellir, plus a stop at Kerið crater and a farm visit with free ice cream. If you have time for just one tour in South Iceland, the Golden Circle is highly recommended to learn about the history and geology of this island.

★ ÞINGVELLIR NATIONAL PARK

Route 36, 47 km/30 mi (45 minutes) northwest of Reykjavík; free entrance, parking 750ISK

The birth of Iceland as a nation happened at Þingvellir. Literally translated to "Parliament Plains," Þingvellir was the site of Iceland's first general assembly, which was said to have been established in the year 930, and was the meeting place of the Icelandic parliament until 1798. Many significant sights are at Þingvellir, including **Almannagjá** (All Man's Gorge) and **Lögberg** (Law Rock). Þingvellir was established as a national park in 1930.

Visitors also come to the area for its geological significance, as it is the site of a rift valley that marks the crest of the **Mid-Atlantic Ridge.** It's also home to **Þingvallavatn,** the largest natural lake on the island, which has a surface area of 84 square kilometers (32 sq mi).

Sights

ÞINGVELLIR INTERPRETIVE CENTER

tel. 354/482-2660; www.thingvellir.is; 9am-8pm daily May-Aug., 9am-4pm daily Sept.-Apr., adults 1,000ISK, children free

The Þingvellir Interpretive Center gives a great overview of the national park, its history, and its geological significance. Stop in to see the interactive display and then pick up hiking maps at the information center next door.

ALMANNAGJÁ

footpath from visitors center leads to the gorge

The park's stony, moss-covered landscape is home to Almannagjá (All Man's Gorge), which is the tallest cliff face in the national park and the original backdrop to Iceland's first parliament. This rock structure is considered the edge of the North American plate, which visitors can view up close. It's an impressive sight, so be sure you have your camera ready.

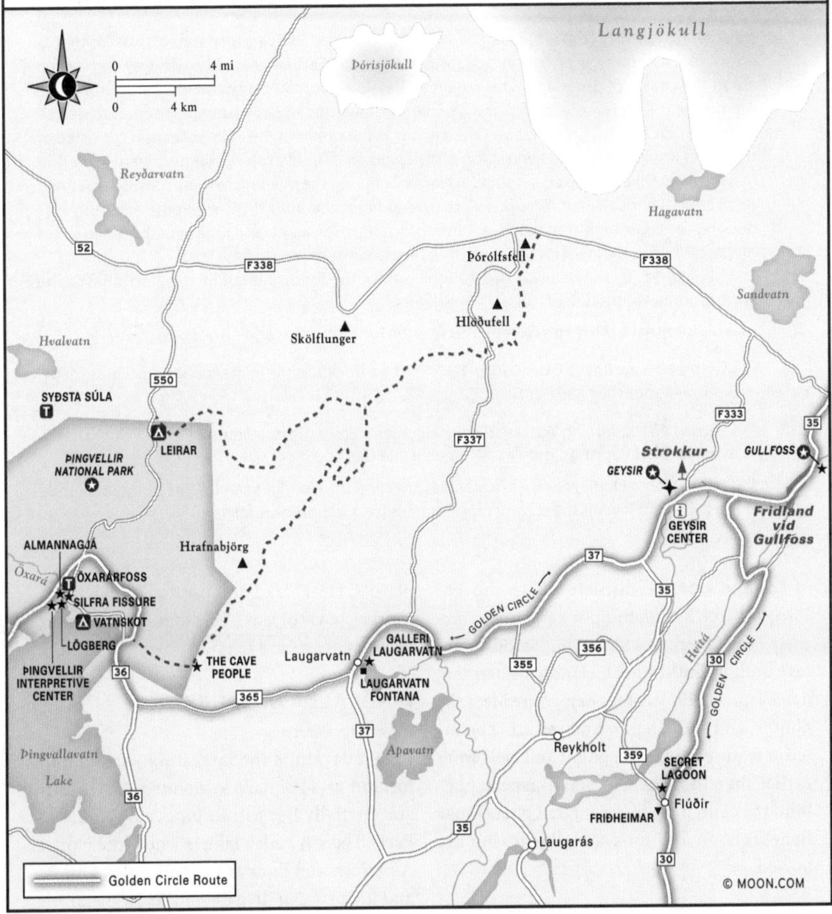

LÖGBERG

footpath from visitors center

Lögberg (Law Rock) is where Icelandic democracy began. Iceland's Commonwealth period ran from 930-1262, and during that time, the Law Rock was the center of the Alþing (parliament). Members of the Alþing gave speeches and held events at the rock, including confirming the year's calendar and issuing legal rulings. A man known as the "law speaker," who was responsible for understanding all laws and required to memorize them, read the procedural laws aloud every summer standing on the rock.

ÖXARÁ RIVER

www.thingvellir.is/en

The Öxará (Axe) River flows over seemingly endless lava fields, emitting a haunting mist in the winter months. It's serene and eerie until it reaches **Öxaráfoss,** where the water tumbles and roars over the cliffs. At the river's edge are a church and farmhouse, the latter of which is the official summer residence

The Birth of Iceland

Iceland's government dates back to the year 930, when the **Alþing** (parliament) was formed as an outdoor assembly just a few decades after settlement. Settlers came from Norway and settled along the coasts of the island. This makes it the oldest continuous parliament in history. The Alþing was formed by the island's most powerful chieftains and its main purpose was to decide on legislation. The **Lögrétta** (Law Council) was at the center of the assemblies and consisted of the chieftains and bishops. Legislation was passed on majority rule. Icelanders were invited to join the assemblies and lived in camps in Þingvellir during the meeting sessions; it was something of an annual family event. Sessions were held at Þingvellir until 1800, when the assembly was disbanded. A new high court was established in 1800 in Reykjavík and took over the functions of Alþingi. When parliament reconvened in 1844, meetings moved to Reykjavík.

While you're in Þingvellir, be sure to look out for the following landmarks, essential to the ancient annual gathering of Iceland's legislators:

- **Almannagjá** (All Man's Gorge): This was the location of Iceland's first parliament.
- **Lögberg** (Law Rock): From 930 to 1262, the Law Rock was the center of Alþing, where members gave speeches and held events.
- **Laugarvatn** (Bathing Waters): Historically, members of the Icelandic parliament would bathe in these nearby springs, between Þingvellir and Geysir.

Still today, Þingvellir plays a role in Icelandic government, even if it's small: The farmhouse visible along the Öxará River is the summer residence of Iceland's prime minister.

of Iceland's prime minister. The church, **Þingvallakirkja** (9am-5pm daily mid-May-early Sept.; free), is a charming wood structure built in traditional Icelandic design that dates from 1859. Visitors can go inside, take photos, and sit on a pew and reflect. The interior features a wooden pulpit and bells from earlier churches. There's a small cemetery behind the church where celebrated poets Einar Benediktsson and Jonasa Hallgrimsson are buried.

SILFRA FISSURE

about 60 km/37 mi from Reykjavík, inside Þingvellir National Park, off Route 36

The Silfra fissure, filled with fresh spring water, is a popular site for diving and snorkeling tours. The crystal-clear water reveals an underwater world with jagged canyon walls, plant life, and fish. The fissure is said to have opened in 1789 as a result of moving tectonic plates. It never freezes—fresh water constantly enters the fissure, so it never settles to freeze—and keeps a constant temperature of 2-3°C (35-37°F). For those that would like to snorkel, www.dive.is offers tours to those over 16 years of age and in good physical health.

ÞINGVALLAVATN LAKE

www.thingvellir.is/en

Þingvallavatn is the largest natural lake in Iceland at 84 square kilometers (32 sq mi) and partially lies within Þingvellir National Park. The rift valley lake is where the North American and Eurasian tectonic plates meet, and tourists can dive or snorkel in the Silfra fissure.

Hiking

Þingvellir is lovely for the casual hiker, a natural place to roam. Acres of flat lava fields make hiking conditions easy, with plenty of walking paths, interesting rock formations, and rugged terrain to see. Just be sure to watch for open rock fissures along the way; it's easy to fall in. You can get information about trails and the surrounding area, as well as free, detailed maps, at the **visitors center.**

Self-Driving the Golden Circle

PLANNING YOUR TIME

In total, the Golden Circle is an approximately 300-kilometer (200-mi) paved circular route, leaving from and returning to Reykjavík. It's good to allocate **6-8 hours** if you're driving it yourself.

WHERE TO STAY

It makes the most sense to overnight in **Selfoss** or **Hvolsvöllur** if you do not plan to return to Reykjavík for the night.

THE ROUTES

With your rental car from Reykjavík, take **Route 1** to **Route 36** for Þingvellir. Continue on Route 36, then **Routes 365, 37,** and **35** to Geysir. From Geysir continue on Route 35 to Gullfoss before looping back toward Reykjavík, heading southwest on well-signed Routes 35 and 1.

SYÐSTA SÚLA

Distance: *13 km (8 mi) round-trip*
Hiking Time: *7 hours round-trip*
Information and Maps: *www.south.is*
Trailhead: *Left turn on Route F-550*

If you're looking to scale some small mountains, check out Syðsta Súla, which reaches 1,085 meters (3,559 ft) in the northern region of the park and is the park's easiest peak to climb. The view from the top over the park is spectacular. Always be sure to check weather conditions before any hike, and make sure you have proper waterproof outer layers, sturdy footwear, a charged mobile phone, and drinking water. The ideal time to hike is the summer, as in the winter you will need proper snow gear.

ÖXARÁRFOSS

Distance: *4.5-km (2.7-mi) loop*
Hiking Time: *1.5 hours*
Information and Maps: *www.south.is*
Trailhead: *Þingvellir National Park parking lot*

Enjoy this short hike to the Öxarárfoss waterfall on a flat, even path. The trail is signposted throughout and the scenery along the way is breathtaking, from views of Hengill (an active volcano) south of the park to the sweeping, open landscape of jagged rocks covered with moss. The waterfall is quite beautiful as it looks as if the water is escaping from the rocks, falling meters below.

Fishing and Watersports

Scuba diving or **snorkeling** in the naturally filtered, pure water of Þingvallavatn lake is sublime. Surveying the underwater basalt walls, multicolored algae, and sloping sands is magical and unique—you're able to snorkel or scuba in the **Silfa fissure,** the enormous crack between the Eurasian and North American continental plates. Don't even think about going in without a dry suit, as the water temperature hovers around 3°C (37°F). Diving is possible year-round, but there are rules to obey, so don't attempt to go without a guide.

Boats are not allowed on the lake, but **fishing permits** are sold at the information center, and they rent equipment too. Tourists have a chance of catching arctic char and brown trout. Be sure to obey the rules and pay for the permit. The fishing season at the lake runs May 1-September 30, and permits are about 8,000ISK.

DIVE ICELAND

Ásbúðartröð 17, Hafnarfjörður; tel. 354/699-3000; www.dive.is

Dive Iceland offers a Silfra diving tour for 31,490ISK. Travelers must be dry-suit certified to dive and must present their certification card. Snorkeling tours start at 15,490ISK.

Horseback Riding

Þingvellir is a popular spot for riding horses,

with several trails that offer the chance to check out some of the more beautiful and geologically significant areas of the park.

REYKJAVÍK EXCURSIONS

tel. 354/580-5400; www.re.is; 20,399ISK

Reykjavík Excursions offers a year-round horse-riding day tour in Þingvellir.

Camping

There are no hotels within Þingvellir National Park. However, there are accommodations in nearby Laugarvatn and Selfoss. If you would like to stay within the park limits, your only option is camping at one of Þingvellir's five campgrounds, spread across two areas of the park: the **Leirar** section and the **Vatnskot** section. All campsites have access to toilets, electricity, and cooking facilities. The difference in the two sections is not access to amenities, but whether you want to camp close to the lake or stay near the information center. Both sections have great views and spacious fields. Campers must bring their own tents.

LEIRAR CAMPGROUND

GPS coordinates N 64.1648 W 21.5174; www.tjalda.is; June 1-Sept. 30; 1,300ISK per person

The Leirar section is a five-minute walk from the Þingvellir information center. The Leirar campground is divided into four campsites: **Fagrabrekka, Syðri-Leirar, Hvannabrekka,** and **Nyrðri-Leirar.**

VATNSKOT CAMPGROUND

GPS coordinates N 64.1440 W 21.5220; www.tjalda.is; June 1-Sept. 30; 1,300ISK per person

Meanwhile, the Vatnskot section, which is by Lake Þingvallavatn, is situated at an abandoned farm by the lake.

Information and Services

TOURIST INFORMATION CENTER

tel. 354/482-2660; www.thingvellir.is; 9am-4pm daily

The tourist information center is close to the car park. Be advised that there is a service fee of 200ISK to use the **restrooms.** There is also a small **cafeteria** to purchase snacks and drinks.

Getting There and Around

Þingvellir is 46 kilometers (29 mi) northeast of **Reykjavík.** By car, it's about a 45-minute drive; take **Route 1** to **Route 36,** which will take you to the northern part of the park.

While there is no public transportation available to get to the park, a number of tours include a stop at **Þingvellir.** The park's attractions are all within a walkable distance, so plan to be **on foot.**

LAUGARVATN

Route 37, 32 km/20 mi (30 min) from Þingvellir

Laugarvatn, or "Bathing Waters," is a lake situated between Þingvellir and the geothermal hot spot of Geysir. Historically, members of Iceland's parliament (Alþing) visited the springs due to their proximity to where parliament met at Þingvellir for hundreds of years. The lake's water temperature hovers around 40°C (104°F), making it a unique and warm swimming experience.

Sights

THE CAVE PEOPLE

Laugarvatnshellir; tel. 354/ 888-1922; www.thecavepeople.is; 10am-6pm daily; 2,100ISK

A fascinating addition to the region, The Cave People offers a look at how Icelanders lived within the earth just 100 years ago. Here you can take a guided tour of two manmade caves that were inhabited by young Icelandic couples in the years 1910-1911 and 1918-1922. The residents had some horses, a cow, and a few sheep, and grew potatoes and harvested fresh berries. Tours are available every 30 minutes, and tickets can be purchased in advance online.

Pools and Hot Springs

LAUGARVATN FONTANA

Hverabraut 1; tel. 354/486-1400; www.fontana.is/en; 11:30am-7pm Sun.-Wed., 11:30am-9pm Thurs.-Sat.;

1: Þingvellir National Park **2:** The Cave People

adults 3,950ISK, children 13-16 2,000ISK, children 12 and under free

The Laugarvatn Fontana is worth a stop before or after you visit Geysir. The facility's sauna captures the steam just as it escapes from the earth. You can bask in the natural sauna and hot springs, enjoying the geothermal energy up close and personal. Towels, bathing suits, and bathrobes can be rented at the spa.

For an experience unique to the region, each day at 11:45am and 2:30pm there is a walk from the reception area to the on-site geothermal bakery (1,700ISK). Visitors can watch as the staff digs out rye bread that's been buried in the ground, left to bake naturally in the geothermally heated earth. You can try the bread, served hot from the ground with some butter—it's delicious!

LAUGARVATN SWIMMING POOL

Hverabraut 2; tel. 354/486-1251; 10am-9pm Mon.-Thurs., 10am-6pm Fri.-Sun.; 1,000ISK

Situated downtown, the Laugarvatn Swimming Pool is popular among locals, and it's a nice break from the summer tourist rush at the Fontana spa nearby. Head here if you would like a quiet spot to take a dip.

Shopping

GALLERI LAUGARVATN

Haholt 1; tel. 354/486-1016; www.gallerilaugarvatn.is; 1pm-5pm daily

When not enjoying the soothing hot springs or the vistas, steal away for a few minutes at Galleri Laugarvatn, a charming little gallery that features local handicrafts, ranging from glass tea light holders to unique paper crafts. There is also a **café** (sandwiches from 950ISK) and **guesthouse** (double room with shared bathroom from 19,000ISK) on-site.

Food and Accommodations

RESTAURANT LINDIN

Lindarbraut 2; tel. 354/486-1262; www.laugarvatn.is; noon-9pm daily; entrées from 3,700ISK

At Restaurant Lindin, owner and head chef Baldur Öxdal Halldórsson has created an upscale, fine-dining experience in a town with fewer than 300 residents. Diners have a lot of choices, from Icelandic mainstays to more exotic fare, with dishes ranging from reindeer meat burgers and pan-fried arctic char to tender lamb fillets and smoked cod. The classic decor and friendly staff make this little restaurant a treasure.

GOLDEN CIRCLE APARTMENTS

Laugarbraut; tel. 354/487-1212; www.goldencircleapartments.is; apartments from 22,000ISK

Golden Circle Apartments offers 25 apartments that are modern and perfect for families, with fully equipped kitchens, private bathrooms, a TV, free Wi-Fi, and free parking. Apartments are spacious, have new appliances, and are close to town attractions. They range from studios to three-bedroom family apartments.

EFSTIDALUR II

Bláskógabyggð; tel. 354/486-1186; www.efstidalur.is; rooms from 29,000ISK

Efstidalur II is a charming farmhouse bed-and-breakfast with an in-house restaurant, friendly staff, and horse rentals. Situated close to the Fontana spa, the B&B is also in proximity of the Golden Circle. On the farm, guests can meet dogs, cows, and horses, and can try fresh homemade ice cream.

Getting There

Laugarvatn is just 77 kilometers (48 mi) northeast from **Reykjavík,** a 1-hour-15-minute drive, and is easily accessible by car and bus via **Route 36** to **Route 365.** If driving from **Þingvellir,** take **Routes 36** and **365** to **Route 37.** The 32-kilometer (10-mi) drive takes about 30 minutes.

★ GEYSIR

Route 35, 28 km/17 mi (22 min) from Laugarvatn

Iceland's geysers are the most obvious demonstration of the island's natural geothermal energy, and historically, Geysir is the country's

1: Geysir **2:** Gullfoss

1
2

most famous example of the phenomenon—it's actually the source of the word "geyser." Geologists theorized that in the 13th century earthquakes stirred the underground workings of the natural hot springs here, causing them to gush, releasing pressure, steam, and water up to 20 meters (66 ft) into the air.

Visitors to the site today unfortunately aren't going to see the dormant Geysir erupt—it hasn't blown since 2005. But don't fret; Geysir's nearby cousin, **Strokkur** (Churn), erupts every seven minutes or so. Crowds gather to watch the frequent eruptions, and the churning, gurgling pool of hot water turning out a rush of pressure from the clay-like earth is an impressive sight; be sure to have your camera ready. Please be careful and stay behind the ropes or you may get hit with hot spray.

Food and Accommodations

HÓTEL GEYSIR

Geysir; tel. 354/480-6800; www.hotelgeysir.is; rooms from 33,250ISK

You can't stay any closer to the geysers than at the Hótel Geysir. This property features 77 rooms and 6 suites just across the road from Geysir. Guests can also stay in chalets on the property that are essentially double rooms. The decor blends with the scenery in muted colors but modern scheme. Visitors have access to a spa, swimming pool, and hot tub. The in-house **restaurant** serves up delicious dishes ranging from fresh Icelandic cod to lamb and beef entrées.

Hótel Geysir also operates a campground 100 meters (300 ft) from the Geysir area, with hot showers (500ISK), pool access, and a common barbecue area; you can pay for your campsite (1,800ISK) at the Geysir shops just across from the campground. An additional 900ISK gives you access to electricity.

Information and Services

GEYSIR VISITORS CENTER

10am-8pm daily

After walking around the geothermal area, stop at the visitors center. It has a short multimedia exhibition about the geology of the region, a small **café** serving refreshments, and a **souvenir shop.**

GEYSIR CENTER

Biskupstungnabraut; tel. 354/519-6020; www.geysircenter.com; 9am-10pm daily June 1-Aug. 31, 9am-6pm daily Sept. 1-May 31

The Geysir Center is your one-stop shop for all your Geysir-related needs. There is a **cafeteria** that sells light meals and drinks, **bathrooms,** a large **gift shop,** and information and maps about attractions in the region.

Getting There

Geysir is about a 1.5-hour drive east from **Reykjavík.** You start out on **Route 1** and then take **Route 35,** which brings you directly to the site.

If following the **Golden Circle** route, continue from **Laugarvatn** on **Route 37** to **Route 35** for Geysir. The drive is just over 20 minutes.

★ GULLFOSS

Route 35, 10 km/6 mi (10 min) from Geysir

The thundering, roaring waterfall of Gullfoss (Golden Falls) epitomizes the raw beauty of Iceland. Gullfoss tumbles into the Hvíta (White) River, which is a perfect name given the turbulent white water. There are three levels of water at the falls, ranging 11-21 meters (36-69 ft), meeting at a 70-meter (230-ft) gorge. If you get too close, expect to get soaked.

Because of Iceland's changing weather, you have a good chance to see a rainbow over the falls, making for a perfect snapshot of your visit. Plan to walk around the site, enjoying not only the wonder of the falls but also the beautiful surrounding landscape. In the summer, there are miles of lush green grass and frequent rainbows on sunny/rainy days. Be careful; it could be slippery.

No matter what time of year, there are scores of tour buses and independent drivers visiting the falls, and that's for a very good reason: It's gorgeous.

Iceland's Best Waterfalls

Waterfalls can be found in every region of Iceland, and while Gullfoss is arguably the most famous, there are several others that are must-sees for their beauty and unique features. Thundering waterfalls are a constant reminder that water is never in short supply in Iceland, thanks in large part to the mighty glaciers.

- **Seljalandsfoss:** One of the most popular waterfalls on the South Coast, Seljalandsfoss is special as it's the only waterfall in Iceland that you can walk behind (page 120).
- **Skógafoss:** With a width of 25 meters (82 ft) and a drop of 60 meters (196 ft), Skógafoss is big and beautiful. You can walk quite close to the falls, but be prepared to get wet (page 121).
- **Dynjandi:** Located in the remote West Fjords, Dynjandi is a tiered waterfall, resembling a delicate bridal veil. It's one of the most beautiful waterfalls on the island (page 172).
- **Goðafoss:** Situated in the north of Iceland, Goðafoss is striking for its width of 30 meters (98 ft). You can view the falls from the east and west and walk along the edges (page 211).
- **Dettifoss:** Known as the most powerful waterfall in Europe, Dettifoss is stunning year-round. A set of stairs allow you to descend, getting up close to the thrashing falls (page 225).
- **Svartifoss:** An oasis in Skaftafell nature reserve, Svartifoss is an elegant 20-meter-tall (65-ft-tall) waterfall that is surrounded by beautiful basalt rocks (page 262).

Food and Accommodations

GULLFOSS CAFÉ

tel. 354/486-6500; 9:30am-7pm daily; entrées from 1,800ISK

A short walk from the falls and parking area, Gullfoss Café (Gullfosskaffi) is the place to go when you're in the area. The Icelandic lamb meat soup on the menu is a winner, and a favorite among visitors, but sandwiches, cakes, and coffee are also available.

HÓTEL GULLFOSS

Brattholt; tel. 354/486-8979; www.hotelgullfoss.is; rooms from 26,000ISK

Hótel Gullfoss is situated perfectly, just 3 kilometers (2 mi) from the falls in a remote area. The resort-like atmosphere is comfortable and a great place to spend the night while touring the Golden Circle, which can be done in one day. Every room has a private bathroom and is classically furnished with comfortable beds. An in-house **restaurant** and hot tub out back make for a comfortable stay.

★ FRIÐHEIMAR

Bláskógabyggð; tel. 354/486-8894; www.fridheimar.is; noon-4pm daily

On Route 35 between Gullfoss and Selfoss, you might stop for lunch at Friðheimar, located in Reykholt, 30 kilometers (19 mi) south of Gullfoss, about a 30-minute drive. The farm is home to tomato greenhouses and a restaurant, as well as a horse-breeding operation. It's an ideal place to have lunch: Tomatoes don't get any fresher in Iceland, and the menu takes advantage of this with items like tomato soup and creative Bloody Marys. Call ahead for lunch reservations. Groups of 10 or more can take a **tour** of the greenhouse with the owner or a staff member. Tours are offered year-round; email fridheimar@fridheimar.is for more information.

Information and Services

Gullfoss's on-site **café** (tel. 354/486-6500; 9:30am-7pm daily) includes a **souvenir shop** and offers some brochures about the surrounding area.

The Secret Lagoon

The **Secret Lagoon (Gamla Laugin)** (Hvammsvegur; tel. 354/555-3351; www.secretlagoon.is; noon-8pm daily May 1-Sept. 30, 10am-6pm daily Oct. 1-April 30; adults 3,000ISK, children 14 and under free) has become a popular (and cheaper) alternative to the Blue Lagoon. It's located in **Fluðir,** a blip of a village with not much going on, but the Secret Lagoon brings tourists by the thousands while still offering a slightly more intimate, less touristy experience than the Blue Lagoon. The surroundings here are beautiful, with farmland and a geothermal area lush with moss-covered lava stones and natural springs bubbling and steaming, just past the water's edge. You can rent towels and swimsuits here, and there is a café with drinks and snacks for sale.

Secret Lagoon

GETTING THERE

If following the conventional **Golden Circle** route from **Gullfoss** down Route 35 back to Route 1, you'll bypass the Secret Lagoon. But if you make a slightly larger circle, jumping off Route 35 and taking **Route 30** south instead, you'll pass right by Fluðir; it's about 38 kilometers (24 mi) south of Gullfoss, a 30-minute drive, and afterward you can connect from Route 30 back to Route 1 and Reykjavík.

Getting There

By car, Gullfoss is 115 kilometers (71 mi) northeast from **Reykjavík.** The drive takes about 1.5 hours on **Routes 1** and **35.**

Gullfoss is about 10 kilometers (6 mi) from **Geysir** on **Route 35,** a 10-minute drive.

SKÁLHOLT CHURCH

tel. 354/486-8801; www.skalholt.is; 9am-6pm daily; free

The site of the Skálholt church has great significance in Iceland's history and is a sacred site for many Icelanders. Gissur the White, a wealthy political figure, played an important role in the Christianization of Iceland and the growth of the early church. He built the first church in Iceland at Skálholt around the year 1000. His son, Ísleifur (1006-1080), chose Skálholt as the site of the first Episcopal see in Iceland, and the first bishopric was founded here in 1056 for southern Iceland.

In the 12th century, Bishop Klængur Þorsteinsson built a great cathedral at Skálholt, and it served as a cultural center up to the Reformation in 1550. The last Catholic bishop of Iceland, Jón Arason, was executed at Skálholt in 1550, along with his two sons, because he opposed the Reformation forced upon Iceland by King Christian III of Denmark. A memorial stands at the site of the execution. Today, Skálholt is visited for the cathedral, the tomb of bishops, the museum, and the collection of ancient books on view in the tower. The church on the site today dates from 1963 and is a large, stark-white building with a dark top. The design is sharp, clean, and classically Nordic. In the summer months, there are cultural events and concerts open to the public.

There's a church service every Sunday at either 11am or 2pm, as well as morning prayers at 9am Monday-Friday and evening prayers at 6pm Mon.-Fri.

Skálholt is 39 kilometers (24 mi) northeast of Selfoss. The drive takes about 40 minutes on the paved **Route 35.**

SELFOSS

Located close to Gullfoss, Geysir, and Þingvellir, Selfoss is a service hub for South Iceland. Many visitors make a stop here to fill up their gas tanks, get a bite to eat, or rest their heads in one of the town's nice hotels or guesthouses. While the town's proximity to the Ring Road and sights in the countryside is a plus, Selfoss has a few attractions of its own that are worth checking out, too. History buffs will want to drop by the **Heritage Museum,** which features exhibitions of life in the town and the surrounding sights.

Sights

BOBBY FISCHER CENTER

Austurvegur 21; tel. 354/894-1275; www.fischersetur.is; 1pm-4pm May 15-Sept. 15, by appointment rest of the year; 1,000ISK

The Bobby Fischer Center is located in a small white house in the heart of Selfoss. This may sound like an odd museum to find in Iceland, but Bobby Fischer, the famous chess player, lived in the town for a couple of years after applying for asylum in the country (after breaking international sanctions to play a chess match in Yugoslavia). The museum serves as the home of the local chess club, and you'll find Bobby Fischer memorabilia, mostly from his time in Iceland, on display. Bobby lived in Iceland from 2005 until his death in 2008.

SKYRLAND

Eyrarvegur 1; tel. 354/666-0010; www.skyrland.com; 11am-5pm Mon.-Fri., 11:30am-4:30pm Sat., noon-4pm Sun.; 2,490ISK

Opened in 2021, Skyrland is a fascinating museum that explores the history of skyr, Iceland's wildly popular soft cheese. Interactive exhibitions bring the history and significance of this classic Icelandic food to life, and there is an opportunity to taste different flavors of skyr on-site.

KERIÐ CRATER

15 km (9 mi) north of Selfoss; parking fee 400ISK

The Kerið crater, which is just 15 kilometers (9 mi) north of Selfoss, is a cool place to stop and take a photo due to the sheer size of the crater lake. The collapsed scoria cone is 70 meters (230 ft) deep and is used for farming fish. There's a nice **path** along the rim (about a 30-minute walk) with good views; use caution and stay on the path.

Sports and Recreation

SÓLHESTAR

Borgargerdi; tel. 354/892-3066; www.solhestar.is

Sólhestar offers year-round horse tours ranging from one-hour rides for 9,000ISK to customized all-day tours for 24,000ISK. Tours feature trails along scenic hot springs, volcanoes, remote beaches, and gorgeous waterfalls.

SUNDHÖLL SELFOSS

Bankavegur; tel. 354/480-1960; 6:30am-9:30pm Mon.-Fri., 9am-7pm Sat.-Sun.; 1,050ISK

The Sundhöll Selfoss pool is open year-round; towel and swimsuit rentals are available.

Food

THE OLD DAIRY SELFOSS

Eyravegur 1; www.mjolkurbu.is; 11am-10pm daily; entrées from 1,600ISK

The Old Dairy Selfoss is a new food hall that opened in 2021 with eight restaurants and two bars. The property was built to look like historic houses, and it has quickly become a hit with the locals. Cuisines served include dim sum, Italian street food, tacos, pizza, and skyr. The food hall is highly recommended, especially for those traveling with kids.

KAFFI KRÚS

Austurvegur 7; tel. 354/482-1266; www.kaffikrus.is; 11:30am-9pm daily; entrées from 2,400ISK

Kaffi Krús is a favorite neighborhood joint that has something for everyone. Pizza is their specialty, but they also serve salads, soups, pasta dishes, burgers, and fish and chips, as well as lamb and fish entrees. You can't go wrong with their pizza, especially their duck pizza pie, with duck confit, mushrooms, red onions, chutney, sauce, and cheese topped off with truffle mayo.

★ KRISP RESTAURANT

Eyravegur 8; tel. 354/482-4099; www.krisp.is/en; 11:30-9pm daily; entrées from 2,890ISK

Krisp is a wonderful addition to Selfoss, with an inventive menu with a lot of surprises. You will find mainstays like burgers, cod, lamb, and salmon, but also Asian-influenced dishes like barbecue pork ribs with sesame seeds, steamed buns, butter-fried edamame, and wolffish skewers. Krisp also serves burritos and several vegan dishes.

Accommodations

SELFOSS HOSTEL

Austurvegur 28; tel. 354/660-6999; www.hostel.is; private rooms from 12,500ISK, beds from 3,300ISK

One of the nicer hostels on the island, this 60-bed facility has spacious rooms, a common kitchen, small gym, and helpful staff. The hostel has a friendly atmosphere. Guests often meet up with fellow travelers and plan excursions together. Washing machines are available for use, and sheets are provided. A hot tub out back is a nice touch.

HOTEL SOUTH COAST

Eyravegur 11-13; tel. 354/464-1113; www.hotelsouthcoast.is; rooms from 33,000ISK

Located adjacent to the new city center in the heart of Selfoss, Hotel South Coast opened its doors in 2021. The hotel, which offers 72 rooms, including 7 deluxe rooms and 8 wheelchair-accessible rooms, also has an in-house restaurant, a spa, and a fitness center. Rooms are clean and comfortable and are decorated in a minimalist design. The hotel spa includes two hot tubs, one round cold tub, and a Finnish sauna. The hotel guest rate for the spa and fitness center is 3,000ISK per adult.

HÓTEL SELFOSS

Eyrarvegur 2; tel. 354/480-2500; www.selfosshotel.is; rooms from 36,000ISK

Hótel Selfoss has the sort of stylish interior you'd expect in Reykjavík, so it comes as a delightful surprise in the countryside. The 99-room hotel has large rooms, including spacious bathrooms, and chic decor. Ten rooms are specifically designed for people with disabilities, and it is one of the most wheelchair-friendly hotels on the island. Business travelers are attracted to the hotel for its conference center, while those looking for luxury are thrilled about the in-house spa, which offers a number of treatments. The staff aim to please and are happy to chat and give recommendations about local sights.

Traustholtshólmi yurt

360 BOUTIQUE HOTEL

Mosató 3; tel. 354/562-2900; www.360hotel.is; rooms from 65,000ISK

Located just outside Selfoss, 360 Boutique Hotel offers striking views and lots of privacy. The hotel offers 10 deluxe rooms, two junior suites, and one large suite, with luxurious furnishings and a modern feel. Each room has large windows and a patio where you can enjoy the views. There's an in-house restaurant and thermal baths where you can relax and soak in the geothermally heated water.

★ TRAUSTHOLTSHÓLMI

tel. 354/699-4256; www.thh.is; yurt for two from 65,000ISK

Traustholtshólmi, located on a private island in the Þjórsá River, is a passion project of the island's owner, Hakón. This one-of-a-kind experience for travelers offers three Mongolian yurts that can sleep two adults and 1-2 children each. Hakón will collect you at a meeting place, which he will email to you, and you will be transported to the island on a four-minute boat ride. The yurts are warm, comfortable, and pleasing to the eye, with bright doors and tasteful, rustic decor. Toilets and showers are close by. A stay on the island allows you to feel one with nature, soaking in the silence and tranquility.

Included in an overnight stay is a tour of the island by Hakón and his friendly sheepdog Skuggi, the chance to participate in catching and tasting wild salmon straight from the river, and a dinner of fresh fish and island-grown potatoes along with the tastiest rhubarb dessert. After a restful night, breakfast is served in the service yurt and you will have time to roam the island before being returned to the mainland. It's a truly unbeatable experience.

Information and Services

SELFOSS TOURIST INFORMATION CENTER

Austurvegur 2; tel. 354/480-1990; www.south.is; 9am-6pm Mon.-Fri., 10am-4pm Sat., closed Sun.

The tourist information center is a great place to pick up pamphlets, arrange tours, and ask questions of the staff.

Getting There

By car, Selfoss is off the familiar **Route 1,** 57 kilometers (35 mi) southeast from **Reykjavík.** The drive takes about 45 minutes.

If you're traveling by bus, the **Strætó 51 bus** (tel. 354/540-2700; www.straeto.is) leaves from bus station Mjodd in Reykjavík several times a day. The ride takes about one hour and costs 1,960ISK. Buses stop and pick up near the **main circle (Austurvegur)** downtown.

HVERAGERÐI

Some Icelanders affectionately call Hveragerði the "Capital of Hot Springs." It's just 30 minutes outside of Reykjavík, so tourists have no reason not to stop, especially as the town is on the way to the Golden Circle of Gullfoss, Geysir, and Þingvellir. Given its proximity to Reykjavík and its healing hot springs, the town is an all-year destination. After a visit to the springs, think about taking a peek at some of the local greenhouses populating the geothermal area. Tomatoes, cucumbers, and bell peppers are popular greenhouse-grown veggies in the region.

Sights

LÁ ART MUSEUM (Listasafn Árnesinga)

Austurmork 21; tel. 354/483-1727; www.listasafnarnesinga.is; noon-5pm daily May 1-Sept. 10, limited hours during winter; free

The LÁ Art Museum offers several different exhibitions throughout the year, ranging from modern to traditional art from Icelandic artists local to the region. The museum also has a children's section, focusing on art for young visitors. It's a cute place to visit, especially if you are traveling with kids.

HVERAGERÐI BOTANICAL GARDEN

Breiðamörk; tel. 354/483-4000; open 24/7; free

Located in the center of town, this is a favorite spot for locals and tourists to stroll and enjoy nature. Guests can find a lot of trees (a rarity in Iceland) and walk along the mighty river Varmá. When the weather is good, it's common to see locals chatting and walking the trails, and tourists taking photos of the surroundings. It's also a great spot for bird-watching in the summer.

Pools and Hot Springs

HVERAGARÐURINN GEOTHERMAL PARK

Hveramörk 13; 9am-6pm Mon.-Sat., 10am-4pm Sun.; free

People flock to Hveragerði for one reason: hot springs. Whether they're under blue skies and sunshine or beset by rain, wind, and snow, the hot springs beckon visitors from around the world. The central geothermal area is in the center of town. The natural phenomenon is hypnotizing to watch, as water bubbles to the surface. It's a constant reminder that Iceland sits on a hotbed of natural geothermal energy. Follow the path between geysers and hot pools, and at the end of the walk, you can soak your feet in one of the hot springs.

LAUGASKARÐ

Reykjamörk; tel. 354/483-4113; 6:45am-9:30pm Mon.-Fri., 9am-7pm Sat.-Sun.; 950ISK

If hot springs aren't your bag, there's a lovely heated swimming pool downtown.

Hiking

HENGILL

Distance: *5 km (3 mi) round-trip*
Hiking Time: *3 hours round-trip*
Information and Maps: *www.south.is*
Trailhead: *Parking area by the viewing platform overlooking Þingvallavatn*

Several trails between Hveragerði and Þingvallavatn lead up to Mount Hengill, which is 68 kilometers (42 mi) north of Hveragerði. The 803-meter (2,635-ft) mountain gives hikers a view of the vast volcanic landscape. Bring your camera and a good pair of boots. There are several active hot spots along the way, so be sure to stick to the trail.

★ REYKJADALUR

Distance: *7 km (4 mi) round-trip*
Hiking Time: *90 minutes round-trip*
Information and Maps: *www.south.is*
Trailhead: *Parking lot, GPS N 64.03309, W 21.21602*

Located just outside of Hveragerði, the Reykjadulur hike has become quite popular the last few years. Hikers get to enjoy the beautiful mountain scenery amid the bubbling hot springs, and are rewarded with the chance to bathe in a part of the river that blends ice cold spring water with hot springs, making for a relaxing soak to soothe your muscles. The hike is best in the summer months, but it's doable in the winter, if conditions are favorable. It is important to check weather conditions before you head out on the hike, and make sure you are wearing proper clothing, and carrying water and a charged mobile phone.

You can reach the trailhead by driving on **Route 1** through Hveragerði to a gravel road that leads to the **parking lot.** The hike starts just past the car park.

Other Sports and Recreation

HVERAGERÐI GOLF COURSE

Gufudalur; tel. 354/483-5090; May-Aug.; greens fees 4,500ISK

The Hveragerði Golf Course is a nine-hole course in a picturesque part of town, set against a backdrop of hot springs. It rents clubs and golf carts, and runs a café with light meals. Call ahead for a tee time.

Food

ALMAR BAKARI

Sunnumörk 2; tel. 354/483-1919; 7am-5pm daily; pastries from 700ISK

Almar Bakari is an ideal spot to grab some bread and pastries, and enjoy light meals like sandwiches, soups, and salads.

ÖLVERK PIZZA & BREWERY

Breiðamörk 2; tel. 354/483-3030; www.olverk.is; entrées from 2,450ISK

Ölverk is a comfortable neighborhood haunt where locals dine on delicious pizza and enjoy cold beer. The specialty is pizza, but you will also find salads, sweet potato waffle fries, and pretzels with cheese dip on the menu. There are eight beers on tap, brewed from their own on-site microbrewery.

HVER RESTAURANT

Breiðamörk 1C; tel. 354/483-4700; www.hverrestaurant.is/en; 4pm-10pm daily; entrées from 3,100ISK

Hver Restaurant is located in Hotel Örk. The restaurant is casual and the staff are friendly. The menu has lamb and fish dishes, soups, sandwiches, and a couple of vegetarian options. Sample courses include arctic char with barley and lightly salted cod with mashed potatoes. The bar has a good selection of local and foreign beers as well as wine and cocktails.

Accommodations

HOTEL ORK

Breiðamörk 1; tel. 354/483-4775; www.hotelork.is; rooms from 24,000ISK

Hotel Ork offers 76 bright and airy standard rooms and 9 superior rooms that are larger. The decor is dated with blue carpeting, but rooms are clean, with private bathrooms, TVs, mini refrigerators, complimentary tea and coffee, and free Wi-Fi. The hotel has an outdoor swimming pool, hot tubs, and a sauna. Breakfast is included in the price of the room.

★ FROST & FIRE HOTEL

Hverahvammur; tel. 354/483-4959; www.frostandfire.is; rooms from 34,000ISK

The 17-room Frost & Fire Hotel is nestled in the heart of Hveragerði. Each room in the boutique hotel is adorned with works from local Icelandic artists and has private shower facilities and comfortable beds. Guests have access to a spa next to the river that offers treatments, hot tubs, and a swimming pool. The included breakfast is delicious.

HVERAGERÐI CAMPSITE

Reykjamork; tel. 354/483-4605; tjalda.is/hveragerdi; open year-round; 1,750ISK

This campsite is just two minutes from the swimming pool. Visitors have access to a washing machine, dryer, toilets, and 220-volt electricity. There are about 80 spots on the large field, and the campsite accommodates tents, RVs, and campers. Electricity costs an extra 1,000ISK, and washing machines are 800ISK per wash.

Information and Services

SOUTH ICELAND REGIONAL INFORMATION CENTER

Sunnumörk 2-4; tel. 354/483-4601; www.south.is; 8:30am-5pm Mon.-Fri.

The South Iceland regional information center is right off Route 1 in Hveragerði.

Getting There

Hveragerði is 40 kilometers (25 mi) southeast of **Reykjavík.** The drive takes about 35 minutes on **Route 1.**

The **Strætó 51 bus** (tel. 354/540-2700; www.straeto.is) from Mjodd bus station in Reykjavík makes about 10 daily trips to Hveragerði year-round, stopping at the **Shell gas station** downtown. The bus ride is about 40 minutes and costs 1,470ISK.

The South Coast

If you're after hot springs and quirky museums, and you have some time to spend before or after you head to the Golden Circle, look no farther than the southern coast. Small towns like Hveragerði, Selfoss, and Vík have unique charm. Hveragerði is famed as the hot springs capital of Iceland. Selfoss is frequently used as a home base when exploring the Golden Circle, but it also has a couple of museums to check out. Vík boasts black-sand beaches. Outdoor activities like hiking, bird-watching, and Jeep tours are popular in this region.

STOKKSEYRI

This small town was home to a thriving fishing industry, but today it's more of a tourist town with a couple of kitschy museums.

Sights

THE GHOST CENTRE

Hafnargata 9; tel. 354/895-0020; www.icelandicwonders.is; 1pm-6pm daily July 1-Aug. 31; 2,000ISK

This small, fun museum is dedicated to Iceland's most famous ghosts and their stories. During the tour, which takes about 40 minutes, you hear 24 ghost stories through a device and headphones that can be listened to in English, French, German, Russian, Japanese, or Icelandic. While you listen to the ghost stories, you look at displays about the various spirits. The phantoms include mountainside ghosts, ancient ghosts, ghosts in animal disguises, infant ghosts, and sea ghosts. The Ghost Bar is at the end of the tour, where you can order a drink and absorb everything you just took in. It's all in good fun, but it's not recommended for children under age 12.

ICELANDIC WONDERS

Hafnargata 9; tel. 354/895-0020; www.icelandicwonders.is; 1pm-6pm daily July 1-Aug. 31; 2,000ISK

Icelandic Wonders is next door to the Ghost Centre. Instead of ghosts, this exhibition focuses on Iceland's rich folklore, including elves, trolls, the Yule Lads (Iceland's version of Santa Claus), and northern lights. There's something for everyone at this charming museum, and it is much more child friendly than the Ghost Centre.

Food

★ FJÖRUBORÐIÐ

Eyrarbraut 3A; tel. 354/483-1550; www.fjorubordid.is/english; noon-9pm daily; entrées from 3,990ISK

If you are in the mood for seafood, this is your place. Fjöruborðið, which means "seashore," specializes in tasty langoustines, from their langoustine soup, to langoustine tails sautéed in garlic and butter. The fish is fresh, tender, and full of flavor. If you aren't in the mood for seafood, don't fret; there is a beef carpaccio salad on offer as well as a vegetarian dish and roasted fillet of local lamb. There's a three-course menu available for 11,650ISK, which includes langoustine soup, followed by langoustine tails, then dessert. For the kids, there are chicken nuggets with fries and a ham and cheese sandwich.

Getting There

Stokkseyri is 65 kilometers (40 mi) southeast of **Reykjavík** and accessible by **Route 1.** The drive takes about 55 minutes.

MOUNT HEKLA

Hekla's claim to fame is being the most active volcano in the country today (no easy feat, as there are currently 35 active volcanoes in Iceland). Hekla (Hood) should not be confused with nearby Eyjafjallajökull, which wreaked havoc on transatlantic air travel in 2010. Climbing 1,491 meters (4,891 ft), Hekla has erupted five times in the last hundred years and more than 20 times since Iceland was settled in the 10th century. Its last eruption was in 2000, and local scientists expect it

The South Coast

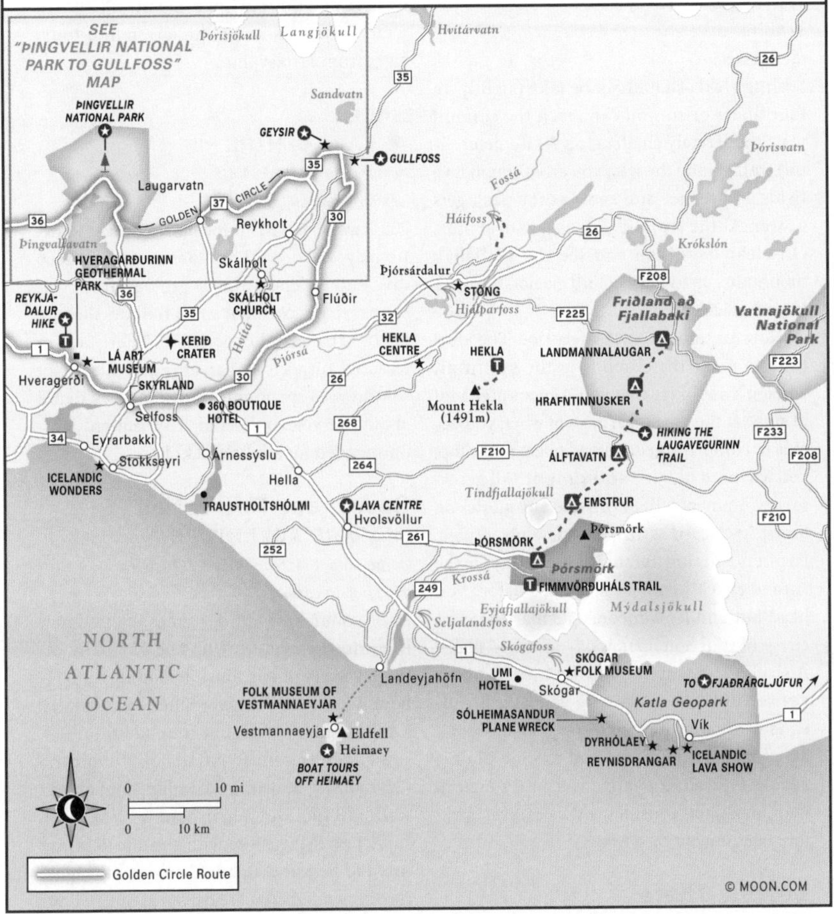

to erupt in the near future. What makes Hekla somewhat unique is that it's a cone volcano, which is less common in Iceland than fissure volcanoes.

Sights

HEKLA CENTER

Leirubakki; tel. 354/487-8700; www.leirubakki.is; 10am-9pm daily May-Sept.; 900ISK

The Hekla Center gives visitors a comprehensive look at one of the island's most active volcanoes. The exhibition emphasizes the influence of the volcano on the inhabited areas close to it, including Landsveit, Holt, and Rangárvellir. The center has special educational materials for children as well as tourist information in English. An on-site **café** offers light meals and coffee. It's an essential place to stop and read up on the region.

Hiking

HIKING HEKLA

Distance: *7 km (4 mi)*

Hiking Time: *8 hours round-trip*

Information and Maps: *Hella Tourist Information Center (Thrudvangur 6; tel. 354/487-4800)*
Trailhead: *Parking lot at southeastern corner of the mountain*

Scaling Hekla should not be taken lightly. In four hours or so, you can reach the summit via a moderately challenging 7-kilometer (4-mi) trail. Along the way, you cross rough lava fields and see ice and snow as the peak gets nearer. At the top, the view is jaw-dropping. On clear days, you can see the Fjallabak mountains up to Vatnajökull glacier, Europe's largest glacier.

Now for some crucial safety tips. The ideal time to make the climb is in the **summer,** when it's not likely that you'll encounter a lot of snow at the top. Regardless of when you decide to climb, if you do intend to get to the top, you will need **glacier equipment.** All necessary equipment will be provided by guides on tours. **Arctic Adventures** (www.adventures.is) offers a hiking tour of Hekla. Always make sure to check weather conditions before you head out and let someone (such as the concierge of your hotel) know of your travel plans. Also check in with the **tourist information center** in Hella. Make sure you have an adequate amount of drinking water, appropriate clothing, and a charged mobile phone. Mount Hekla is an active volcano, so check with locals and consult www.safetravel.is before heading out on a hike.

Getting There

By car from **Reykjavík,** head southeast on **Route 1** and take unpaved **Route 26** toward the town of Hella. There is parking by the trailhead. The journey from Reykjavík is 93 kilometers (58 mi), which takes about 1.5 hours.

HVOLSVÖLLUR

Hvolsvöllur is a small town about 100 kilometers (62 mi) from Reykjavík, home to less than 2,000 people. Close to the Golden Circle route, and a growing interest in tourism, Hvolsvöllur houses a fascinating **Lava Centre** and the tourism company **Midgard,** which provides accommodation and tours right from Hvolsvöllur.

Sights

★ LAVA CENTRE

Austurvegur 14; tel. 354/415-5200; www.lavacentre.is; 9am-4pm daily; 3,990ISK

The Lava Centre is informative, fun, and extremely well done. The museum takes a deep dive into Iceland's unique geology, from volcanoes to the constant small tremors that are part of the island experience. There are interactive displays and an engaging film; a lot of time was spent on capturing every detail about this volcanic island. This is highly recommended for adults and kids.

Sports and Recreation

MIDGARD ADVENTURE

Dufþaksbraut 14; tel. 354/578-3180; www.midgardbasecamp.is

Hvolsvöllur-based Midgard has injected new life into the small town. The company offers a variety of day tours, including a 10-14-hour hike along Fimmvörðuháls (40,000ISK), a bike and lava caving tour (25,000ISK), snowmobiling on Eyjafjallajökull volcano (26,900ISK), and an ice-climbing and glacier walk (21,490ISK). Their popular Þórsmörk super Jeep (a huge Jeep with gigantic tires outfitted to handle rough terrain) tour is highly recommended: You are driven about an hour from Hvolsvöllur into Þórsmörk, where you will see waterfalls and canyons, cross rivers, and get up close and personal with a glacier. The 6-8-hour tour costs 32,000ISK.

HVOLSVÖLLUR SWIMMING POOL

Vallarbraut; tel. 354/488-4295; 6am-9pm Mon.-Fri., 10am-7pm Sat.-Sun.; 1,000ISK

Hvolsvöllur has a large outdoor swimming pool, with a slide for kids, as well as a gym, sauna, and hot tubs.

Food and Accommodations

VALHALLA RESTAURANT & SAGA CENTER

Hlíðarvegur 14; tel. 354/487-8781; 5pm-10pm daily; entrées from 1,800ISK

Valhalla Restaurant is a family-friendly spot that offers casual food like hamburgers, smoked barbecue ribs, and pulled pork sandwiches. The menu is small and simple, centered around their charcoal grill. There is a veggie burger on the menu as well as a kids' burger. The restaurant has a Viking theme that is kitschy and fun. They even offer a place to practice your axe-throwing skills.

MIDGARD BASE CAMP

Dufþaksbraut 14; tel. 354/578-3180; www.midgardbasecamp.is; beds from 4,000ISK, private rooms from 24,900ISK

The same family that operates Midgard Adventure runs Midgard Base Camp, a relaxed, friendly hostel that offers dorm room accommodations as well as private rooms. Dorm rooms have design-forward bunk beds with a bedside light, charging sockets, and a privacy curtain, along with shared bathroom facilities. Private rooms can accommodate two travelers and have private bathrooms with a shower. All guests have access to a rooftop sauna and hot tub to relax in after a long day of adventure. There's a large common lounge area and an in-house **bar** and restaurant. The **restaurant** (breakfast 7am-11am, dinner 4pm-10pm; entrées 2,600ISK) serves up options like a tasty lamb prime rib and local pan-fried salmon, as well as burgers, salads, and vegan dishes.

UMI HOTEL

Leirnavegur 243; tel. 354/518-4001; www.hotelumi.is; rooms from 50,000ISK

UMI Hotel is a new, modern hotel with 28 rooms that have gorgeous views of the South Coast. The rooms are decorated in an elegant, Scandinavian style with a minibar, a coffee and tea set, a bathrobe, and complimentary toiletries from the popular local Sóley Cosmetics. There's an in-house restaurant open year-round.

Getting There

By car from **Reykjavík,** head southeast on **Route 1** and take it to Hvolsvöllur. The journey from Reykjavík is 107 kilometers (67 mi), which takes about 1.5 hours.

ÞJÓRSÁRDALUR

Þjórsárdalur is a flat, lush valley near the Þjórsá River with a number of stunning waterfalls. The region has a lot of pumice because of the numerous eruptions of Mount Hekla over the years, evidenced by **Stöng,** a reconstructed settlement-era farm that was completely buried by Hekla's eruption in the year 1104.

Sights

HÁIFOSS

Route 32

Háifoss, a beautiful waterfall near Mount Hekla, drops from a height of 122 meters (400 ft), making it the second-highest waterfall on the island. Set against the backdrop of the Þjórsá River, Háifoss is a wonderful place to stop and take photos. It is possible to **hike** to the waterfall from the farm Stöng, a moderate, six-hour, 18-kilometer (11-mi) round-trip hike, but there is a **parking lot** above the cascade, which makes it a car-friendly stop along the way to your next destination.

If you are planning to hike it, make sure you have proper footwear and adequate drinking water. From **Selfoss,** take **Route 1** for 14 kilometers (9 mi) to **Route 30;** follow Route 30 for 18 kilometers (11 mi) to **Route 32,** for another 43 kilometers (27 mi). All routes are paved.

HJÁLPARFOSS

from Route 32, drive about 20 minutes until you see a sign by the road that says Hjálparfoss

Hjálparfoss is another gorgeous waterfall near Mount Hekla. While not particularly tall, the waterfall is special as it's where the Þórsa and Fossa rivers meet, and the falls are split in two.

It is about 30 kilometers (19 mi) east of the village Flúðir and can be reached by a gravel road between **Route 30** to **Route 32** that winds through the Vikrar lava fields. From Route 32, drive about 20 minutes until you see a sign by the road that says Hjálparfoss.

STÖNG

tel. 354/488-7713; www.thjodveldisbaer.is/en; 10am-5pm daily June 1-Aug. 31, remainder of the year open by appointment; adults 1,000ISK, children up to 16 free

Stöng, a settlement-era farm, was completely buried by Hekla's eruption in the year 1104. A reconstructed 11th-century longhouse called Þjóðveldisbær was erected in this protected valley. For those looking to see a traditional "turf house" with grass on the roof, this is the place to go. The farm, as legend tells it, was the residence of Gaukur á Stöng from *Njál's Saga*. History buffs will want to make a stop, and visitors are welcome to go inside and take a look.

Sports and Recreation

ÞJÓRSÁRDALUR SWIMMING POOL

tel. 354/488-7002; 10am-9pm daily June-Aug.; 1,000ISK

After erecting the local dam, the Búrfell hydroelectric station used its extra cement to build the open-air Þjórsárdalur Swimming Pool.

Getting There and Around

Þjórsárdalur is 118 kilometers (73 mi) east of **Reykjavík.** It's accessible by unpaved **Route 32;** a **four-wheel-drive** Jeep is recommended to get around some choppy parts of the road. It is not recommended to venture out in a compact car, as the likelihood of getting stranded is high. The drive takes about 1.5 hours. Be sure to check weather forecasts before heading out on your journey.

ÞÓRSMÖRK AND LANDMANNALAUGAR

The spectacular Þórsmörk (Thor's Woods) region offers landscapes ranging from towering mountains to scores of glacial streams and miles of black sand. Þórsmörk is not an easy region to get to, as there are river crossings and you need a vehicle that has a high enough clearance to cross. The region is dotted with waterfalls, canyons, lush vegetation, and vast open spaces. Making it here is no easy feat. Do not venture out in a compact car. Because of the **Krossá River,** this is a wet and turbulent ride that requires a Jeep.

Nearby Landmannalaugar is a major hub for hikers, and for very good reason. There are several well-maintained trails throughout the region that range from day hikes to multiday treks. The landscape is one of wonder, with vast valleys, colorful rhyolite mountains, hot springs, and riverbanks. Landmannalaugar is a three-hour drive from Reykjavík, and an F-road approved vehicle is necessary to drive in the highlands. From Reykjavík, you drive on Route 1 to Road 26, followed by the mountain roads F225, F208, and F224. While not an easy route, Landmannalaugar is not as challenging to reach as Þórsmörk.

The wildly popular **Laugavegurinn hiking route** from the Landmannalaugar region to the Þórsmörk area is a 55-kilometer (34-mi), four-day hike that attracts backpackers and hikers from around the world. If you're coming to Iceland to hike just one trail, this is the one. Its popularity stems from the variety of landscape along the way: bubbling hot springs, vast glaciers, beautiful mountains, stunning waterfalls, and roaring rivers.

TOP EXPERIENCE

★ Laugavegurinn Trail

DAY 1: LANDMANNALAUGAR TO HRAFNTINNUSKER

Distance: *12 km (7 mi)*

Hiking Time: *4-5 hours*

Trailhead: *Landmannalaugar huts*

The Landmannalaugar-Hrafntinnusker leg of the hike is considered moderately challenging. The trail goes through a rugged lava field,

---

1: Landmannalaugar **2:** Þórsmörk

1
2

Hiking Laugavergurinn: Packing, Getting There, and Other Tips

For general information about the Laugavegurinn Trail, contact the **Iceland Touring Association (Ferðafélag Íslands)** (www.fi.is).

WHEN TO GO

The ideal months for this hike are **June** and **July,** but **August** is possible as well. The region is inaccessible the rest of the year due to snow levels and impassable roads, so if you want to attempt this hike, summer is your only option.

WHAT TO PACK

- **Clothing:** Waterproof pants, waterproof jacket, mid-layer, waterproof boots, gloves, hat, wool socks, sunglasses, gaiters, wool or synthetic base layers
- **Gear:** Sleeping bag, mattress, pillow, three-season tent, camping stove, lighter, gas, utensils, cooking pot, knives
- **Food:** All the food needed for duration of the journey, plus an extra emergency day, snacks, granola bars
- **Personal hygiene:** Toothbrush, toothpaste, toilet paper, sunscreen, towel
- **Other necessities:** Maps, GPS, water bottle, small first-aid kit

BEFORE YOU GO

Precaution is needed when hiking in the highlands. The region is remote, unforgiving, and lacks conveniences like stores, or shelter. Therefore, before you head out, make sure you have informed someone of your plan; you can **register** your information at www.safetravel.is. It is imperative that you have the **proper clothing and footwear,** enough **food** and **water, camping gear** that can sustain fierce weather, or booked accommodation at **mountain huts** if you are not camping in designated campsites. Also, make sure you have **maps** and a **charged mobile phone.**

which makes this leg a bit more difficult, to the slopes of the volcano Brennisteinsalda. The landscape offers every color of the rainbow, from deep green moss to the bluest skies to yellow and red earth. After about four hours, you will reach a hot spring, Stórihver, which surges with activity, steam bubbling to the surface. The remainder of the trail to the Hrafntinnusker hut at Höskuldsskáli might be challenging depending on weather conditions, so be sure to monitor the forecast for snow and wind.

DAY 2: HRAFNTINNUSKER TO ÁLFTAVATN

Distance: *12 km (7 mi)*

Hiking Time: *5 hours*

Trailhead: *Hrafntinnusker hut*

The Hrafntinnusker-Álftavatn part of the trail is also moderately challenging, starting out through a valley with some small gorges and dips in the land. If the weather is good, a climb up Mount Háskerðingur (1,032 m/3,386 ft tall) will treat you to a spectacular view of the landscape and the road ahead. The trail continues through a region rich with mountains and glaciers. As you get closer to the Grashagakvísl River, the colors become more vibrant, with bright green moss and lichen alive along the riverbanks. It's a beautiful place to stop, take some pictures, and soak up the scenery.

GETTING THERE (AND GETTING BACK)

Starting in Landmannalaugar

From Reykjavík, Landmannalaugar is about 200 kilometers (124 mi). By rental car, drive on **Route 1** to **Route 30** to **Route 26.** Next, take **Route 208** until you reach Landmannalaugar. The routes are signposted along the way. For those who wish to travel by bus, the company **Trex** (www.trex.is) operates buses for 9,400ISK one-way. The trip from Reykjavík takes 4 hours 15 minutes.

Starting in Þórsmörk

If starting the hike at Þórsmörk, it's important to note that it is not easy to reach, though it's worth the effort if you're looking for untouched and unspoiled land. There are significantly fewer visitors to Þórsmörk. You will need a Jeep with high clearance to cross rivers to navigate these roads; do not attempt the trip in a compact car or city SUV. To reach Þórsmörk by car, drive on **Route 1** to **Route 249** to **F249.**

Arranging Your Return Trip

There are buses that return to Reykjavík through **Trex** (www.trex.is) from both Landmannalaugar and Þórsmörk. One-way fares are 9,400ISK and tickets can be purchased online.

MOUNTAIN HUTS AND CAMPSITES

At night, hikers on the Laugavergurinn Trail rest their heads in **mountain huts,** which mark the starting and ending points of each leg of the trail. The huts are run by **Volcano Huts** (www.volcanohuts.com), and can sleep 2-16 people (beds start at 7,140ISK). They have running water, cooking facilities, a sauna, pool, and showers. It's required to **call ahead** for a spot in the mountain huts.

There are **campsites** that adjoin the mountain huts that are also operated by Volcano Huts. The facilities include a cooking area, toilets, and running water. It's always a good idea to **call ahead** for camping.

DAY 3: ÁLFTAVATN TO EMSTRUR

Distance: *15 km (9 mi)*

Hiking Time: *7 hours*

Trailhead: *Brattháls ridge*

This moderately challenging trail starts out over the ridge Brattháls, passes into the Hvanngil gorge, and crosses the Bratthálskvísl River by bridge. The landscape is vast and serene. As you continue on to the Kaldaklofskvísl River, there is a bridge for hikers. Past the bridge, you have two options as the trail splits. One branch leads east to Mælifellssandur, and the other path leads south to Emstrur. Most people opt for the southern trail to Emstrur because it's a bit more scenic, with mountain views and an interesting rocky landscape. Less than one kilometer (0.6 mi) from Kaldaklofskvísl from the southern trail, there's another river, Nyrðri Emstruá, where there is a bridge to cross.

DAY 4: EMSTRUR TO ÞÓRSMÖRK

Distance: *15 km (9 mi)*

Hiking Time: *7 hours*

Trailhead: *Emstrur huts*

The last leg of the hike, from Emstrur to Þórsmörk, starts out navigating the canyon of Syðri-Emstruá. The path down to the bridge is steep, so stay aware and be careful where you step while descending. Next, hikers come across the Almenningar region and will have to ford the Þröngá River. After wading through the river, it's a 30-minute walk to the Langidalur huts in Þórsmörk.

Getting There

Landmannalaugar is 193 kilometers (119 mi) southeast of Reykjavík. Take **Route 1** to **Route 26** to **F225;** the latter two roads are unpaved. It's about a 3.5-hour drive.

Þórsmörk is 157 kilometers (97 mi) southeast from Reykjavík. It's reachable by **Jeep** via **Route 1** and **Route 249.** The drive takes about 3.5 hours.

By bus, **Trex** (tel. 354/587-6000; www.trex.is) has daily departures in the summer from Reykjavík to Þórsmörk (9,400ISK per person) and Reykjavík to Landmannalaugar (9,400ISK per person). Both rides take about 4 hours.

SELJALANDSFOSS

The mighty Seljalandsfoss is a highlight for many visitors to the South Coast. Tourists delight in the spray from the 40-meter (131-ft) falls, and rainbows are frequently seen here due to the changing weather and frequent rain showers. The long stream of thundering water cascades over a rocky cliff, tumbling meters below. During the summer, the area around the falls is lush with bright green grass, a heavenly sight on bright days. In the winter months, the waterfall is moodier; it can be quite beautiful when it snows and you see the falls against a stark white contrast. What makes this waterfall unique in a land of spectacular waterfalls is that there's a path that lets you walk behind it. Those who do so are treated to a memorable view, but be prepared to get wet and be sure to wear appropriate footwear. Use caution during the winter, as it can be especially slippery. There is a path on the right side of the falls that leads to the top, but the best viewpoint is right in front.

Getting There

Seljalandsfoss is about 120 kilometers (76 mi) southeast of **Reykjavík,** about a 1-hour-15-minute drive, and is right off **Route 1.**

EYJAFJALLAJÖKULL

Eyjafjallajökull became Iceland's most famous volcano after its eruption in 2010 halted air travel across Europe, stranding tens of thousands of people. For locals, it was a treat to hear foreign newscasters struggle to pronounce the name of the volcano on the nightly news. Clips were regularly shown on Icelandic TV. (For the record, it's pronounced EYE-ya-fyat-lah-YOH-kuht.)

Before Eyjafjallajökull made worldwide headlines, the volcano had been a popular destination to explore, and it remains so today, with a rugged and icy landscape. Never attempt to climb a glacier on your own. Eyjafjallajökull is completely covered by an ice cap; magma hitting the ice created the tremendous ash cloud during the eruption. The ice cap covers an area of about 100 square kilometers (39 sq mi), which feeds several outlet glaciers. When people joke that "Iceland is green, and Greenland is icy," those who visit the Eyjafjallajökull region will think again. There is a lot of ice in Iceland. The ice cap is the island's fourth-largest glacier.

Eyjafjallajökull is a stratovolcano that ascends to 1,651 meters (5,417 ft) at its highest point. The volcano is fed by a magma chamber under the mountain, and it is part of a chain of volcanoes stretching across Iceland. Its nearest active neighbors are Katla to the north and Heimaey and Eldfell to the south. The volcano is thought to be related to Katla, in that eruptions of Eyjafjallajökull have generally been followed by eruptions of Katla. However, Katla did not erupt following Eyjafjallajökull's 2010 eruption. Scientists closely monitor the volcanoes' activity, measuring the size and frequency of the tremors.

Getting There

Eyjafjallajökull is on the Ring Road, **Route 1,** and is 140 kilometers (87 mi) east of **Reykjavík.** Buses do not stop near the volcano, so if you want to get up close and personal, you need access to a car.

SKÓGAR

Skógar is a tiny village of fewer than 40 people. The town suffered a major setback in the aftermath of the Eyjafjallajökull eruption, as it was covered in ash and life ground to a halt. The town has since recovered, and tourism to the region is back in full swing. The **Skógafoss** cascade is the main draw, but there is also a folk museum worth checking out.

Sights

SKÓGAFOSS

Skógafoss is an epic waterfall, one of the biggest in the country. It looms 25 meters (82 ft) high and has a drop-off of 60 meters (197 ft). The sheer width of the falls makes it unique, as well as the option to scale a set of stairs to the top. In the summer, Skógafoss is surrounded by deep greens and hints of purple from the wild lupines. According to Viking lore, a local settler buried a treasure chest in a cave behind the waterfall. It was said that locals discovered the chest years later, but it quickly disappeared before they could grasp it. Because of the amount of spray the waterfall produces, as well as the changing weather from sun to rain, it's common to see rainbows over the falls; be sure to have your camera ready. The waterfall is in town, near the southern Ring Road.

SKÓGAR FOLK MUSEUM

(Skógasafn)

Austur-Eyjafjöllum; tel. 354/487-8845; www.skogasafn.is; 9am-6pm daily June 1-Aug. 31, 10am-5pm daily Sept. 1-May 31; adults 2,000ISK, children 12-17 1,200ISK, children under 12 free

Skógar Folk Museum is a charming initiative that started in 1949 at the behest of resident Þórður Tómasson, who curated the museum from its inception until his retirement in 2013, at the age of 92. The museum, which houses relics of the past, including tools, fishing equipment, and a fishing boat, does a great job of showing what life has been like in Skógar over the last several decades. A little coffee shop serves a great cup of coffee and delicious pastries.

SÓLHEIMASANDUR PLANE WRECK

GPS: N63.4595, W19.3646

The Sólheimasandur plane wreck is one of the more unexpected tourist attractions in Iceland. In 1973, a U.S. Navy Douglas DC-3 plane crash-landed on the stark black sands of Sólheimasandur, and the shell of the plane remains on the sands, a popular photo opportunity for many travelers. Visitors should park their car at the "plane wreck parking lot" and walk the 4 kilometers (2 mi) to the plane's location The wreck's parking area is about 9 kilometers (5.5 mi) from Skógar on Route 1, about a 10-minute drive. The hike is about 1 hour each way on a well-marked path. For those that don't want to walk, a **shuttle service** (www.arcanum.com) provides about a dozen departures to and from the wreck per day (2,500ISK). The shuttle takes about 15 minutes each way.

Hiking the Fimmvörðuháls Trail

The trek through the Fimmvörðuháls pass from Skógar to **Þórsmörk** is one of the most popular hiking routes in the country. The trail takes hikers up from Skógar, along the **Skógá River** and its wondrous waterfalls, and up between the two enormous glaciers: **Eyjafjallajökull** and **Mýrdalsjökull.** There, hikers can see recently formed lava and craters. Heading down from the craters to the stunning Þórsmörk glacier valley, there are some amazing views over the highlands and the surrounding glaciers. The trek is only safely accessible from around **mid-June** to early **September.**

This is a demanding hike, with an elevation gain of over 1,000 meters (3,000 ft) and a total distance of about 25 kilometers (16 mi). It takes about 8-10 hours. Most tourists hike it in **one day,** but it can be done over two days as well. For those who want to take the **bus** back, check out www.trex.is for the timetable and rates. It's recommended that you start the hike at Skógar and end at Þórsmörk; starting at Skógar is more popular than starting in Þórsmörk because it's

1
2
3

easier to get to. There are no facilities along the route, so be sure to have enough food and water, as well as proper gear. Good hiking boots and waterproof clothing are required, and having layers is strongly recommended. You can encounter all types of weather, so be prepared.

Experienced independent hikers may opt to take a bus run by **Reykjavík Excursions** (tel. 354/580-5400; www.re.is) to Skógar, which leaves twice daily from Reykjavík June 1-August 31. The one-way fare is 7,999ISK. Upon completing the hike, travelers can take a Reykjavík Excursion bus back to Reykjavík from the Básar campsite, in the vicinity of Þórsmörk, for 7,999ISK.

DAY 1: SKÓGAR TO FIMMVÖRÐUSKÁLI HUT

Distance: *12 km (7 mi)*

Hiking Time: *5-6 hours*

Trailhead: *Skógafoss waterfall; GPS coordinates N 63.37.320, W 19.27.093*

The trek starts at the epic waterfall Skógafoss, where you'll want to spend some time exploring the area and admiring the thundering falls. The trail officially begins after climbing the makeshift stairs along the waterfall. You'll see a river ahead and a path, and you'll encounter myriad colors in the landscape, from lush greens in the first 7-8 kilometers (4-5 mi) to the muted grays and browns of the rugged, rocky terrain. Eyjafjallajökull and Mýrdalsjökull glaciers loom ahead as you make your way past gravelly ruts and fields of snow. Keep in mind that even in the summer, you will see snow. The Fimmvörðuskáli Hut, which is signposted and about 30-40 minutes west of the trail, is the halfway mark. The hut (tel. 354/562-1000; www.utivist.is; 7,600ISK) is open mid-June to August 31 and can accommodate 20 people. It has bathrooms, a gas stove, and kitchen accessories.

1: Seljalandsfoss **2:** Skógafoss waterfall **3:** eruption at Eyjafjallajökull

DAY 2: FIMMVÖRÐUSKÁLI HUT TO ÞÓRSMÖRK

Distance: *13 km (8 mi)*

Hiking Time: *5-6 hours*

Trailhead: *Fimmvörðuskáli Hut*

After a hopefully restful evening and soon after getting back on the trail, you'll make your way between the two glaciers—for many this is a highlight. Observe the smooth curves and jagged edges of the glaciers before getting ready to encounter snow as the elevation rises. The highest point is between the two mountains, Magni and Móði. Pressing ahead, you will encounter the site of the 2010 Eyjafjallajökull eruption and new lava fields created in its aftermath. The path continues through rocky plateaus before descending into valleys as you enter Þórsmörk.

Food and Accommodations

★ HOTEL SKOGAR

Skogum; tel. 354/487-4880; www.hotelskogar.is; rooms from 33,000ISK

Just a five-minute walk from Skógafoss waterfall, at the foot of Eyjafjallajökull, Hotel Skogar offers 12 rooms in a minimalist Nordic design. Rooms are bright and airy, with wood furniture and shockingly white bedding. It's clean, comfortable, and has a beautiful in-house restaurant in a killer location with stunning views. Breakfast is included, and guests have access to a sauna and outdoor hot tub. The **Hotel Skogar Restaurant** (breakfast 8am-10am daily year-round, lunch noon-3pm daily June-Aug., dinner 6pm-10pm daily year-round; entrées from 3,100ISK) offers a delicious selection of choice local meats and fish and other fresh ingredients.

Getting There

The tiny village of Skógar is 154 kilometers (96 mi) southeast of **Reykjavík** and is accessible by **Route 1.**

VÍK

Vík, home to fewer than 400 people, has a small-town feel. The main tourist draws are the **Katla Geopark**—the region surrounding the mighty **Katla volcano**—and the area's hauntingly beautiful black-sand beaches.

Sights

ICELANDIC LAVA SHOW

Víkurbraut 5; tel. 354/823-7777; 1:30pm and 5pm shows daily; adults 5,900ISK, children 2-12 3,500ISK, children under 2 free

The Icelandic Lava Show is the only place in Iceland to see hot molten lava up close when there isn't a volcanic eruption. This show creates the conditions of an eruption, with molten lava seeping down a display. Guests get to see the lava, which reaches a temperature of 1,093°C (2,000°F); feel the staggering heat emitting from it; and hear the lava crackle and sizzle. This is a fun experience, and a winner for kids.

REYNISDRANGAR

Reynisdrangar is a cluster of striking basalt sea stacks that jut out from a sandy beach. The stacks sit under the mountain Reynisfjall just outside Vík. It's popular to climb on the stacks and take photos, then roam the black-sand beach, picking up stones and admiring the rock formations. Reynisdrangar is about 10 kilometers (6 mi) south of Vík and can be reached by Route 1 and Route 215, both paved roads.

REYNISFJARA

Reynisfjara, from which Reynisdrangar is visible, is probably the most famous black-sand beach in Iceland. The juxtaposition of the white waves crashing on the stark black sand and pebbles is beautiful, with towering basalt columns along the shore next to a small cave. As a popular sight in the south, there tends to be a lot of foot traffic in the area. Pay close attention to the warning signs in the parking lot, as there are sneaker waves that can drag you out to sea; there have been fatal accidents here in recent years. Reynisfjara is also about 10 kilometers (6 mi) south of Vík and can be reached by Route 1 and Route 215, both paved roads.

DYRHÓLAEY

Route 218

Dyrhólaey is a unique rock formation near Reynisfjara. The rock arch rises from the sea, peaking at 120 meters (394 ft), and offers views of the Reynisfjara black-sand beach, basalt columns, the ocean, and during the summer, seabirds, including puffins. You can drive to Dyrhólaey from Reynisfjara, which is about 20 kilometers (12 mi) west, taking paved Route 215 to paved Route 1 to unpaved Route 218. Visitors can walk to the arch from the small carpark.

Sports and Recreation

KATLA GEOPARK

www.katlageopark.com

Vík is the gateway to the Katla Geopark. Iceland's first geopark was designated in 2011 to protect the natural environment, promote local sustainable development, introduce local culture, and emphasize nature tourism. The name comes from one of the island's volcanoes, **Katla,** which is situated under the glacier **Mýrdalsjökull.** The geopark is 9,542 square kilometers (7,545 sq mi), which is 9.3 percent of the total area of Iceland. Within the geopark are glaciers, volcanoes, mountains, rivers, waterfalls, and miles of lava fields. Visitors can enjoy hiking, caving, angling, horse riding, glacier walking, and ice climbing. The geopark is open year-round.

TRUE ADVENTURE

Suðurvíkurvegur 5; tel. 354/698-8890; www.trueadventure.is; adults 14,900ISK, children ages 8-16 7,500ISK

Vík-based True Adventure runs a zipline tour in a region surrounded by sweeping valleys and waterfalls. You will start off with an easy hike through a canyon, followed by two zipline rides. The first zipline spans 235 meters (771 ft), followed by a shorter zipline at 135 meters (443 ft). The guide will provide all the necessary equipment and will give you a safety briefing.

1: puffin in Vík **2:** the Reynisdrangar sea stacks **3:** Skool Beans **4:** view from Reynisfjara beach

1
2
SKOOL BEANS CAFE
3
4

Food

HALLDÓRSKAFFI

Víkurbraut 28; tel. 354/487-1202; www.halldorskaffi.is; noon-9pm daily; entrées from 2,690ISK

Halldórskaffi has it all for a tiny café. There are soups, sandwiches, pizza, hamburgers, and more upscale fish and lamb dishes. A children's menu offers chicken nuggets and hamburgers. The food is eclectic for a local café, and the owner is a big fan of garlic. The lamb sandwich with fresh marinated meat in pepper sauce with a salad and french fries hits the spot.

★ SKOOL BEANS

Klettsvegur; tel. 354/830-0079; www.skoolbeans.com; 9am-5pm Tues.-Fri., 10am-5pm Sat.-Sun.

Skool Beans was the most unexpected addition to Vík in 2020, a bright yellow school bus serving coffee, hot chocolate, and snacks. If you find yourself in Vík, you must stop by to sample a classic coffee or latte, or something more interesting like a white chocolate and fennel hot chocolate or a chocolate and peanut butter hot chocolate. The owner, who roasts the coffee herself, is lovely and sells local crafts and art in the bus.

SUÐUR-VÍK RESTAURANT AND CAFÉ

Suðurvikurvegur 1; tel. 354/487-1515; noon-9pm daily; entrées from 3,900ISK

Suður-Vík Restaurant and Café brings some much-needed food diversity to Vík. The menu is eclectic and includes some tasty Thai dishes that are perfectly spiced. The restaurant is situated in an old house on the top of a hill with amazing views of the landscape, including the sea and mountains.

STRONDIN PUB

Austurvegi 18; tel. 354/790-1442; www.strondin.is; noon-11pm daily; entrées from 2,790ISK

Strondin Pub is a cozy gastropub in the heart of Vík and a great place to stop for home-cooked comfort food. The small restaurant features wood furnishings and decor that conjures the atmosphere of a lodge, with a warm, friendly staff and a diverse menu. Guests can choose from pizzas, salads, and main courses like Icelandic cod stew, pan-fried arctic char, and grilled lamb fillet.

Accommodations

HOTEL KATLA

Hofdabrekku; tel. 354/487-1208; www.keahotels.is; rooms from 40,000ISK

Hotel Katla offers 103 rooms that feel a bit dated, but they are large and great for a short stay. Guests have free access to an outdoor geothermal pool, sauna, and gym, as well as an in-house restaurant. Options include lamb, fish, chicken, turkey, pork, and vegetarian main courses, as well as a salad bar, cold cuts, soup, fresh-baked bread, and an array of desserts.

HOTEL KRÍA

Sléttuvegur 12-14; tel. 354/416-2100; www.hotelkria.is; rooms from 41,000ISK

Hotel Kría is a stylish hotel, with 70 rooms and one suite, close to everything in Vík. Rooms are spacious with fantastic mountain views and amenities like a private bathroom, hair dryer, kettle with tea and coffee, and LCD satellite television. The in-house restaurant, **Drangar,** serves up traditional Icelandic food with a modern take. You will find fresh fish, local lamb, and seasonal vegetables on the menu.

HOTEL VÍK Í MÝRDAL

Klettsvegur 1-5; tel. 354/487-1480; www.stayinvik.is; rooms from 40,000ISK

Hotel Vík í Mýrdal is in a fantastic location, just a 10-minute walk to the black-sand beach. There are 78 guest rooms with either mountain, beach, or ocean views, and the decor is modern and comfortable with soft, muted colors and light wood floors. Each room features a large bathroom with organic skincare products that are made in Iceland. The in-house restaurant, Berg Restaurant, features fresh fish, lamb, beef, and vegetarian options, as well as an impressive cocktail menu.

Getting There

By car, Vík is 185 kilometers (115 mi) southeast of **Reykjavík** by **Route 1.** It's about a 2.5-hour drive.

KIRKJUBÆ-JARKLAUSTUR

Kirkjubæjarklaustur is a small village located between Vík and Höfn. The village, referred to as Klaustur by locals, is home to fewer than 150 people. Many tourists who struggle to find accommodations in Vík choose to stay here.

Sights

★ FJAÐRÁRGLJÚFUR

about 4 km (2.5 mi) from Route 1

Fjaðrárgljúfur is a large canyon that was a little-visited site until a couple of years ago when Canadian pop superstar Justin Bieber filmed a video there. Since then, tourism to the site has been on the rise. The canyon, which is believed to be formed during the last ice age, has been hollowed over millions of years by the Fjaðrá river, creating narrow walls. The canyon is about 2 kilometers (1.2 mi) long and about 100 meters (328 ft) deep, and visitors can walk on a footpath along the canyon's edge to admire the view and take photos. The contrasts are striking as the river weaves through towering rock formations that are lush in the summer months. Please be advised that it's important to stay on the path. The canyon is situated about 4 kilometers (2 mi) from Route 1. If you are driving toward the east, you will see a sign indicating Fjaðrágljúfur is on the left, leading you to a parking lot.

DVERGHAMRAR

Route 1, GPS coordinates N63.5056 W17.5141; www.katlageopark.com

Just east of Kirkjubæjarklaustur, you can find Dverghamrar (Dwarf Cliffs), which is a small canyon that geologists believe was shaped during the last ice age. Higher sea levels would have hammered the canyon, creating the interesting jagged basalt columns. The cliffs can be found just off Route 1.

Sports and Recreation

KIRKJUBÆJARKLAUSTUR SWIMMING POOL

Kirkjubær; tel. 354/487-4656; 10am-8pm daily; 900ISK

This popular outdoor swimming pool in the center of town has two hot tubs.

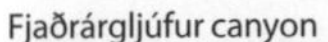

Fjaðrárgljúfur canyon

ICELAND BIKE FARM

Mörtunga 2; tel. 354/692-6131; www.icelandbikefarm.is; tours from 25,000ISK

Iceland Bike Farm is a family-run business that offers guided mountain bike tours on an array of tracks that pass canyons, waterfalls, and hills. Their single track full-day tour (25,000ISK), which is for advanced riders, starts with a super Jeep ride up the mountains before riding 15-25 kilometers (9-15 mi) over 4-6 hours.

Food and Accommodations

FOSSHOTEL NÚPAR

Núpar; tel. 354/517-3060; www.islandshotel.is; rooms from 36,000ISK

Fosshotel Núpar has 99 rooms, with some boasting a view of the glacier Vatnajökull. Rooms are clean, each with a private bathroom, simple desk, and bedside table. There's an in-house **restaurant and bar** (11am-9pm daily, entrées from 3,200ISK), and breakfast is included in the price of the room.

HOTEL KLAUSTUR

Klausturvegur 6; tel. 354/487-4900; www.hotelklaustur.is; rooms from 37,000ISK

Hotel Klaustur is a 57-room hotel just off the Ring Road, making this a convenient place to stay when exploring the South Coast. It offers twin and queen rooms as well as king junior suites. The rooms feel a little dated, with green carpeting and bright bed linens, but it's an adequate three-star hotel. The in-house **restaurant** offers a breakfast buffet every morning (7:30am-9:30am daily), and dinner (6:30pm-9pm daily). Main courses start at 2,900ISK and include grilled arctic char, lamb fillet, and pasta dishes.

MAGMA HOTEL

Tunga; tel. 354/420-0800; www.magmahotel.is, rooms from 34,000ISK

Magma Hotel is a stylish addition to the area. The 14 self-contained cottage-style rooms are modern, chic, and heavy on Nordic design. Each room is tastefully decorated in muted colors with quality linens, wood furniture, and hardwood floors. All rooms have huge windows as well as a patio. Rooms range from doubles to family rooms and have a flat-screen TV with access to Netflix, Marshall speakers, free Wi-Fi, and a private bathroom.

Getting There

By car, Kirkjubæjarklaustur is about 250 kilometers (155 mi) southeast of **Reykjavík** on **Route 1**, an approximately three-hour drive.

Heimaey

The Westman Islands (Vestmannaeyjar) are chock-full of rocky ridges and bird-watching opportunities. Heimaey, the only inhabited island, is where all of the sights, restaurants, and museums are located. With fewer than 5,000 residents, it's an isolated community, surrounded by beauty. The other islands remain uninhabited but can be seen from the sea during a boat tour. In the summer months, Heimaey is a popular spot for puffin-watching.

SIGHTS

Eldfell

www.visitwestmanislands.com

Eldfell, which means "fire mountain" in Icelandic, is a volcanic cone that reaches 200 meters (656 ft) high. It was formed after the 1973 volcanic eruption on Heimaey, which came without warning and displaced more than 3,000 Icelanders. Ash from the eruption fell for weeks, destroying homes, livestock, and personal possessions. Most of Heimaey's residents left by boat, and thankfully there were no deaths.

Tourists can take a 30-minute **ferry** ride from **Landeyjaharbor** in the southern town of **Hvolsvöllur** to Heimaey to get a close look at Eldfell, which is possible to hike. Ferries (www.visitwestmanislands.com) depart seven times a day May-September (4,000ISK round-trip without a car).

Eldheimar

Gerðisbraut 10; tel. 354/488-2700; www.eldheimar.is; 1:30pm-4:30 daily; adults 2,600ISK, children 10-18 1,300ISK, children 9 and younger free

Eldheimar is a fascinating interactive museum about Heimaey's 1973 volcanic eruption. It includes photos, surviving structures, and an overview of the volcanic geology of the region. Videos illustrate the force of the volcanic eruption and destruction left in its wake, and maps light up on the walls, pointing out volcanoes around the island.

Folk Museum of Vestmannaeyjar

Safnahúsinu við Ráðhúströð; tel. 354/488-0100; www.sagnheimar.is; 11am-5pm daily; 1,000ISK

The Folk Museum of Vestmannaeyjar contains an interesting group of permanent exhibits that include the 1973 volcanic eruption on Heimaey; the annual Vestmannaeyjar festival, which has been held every year since 1874; the role of women in the fishing station over the years; and an exhibit about the harbor area.

SPORTS AND RECREATION

★ Boat Tours

VIKING TOURS

tel. 354/488-4884; www.vikingtours.is; May 15-Sept. 15; adults 9,990ISK, children 4,990ISK

Viking Tours offers a lovely boat tour departing from Heimaey harbor daily at 2:15pm. On the 1.5-hour tour, you'll see the rugged lava coastline, bird cliffs, and ocean caves. Near its conclusion, you'll enter a cave along the harbor, where you'll listen to instrumental music that takes advantage of the cave's acoustics. It's a wonderful way to spend a couple of hours.

RIBSAFARI

Basaskersbryggja 6; tel. 354/661-1810; www.ribsafari.is; tours for adults from 14,900ISK, children from 7,900ISK

From mid-May to mid-September you can take a thrilling ride on a RIB speedboat, zooming over waves off the shores of the Westman Islands. During the tour you get

Heimaey

to explore sea caves that are only accessible by small boats, as well as spot seabirds like puffins, gannets, and fulmars. This is a great tour for adrenaline junkies who also want to see some nature by sea.

BELUGA WHALE SANCTUARY

Ægisgata, Vestmannaeyjabær; www.visitwestmanislands.com; Apr.-Oct.; 3,050ISK

The Westman Islands' latest attraction is the arrival of Little Grey and Little White, two beluga whales that were moved from China to Iceland in 2019. Sea Life Trust, a nonprofit, is behind the sanctuary, and guests can join a boat tour (8,500ISK) of the bay the whales now call home. The two-hour tour includes the boat tour and a stopover to the **visitors center** and the **aquarium.** Tours run from April-October.

Bird-Watching

The island's puffin population is the main attraction for tens of thousands of visitors. The **puffins** are cute, charismatic, and classically Icelandic. Their bright orange feet, round bodies, and striped bills are irresistible to children and adults alike. Take a walk along the sea cliffs and spend some time with the adorable birds. Prime puffin-watching season is **June-August.** The best viewing area is by the cliffs close to the harbor.

Hiking

Heimaey has a little bit of everything. Because of its small size, it's impossible to get lost, but there are moments when you will feel completely isolated, and serene, if you choose to go on a hike. Many decide to roam the base of the Eldfell volcano, watch the personality-packed puffins in the summer, and stroll downtown. You won't find a plethora of arduous treks, but the island is an opportunity for casual strolls and prime picture-taking. There are about 12 kilometers (7 mi) of trails along the coast. You can find out more about the hikes at www.visitwestmanislands.com.

ELDFELL

Distance: *3 km (2 mi) round-trip*
Hiking Time: *2 hours*
Information and Maps: *www.south.is*
Trailhead: *Path at the base*

Walking up Eldfell is a lovely way to spend a couple of hours in the Westman Islands. This is a rare opportunity to hike on a volcano that erupted less than 50 years ago. The earth is still warm enough in places to bake bread. The easy hike on the 220-meter-high (723-ft-high) volcanic cone has a well-marked path from the trailhead to the top. You can walk to the trailhead from town, and on clear days you have an outstanding view over the town.

Pools and Hot Springs

HEIMAEY SWIMMING POOL

Vestmannaeyjabær; 6:15am-9pm Mon.-Fri., 9am-6pm Sat.-Sun.; 950ISK

The Heimaey Swimming Pool has a large indoor swimming pool, three hot tubs, a sauna, and a gym. There's a slide for children, and the pool is family friendly. It's open all year.

FOOD

GOTT

Bárustígur 11; tel. 354/481-3060; www.gott.is; 11:30am-9pm daily; entrées from 2,690ISK

GOTT is a bright eatery that uses fresh ingredients in creative ways. The menu features cod fillet with wild mushroom crust, handmade pasta with lobster, and a spicy chicken burger. There are also salads, soups, and more burgers on the menu.

★ SLIPPURINN

Strandvegur; tel. 354/481-1515; www.slippurinn.com; 5pm-11pm Wed.-Sun. May 1-Aug. 31; entrées from 3,950ISK

If you want fine dining on the island, Slippurinn is your place. Only open during the summer months, the restaurant is a mix of modern and rustic, housed in an old machine warehouse near a shipyard. Local ingredients are featured in its scratch-made dishes. Guests will find divine seafood entrées like lobster soup, lemon sole, and a pan-fried fish of the day. Meat eaters can choose from lamb, beef, chicken, and even minke whale. Vegetarian options are limited.

ACCOMMODATIONS

GUESTHOUSE HAMAR

Herjólfsgötu 4; tel. 354/659-3400; www.guesthousehamar.is; rooms from 24,605ISK

Guesthouse Hamar is a small family-run guesthouse just 250 meters (820 ft) from the harbor. Rooms are spacious and have private bathrooms, and some rooms have a view of Eldfell volcano.

★ HOTEL VESTMANNAEYJAR

Vestmannabraut 28; tel. 354/481-2900; www.hotelvestmannaeyjar.is; rooms from 31,500ISK

Hotel Vestmannaeyjar offers 43 clean, small rooms with private bathrooms. The hotel has a restaurant and bar, as well as a tour desk that can book excursions. There is also a spa on the lower floor that has hot tubs and a sauna, with massages and other treatments on offer. Breakfast is included in the price of the room.

INFORMATION AND SERVICES

HEIMAEY TOURIST INFORMATION CENTER

Bárustígur 2; tel. 354/482-3683; www.vestmannaeyjar.is; noon-5pm daily beginning of May to end of Aug.

The tourist information center is housed in the town's **Eymundsson bookshop** and is ground zero for pamphlets and booking tours.

GETTING THERE

By Air

HEIMAEY AIRPORT

tel. 354/481-3300

Heimaey Airport, which is roughly 3 kilometers (2 mi) from downtown Heimaey, hosts **Eagle Air** (tel. 354/562-4200; www.eagleair.is) with daily flights to and from Reykjavík. Flights are about 25 minutes and cost 20,000ISK each way.

By Ferry

Visitors can get to the island through the ferry **Herjólfur** (Básaskersbryggju; tel. 354/481-2800; www.herjolfur.is; 2,000ISK), which has frequent year-round service, daily May-September. Travelers can bring their cars on the ferry for an extra fee. The Herjólfur ferry departs from **Landeyjahöfn** in South Iceland, and the ferry ride is about 40 minutes. Landeyjahöfn is 137 kilometers (85 mi) southeast of **Reykjavík,** about 2 hours, accessible by **Route 1.**

GETTING AROUND

The island is **walkable** and bringing your rental car is not necessary, especially if you are taking tours. The restaurants, cafés, shops, and attractions are a short walk from where you disembark the ferry.

Snæfellsnes Peninsula and the Westfjords

A trip to West Iceland is ideal if you have limited time but want to see some of the countryside. Black-sand beaches, hot springs, quiet fishing towns, and a glacier accessible by foot await you, just 40 minutes up the West Coast from Reykjavík.

Perhaps the most beautiful park in Iceland, Snæfellsjökull National Park is the ultimate tourist treat. The glacier's ice-capped glory invites visitors to put on a pair of crampons and see it for themselves.

On the Snæfellsnes Peninsula, you can see the small fishing towns that serve as the backbone of the country, sustaining the island over the centuries. Without fish, there wouldn't be an Icelandic economy to speak of.

If you are in Iceland for an extended period of time, don't miss the

Highlights

Look for ★ to find recommended sights, activities, dining, and lodging.

★ **Settlement Center:** This museum in Borgarnes offers a crash course in the sagas and earliest days of Icelanders (page 142).

★ **West Iceland's Natural Pools:** Take some time in between sightseeing to bathe in two of West Iceland's newest warm pools, **Guðlaug** in Akranes (page 140) and **Krauma** near Húsafell (page 146).

★ **Hiking in Húsafell:** Húsafell is a gem of a town in the West, with well-maintained hiking trails offering spectacular views of mountains and glaciers (page 147).

★ **Snæfellsjökull National Park:** Explore the giant glacier that was the setting for Jules Verne's *Journey to the Center of the Earth,* as well as lava-formed landscapes (page 150).

★ **Westfjords Alps Hike:** This gorgeous, moderate hike offers an uncrowded chance to explore the mountains (page 170).

★ **Bird-Watching at the Látrabjarg Cliffs:** Visit one of the best spots on the island to see puffins (page 174).

Snæfellsnes Peninsula and the Westfjords

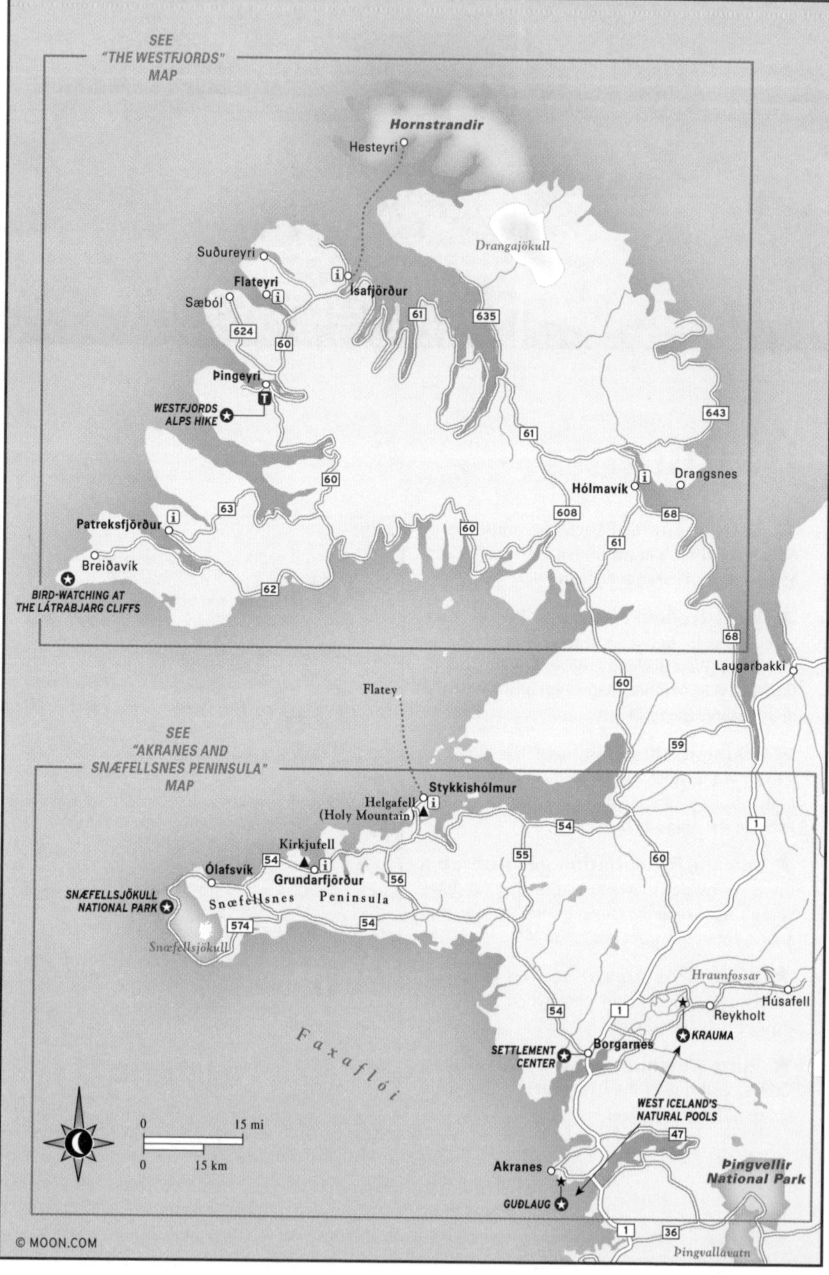

Westfjords, where you'll find steep cliffs with millions of nesting birds, well-maintained hiking paths, quirky museums, and some of the most striking beauty on the island.

PLANNING YOUR TIME

Tourism in the West is still growing, especially in the **Westfjords.** Independent travelers who **rent a car** for a day out of Reykjavík frequently make their way to **Akranes, Borgarnes,** and the **Snæfellsnes Peninsula,** which gives casual day-trippers a great taste of what the West has to offer, including **mountains** and **charming fishing villages.** A trip farther northwest will treat you to pure beauty, along with everything from whale-watching excursions to quirky museums to mountain climbing.

A day is enough for a taste of the West Coast. To get a true sense of the western coast and the Westfjords, plan for at least **5-6 days,** with one day in Akranes/Borgarnes, two days in the Snæfellsnes Peninsula, and 2-3 days in the Westfjords. While buses stop at several towns, you need a car to see some choice spots in the Westfjords—**Hólmavík** and **Hornstrandir** in particular.

Itinerary Ideas

DAY 1: AKRANES AND BORGARNES

1 Start your morning in Akranes with a relaxing soak at **Gúðlaug natural pool.**

2 Walk along Langisandur beach followed by a walk around Akranes, stopping by the **David Bowie Wall** for some photos.

3 Visit **Café Kaja** for a delicious bowl of fish soup, or some avocado on toast, followed by a latte.

4 Stop by the **Akranes Lighthouse** for a chat with the lighthouse keeper before climbing to the top for panoramic views over the town, mountains, and ocean.

5 Make the 35-minute drive to Borgarnes and spend some time at the **Settlement Center** to learn about the founding of Iceland.

6 Grab a coffee and a tasty pastry at **Geirabakarí Kaffihus.** For a local treat, try a fresh kleina (an Icelandic donut). Take a drive around the town, stopping for photos along the waterfront, which is especially lovely on sunny days.

7 Have dinner at **La Colina;** the restaurant's scrumptious pizzas make it a favorite among locals.

TWO DAYS ON THE SNÆFELLSNES PENINSULA

Day 1

1 Start your tour of the scenic Snæfellsnes Peninsula, a region known as "Iceland in miniature" for its diverse landscapes. Start with a glacier hike on **Snæfellsjökull Glacier** with Arctic Adventures, getting up close and personal with the glacier made famous by Jules Verne in *Journey to the Center of the Earth.*

Previous: Kirkjufell; Hraunfossar waterfalls and Hvita river in Húsafell; Arnarstapi Cliffs at Snæfellsjökull National Park.

Itinerary Ideas

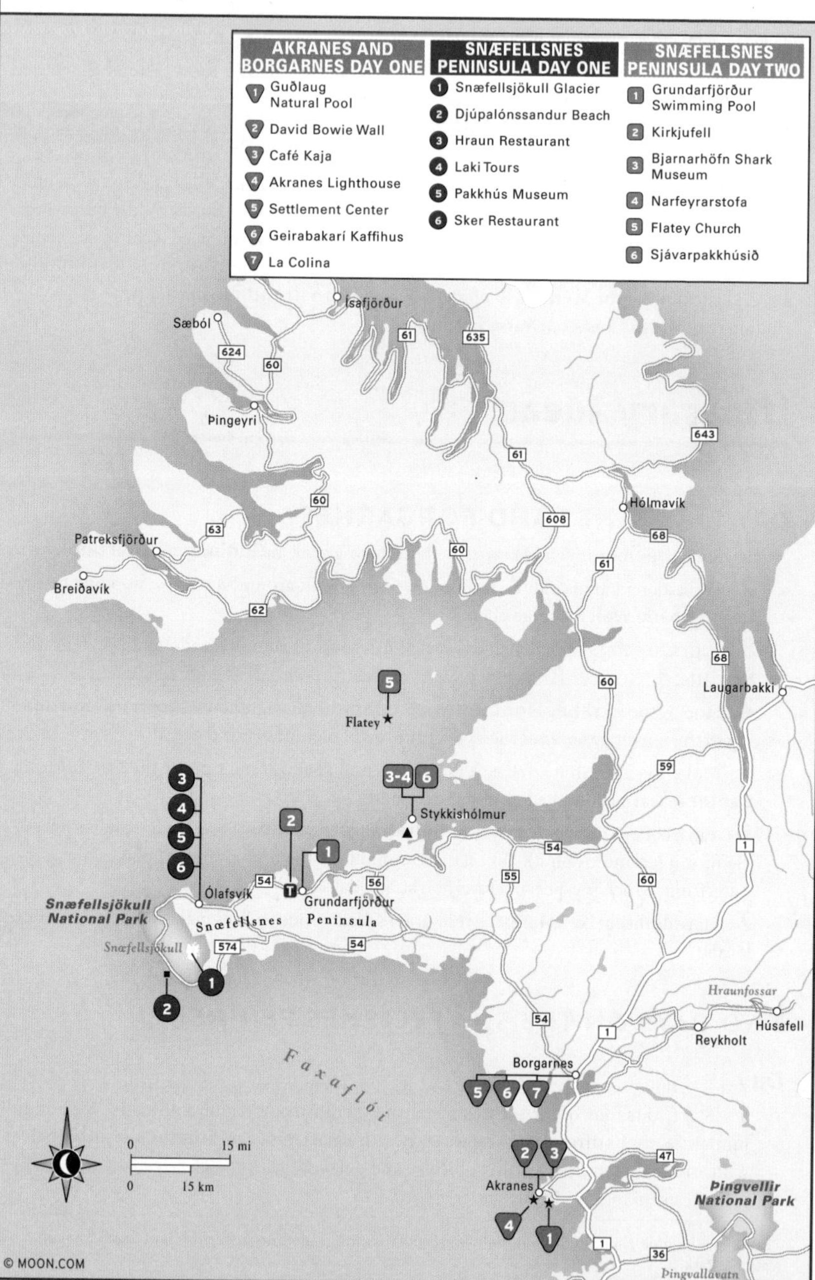

2 Continue to **Djúpalónssandur Beach,** a black-sand beach dotted with lifting stones, which fishermen used in the old days to prove their strength.

3 Stop by **Hraun Restaurant** in Olafsvík for a hearty lunch. Their Icelandic meat soup really hits the spot.

4 Go for a whale-watching tour after lunch in Olafsvík with **Laki Tours** for a chance to spot killer whales.

5 Visit the **Pakkhús Museum** for a glimpse into the region's history, from the days of settlement to today.

6 Have dinner at **Sker Restaurant,** which is known for its enticing fish dishes, but also serves up a mean lamb steak.

Day 2

1 Do as the locals do by visiting a swimming pool to begin your day. The **Grundarfjörður Swimming Pool** is a lovely place to relax.

2 Be sure to stop by the shark fin-like mountain peak of **Kirkjufell** for a photo before continuing on your way.

3 Hit the road and head to Stykkishólmur, arguably the prettiest town in Snæfellsnes. In Stykkishólmur, stop by the **Bjarnarhöfn Shark Museum** to learn about the region's long history of shark fishing.

4 Have lunch at **Narfeyrarstofa** before heading to the ferry terminal to board the ship to Flatey, an island between Snæfellsnes and the Westfjords.

5 Spend the afternoon in Flatey walking along the one road, visiting **Flatey Church** and watching countless birds, before returning to Stykkishólmur.

6 Enjoy an elegant seafood dinner at **Sjávarpakkhúsið** before calling it a night.

Akranes and Inland

Charming little towns await travelers who pass through the Hvalfjarðargöng (Hvalfjörður Tunnel) from Reykjavík. Before heading to the Snæfellsnes Peninsula, spend some time exploring the region's small fishing villages.

AKRANES

Just a 40-minute drive from Reykjavík, Akranes is a popular detour for those looking to explore the West Coast. A town of 7,000 people, Akranes is a classic fishing village that also has deep industrial roots. It was once home to the country's only cement factory, and an aluminum smelter lies just outside the town. The town is peaceful and friendly, and it's home to a **lighthouse** open to the public; it offers spectacular views of Snæfellsnes on clear days.

Sights

AKRANES LIGHTHOUSE (Akranesviti)

Breið 2; opening times vary; 300ISK

This lighthouse is a delightful place to visit any time of year. Away from bright lights, tourists and townsfolk flock to the site in winter to catch a glimpse of the northern lights dancing in the sky. In the summer, locals picnic outside the lighthouse, and when it is open, guests are invited in and can climb to the top (check the lighthouse's Facebook page for opening hours). On clear days you

Akranes and Snæfellsnes Peninsula

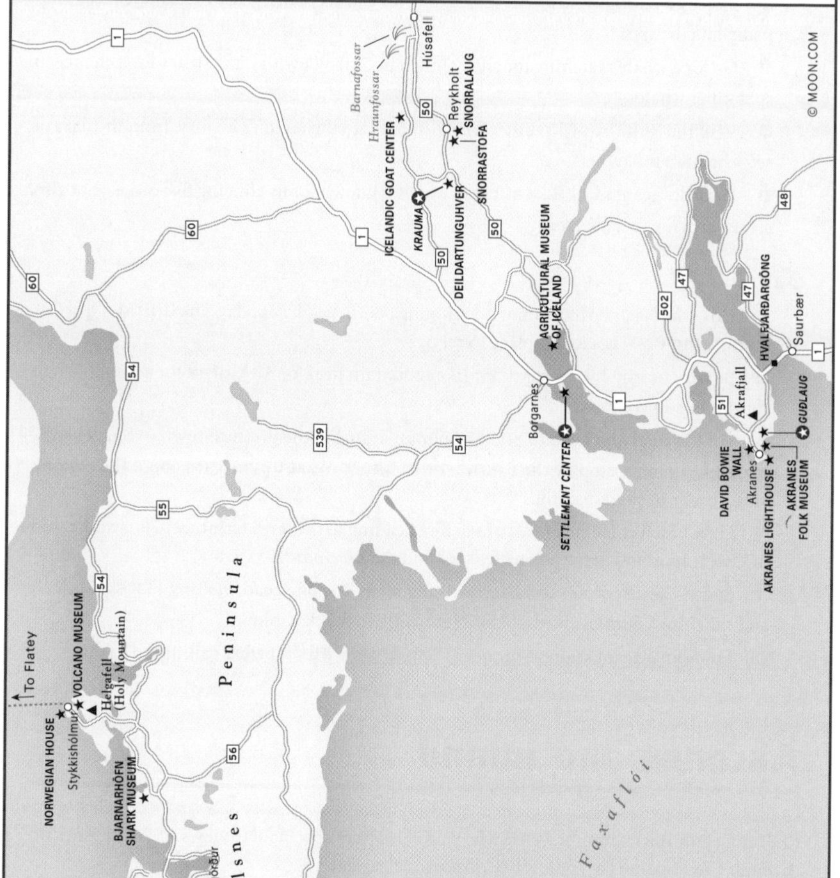
Húsafell
Barnafossar
Hraunfossar
Reykholt
SNORRALAUG
SNORRASTOFA
ICELANDIC GOAT CENTER
KRAUMA
DEILDARTUNGUHVER
AGRICULTURAL MUSEUM OF ICELAND
Borgarnes
SETTLEMENT CENTER
Akrafjall
HVALFJARÐARGÖNG
Saurbær
GUÐLAUG
DAVID BOWIE WALL
Akranes
AKRANES LIGHTHOUSE
AKRANES FOLK MUSEUM
To Flatey
NORWEGIAN HOUSE
Stykkishólmur
VOLCANO MUSEUM
Helgafell (Holy Mountain)
BJARNARHÖFN SHARK MUSEUM
Grundarfjörður
Kirkjufell
KIRKJUFELL HIKE
Snæfellsnes Peninsula
Faxaflói
Arnarstapi Cliffs
SNÆFELLSJÖKULL NATIONAL PARK VISITORS CENTER
Hellnar Cliffs
Lóndrangar Cliffs
LÓNDRANGAR
SNÆFELLSJÖKULL
Hellnar
SNÆFELLSJÖKULL GLACIER
VATNSHELLIR CAVE
Djúpalónssandur Beach
Dritvík Cove
RAUÐHÓLL
SNÆFELLSJÖKULL NATIONAL PARK
Ólafsvík
Hellissandur
HELLISSANDUR MARITIME MUSEUM
1
50
60
54
539
55
56
576
574
47
48
502
51
10 mi
10 km
0
© MOON.COM

can see the Snæfellsnes Peninsula and a spectacular view of Mount Akrafjall. Built in 1947, the lighthouse has been used in recent years to host concerts and art exhibitions. In 2013, the Icelandic band Amiina filmed a video here for a single off their album *The Lighthouse Project.*

AKRANES FOLK MUSEUM
(Safnasvæðið á Akranesi)

Garðarholt 3; tel. 354/433-1150; www.museum.is; 10am-5pm daily June 2-Sept. 15, limited hours during winter; adults 1,000ISK, seniors 700ISK, 17 and under free

This folk museum is dedicated to exploring what Akranes was like in the days of settlement in the 10th century. It reopened in 2020 after extensive renovation, with a revamped museum hall featuring multimedia exhibitions, and historical and cultural artifacts from the town. There's an audio guide available in the price of admission.

Outdoors, there are a few houses and boats that are key to the history of the town. One house, the red **Neðri-Sýrupartur,** was built in 1875, and it's considered the oldest wooden house in the town. Visitors can go inside the houses and explore. A wood building hosts the annual Nordic blacksmithing competition.

DAVID BOWIE WALL

Kirkjubraut 8

This mural was painted in 2017, when two local David Bowie fans, Bjorn Luðviksson and Halldor Lárusson, were inspired to memorialize Bowie after his passing in 2016. The Akranes mural, which features several Bowie personas throughout the years, joins the likes of Bowie wall tributes in Jersey City, Seattle, London, and Warsaw.

Hiking

The mountain **Akrafjall** is the pride and joy of Akranes residents. Many locals have fond memories of foraging for gull eggs and playing on the mountain as children. The mountain can be reached by **Route 51** and is 11 kilometers (7 mi) east of town. It's known as a relatively easy climb, especially from the Akranes Water Works car park. There are two routes: Haihnukur and Geirmundartindur.

Other than Akrafjall, another hike in the area is to **Glymur,** Iceland's tallest waterfall. It's a worthwhile detour before heading to Akranes from Reykjavík.

HAIHNUKUR

Distance: *6 km (4 mi) round-trip*

Hiking Time: *2.5 hours round-trip*

Akranes Lighthouse

Information and Maps: *www.west.is*
Trailhead: *The Akranes Water Works parking lot near the dam*

A shorter climb on Mount Akrafjall takes you to the top of Haihnukur, which, at 555 meters (1,820 ft), has a nice view of the outskirts of town.

GEIRMUNDARTINDUR

Distance: *6.4 km (4 mi) round-trip*
Hiking Time: *5 hours round-trip*
Information and Maps: *www.west.is*
Trailhead: *The Akranes Water Works parking lot near the dam*

If you're up for a longer climb on Mount Akrafjall, the highest peak is Geirmundartindur, at 643 meters (2,109 ft). The views from the top are breathtaking, especially on clear days when you can see Snæfellsjökull.

GLYMUR

Distance: *7.5 km (4.6 mi) round-trip*
Hiking Time: *3.5 hours round-trip*
Information and Maps: *www.west.is*
Trailhead: *Parking lot along Botnsa river*

Glymur, which stands at 198 meters (650 ft), sits along the Botnsá river, with white water thrashing down the side of **Hvalfell mountain.** The hike up to the top of the waterfall is challenging, with uneven terrain and steep sections. But the view from the top, over Hvalfjörður, is worth it on a clear day. Make sure you have sturdy hiking boots and check the weather forecast before heading out.

Take paved **Road 47** to the parking area. You will see the hiking path marked by a large boulder that looks like an anvil.

Pools and Hot Springs

★ GUÐLAUG NATURAL POOL

Langisandur; gudlaug@akraneskaupstadur.is; hours vary; 500ISK

Guðlaug, which opened in 2019, is a heated natural pool situated along Akranes's sandy beach, **Langisandur.** The two-tier concrete structure is the perfect place to relax during a stop in the small town. The pool has a small fee to enter, and the changing room is steps away. Hours are limited during the winter. The pool is open year-round but hours vary; check www.akranes.is for opening hours.

JADARSBAKKAR POOL

Innesvegur; tel. 354/433-1100; hkj@akranes.is; 6:15am-9pm Mon.-Fri., 9am-6pm Sat.-Sun.; 700ISK

The Jadarsbakkar Pool is a splendid outdoor pool with views of Mount Akrafjall. Take a dip in the geothermally heated waters or soak in one of the hot tubs.

Golf

GARÐAVÖLLUR

Garðar; tel. 354/431-2711; www.golficeland.org; 8am-6pm May 1-Sept. 30; 4,000-6,000ISK

This is a challenging 18-hole course with beautiful scenery: Mount Akrafjall, sheep, and horses dot the background. Clubs and golf carts are available to rent. Greens fees vary by tee time, so call ahead to book.

Food

FRYSTIHÚSIÐ

Kirkjubraut 2; tel. 354/419-0770; scoops from 350ISK

Frystihúsið (The Freezer House) serves up delicious ice cream cones, sundaes, shakes, and coffee beverages in the heart of Akranes. Opened in 2021, this quickly became a hot spot in town. Their Frappó shake is divine, with two shots of espresso, ice cream, and caramel sauce.

CAFÉ KAJA

Stillholt 23; tel. 354/840-1665; www.kajaorganic.com; 9am-6pm Mon.-Fri., 10am-4pm Sat., noon-4pm Sun.; snacks from 800ISK

Akranes's first and only organic café and market, Café Kaja offers salads, sandwiches, cakes, juices, and coffee drinks, plus a shop for local organic produce. Kaja's fish soup is divine. The atmosphere is charming, with cozy furniture and friendly staff.

GRJÓTIÐ BISTRO-BAR

Kirkjubraut 10; tel. 354/792-9222; open daily 11am-11pm; entrées from 2,100ISK

Grjótið Bistro-Bar opened its doors in 2021 and is a welcome addition to Akranes. The laid-back bistro offers an eclectic menu ranging from tacos to burgers to Asian-inspired dishes. On weekdays there are lunch specials, pulled from the menu, for 1,900ISK. At night, the bistro transforms to a bar, serving tourists and locals beers on tap, wine, and cocktails. Be sure to check out the Bowie Wall on the side of the restaurant.

★ GALITO RESTAURANT

Stilholt 16-18; tel. 354/430-6767; www.galito.is; 11:30am-9pm Mon.-Wed., 11:30am-10pm Fri., noon-10pm Sat., 4pm-9pm Sun.; entrées from 2,450ISK

Galito Restaurant is the most upscale restaurant in Akranes, but its prices are reasonable. Diners can choose from traditional options like shrimp soup and saltfish entrées, or hamburgers, pizza, sushi, and an array of sandwiches. The decor is modern and the staff is friendly.

GAMLA KAUPFELAGID

Kirkjubraut 11; tel. 354/431-4343; www.gamlakaupfelagid.com; 11:30am-2pm Mon.-Fri.; entrées from 2,500ISK

Gamla Kaupfelagid is a cozy restaurant situated downtown, open only for lunch on weekdays. The food is outstanding. There's a set menu that includes a meat and fish option as well as salads, potatoes, and vegetables. Expect fresh, local ingredients creating classically Icelandic dishes.

Accommodations

AKRANES HI HOSTEL

Sudurgata 32; tel. 354/868-3332; www.staywest.is; rooms from 10,200ISK

This hostel offers single, double, triple, and family rooms as well as dormitory-style accommodations. Rooms are clean, bright, and cozy, and all have shared bathrooms. The hostel also has two fully equipped kitchens, a television lounge, free Wi-Fi, and laundry facilities.

AKRA GUESTHOUSE

Skagabraut 4; tel. 354/587-3901; rooms from 10,800ISK

Akra Guesthouse is a small, family-run guesthouse with countryside charm. The five rooms are large and make you feel like you're staying with grandparents. Akra features wood floors, muted wallpaper, and a friendly staff. There's a common dining room for guests as well as an outdoor eating area and shared bathrooms.

TEIGUR GUESTHOUSE

Háteigur 1; tel. 354/431-2900; www.teigur-akranes.com; rooms from 12,000ISK

Teigur Guesthouse is a two-room guesthouse with the comforts of home. Guests have access to a full kitchen, washing machine, garden, and large terrace. A common living room has a TV, DVD player, and free Wi-Fi.

Information and Services

AKRANES INFORMATION CENTER

Breið 2; 11am-6pm daily May 1-Sept. 15, 11am-5pm Tues.-Sat. Sept. 16-Apr. 30

The Akranes Information Center is located in the Akranes Lighthouse. In addition to its regular hours, it's also open upon request for groups.

Getting There

Akranes is about a 40-minute, 48-kilometer (30-mi) drive from **Reykjavík** on paved **Route 51.**

Many people stop in Akranes before making the 39-kilometer (24-mi) journey to **Borgarnes,** which takes about 30 minutes.

The **Strætó 57 bus** (www.straeto.is; 980ISK) runs from the bus station Mjodd in Reykjavík to Akranes in a little over an hour.

BORGARNES

About a 75-minute drive from Reykjavík, Borgarnes is a picturesque town of about 2,000 people. Those traveling on the **Ring Road** will reach the town by Borgarfjarðarbrú, one of the longest bridges on the island, considered one of the country's largest architectural feats. Fans of the sagas will want to visit the town, as much of *Egil's Saga* takes place in the region. Film buffs may recognize Borgarnes from scenes in Ben Stiller's 2013 movie *The Secret Life of Walter Mitty.*

Sights

★ SETTLEMENT CENTER (Landnámssetur)

Brákarbraut 13-15; tel. 354/437-1600; www.landnam.is/eng; 10am-5pm daily; adults 2,500ISK, students and seniors 1,900ISK, children under 14 free

This is the place to get a crash course in the sagas and the earliest days of Icelanders during the settlement—including what everything on the newly discovered island was like, ranging from food to fashion. Interactive displays and replica dwellings are on exhibit. Audio guides are available in 10 languages. A gift shop sells everything from gourmet salts to woolen goods, and a restaurant serves up lamb, fish, and sandwiches.

AGRICULTURAL MUSEUM OF ICELAND (Landbúnaðarsafn Íslands)

Hvanneyri; tel. 354/844-7740; www.landbunadarsafn.is; 11am-5pm daily June-Aug.; 1,400ISK

The Agricultural Museum of Iceland is dedicated to the farming history of Iceland during the 19th and 20th centuries. The museum holds an extensive collection of farm artifacts, including the first plows and other horse-driven equipment used in Iceland. The museum also has the first tractors imported to Iceland, as well as farming equipment of the present day.

BORGARNES MUSEUM (Safnahús Borgarfjarðar)

Bjarnarbraut 4-6; tel. 354/433-7200; www.safnahus.is; 1pm-5pm daily May 1-Aug. 31, 1pm-4pm Mon.-Fri. Sept. 1-April 30; 500ISK

This is a nice spot to spend a couple of hours, with two exhibitions: One features photography focusing on Iceland's 20th-century history, and the other is a collection of stuffed birds in a beautiful environment designed by the artist Snorri Freyr Hilmarsson. The museum is also home to the town's library and archives.

Sports and Recreation

BORGARNES SWIMMING POOL

Þorsteinsgata 1; tel. 354/433-7140; 6am-10pm Mon.-Fri., 9am-6pm Sat.-Sun.; 970ISK

The Borgarnes Swimming Pool is open year-round and has indoor and outdoor swimming pools, a slide, hot tub, and gym.

BORGARNES GOLF CLUB (Golfklúbbur Borgarness)

Hamar; tel. 354/437-1663; www.gbgolf.is; May-Sept.; greens fees 10,000ISK

Borgarnes Golf Club is 18-hole course situated on the property of Icelandair Hótel Hamar. The course, which is great for beginners, also has a driving range area and an 18-hole putting course. It's also easy to walk. Call ahead for a tee time.

Shopping

LJÓMALIND FARMERS MARKET

Brúartorg 4; tel. 354/437-1400; www.ljomalind.is; 10am-6pm daily

Ljómalind Farmers Market is a farmers market collective started by a group of 10 women in 2013. Situated on the main stretch of road in Borgarnes, the market sells fresh cream, eggs, jam, local meat, fresh produce, woolen goods, and souvenir trinkets. In the summer, you can find sunflowers and local tomatoes on offer.

Food

GEIRABAKARÍ KAFFIHUS

Digranesgata 6; tel. 354/437-1920; geirabak@internet.is; 8am-5pm daily; pastries from 600ISK

Geirabakarí Kaffihus offers light meals, including soups and sandwiches and an array of classic Icelandic cakes and pastries. The coffeehouse was used to film scenes from Ben Stiller's 2013 movie *The Secret Life of Walter Mitty.* Photos taken during filming are displayed throughout the space.

KAFFI KYRRÐ

Skúlagata 13; tel. 354/861-2232; www.blomasetrid.is; 11am-6pm daily; pastries from 800ISK

Kaffi Kyrrð is located inside Blómasetrið, a cute flower shop popular with locals. The café serves light meals like waffles, soups, and quiches, and well as coffee, tea, soft drinks, and beer.

LA COLINA

Hrafnaklettur 1b; tel. 354/437-0110; noon-9pm daily; entrées from 2,100ISK

La Colina opened its doors in 2016, and the warm and cozy pizzeria offers delicious pies. Pizzas range from a classic Margherita to creative pies with shrimp, tuna, and lobster.

★ SETTLEMENT CENTER RESTAURANT

Brákarbraut 13-15; tel. 354/437-1600; 11:30am-9pm daily; entrées from 2,600ISK

The restaurant housed above the Settlement Center features a menu full of Icelandic staples like fish soup, mashed fish, and Icelandic meat soup. Burgers and sandwiches are on the menu as well, and there are vegetarian options and a kids' menu. For a quick snack, the freshly baked cakes are delicious. The restaurant serves a vegetarian lunch buffet on weekends for 2,500ISK, and is one of the best meals on Iceland's West Coast.

Accommodations

HÓTEL BORGARNES

Egilsgata 16; tel. 354/437-1119; www.hotelborgarnes.is; rooms from 15,000ISK

This 75-room no-frills hotel is perfect for short stays. It offers small, comfortable rooms with private bathrooms, and an in-house restaurant serves up a delicious breakfast buffet included in the price of the room.

BORGARNES HOSTEL

Borgarbraut 9-13; tel. 354/695-3366; www.borgarneshostel.is; rooms from 14,800ISK, beds from 4,600ISK

Borgarnes Hostel offers 20 rooms ranging from singles to triples. It has private rooms with private bathroom, private rooms with shared bathroom, and dorm accommodations with shared bathroom options. The hostel is centrally located, just a quick walk from the harbor and Settlement Center. Guests have access to two fully equipped kitchens, laundry facilities, a computer room, free Wi-Fi, and a common living room.

ICELANDAIR HÓTEL HAMAR

Hamar, 310 Borgarnes; tel. 354/433-6600; www.icelandairhotels.com/en/hotels/hamar; rooms from 24,000ISK

Icelandair Hótel Hamar was built on an 18-hole golf course and is in an especially scenic part of Borgarnes. Situated among waterfalls and lava fields, the 44-room hotel offers comfortable rooms with double beds and private bathrooms. There is an abundance of local art around the hotel, and it has a modern yet country atmosphere. The in-house **restaurant** is open noon-9pm daily, serving everything from an Asian-inspired cod dish to lamb fillets.

B59 HOTEL

Borgarbraut 59; tel. 354/419-5959; www.b59hotel.is; rooms from 24,000ISK, beds in a dorm from 3,500ISK

B59 Hotel, opened in 2018, is a sleek, modern addition to Borgarnes's hotel scene. Rooms are spacious, tastefully decorated in muted colors and high-quality linens, and feature flat-screen TVs, a mini fridge, free Wi-Fi, and organic Icelandic soaps in the bathrooms. The in-house spa, which is open to all guests for a small fee, has a sauna, hot tub, and indoor pool. Spa treatments are available by request. Breakfast is included in the price of the room.

ENSKU HÚSIN

Hótel við Langá; tel. 354/437-1826; www.enskuhusin.is; rooms from 23,000ISK

This former fish lodge has been transformed into a guesthouse and space for special events. There are 11 bedrooms that each accommodate two people, with a mix of private and shared bathroom facilities. Rooms are no-frills, but are clean and comfortable, and the friendly staff make you feel at home. The hotel is located along the river Langá.

Information and Services

WEST ICELAND INFORMATION CENTER

Borgarbraut 58-60; tel. 354/437-2214; www.westiceland.is; 9am-5pm daily

Located in the Hyrnutorg shopping center, the West Iceland Information Center has brochures, tour information, and a gift shop.

Getting There

Borgarnes is about a 75-kilometer (47-mi) drive north from **Reykjavík,** about 1 hour 15 minutes on **Route 1,** and 39 kilometers (24 mi) from **Akranes,** about 35 minutes on Route 1.

REYKHOLT

Reykholt is a placid, sleepy town about an hour from Borgarnes. Its laid-back, quiet atmosphere is part of the town's charm. A couple of sights are connected to Snorri Sturluson, one of the most famous and important figures in Icelandic literature. Snorri penned *Edda, Egil's Saga,* and *Heimskringla* before his death in 1241. Tourists might also want to take a look at **Deildartunguhver,** the largest hot spring in Europe, and explore the lava cave **Víðgelmir.**

Sights

ICELANDIC GOAT CENTER (Íslenska Geitin)

Haafell; tel. 354/845-2331; 1pm-6pm daily June 1-Aug. 31; adults 1,500ISK, children 7-17 750ISK, children under 7 free

The Icelandic Goat Center was established to protect and maintain the goat stock in Iceland—believe it or not, the Icelandic goat is an endangered species. Tourists are welcome to visit the grounds and meet the goats as well as other animals on the farm, including sheep, horses, and chickens. Workers at the center show an enormous amount of care for the animals. It's an especially great place to visit if you're traveling with children. The local food store sells many goat products, including sausages, cheeses, soaps, books, and handicrafts.

DEILDARTUNGUHVER

off Route 50, GPS coordinates N 64.6631, W 21.4112

Geology buffs will want to take a look at Deildartunguhver, which is considered Europe's most powerful hot spring. It provides 200 liters (52 gallons) per second of 100°C (212°F) water. Most of the water used for central heating in the towns of Akranes and Borgarnes is taken from Deildartunguhver. The hot-water pipeline to Akranes stretches 64 kilometers (40 mi), the longest in Iceland. The water is about 78-80°C (172-176°F) when it reaches the town. Be sure to keep your distance, as there is a chance of getting splashed if you get too close. Visitors will see water bubbling up and splashing against moss and rock.

SNORRASTOFA

GPS coordinates N 64.6648, W 21.2937; tel. 354/433-8000; www.snorrastofa.is; 10am-5pm daily May 1-Aug. 31, 10am-5pm Mon.-Fri. Sept. 1-Apr. 30; 1,500ISK

Snorrastofa is the cultural hub of Reykholt. It was established in 1995 as an independent research center to investigate and collect information on the medieval era in Iceland, with particular focus on the legendary saga writer and politician Snorri Sturluson, who lived in Reykholt until his death in 1241. The building also holds a tourist information center, an exhibition on Snorri Sturluson's sagas, and a public research library, and it hosts courses and lectures. A gift shop sells books, CDs, and handicrafts.

SNORRALAUG

GPS coordinates N 64.664, W 21.2912, Route 518

Snorralaug, or "Snorri's Pool," is a geothermally heated pool preserved from Iceland's medieval period and is one of Reykholt's

1: ship at the Akranes Folk Museum **2:** Haafell goat **3:** Snorralaug (Snorri's Pool)

SIGURFARI
1
2
3

oldest structures. The hot tub was built with hand-hewn lava from the 10th century, cut and shaped to exact measurements. The hot water in the pool comes from the Skrifla hot spring through a canal. The site is open to the public, but visitors cannot enter the pool to bathe.

Sports and Recreation

THE CAVE

Fljotstunga; tel. 354/783-3600; www.thecave.is; 9am-6pm June-Aug., 10am-4pm Mar.-Oct., 10am-3pm Dec.-Feb.; adults 7,000ISK, children 7-15 3,800ISK, children 6 and under free

Reykholt is home to the largest cave in Iceland, **Víðgelmir,** which is only accessible through a tour. The Cave can take you to explore the beautiful ice formations, including scores of stalactites and stalagmites. There is a walking path inside most of the cave, but there are uneven surfaces, so take care. You will be provided a helmet with a headlight. The tour is 1.5 hours long.

★ KRAUMA

Deildartunguhver; tel. 354/555-6066; www.krauma.is; 11am-9pm daily; adults 4,500ISK, children 13-16 2,250ISK, children 12 and under free

Adjacent to Europe's most powerful hot spring, Deildartunguhver, Krauma is a geothermal bath and spa, a welcome addition to West Iceland. Krauma has six baths at the facility: five of varying warm temperatures and one cold bath. Guests also have access to two steam baths and a relaxation room that contains comfortable lounge chairs, a roaring fireplace, and soothing music.

Food and Accommodations

HVERINN RESTAURANT

Kleppjárnsreykir; tel. 354/571-4433; www.hverinn.is; 10am-9pm Sun.-Thurs., 10am-11pm Fri.-Sat. May 1-Oct. 1; entrées from 2,600ISK

Hverinn Restaurant is a quaint farm-style restaurant serving up comfort food. It uses organic ingredients from its farm and local meats in each dish, ranging from soups and salads to lamb and fish dishes. Sandwiches, hamburgers, and pizza are also on the menu.

HÓTEL Á

Kirkjuból; tel. 354/435-1430; www.hotela.is; rooms from 24,000ISK

This former farmhouse was converted into a guesthouse with 22 double rooms and three family rooms. The decor is rustic and the staff friendly, and common rooms contribute to the laid-back vibe. Breakfast is included in the price of the room. The hotel also has an in-house **restaurant** (5pm-10pm daily) that offers meat (9,200ISK) and fish (8,100K) three-course dinners featuring local ingredients.

FOSSHOTEL REYKHOLT

Hálsasveitavegur; tel. 354/435-1260; www.islandshotel.is; rooms from 31,000ISK

Fosshotel Reykholt used to be the only hotel in the region. The 53-room property has dated furniture, and some rooms with carpeting, which is not common in Iceland. However, the dreary decor is made up for with free Wi-Fi, private bathrooms, free parking, and outdoor hot tubs. The included breakfast is adequate, but nothing to write home about.

Information and Services

Housed in the Snorrastofa complex, the **Reykholt Information Office** (tel. 354/433-8000; www.snorrastofa.is; 10am-5pm daily May 1-Aug. 31, 10am-5pm Mon.-Fri. Sept. 1-Apr. 30) offers tourist brochures and art exhibitions and hosts occasional lectures and concerts. The GPS coordinates are N 64.6648, W 21.2937.

Getting There

Reykholt is 41 kilometers (25 mi) northeast of **Borgarnes** on **Route 518,** which is paved.

HÚSAFELL

Húsafell is a tiny village surrounded by glaciers, ample hiking opportunities, and miles of lava fields. Most tourists make a stop to camp, visit two beautiful waterfalls, **Hraunfossar** and **Barnafossar,** and check out some lava caves in nearby Reykholt or explore the **Langjökull** ice tunnel. Organized trips with a tour operator to Langjökull glacier are available from Húsafell throughout the year.

Sights

HRAUNFOSSAR

6.4 km (4 mi) west of Húsafell on Route 518, GPS coordinates N 64.7028, W 20.9777

Hraunfossar (Lava Waterfalls) is a series of waterfalls streaming over 900 meters (2,950 ft) out of a lava field. The lava flowed from an eruption from a volcano lying under the Langjökull glacier. The falls are beautiful to visit in any season, and rainbows are frequently seen near the falls on both rainy/sunny days. There is a parking area to the left of the falls, and it's a short walk to a platform overlooking Hraunfossar.

BARNAFOSSAR

GPS coordinates N 64.7015, W 20.9727

Two kilometers (1.2 mi) west of Húsafell on Route 518, Barnafossar (Children's Falls) is a stunning waterfall, wide with water rushing over a rocky landscape creating several cascades. It was named for children who disappeared from a nearby farm and drowned in the river, and lore has it that the mother of the disappeared children put a curse on the falls that people should not cross the river. Barnafossar shares the same parking area as Hraunfossar, and it is a short walk to the falls.

★ Hiking

Hikers have a number of options in Húsafell, ranging from easy walks to more challenging climbs. Before you set out, be sure to check the weather forecast, bring the proper gear and plenty of drinking water, and let people know your whereabouts. The prime hiking season is **June-August.**

MOUNT STRÚTUR

Distance: *2 km (1.2 mi) round-trip*
Hiking Time: *2 hours round-trip*
Information and Maps: *www.west.is*
Trailhead: *Low hill north of Kalmanstunga*

While the climb to the summit of the 938-meter (3,077-ft) Mount Strútur, with an elevation gain of 469 meters (1,539 ft), isn't very difficult, it is quite long, several hours depending on the weather and your endurance. It is recommended you start from the low hill north of the farm **Kalmanstunga** and follow a signposted track that leads up the mountain. The payoff for reaching the top is a spectacular view of mountains and the Borgarfjörður fjord. Kalmanstunga is 17 kilometers (11 mi) north of Húsafell and can be reached by Route 518.

ODDAR

Distance: *4 km (2.5 mi) round-trip*
Hiking Time: *1.5 hours round-trip*
Information and Maps: *www.husafell.is*
Trailhead: *Summerhouse settlement*

The summerhouse settlement (a collection of summerhouses) in the center of Húsafell is the starting point for wooded paths heading westward for an easy walk along **Oddar,** a group of brooks with diverse birdlife. From there it is just a short walk upriver to the meeting point of two rivers: the **Norðlingafljót** and **Hvítá.** Just below Hvítá is the waterfall **Hundavaðsfoss,** a great place to stop and marvel at the beauty. The route then leads southeast along the sands just past the waterfall to a path leading back to the summerhouse settlement. The walk is very easygoing.

Other Sports and Recreation

INTO THE GLACIER

Viðarhöfði 1; tel. 354/578-2550; www.intotheglacier.is; tours from 22,000ISK

For those looking for a little ice in Iceland, Into the Glacier offers 3-4-hour tours to the world's largest human-made ice cave, **Langjökull.** A super truck picks up visitors close to **Hotel Húsafell** for a breathtaking journey across Langjökull to the tour company's base camp,

1
2
3

which takes 25 minutes. The cave itself is an engineering feat in which visitors are treated to views of crevices and the smooth ice walls. LED lighting embedded in the walls illuminates the ice nicely, and benches are scattered throughout the tunnel.

HÚSAFELL SWIMMING POOL

Stórarjóður; tel. 354/435-1552; www.husafell.com; 10am-10pm daily June-Sept., 1pm-5pm Sat.-Sun. Oct.-May; 1,500ISK

The Húsafell Swimming Pool has two pools, two hot tubs, and a big waterslide for kids.

HÚSAFELL GOLF COURSE

GPS coordinates N 64.6991, W 20.8709, Stórarjóður; tel. 354/435-1552; www.husafell.is; 8am-6pm daily May-Sept.; greens fees 4,000ISK

This nine-hole course is situated on a gorgeous patch of land overlooking mountains and lava fields. You must call ahead for a tee time.

Food and Accommodations

HRAUNFOSSAR RESTAURANT-CAFÉ

Hraunás 4; tel. 354/862-7957; www.hraunfossar.is; 10am-6pm daily; 2,200ISK

Located at the Lava Waterfalls, Hraunfossar Restaurant-Café has a good selection of light meals and snacks. Sit on the eatery's porch to enjoy coffee, cakes, ice cream, and sandwiches, along with a nice view.

★ HOTEL HÚSAFELL

Borgarbyggd; tel. 354/435-1551; www.hotelhusafell.com; rooms from 40,000ISK

This modern 48-room hotel opened in 2015. The location is unbeatable, as it is nestled in a scenic spot with stunning views of the mountain landscape, close to lava caves and glaciers. Rooms feature comfortable beds, private bathrooms, and modern design accents, including wood furnishings and large windows. A breakfast buffet is included in the room price, and 24-hour room service is available. A pool and hot tubs are on-site, and the in-house **restaurant** (11:30am-10pm daily; entrées from 5,500ISK) is not to be missed. The menu features everything from tender lamb fillet to fresh fish.

HUSAFELL CAMPGROUND

tel. 354/435-1551; www.husafell.com; adults 1,600ISK, children 900ISK

The Husafell Campground is an open campground surrounded by trees, which cuts down on the wind a bit. RVs and tents are welcome, and the facilities include restrooms, showers, hot and cold water, and laundry machines. The site is a short distance to the swimming pool, golf course, and hiking trails.

Getting There

Húsafell is 25 kilometers (15.5 mi) east from **Reykholt** on **Route 518,** which is paved.

Snæfellsnes Peninsula

Snæfellsnes is considered the jewel of the western coast, in part because the region has a taste of everything: mountains, glacier walks on Snæfellsnesjökull, and whale-watching. Many locals refer to the area as "Iceland in miniature."

The western edge of the Snæfellsnes Peninsula is home to Snæfellsjökull National Park and small towns like Hellissandur, Ólafsvík, and Grundarfjörður. The Snæfellsjökull glacier, which lies on top of a volcano in the center of the national park, is the main event for many. You can book tours to walk on the glacier and explore some actual ice in Iceland. Charming fishing villages dot the peninsula and offer ample hiking routes and quirky museums.

1: Hraunfossar waterfalls **2:** the Langjökull glacier **3:** Hotel Húsafell

PLANNING YOUR TIME

If you intend to add Snæfellsnes to your trip around the **Ring Road,** plan to spend some time here—at least **two full days.** The breathtaking landscape, with its long volcanic ridge spanning miles of rocky lava fields and towering mountains, demands more than a quick detour. The area is many Icelanders' favorite place on the island. Traveling to the region is not difficult, as there are numerous **tours** going to Snæfellsnes, as well as **buses.** For a more leisurely visit, **rent a car.** I would recommend staying the night in **Stykkishólmur.**

★ SNÆFELLSJÖKULL NATIONAL PARK

The Snæfellsjökull glacier became world famous after author Jules Verne described it as the starting point for the titular journey in *Journey to the Center of the Earth.* There is plenty to explore inside the park, such as beaches, cliffs, and views of the glacier. Take some time, wear comfortable yet sturdy footwear, and bring your camera. Plan at least two days in the region.

Sights

ARNARSTAPI CLIFFS

Arnarstapavegur, off Route 574

The seaside cliffs in the small fishermen's town of Arnarstapi, at the gateway to Snæfellsjökull National Park, are spectacular, with basalt formations including holes and arches carved out by surf. The cliffs are a nesting ground for the artic tern, and you'll love taking photos with a huge stone statue of Bárður Snæfellsás with its back to the ocean not far from the parking lot. Easy paths weave through the cliffside area, making it a lovely place to spend 45 minutes or so.

HELLNAR CLIFFS

Route 5730, off Route 574

Continuing just a few kilometers west down Route 574 from the Arnarstapi Cliffs, Hellnar is another small fishing village with beautiful seaside rock formations. A 4-kilometer (2.5-mi) walking path connects the two cliff areas.

LÓNDRANGAR CLIFFS

parking area off Route 574

Yet another place to stop and have your breath taken away overlooking seaside cliffs, farther west on Route 574 from Arnarstapi and Hellnar, in this case the basalt cliffs that are the vast remains of a crater eroded by the sea. Two stacks (the taller at 75 m/246 ft, the lower at 61 m/200 ft) are visible, home to puffins and fulmars in the summer.

TOP EXPERIENCE

SNÆFELLSJÖKULL GLACIER

near route 574

The Snæfellsjökull glacier lies on top of a volcano, situated in the center of the national park. The glacier's peak is 1,446 meters (4,774 ft) tall, and it can be seen from Reykjavík on a clear day. The volcano is considered active, though the last eruption occurred 1,900 years ago. It takes center stage in the 1864 literary classic *Journey to the Center of the Earth* by Jules Verne, which chooses the summit of Snæfellsjökull as the setting of a fictional passage to the center of the earth.

Travelers can explore the area around the glacier, but should not venture onto the glacier without a guide as it can be dangerous. Plan to spend 1-2 hours here to walk the area, take photos, and enjoy the surroundings.

It's about 190 kilometers (118 mi) from **Reykjavík** to the Snæfellsjökull glacier; the drive takes about 2.5 hours. From Reykjavík, take **Route 1** north through the town of **Borgarnes** and then turn left onto **Route 54.** Head west on **Route 54** across the peninsula for about 98 kilometers (61 mi), connecting to **Route 574.** Continue west on **Route 574** for about 35 kilometers (22 mi). You'll find the road leading up to the volcano on the right-hand side, and signs are posted all the way up to a **parking lot.** It's essentially

1: Snæfellsjökull glacier **2:** Djúpalónssandur beach

1

2

an enormous mountain with an ice cap. Given its literary history, many people like to visit the area and get a view of the volcano. Be sure to check the forecast before heading out and be advised that roads leading to the volcano are unpaved.

VATNSHELLIR LAVA CAVE

near Route 574

The Vatnshellir lava cave, opened to the public in 2011, is another highlight. Scientists believe the 200-meter-long (656-foot-long) cave was created in an eruption 6,000-8,000 years ago. The cave has two main sections: the upper section, which showcases unique lava formations that are curved on the sides of the lava tube, and the lower part, which can be reached by a long and narrow but well-maintained staircase, and takes tourists about 35 meters (115 ft) underground to a place hidden from the outside world for thousands of years.

The cave is accessible only through a guided tour from **Summit Guides** (tel. 354/787-0001; www.summitguides.is; 45-minute tours for adults 3,750ISK, students and seniors 3,000ISK, children 12-17 1,500ISK, children 3-11 free). Tourists are required to have hiking boots, gloves, and warm clothing. The tour guide provides helmets and flashlights. The Vatnshellir cave is located in the southern end of the park, near Route 574.

DJÚPALÓNSSANDUR BEACH AND DRITVÍK COVE

near Route 574, GPS coordinates N 64.7493, W 23.9122

Djúpalónssandur beach, on the southwestern edge of the Snæfellsnes Peninsula, is one of the region's highlights. The vast beach is covered by small black stones that were shaped by the force of the tides and whipping of the wind. Visitors love to wander among the frozen lava landscapes and the interesting rock formations. Plan to spend an hour at the beach. A short, paved road through lava fields leads directly from **Route 574** to Djúpalónssandur beach.

From Djúpalónssandur, you can access Dritvík Cove via an easy hike. You'll see the remains of fishermen's huts in the cliffs above the beach.

Hiking

Many Icelanders consider the hiking of Snæfellsnes unrivaled, calling the region their favorite place in the country. Why? Snæfellsnes has it all. There are mountains to climb, lava fields to explore, and glaciers to scale, all accessible by countless hiking trails with varying degrees of difficulty. Specific information on trails can be found at the park's visitors center.

Feel free to roam and take in the sights. Whether you head out alone, with a small group, or with a tour, always go out for a hike prepared: Check the weather forecast, bring proper gear and drinking water, and let people know your whereabouts.

RAUÐHÓLL

Distance: *2.3-km (1.4-mi) loop*
Hiking Time: *45 minutes*
Information and Maps: *www.west.is*
Trailhead: *Unnumbered road off of Route 570*

Rauðhóll is a leisurely hike within the park, which takes hikers around a vast, jagged lava field and a treeless plain, giving unobstructed views of the glacier looming in the distance. The 2.3-kilometer (1.4-mi) loop hike is easy, on relatively flat ground, and takes about 45 minutes. The landscape is filled with moss and lichen-covered lava stones and lava tubes, where lava once flowed out of the volcano.

Coming from Hellissandur, you'll find the hiking path down an unnumbered road off of Route 570 (which is unpaved but no longer an F road); look for a sign that says "Eysteinsdalur Snæfellsjökull" and turn left. On the south side of the road is a signpost for the Rauðhóll trail, and red stakes along the path mark the way.

LÓNDRANGAR

Distance: *1 km (0.6 mi)*
Hiking Time: *30 minutes*
Information and Maps: *www.west.is*

Trailhead: *Parking area off Route 574, 25 minutes (28 km/17 mi) from Hellissandur*

From the parking area, set off on the marked path called Þufubjarg. It's an easy path and a quick walk to the seaside cliffs, which are the remains of a crater eroded by the ocean. You have sweeping views of the beach and of the two stacks, which are flush with birdlife in the summer months.

Tours

ARCTIC ADVENTURES

tel. 354/562-7000; www.adventures.is; Mar.-Oct.; 22,000ISK

Snæfellsjökull, rising 1,446 meters (4,774 ft) from the western tip of the Snæfellsnes Peninsula, offers gorgeous views during a challenging trek, on which you can embark with a guided tour (this hike isn't recommended as an independent trek). The adventure starts and ends at the small fishing village of **Arnarstapi,** off **Route 54** down **Útnesvegur.** Arctic Adventures takes you to the **Jökulháls pass,** where you'll start your hike toward the summit of the glacier. The first part of the hike is over volcanic rock, but as you climb, the snow and ice increases, and crampons become necessary near the top. The hike is about 7-8 kilometers (4-5 mi), with a total elevation gain of 760 meters (2,500 ft), and it takes about 3-5 hours, depending on the conditions and weather.

Remember to bring warm outdoor clothing, a waterproof jacket and pants, a hat, and gloves. Good hiking shoes are essential on this tour. Waterproof outerwear and sturdy hiking shoes can be rented from the tour company with advance notice.

REYKJAVÍK EXCURSIONS

tel. 354/580-5400; www.re.is

If you're after other structured, guided tours, some companies offer excursions. Check out Reykjavík Excursions for a list, including a 12-hour **"Wonders of Snæfellsnes"** tour year-round from Reykjavík visiting **Snæfellsjökull** glacier, sandy beaches, craters, and fishing villages (adults 16,999ISK, children 12-15 8,499ISK, children under 12 free).

Food and Accommodations

GUESTHOUSE LANGAHOLT

Ytri-Garðar Staðarsveit; tel. 354/435-6789; www.langaholt.is; rooms from 18,800ISK

Guesthouse Langaholt is a 20-room family-run guesthouse with spacious rooms, classic decor, free Wi-Fi, and a shared terrace. Amenities include an on-site restaurant, nearby golf course, plenty of free parking, and on-site camping facilities for budget travelers.

FOSSHOTEL HELLNAR

Brekkubær; tel. 354/435-6820; www.islandshotel.is; May-Oct.; rooms from 33,000ISK

Fosshotel Hellnar is a beautiful 39-room country hotel that takes pride in the small things. Guests can find fresh flowers throughout the hotel, a warm staff, and a splendid in-house restaurant. Each room has a private bathroom, comfortable bed, and television. The **restaurant** (8am-9pm daily; entrées from 3,200ISK), open for breakfast, lunch, and dinner in the summer, uses fresh, organic ingredients with lots of fish and meat options, along with options for vegetarians as well.

★ HÓTEL BÚÐIR

Búðir; tel. 354/435-6700; www.hotelbudir.is; rooms from 43,600ISK

Guests at Hótel Búðir are treated to a comfortable stay with spectacular views of the Snæfellsjökull glacier. The 20-room boutique hotel features clean and cozy rooms with private bathrooms. The hotel's top-notch breakfast is included in the price. It frequently hosts weddings and conferences. The **restaurant** (8am-9pm daily; entrées from 4,590ISK) features Icelandic staples like fresh cod and lamb dishes, but the chef likes to mix up the menu selections depending on the season. Expect shellfish on the menu. The food is fresh, elegant, and memorable. The hotel is 27 kilometers (17 mi) southeast of Ólafsvík on Route 54.

Information and Services

SNÆFELLSJÖKULL NATIONAL PARK VISITORS CENTER

Malarrif; tel. 354/436-6888; 10am-5pm daily mid-May-mid-Sept., noon-4pm daily mid-Sept.-mid-May

The Snæfellsjökull National Park visitors center gives an overview of the history, flora, fauna, and geology of the park. The center also provides information on hiking paths and the wildlife that can be seen in the park.

Getting There

Snæfellsjökull National Park can be reached by **Route 574,** which spans the perimeter of the park along the coastline. A regular two-wheel-drive car will be fine on the unpaved road, but it's not feasible for cyclists.

The park is 197 kilometers (122 mi) from **Reykjavík**, about three hours taking **Route 1** to **Route 574.**

Tour companies such as **Reykjavík Excursions** (tel. 354/580-5400, www.re.is) include stops at Snæfellsjökull.

HELLISSANDUR

Hellissandur is a blink-and-you'll-miss it kind of town, but it's home to an interesting fishing museum that's worth a stop if that strikes your fancy.

Sights

HELLISSANDUR MARITIME MUSEUM

(Sjómannagarður)

Útnesvegur; tel. 354/436-6961; 10am-5pm daily June 1-Sept. 30; 1,300ISK

Hellissandur Maritime Museum was established by the Council of Seamen of the towns of Hellissandur and neighboring Rif to preserve the history of fishers and fishing stations in the region. One-stroke engines, a fisherman's house (called Þorvaldarbúð), and Iceland's oldest preserved fishing boat, *Bliki,* are on display, showing the rich fishing history of the town. The well-curated museum is a must-see for those interested in fishing history.

INGJALDSHÓLSKIRKJA

Route 574, east of Hellissandur; tel. 354/436-6970

The other big draw in Hellissandur is Ingjaldshólskirkja, or Ingjaldshóls Church, which was, according to legend, the site where Italian explorer Christopher Columbus traveled in 1477 to meet with Icelanders. Columbus was interested in speaking with islanders whose ancestors had traveled to America. In the basement of the church is a mural of Columbus's meeting with the Icelanders. The church is a classic Icelandic structure built in 1903, with a white exterior and a red roof. However, the land has been a church site since the year 1317.

Hiking

EYSTEINSDALUR VALLEY HIKE

Distance: *20 km (12 mi) round-trip*
Hiking Time: *5 hours round-trip*
Information and Maps: *Hellnar tourist information office, www.west.is*
Trailhead: *Unmarked gravel road between campground and Maritime Museum*

A great moderate, five-hour round-trip day hike of around 20 kilometers (12 mi) total leads from Hellissandur village into the Eysteinsdalur valley. Hikers should take the unmarked gravel road between the Hellissandur campground and Hellissandur Maritime Museum, which leads toward **Snæfellsjökull.** The road becomes a hiking trail after about one kilometer (0.6 mi) and leads you to the **Prestahraun** lava field. Follow the trail to see a red scoria crater and rifts in lava and basalt rocks. The trail continues past waterfalls, the glacial river **Ljósulækir,** and breathtaking views of the glacier. Detailed hiking maps are available from the **tourist information office** in **Hellnar.**

Food and Accommodations

THE FREEZER HOSTEL

Hafnargata 16; tel. 354/833-8200; www.thefreezerhostel.com; beds from 3,700ISK

The Freezer Hostel, located in Rif, several kilometers east of Hellissandur off Útnesvegur, is a former fish factory that's been converted into one of the coolest spots in the region. It's a hostel that offers dorm beds, apartments, a culture center, and an artist residency. The space is stripped down yet comfortable and serves as a social spot for tourists and locals alike. The Freezer hosts theater performances and concerts throughout the year. The owners of Freezer Hostel opened apartments for short-term rent for guests who would like a little more privacy. Apartments start at 40,000ISK.

WELCOME HOTEL

Klettsbúð 9; tel. 354/487-1212; www.hellissandur.welcome.is; rooms from 24,400ISK

Welcome Hotel is a 20-room hotel with standard double rooms featuring private bathrooms and free Wi-Fi. Rooms are big but sparsely decorated, and the in-house restaurant serves adequate meals.

Getting There

Hellissandur is 9 kilometers (6 mi) northwest of **Ólafsvík** and 35 kilometers (22 mi) north of **Hellnar.** By car, take **Route 574** to Hellissandur; this stretch is paved.

ÓLAFSVÍK

Ólafsvík is a charming fishing village situated on the western end of the Snæfellsnes Peninsula. The small town has approximately 1,100 residents, and is the main town of the Snæfellsbær municipality, which includes the villages of Hellissandur and Rif. Because of its proximity to the **Snæfellsjökull National Park,** Ólafsvík, which means "Olaf's bay," is often used as a base camp where travelers can get a bite to eat and gas up the car. Ólafsvík also might be the best whale-watching spot in West Iceland.

Sights

PAKKHÚS MUSEUM

12 Ólafsbraut; tel. 354/433-6929; www.snb.is; noon-5pm daily June 5-Aug. 31; 800ISK

A former trading store built in 1844, the Pakkhús Museum is a national monument. The second and third floors house the Snæfellsbær regional museum, where guests can see items from as early as the days of Iceland's settlement, including fishing equipment and household goods. The museum gives insight into how Icelanders lived in this region of the island, managing on very little. On the ground floor, you'll find a general store and handicraft shop.

Sports and Recreation

ÓLAFSVÍK SWIMMING POOL

Ennisbraut 11; tel. 354/433-9910; 7:30am-9pm Mon.-Fri., 10am-5pm Sat.-Sun.; 1,000ISK

The Ólafsvík Swimming Pool is popular among locals as well as tourists passing through. Amenities include an indoor swimming pool, hot tubs, and an outdoor area for catching some sun (when it's out).

LAKI TOURS

tel. 354/546-6808; www.lakitours.com; 10am and 2pm daily Feb. 15-Sept. 30; adults 10,400ISK, children 12-15 5,200ISK, children under 11 free

Laki Tours operates three-hour whale-watching tours from Ólafsvík; if luck is on your side, you'll catch a glimpse of sperm whales or killer whales. This is the only area in Iceland where you can see them. Seeing these majestic creatures with the Snæfellsnes Peninsula behind them is breathtaking—the towering mountains, migrating birds, and looming glacier are gorgeous. If you strike out with killer or sperm whales, you also have a chance to spot minke, humpback, blue, and fin whales along with harbor porpoises and dolphins. Make sure you dress warmly and bring your camera!

Food

HRAUN RESTAURANT

Grundarbraut 2; www.hraunrestaurant.com; 11:30am-9pm Sun.-Thurs., 11:30am-10pm Fri.; entrées from 2,400ISK

Hraun is a neighborhood haunt worth a visit. The restaurant serves staples you would expect like Icelandic meat soup, lamb steaks, and pan-fried cod, but there are also some surprises on the menu. You can choose to partake in trout ceviche, Icelandic scallop tacos, duck salad, or tiger prawn skewers. There are also burgers, pizza, and fish and chips on offer.

★ SKER RESTAURANT

Ólafsbraut 19; tel. 354/436-6625; 11:30am-9pm daily; entrées from 3,190ISK

Sker opened in 2018 to rave reviews among locals. The casual eatery offers fish dishes like grilled salmon and smoked haddock; meat entrées including lamb steak, beef tenderloin, and burgers; and pizza and vegetarian options.

Accommodations

VIÐ HAFIÐ GUESTHOUSE

Ólafsbraut 55; tel. 354/436-1166; vid.hafid@hotmail.com; rooms from 19,000ISK

Við Hafið Guesthouse, close to the harbor and on the town's main street, has dorm beds as well as double, triple, and family rooms, all with shared bathroom facilities.

NORTH STAR HÓTEL ÓLAFSVÍK

Ólafsbraut 20; tel. 354/487-1212; rooms from 22,000ISK

North Star Hótel Ólafsvík offers 48 rooms in the center of town near the harbor. The rooms are large, bright, and comfortable. The decor is traditional and the staff is friendly. Most rooms have private bathrooms, and breakfast is included in the price. The hotel's **restaurant** (dinner 6pm-10pm daily; entrées from 3,100ISK) is the only option for fine dining in the town, but it shines even without competition. The menu features fresh, local ingredients, with an emphasis on fish, including cod, salmon, haddock, and langoustines. There are also meat dishes as well as a couple of vegetarian options.

Getting There

Ólafsvík is 26 kilometers (16 mi) west of **Grundarfjörður.** By car from Grundarfjörður, Ólafsvík is reachable by **Route 54** connecting to **Route 574,** both paved roads. Hellissandur is just 9 kilometers (6 mi) from Ólafsvík on Route 574.

GRUNDARFJÖRÐUR

Centrally located on the northern coast of the Snæfellsnes Peninsula, Grundarfjörður is situated in a spectacular mountain range that includes **Mount Kirkjufell,** which has a steep and treacherous-looking peak. Exploring the town by foot is far and away the most popular activity for tourists. Those interested in spotting orcas have a great shot in Grundarfjörður, as the majestic whales are known to feast on herring off the shores of the town. The town has a few interesting museums and a lot of hiking opportunities.

Sights

KIRKJUFELL

Parking area 3-minute drive (2.5 km/1.5 mi) west from Grundarfjörður on Route 54

Kirkjufell, which means "Church Mountain" in Icelandic, is a favorite subject for photographers due to its unique shape: sharpened at the top and long sloping sides. The mountain formed over millions of years, gaining its shape from glacial erosion, and peaking at 463 meters (1,5,19 ft). It also draws *Game of Thrones* fans, as the mountain appeared on the show as Arrow Head Mountain.

Sports and Recreation

LÁKI TOURS

Nesvegur 5; tel. 354/546-6808; www.lakitours.com; 10,400ISK

Láki Tours operates three-hour tours from Grundarfjörður (Dec. 20-Mar. 31). Guests have a good chance of spotting sperm whales and orcas in this region, as well as humpbacks, minke whales, dolphins, and porpoises.

HIKING KIRKJUFELL

Distance: *4 km (2.5 mi) round-trip*
Hiking Time: *4 hours round-trip*
Information and Maps: *www.west.is*
Trailhead: *Parking lot on the side of the road opposite the mountain; arriving from the east, it will be on your left*

Iceland's Best Photo-Ops

Kirkjufell

One could argue that every spot in Iceland is a photo-op, and they wouldn't be wrong. Iceland is beautiful, offering everything from looming mountains to wondrous waterfalls to interesting architecture. Below are just a few suggestions for places to snap a memorable photo.

- **Kirkjufell:** The towering mountain with a sharpened top and steep sloping sides is a favorite among photographers (page 156).
- ***Sun Voyager:*** This stainless steel statue along the coast of Reykjavík is said to look like a Viking ship (page 45).
- **Hallgrímskirkja:** Standing 73 meters (239 ft) high, Hallgrímskirkja is the largest church in Iceland and one of the most striking, with its basalt lava-inspired columns adorning the exterior (page 40).
- **Dettifoss:** The most powerful waterfall in Europe, Dettifoss is an ideal place to visit and snap photos when visiting North Iceland (page 225).
- **Blue Lagoon:** It may be the most famous attraction in Iceland, but it's for good reason. The Blue Lagoon's milky blue water is a geothermal wonder (page 92).
- **Jökulsárlón:** Put the "ice" in "Iceland" when you visit Jökulsárlón, the glacier lagoon. The massive chunks of glacial ice bobbing in the lagoon are majestic (page 260).

At the center of it all is Mount Kirkjufell, which looms 463 meters (1,519 ft) high. From a distance the mountain looks quite daunting, and it is a difficult climb, with the trickiest points near the top as it gets quite steep. The hike is about four kilometers (2.5 mi) and takes about four hours round-trip. It's advisable to go during the summer months, but it's still important to check weather conditions and bring proper gear with you regardless of the time of year. If you arrive in winter and the weather is good, a walk along the base of the mountain is nice, but don't attempt a climb on your own as it can be very dangerous.

KIRKJUFELLSFOSS

Distance: *1 km (0.6 mi) round-trip*
Hiking Time: *40 minutes*

Information and Maps: *www.west.is*
Trailhead: *Parking area*

Kirkjufellsfoss is a beautiful waterfall close to Kirkjufell mountain; it's a favorite among photographers who like to capture the falls with the mountain in the background. From the parking area, you walk a short distance to the waterfall and can view it from the top and follow a set up steps to a lower viewpoint. It's lovely to spend some time viewing the falls and mountain from different angles.

GRUNDARFJÖRÐUR SWIMMING POOL

Borgarbraut 19; tel. 354/430-8564; 7am-9pm Mon.-Fri., 10am-6pm Sat.-Sun.; 900ISK

The Grundarfjörður Swimming Pool is a lovely local spot with a 16-meter (52-ft) outdoor pool, hot tubs, and a section for children.

Food and Accommodations

GRUNDARFJÖRÐUR HOSTEL

Hlíðarvegur 15; tel. 354/562-6533; www.hostel.is; rooms from 11,000ISK, beds from 5,000ISK

Grundarfjörður Hostel is in a cute countryside building that is painted bright red. In other words, you can't miss it. The staff are friendly and eager to give tips and help set up tours. Guests have access to a fully equipped kitchen, shared bathroom facilities, free Wi-Fi, and a common TV room.

KIRKJUFELL HOTEL

Nesvegur 8; tel. 354/438-6893; www.kirkjufellhotel.is; rooms from 25,000ISK

Kirkjufell Hotel offers 29 rooms, renovated in 2018, with glorious views of the Snæfellsnes Peninsula. The room decor is effortless and authentically Scandinavian. All rooms come with a private bathroom, free Wi-Fi, and access to a sauna and hot tub. The in-house **restaurant** (breakfast 7am-10am, dinner 5pm-9pm daily; entrées from 2,800ISK) is more than a hotel restaurant; it has a reputation among locals for delicious fish dishes. You will find fresh cod, salmon, and mackerel on the menu, but if you're not into fish, it offers lamb dishes as well as vegetarian options.

Information and Services

TOURIST INFORMATION CENTER

Grundargata 35; tel. 354/438-1881; www.grundarfjordur.is; 1pm-5pm daily

The tourist information center is housed in the **Grundarfjörður Heritage Center.**

Getting There

Grundarfjörður is 39 kilometers (24 mi) southeast from **Stykkishólmur** on paved **Route 54.** Grundarfjörður is 26 kilometers (16 mi) from **Ólafsvík** on Route 54.

STYKKISHÓLMUR

Stykkishólmur is a placid seaside town that hit it big when Ben Stiller decided to shoot crucial scenes of his 2013 film *The Secret Life of Walter Mitty* there. Since the movie's release, tourists have been flocking to the otherwise quiet town in droves. It's full of West Coast charm, with brightly colored houses and quaint guesthouses at the base of a mountain range.

Sights

NORWEGIAN HOUSE (Norska Húsið)

Hafnargata 5; tel. 354/433-8114; www.norskahusid.is; 10am-5pm daily May-Aug., 11am-4pm Mon-Sat. Sept.-Apr.; adults 1,300ISK, 18 and under free

The Norwegian House is the local museum of Snæfellsnes. Rotating exhibits focus on the fishing industry, the region's history, and art from regional artists. The building started out as the home of Árni Thorlacius, a 19th-century local trader. It was built in 1832, and was extraordinary at the time as the first two-story home on the island.

BJARNARHÖFN SHARK MUSEUM (Bjarnarhöfn Hákarlasafnið)

Bjarnarhöfn; tel. 354/438-1581; www.bjarnarhofn.is; 10am-5pm daily; 1,400ISK

The Bjarnarhöfn Shark Museum is one of those interesting museums you won't see anywhere but Iceland. The museum is located on the farm of a family that has been shark fishing and processing shark meat for generations. The owners provide a guided tour of the museum, where you will see fishing boats and equipment used in shark fishing. Guests are then taken to the drying house, where you can witness the process of preserving shark meat. You can even take a taste if you dare. If you'd like to take some with you, shark meat (*hákarl*) and dried fish (*harðfiskur*) may be purchased at the museum.

VOLCANO MUSEUM
(Eldfjallasafn)

Aðalgata 6; tel. 354/433-8154; www.eldfjallasafn.is; 10am-5pm daily; adults 1,000ISK, 17 and under free

The Volcano Museum showcases works of art, old and new, that depict volcanic eruptions, as well as artifacts and volcanic rocks. The museum is focused on volcanoes around the world, not just those in Iceland. If you would like an in-depth tour on the science behind volcanoes, the museum offers geology excursions on Mondays and Tuesdays, which take you to interesting locales along the Snæfellsnes Peninsula. Contact the museum for departures and price information.

HELGAFELL

Road 58

Helgafell, or "Holy Mountain" in English, stands at 73 meters (240 ft) and has a viewing dial at the top, for those who choose to walk up. The view offers panoramas over Breiðafjörður bay, which is lovely on a clear day. Like many mountains in Iceland, there is some folklore to be told. It is said that those who make the climb without looking back or speaking will be granted three wishes, as long as they tell no one else of the wishes and are facing east when making them.

Sports and Recreation

SEATOURS

Smidjustigur 3; tel. 354/433-2254; www.seatours.is; May-Sept.; tours from 7,700ISK

Seatours runs a unique bird-watching tour by boat May-September. The two-hour tour leaves from Stykkishólmur harbor, and tourists have a chance to see white-tailed eagles, shags, puffins (in the summer), eider ducks, and fulmars. While scouting for birds, guests are treated to stunning views of Snæfellsnes, including cool basalt rock formations.

Stykkishólmur harbor

STYKKISHÓLMUR SWIMMING POOL

Borgarbraut 4; tel. 354/438-1150; 7am-10pm Mon.-Thurs., 7am-7pm Fri., 10am-6pm Sat.-Sun.; 1,050ISK

The Stykkishólmur Swimming Pool is an outdoor complex with a heated pool and hot tubs.

Food

SJÁVARPAKKHÚSIÐ

Sæbraut 2; tel. 354/438-1800; www.sjavarpakkhusid.is; noon-10pm daily; entrées from 3,490ISK

Sjávarpakkhúsið is a place for seafood lovers. The seafood is as fresh as it gets, with local mussels along with cod and a fish of the day. The restaurant is located directly above the marina, and you can see the boats that the catch comes in on. There's a six-course menu available for 8,900ISK per person.

NARFEYRARSTOFA

Aðalgata 3; tel. 354/533-1119; www.narfeyrarstofa.is; 6pm-10pm daily; entrées from 3,650ISK

Narfeyrarstofa is an elegant restaurant serving Icelandic staples and savory comfort food. Guests can choose among Icelandic meat soup, cod fillet, salmon, and lamb dishes, among many other tasty choices. Minke whale steaks and guillemot are also on the menu, as are hamburgers and fried fish. The meat soup is divine.

Accommodations

HOFÐAGATA GUESTHOUSE

Hofðagata 11; tel. 354/831-1806; www.hofdagata.is; rooms from 18,000ISK

Hofðagata Guesthouse is known as the oldest guesthouse in town. The concrete structure might not be much to look at from the outside, but inside it is warm and inviting. Rooms are decorated with great care, mixing warm hues with classic Scandinavian comfort. The four rooms include shared bathrooms, free Wi-Fi, and a hearty breakfast.

FOSSHOTEL STYKKISHÓLMUR

Borgarbraut 8; tel. 354/430-2100; www.islandshotel.is; rooms from 31,000ISK

Fosshotel Stykkishólmur is chic, stylish, and inviting. All 79 rooms have private bathrooms and large, comfortable beds. Guests have access to free Wi-Fi, free parking, an included breakfast buffet, and a hotel bar. The hotel **restaurant** (breakfast 7am-10am, dinner 6pm-10pm daily; entrées from 3,400ISK) is delicious fine dining at its best. It has a playful, eclectic menu featuring meat, fish, and vegetarian options using traditional, fresh Icelandic ingredients.

Information and Services

TOURIST INFORMATION CENTER

Borgarbraut 4; tel. 354/433-8120; www.westiceland.is; 10am-5pm daily

The tourist information center, located at the ferry terminal, provides brochures on local sights as well as places to see in the surrounding area.

Getting There

Stykkishólmur is approximately a two-hour drive from **Reykjavík,** traveling north along **Route 1** and then west along paved **Route 54,** 165 kilometers (103 mi) via the **Hvalfjörður** tunnel. Stykkishólmur is 37 kilometers (23 mi) from **Grundarfjörður** on Route 54.

The ferry to the Westfjords, *Baldur,* crosses the Breiðafjörður bay from Stykkishólmur. The ferry terminal is located on the harbor and is operated by Seatours (Smiðjustigur 3; tel. 354/433-2254; www.seatours.is). It sets sail once daily and takes about 1.5 hours to reach Flatey (4,180ISK one-way). The ferry arrives in Brjanslaekur in the Westfjords, and the full trip to the Westfjords takes 2.5 hours (6,130ISK one-way). Driving would take around 5 hours.

FLATEY

Flatey (Flat Island) is the largest of the western islands in **Breiðafjörður,** a bay that separates the Westfjords from the southern part of the country. It is reachable only by ferry. The small island, which is north of the Snæfellsnes Peninsula and about one kilometer (0.6 mi) wide and two kilometers (1.2 mi) long, is an ideal visit for those seeking a spot in Iceland that is as old world as it gets—as in, not much has changed on this island in centuries. The colorful wood houses and single road evoke a simpler time, one that has not been overcrowded with industry.

Flatey is very much a seasonal destination, ideal for leisurely walks, bird-watching, and taking a break from some of the more popular attractions in the Westfjords. Icelanders who own a second home here make regular trips in the summer, and only a handful of people remain during the winter months. The main hotel-restaurant on the island is open for business only during the summer, so plan accordingly if you want to venture out to the island in the winter.

There are no addresses on the island, but don't worry about getting lost—there is just one dirt road.

Sights

FLATEY CHURCH

Eastern end of island

Flatey church, on the eastern end of the island, was erected in 1926. The exterior is classic minimalist Icelandic design, but the inside features works from Spanish painter Baltasar Samper, who captured scenes from the island in the 1960s. Baltasar is the father of renowned filmmaker Baltasar Kormakur, who directed movies like *101 Reykjavík* and *Everest* and the television show *Trapped*. Across from the church is a small cemetery with some graves that are several hundred years old.

Bird-Watching

The island offers unspoiled nature at its best, with hordes of migrating birds coming to nest and few human souls occupying the island. Flatey is a good place to spot **puffins** that migrate to the island in the summer (June-Aug.), as well as other species, including **arctic terns, gulls,** and **oystercatchers.** However, note that part of the island is restricted from mid-May to mid-July to protect nesting birds from outside interference. The best area to see birds is along the cliffs at the end of the very small island.

Food and Accommodations

HÓTEL FLATEY

tel. 354/555-7788; www.hotelflatey.is; June-Aug.; rooms from 35,000ISK

Hótel Flatey is housed in a traditional timber house, a type that is prevalent on the island. The rooms are small yet tastefully decorated in a classic Scandinavian style—wood furniture, quaint white linens, and lots of minimalist charm. Each of the rooms is named after a different bird species that inhabits the island. The staff are accommodating and the house is centrally located. This place is a winner. The in-house **restaurant** (8am-9pm daily in summer; entrées from 4,300ISK) is a favorite among tourists and locals, with a mouthwatering menu that includes lumpfish caviar, mussels, lamb fillets with blueberry salt, and a delicate pan-fried cod dish with lobster sauce. Breakfast is served from 8am-10am, lunch noon-3pm, and dinner 6pm-9pm.

KRÁKUVÖR

tel. 354/438-1451; 1,500ISK

The Flatey Krákuvör campsite is small and as basic as it gets. It's an open area with no shelter, and the weather can be unforgiving. Camping here isn't recommended unless you have top-notch equipment—including a waterproof tent that can withstand high winds.

Getting There

There is one way to get to Flatey—by **ferry.** The *Baldur* ferry is operated by **Seatours** (www.seatours.is; 6,520ISK round-trip) and departs from the harbor in **Stykkishólmur,** where you can buy round-trip tickets. In the summer there are two daily departures and it takes about 1.5 hours to reach the island. The schedule in the winter varies and is dependent on weather conditions. Be sure to check the website for up-to-date timetables.

The Westfjords

In a country full of beauty, the Westfjords may be the most lovely region of all. Endless coastlines, jaw-dropping cliffs, and gorgeous mountain landscapes await those who make the trip. Rent a car to explore the region because bus service is limited. For travelers looking for a shortcut, the *Baldur* ferry leaves from Stykkishólmur, taking 2.5 hours to get to Brjánslækur in the Westfjords.

Driving north from the West Coast, travelers will find that the Westfjords are the most sparsely populated inhabited area on the island, which is part of the region's charm. There is striking nature every which way you turn, from mountains, to empty beaches, to winding roads where you may not encounter another car for hours.

HÓLMAVÍK

Hólmavík, while a small town, is the largest in the **Strandir** area, which makes up the easternmost tip of the Westfjords. It's a popular stop due to the unique **Museum of Sorcery and Witchcraft** and the cute **Sheep Farming Museum,** along with the beautiful coastline. Many travelers use the town as a base for exploring nearby villages.

Sights

MUSEUM OF SORCERY AND WITCHCRAFT

(Galdrasafnið á Hólmavík)

Höfðargata 8-10; tel. 354/897-6525; www.galdrasyning.is; 10am-6pm daily; adults 1,100ISK, children under 15 free

The exhibits at the Museum of Sorcery and Witchcraft are truly unique. They tell the story of Iceland's infamous 17th-century witch hunts; this is the only museum on the island that gives a comprehensive overview of the period. The two-story facility also features wax figures, an audio tour, and information about spells and runes. The museum may be a little unnerving to children under the age of 12, as there are depictions of death and violence. If you still have an appetite, there's a gift shop and museum café that serves coffee and snacks.

SHEEP FARMING MUSEUM

(Sauðfjársetur á Ströndum)

Sævangur; tel. 354/451-3324; www.saudfjarsetur.is; 10am-6pm daily June-Aug.; free

The Sheep Farming Museum is a region-specific museum that's great if you're traveling with children. The museum focuses on Icelandic sheep and sheep-farming methods that have been employed in the Strandir region for centuries. A favorite among kids is feeding young sheep milk from a bottle while learning about the breed. There's also a souvenir shop and small café, where you can grab a coffee or cocoa and a snack.

Sports and Recreation

HÓLMAVÍK SWIMMING POOL

Jakobínutún; tel. 354/451-3560; 9am-9pm daily; 1,025ISK

The Hólmavík Swimming Pool is quiet and gets a bit of traffic in the summer because it's close to the campsite. There are a few hot tubs and a steam bath to enjoy as well.

HÓLMAVÍK GOLF CLUB

Hafnarbraut 18; tel. 354/892-4687; www.golf.is; greens fees 7,000ISK

Hólmavík Golf Club is a nine-hole course with sweeping views of the ocean, valleys, and mountains. Be sure to call ahead for a tee time. The facility is open year-round, but it's wise to confirm hours of operation because they're highly changeable.

Food and Accommodations

CAFÉ RIIS

Hafnarbraut 39; tel. 354/451-3567; 11:30am-9pm Sun.-Fri., 11:30am-3am Sat.; entrées from 3,100ISK

Café Riis is the town's only place for a sit-down

The Westfjords

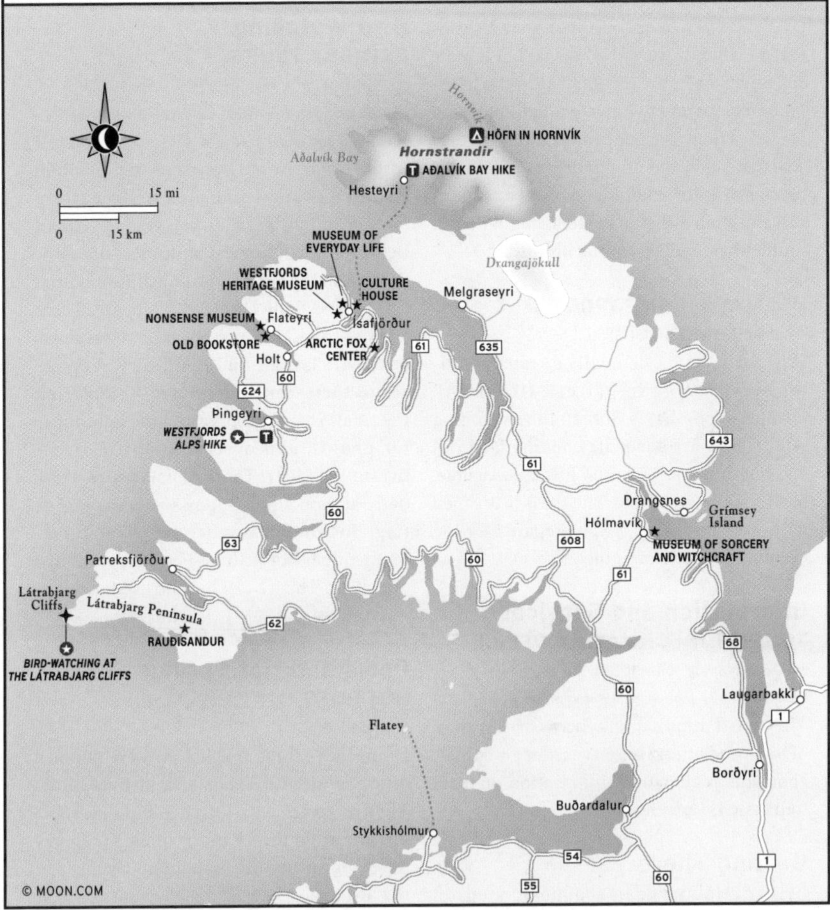

meal. The nondescript green building has a tourist-friendly menu ranging from traditional fish and lamb dishes to pizza, sandwiches, and snacks. On weekends, Café Riis serves as the town's main watering hole, where locals congregate to grab some drinks and let loose, especially late on Saturday nights.

FINNA HOTEL

Borgabraut 4; tel. 354/451-3136; www.finnahotel.is; rooms from 16,000ISK

Finna Hotel is a small guesthouse in a quaint yellow house on a quiet road in the center of town. Rooms are clean, smart, and furnished simply. If you have a choice, request a room on the second floor—those rooms underwent a recent renovation. Amenities include free Wi-Fi, free parking, and shared bathrooms. Room rates with or without breakfast are available.

HÓTEL LAUGARHÓLL

Bjarnarfjörður; tel. 354/451-3380; www.laugarholl.is; rooms from 26,600ISK

Hótel Laugarhóll offers 17 rooms, 11 of which

have private bathrooms. The rooms are bright and tidy, with Wi-Fi access and free parking. The hotel is in a large estate set within a rocky landscape. It's close to town, about 25 kilometers (16 mi) east of Hólmavík, but remote enough to maintain a countryside feel. The in-house **restaurant** (7am-9pm daily) offers a breakfast that's included in the room price, as well as a lunch and dinner menu. The dinner menu starts at 3,900ISK and offers a range of fish and lamb dishes to lighter items like soup, sandwiches, and vegetarian options.

HÓLMAVÍK CAMPGROUND

Jakobínutún; tel. 354/451-3560; 1,600ISK

The town has a centrally located, well-maintained campsite, Hólmavík Campground, that is close to the swimming pool. There are adequate cooking facilities and hot showers. Tents and RVs are welcome, with hookups available. The site is in an open field with no shelter, so be prepared for the elements if you're camping in a tent.

Information and Services

TOURIST INFORMATION OFFICE

Höfðagata 8; tel. 354/451-3111; www.holmavik.is; 9am-5pm daily June-Sept., limited winter hours

The tourist information office is in the center of town and offers Internet access, pamphlets about the region, and information on local tours and horse rentals.

Getting There

By car, Hólmavík is a popular stop on the Westfjords for travelers coming from **Ísafjörður,** as Ring Roaders tend to need gas by this point. **Route 61** is paved and connects Hólmavík, which is 223 kilometers (139 mi) southeast of Ísafjörður, to the **Ring Road.**

DRANGSNES AND GRÍMSEY ISLAND

Drangsnes is a small fishing village with fewer than 70 residents. It has an active harbor, a school, some summer houses, and a couple of popular **hot pots.** Boat tours leave from Drangsnes to Grímsey island, which is a prime spot for puffin-watching in the summer.

Bird-Watching

GRÍMSEY TOURS

tel. 354/419-2801; www.malarhorn.is/boat-trip; ages 13 and over 8,900ISK, children 7-12 4,000ISK, children 6 and under free

Just offshore from Drangsnes, the island of Grímsey is known for its **puffin colony** (about 80,000 nesting pairs) and a small lighthouse. No homes, buildings, or facilities are on the island—just birdlife and pristine nature. From Drangsnes, scheduled boat trips to the island take around 10 minutes, and tours last around four hours. Visitors spend their time independently exploring the small island, stopping by the lighthouse for photos, and observing puffins nesting on the cliffs. Tours depart twice a day daily at 9am and 1:30pm, weather permitting. Booking in advance via phone is recommended, but if there is space, walk-ups are taken. The fee can be paid at Malarhorn guesthouse.

Pools and Hot Springs

HOT POTS

Road 645

Drangsnes's three free hot pots are popular year-round with locals and visitors alike. They're great spots to relax and enjoy the scenery; from their location along the shoreline, you can see the harbor and Grímsey in the distance. They are visible from the road (Route 645), and there's a changing area across the street. Be sure to bring a towel.

DRANGSNES SWIMMING POOL

Grundargata 15; tel. 354/451-3201; sundlaug@drangsnes.is; 10am-9pm Mon.-Thurs. and 10am-6pm Fri.-Sun. June 15-Aug. 30, 4pm-7pm Tues.-Wed. and Fri. and 3pm-5pm Sat.-Sun. Sept. 1-June 14; 900ISK

The Drangsnes Swimming Pool is a small outdoor pool with a hot tub that's popular with locals. It's located close to Malarhorn, the town's only guesthouse.

Food and Accommodations

MALARHORN

Grundargata 17; tel. 354/853-6520; www.malarhorn.is; rooms from 22,000ISK

Malarhorn is the only game in town in Drangsnes. The guesthouse has three buildings with singles, doubles, family rooms, luxury rooms, and self-catering cottages. There are common areas and a mix of shared and private bathrooms. Rooms are comfortable and sparsely decorated with simple wood furniture and bare walls. Guests have access to porches and gas barbecues. Malarhorn's **restaurant,** Malarkaffi, is open from dusk till dawn in the summer, and open by request the rest of the year. Soups, sandwiches, and burgers are on the menu for lunch, and dinner includes pan-fried cod, fish stew, grilled wolffish, and grilled lamb.

Getting There

The only way to get to Drangsnes is by car. From **Hólmavík,** head north on **Route 61** and then east on **Route 643** and south on **Route 645.** The trip is about 33 kilometers (21 mi) on the paved routes and takes 40 minutes.

ÍSAFJÖRÐUR

Ísafjörður is the unofficial capital of the Westfjords, but don't let that "title" fool you; it's just a tiny town of about 4,000 people. It's easy to feel isolated in Ísafjörður, but it's a feeling many tourists relish. Ísafjörður is a good base for exploring the Westfjords. The town itself is quaint, with a small downtown area with shops and restaurants, and with picturesque surroundings, with a bustling harbor and mountains in the background. A short drive outside town, you'll find towering mountains, interesting rock formations, and more sheep than people.

Sights

WESTFJORDS HERITAGE MUSEUM (Byggðasafn Vestfjarða)

Neðstakaupstað; tel. 354/896-3291; www.westfjords.is; 10am-5pm daily May 15-Sept. 15; 1,300ISK

The Westfjords Heritage Museum pays homage to the traditional methods of fishing, with equipment and fishing boats used in the old days on exhibit. The museum is housed in an 18th-century building that sets the tone for the exhibits. There are also ship models on display, informative documentaries on view, and a special exhibition on the processing of sun-dried salted fish and its significance to the town.

CULTURE HOUSE (Gamla Sjúkrahúsið)

Eyrartún; tel. 354/450-8220; www.safnis.is; noon-6pm Mon.-Fri., 1pm-4pm Sat.; free

Originally built in 1925 as the town's hospital, Ísafjörður's Culture House has morphed into Ísafjörður's library, with an art collection and photo archives that have a regional focus. The building itself is striking, with a white exterior and bright green roof. The interior is warm and cozy and a great place to hide out in for a couple of hours when the weather is particularly bad. There are several computers with Internet connection available for use for a small fee, and many treasures wait to be discovered in the archives.

MUSEUM OF EVERYDAY LIFE (Hversdagssafn)

Hafnarstræti 5; tel. 354/770-5503; www.everydaylife.is; 1pm-5pm daily June 1-Aug. 30; 1,000ISK, kids under 16 free

This small, quirky museum houses exhibitions that focus on local life in the Westfjords, including stories about individuals that recently immigrated to the region, and an interactive display of shoes mounted on a wall, accompanied by headphones where guests can listen to stories by the owners of the shoes. This museum isn't for everyone, but if you are after something a little different, it's worth a visit.

ARCTIC FOX CENTER

Eyrardalur 4; tel. 354/456-4922; www.melrakki.is; 10am-6pm daily June 1-Aug. 31; 1,200ISK

The Arctic Fox Center is dedicated to the only

1

2

Wildlife in the West

The west gives you a chance to see wildlife not typically found in other regions of the island, namely arctic foxes, Icelandic goats, and orcas. Get up close and personal on tours and visits to centers housing these magnificent animals.

- **Icelandic Goat Center:** Travelers are welcome to the Icelandic Goat Center to visit the grounds and meet the goats as well as other animals on the farm, including sheep, horses, and chickens (page 144).
- **Horseback riding:** Simbahöllin in Þingeyri gives you an opportunity to view breathtaking nature in the Westfjords by horseback, along the Sanda river (page 172).
- **Orcas:** Láki Tours operates three-hour tours from Grundarfjörður where guests have a good chance of spotting orcas in this region, as well as humpbacks, minke whales, dolphins, and porpoises (page 155).
- **Arctic Fox Center:** For those who want a glimpse of the arctic fox, which is the only native land mammal on the island, go west, to the Arctic Fox Center in the Westfjords (page 165).

native land mammal in Iceland. It features an exhibition focusing on the biology and history of arctic foxes in Iceland, fox farming activities, and how the species has coexisted with Icelanders since the early days of settlement. You can also meet adorable arctic fox cubs on-site.

Sports and Recreation

WILD WESTFJORDS

Hafnarstræti 9; tel. 354/456-3300; www.wildwestfjords.com; 14,800ISK

Wild Westfjords offers a year-round 2.5-hour kayak tour from Ísafjörður; it's perfect for an easy introduction to kayaking. Peacefully paddle and enjoy the stunning mountain surroundings, with a good chance to see birds and seals.

ÍSAFJÖRÐUR SWIMMING POOL

Austurvegur 9; tel. 354/456-3200; 10am-9pm Mon.-Fri., 10am-5pm Sat.-Sun.; 900ISK

If the weather is particularly challenging, escape to the local indoor Ísafjörður Swimming Pool for a couple of hours.

1: Drangsnes hot pots **2:** Hornstrandir Nature Reserve

Food

VIÐ POLLINN

Silfurtorg 2; tel. 354/456-3360; www.isafjordurhotels.is; 11am-9pm daily June 1-Aug. 31, limited hours in the winter; entrées from 3,400ISK

Við Pollinn is located in Hótel Ísafjörður and offers locally sourced options including dishes ranging from lamb to fish to vegetarian options like nut steak. The grilled lamb is divine. A kids' menu is available.

★ TJORUHÚSIÐ

Nedstikaupstadur; tel. 354/456-4419; noon-2pm and 7pm-10pm daily June-Sept.; entrées from 3,500ISK

Tjoruhúsið is a family-run restaurant that serves delicate, fresh fish in inventive ways. The rustic wood interior is cozy, the service is top-notch, and the menu consists of the catch of the day. It could be haddock, cod, salmon, or other fish served with great care alongside fresh veggies. At night, there is an all-you-can-eat buffet for 6,000ISK per person, and it is well worth it.

Accommodations

GAMLA ÍSAFJÖRÐUR GUESTHOUSE

Mánagata 5; tel. 354/456-4111; www.isafjordurhotels.is; rooms from 17,550ISK

Gamla Ísafjörður Guesthouse is a standard

nine-room guesthouse that offers the comforts of home. Rooms are small but clean and comfortable. The common lounge feels like you're visiting Icelandic relatives, with classic Scandinavian furniture and a reading corner with lots of books on the shelves. Guests have access to kitchen and laundry facilities.

HOTEL HORN

Austurvegur 2; tel. 354/456-4111; www.isafjordurhotels.is; rooms from 25,000ISK

Hotel Horn offers standard, deluxe, and family rooms year-round. All rooms have a private bathroom and free Wi-Fi, and family rooms also have a small kitchen. Rooms are tastefully decorated, and the lobby is bright and colorful. Breakfast is included in the rate of the room, and free parking is just outside the hotel.

HÓTEL ÍSAFJÖRÐUR

Silfurtogr 2; tel. 354/456-4111; www.hotelisafjordur.is; rooms from 26,800ISK

Hótel Ísafjörður is the nicest hotel in town, but you will pay for that stay. The 36-room hotel is decorated in standard Scandinavian simplicity and has private bathrooms, free Wi-Fi, free parking, and a staff that is happy to arrange tours and make recommendations. The hotel is centrally located, and all the main attractions are within walking distance.

Information and Services

TOURIST INFORMATION CENTER

Aðalstræti 7; tel. 354/456-5121; www.westfjords.is; 8am-5pm Mon.-Fri., 8am-3pm Sat.-Sun. June 15-Aug. 31, 8am-4pm Mon.-Fri., 9am-noon Sat.-Sun. Sept., 8am-4pm Mon.-Fri. Oct. 1-June 14

The tourist information center offers many services, including the option to rent camping equipment and bicycles. Brochures on the region are available, and many tourists use the outpost as a place to join hiking groups.

Getting There

Ísafjörður is accessible by **Route 61,** which is paved. It's a little over five hours (456 km/283 mi) from **Reykjavík.**

By plane, daily flights are available through **Icelandair** (www.icelandair.com), which is operated at Reykjavík's domestic airport and Ísafjörður (tel. 354/505-0100). Depending on the weather, your 45-minute flight could be eventful due to wind conditions, but the view is amazing. A round-trip flight from Reykjavík is about 28,000ISK. Ísafjörður's very small airport is just a few minutes by car from town.

HORNSTRANDIR NATURE RESERVE

The **Hornstrandir Peninsula** is the northernmost part of the Westfjords, and it is idyllically isolated. The Hornstrandir Nature Reserve, which was established in 1975, lies on the north edge of the peninsula. It's a perfect spot to explore by foot, enjoying hiking paths and observing the rich birdlife. Nature rules in this spot of the Westfjords—you won't find museums or cultural attractions, but who needs them when there are millions of seabirds and arctic fox sightings are common? It isn't just foreign travelers making their way to these parts, but also Icelanders in search of pure solitude and striking beauty.

On bird cliffs in the western end of the region, the subjects of postcard-perfect photos, you can see puffins, kittiwakes, fulmars, and guillemots. A long, sandy beach is the perfect place to roam while basking in the shadows of sharp mountains and the jagged landscape.

Travel to Hornstrandir is very much seasonal, with the high season being from the middle of June to the end of August. Because of its northern locale, the weather can be especially cold, even in the summer, and very wet.

Hiking

Be mindful that this stretch of land is fiercely protected; cars are banned within the reserve limits and fishing is strictly prohibited. Enjoy the land, but be respectful and obey the rules.

The terrain could be treacherous depending on the weather, so it's not ideal for casual hikers, but rather for more experienced trekkers. Good maps are necessary and can be found online at www.galdrasyning.is. Because of its northern locale, the winds can be fierce and the rain plentiful. Make sure you are prepared with a good pair of boots, waterproof gear, and lots of layers because it can get really cold. Use common sense—there are streams that need to be crossed, sections that are slippery with ice, and portions where crampons are necessary. Visitors must bring their own tents if the plan is to camp overnight. Weatherproof equipment is necessary, as snow can be expected at any time of the year and storms can break with little warning. Thick fog often occurs in the region, and it's a good idea to have GPS with you.

If you are a novice hiker or would like the structure of an organized tour, **West Tours** (tel. 354/456-5111; www.westtours.is) offers packages and excursions throughout the year.

AÐALVÍK BAY HIKE

Distance: *12 km (7 mi) round-trip*
Hiking Time: *8 hours round-trip*
Information and Maps: *www.westfjords.is*
Trailhead: *Læknishúsið Guesthouse*

The moderate hike between the small village of **Hesteyri** and **Aðalvík Bay** at the tip of Hornstrandir is the most popular option, and it's about an eight-hour hike at a leisurely pace, during which you can enjoy the cliffs, the rocky landscape, and unspoiled nature. It's about 12 kilometers (7 mi) round-trip with an elevation gain of about 300 meters (984 ft).

Accommodations

HÖFN IN HORNVÍK

GPS coordinates N 66.4232, W 22.4882

The campground Höfn in Hornvík (free) has basic camping facilities, including restrooms, a cooking area, and hot and cold water. Be respectful of the surroundings, dispose of your trash, and leave no trace. The campsite is in an open space with little shelter.

Getting There and Around

There are daily 45-minute flights from Reykjavík's domestic airport to **Ísafjörður** for 28,000ISK, and from Ísafjörður, you can catch a ferry operated by **Sjóferðir** (tel. 354/456-3879; www.sjoferdir.is) that stops at the ports Aðalvík, Hornvík, Grunnavík, and Hesteyri for 10,500ISK each way.

The easiest way to travel to the region is to book an **excursion,** as there are detailed logistics involved and it's best to have a local tour company handle them. There can be delays because of weather, and travelers can avoid headaches by booking a tour. Local tour companies include Ísafjörður-based **West Tours** (tel. 354/456-5111; www.westtours.is), **Arctic Adventures** (tel. 354/456-3322; www.adventures.is), and **Borea Adventures** (www.boreaadventures.com), also in Ísafjörður.

FLATEYRI

Flateyri was established as a trading post in 1792, and in the 19th century was a base of operations for whaling and shark-hunting. Most of the colorful houses on Flateyri's seafront street, **Hafnarstræti,** were built between 1880 and 1915. The town's fishing industry began to wane decades ago when a major fish company closed, and the town has since transformed itself to attract tourists in the summer months. Today, it's popular with sea anglers and kayak enthusiasts. A couple of museums and a stunning landscape of mountains and endless ocean make the tiny town a worthwhile stop when traveling through the Westfjords.

Sights

OLD BOOKSTORE

(Gamla Bókabúðin)

Hafnarstræti 3-5; tel. 354/865-6695; www.gamlabokabudin.is; 10am-5pm daily

Visitors to the Old Bookstore can have a look at an exhibition of the old living quarters of the merchant family who made their home in the building. It's a unique take on what life was like in the town a couple of centuries ago. The nondescript building also has an exhibition about dried fish, which was a big part of the town's history before Flateyri's fishing industry ground to a halt. Used books are sold by the kilo in the store, which also sells souvenirs and toys.

NONSENSE MUSEUM
(Dellusafnið)

Hafnarstræti 11; tel. 354/894-8836; 1pm-5pm daily June 1-Aug. 20, rest of year by appointment only; adults 1,000ISK, 12 and under free

The Nonsense Museum is one of those quirky museums that tend to pop up in the countryside of Iceland. This museum is a labor of love for the owner, and its wackiness is worth a visit. There's no rhyme or reason to the collections, but they are certainly fun and/or unexpected. For instance, there are more than 100 police hats on display, from forces around the world. There are also collections of ship models (including a huge replica of the *Titanic*), teaspoons and sugar packets, matchboxes, salt and pepper sets, and lighters. It's a fun place to peruse when the weather is bad, or if you have planned an extended stay in the region.

Sports and Recreation

FLATEYRI SWIMMING POOL

Tjarnagata; tel. 354/456-7738; 10am-8pm Mon.-Fri., 10am-5pm Sat.-Sun.; 900ISK

The Flateyri Swimming Pool is a central meeting place for locals, and tourists are more than welcome to take a dip and chat with the residents. The facility has a heated pool, hot tub, and sauna.

Food and Accommodations

VAGNINN

Hafnarstræti 19; tel. 354/456-7751; 4pm-11pm Sun.-Thurs., 4pm-3am Fri.-Sat.; entrées from 2,400ISK

Vagninn is your best bet for a bite to eat when in Flateyri—otherwise you will have to settle for fast food at the local gas station. Even though Vagninn is the only game in town, it still goes out of its way to please diners. The food is exceptional, including classic Icelandic fish dishes, and other menu options range from sandwiches and soups to hamburgers. They also have a kids' menu. The atmosphere is fun and easygoing, with live music on the weekends.

HOLT INN

Holt; tel. 354/456-7611; www.holtinn.is; rooms from 27,000ISK

Holt Inn is a charming guesthouse that opened in 2018 owned by a local couple. There are 11 minimalist rooms decorated with soothing blue colors and hardwood floors. The owners are warm, welcoming people, and breakfast is included in the price of the room.

Getting There

Flateyri is about 20 kilometers (12 mi) west of **Ísafjörður** and can be reached via a paved stretch of **Route 60;** after about 12 kilometers (7 mi), turn right onto an unpaved but signposted road and follow it for about 7 kilometers (4 mi).

ÞINGEYRI

Þingeyri is a tiny village of fewer than 300 residents with scenic seaside views of the fjord **Dýrafjörður.** Tourism in the village isn't centered on museums or cultural exhibitions, but rather outdoor activities like hiking, swimming, and horse riding.

Hiking

★ WESTFJORDS ALPS HIKE

Distance: *25 km (16 mi) round-trip*
Hiking Time: *5 hours round-trip*
Information and Maps: *www.westfjords.is*
Trailhead: *Kaldbakur farm*

From Þingeyri, you can hike into the Westfjords Alps, a striking mountain range with pointed peaks unlike the usual flat-topped variety. **Kaldbakur** peak is the tallest mountain in the Westfjords Alps at 998 meters (3,274 ft). This moderate out-and-back hike starts from Kaldbakur, a farm, which you can reach via **Route 60** and then **Route 622,** which you'll drive down for 13 kilometers (8 mi), turning left onto a gravel road where

---

1: Take a horseback riding tour with Simbahöllin. **2:** house in Flateyri **3:** Dynjandi waterfall

1

2

3

you'll be able to **park** your car. The trailhead is at the parking area, and you'll head west to climb **Helgafell.**

This trail is in a stretch of Iceland that doesn't get a lot of tourist traffic; it's possible to be alone on it, which can be very appealing for some hikers. Several peaks, including Kaldbakur, are visible from the well-maintained trail, along with sweeping valleys and lush green vegetation. The highlight is reaching the top of Helgafell, where you'll catch views of the western Westfjords Alps. The round-trip hike takes about five hours, is about 25 kilometers (16 mi), and has an elevation gain of 549 meters (1,801 ft). Be sure to check the weather forecast before attempting the hike. Bring waterproof outer layers, hiking shoes, water, and a charged mobile phone.

DYNJANDI

Distance: *100 m (328 ft) round-trip*
Hiking Time: *30 minutes round-trip*
Information and Maps: *www.westfjords.is*
Trailhead: *Parking lot*

Dynjandi is likened to a bridal veil. The waterfall is 30 meters (98 ft) wide at its highest point and 60 meters (196 ft) wide at its lowest. It's the largest waterfall in the Westfjords, and visiting the chute makes for a beautiful little hike. From a parking area on Route 60, it's a 15-minute walk up to the base of the waterfall. Along the way you'll pass six other smaller falls, so plan on spending more time along the route for photo stops and to enjoy the surroundings.

Dynjandi is about 35 kilometers (22 mi) southeast of Þingeyri via an unpaved stretch of Route 60.

Other Sports and Recreation

SIMBAHÖLLIN

Fjarðargötu 5; tel. 354/869-5654; www.westfjords-horseriding.com

Simbahöllin offers horseback tours daily May 15-September 17. The two-hour tour (9,900ISK) takes travelers along the Sanda river, where you'll see lush vegetation along the calm riverbanks and take in stunning views of the Westfjords Alps. This is an easy tour, suitable for ages 6 and up.

ÞINGEYRI SWIMMING POOL

Þingeyraroddi; tel. 354/456-8375; 8am-9pm Mon.-Fri., 10am-6pm Sat.-Sun.; 900ISK

The Þingeyri Swimming Pool is conveniently located right next to Þingeyri's campsite.

Food and Accommodations

SIMBAHÖLLIN

Fjarðargata 5; tel. 354/899-6659; www.simbahollin.is; noon-6pm daily June 1-Aug. 30; light meals from 1,300ISK

Simbahöllin is a charming countryside café located in a 1915 building that served as a grocery store. The old-fashioned atmosphere is adorable, the cakes and pastries are fresh, and the staff make you feel like family. The specialty is Belgian waffles with fresh rhubarb jam and cream. Your taste buds will thank you.

HOTEL SANDAFELL

7 Hafnarstræti; tel. 354/456-1600; www.hotelsandafell.com; rooms from 20,000ISK

Housed in the center of town, Hotel Sandafell offers 21 spacious rooms with free Wi-Fi and beautiful mountainous views. Some of the rooms have a private bathroom, and breakfast is included in the price of the room. There are six family rooms to accommodate larger traveling groups. The hotel is open mid-May to mid-September.

ÞINGEYRI CAMPGROUND

Þingeyraroddi; tel. 354/450-8470; 1,790ISK

The Þingeyri Campground is close to the swimming pool, so there's a lot of foot traffic in the area. It's a small campsite with an adequate cooking area, toilets, and room for tents and RVs. The campsite is in an open field with no shelter, but it has stunning views of the fjord. It's open mid-May to mid-September.

Information and Services

TOURIST INFORMATION CENTER

Hafnarstræti 5; tel. 354/891-6832; www.thingeyri.is; 11am-5pm daily June-Sept., Mon.-Fri. limited winter hours

The tourist information center has brochures, suggestions for local tour operators, and Internet access.

Getting There

By car, Þingeyri is 49 kilometers (30 mi) southwest of **Ísafjörður** and is accessible via a paved stretch of **Route 60.**

PATREKSFJÖRÐUR

Patreksfjörður is the kind of sleepy fishing town you will come to love and expect as you travel along the Westfjords. Many travelers use the town as a base while heading out on excursions and day trips. Spend some time in Patreksfjörður if you're a sea angler or if you want to check out sights like the harbor area.

Sports and Recreation

PATREKSFJÖRÐUR SWIMMING POOL

Aðalstræti 55; tel. 354/456-1301; 8am-9:30pm Mon.-Fri., 10am-6pm Sat.-Sun.; 1,030ISK

The town has one of the nicest swimming pools in the region. Patreksfjörður Swimming Pool is an outdoor pool with hot tubs, a steam bath, and an indoor gym.

WESTFJORDS ADVENTURES

Aðalstræti 62; tel. 354/456-5006; www.westfjordsadventures.com

The tour company Westfjords Adventures offers bird-watching tours by bicycle to see gorgeous landscapes and seabirds including puffins. The eight-hour "Bird Cliffs and Biking Tour" (36,800ISK per person) is available Tuesday-Saturday May 1-September 15. Tourists are advised to wear layers and comfortable footwear. The company also offers all-day Jeep tours on rocky terrain for action junkies (35,700ISK) as well as a leisurely three-hour hike around town (4,900ISK), with a guide pointing out the major sights, including the scenic harbor area and fish market.

Food and Accommodations

STÚKUHÚSIÐ

Aðalstræti 50; tel. 354/456-1404; www.stukuhusid.is; noon-9pm daily June 1-Aug. 31, limited hours in winter; entrées from 2,750ISK

Stúkuhúsið is a cute café situated just off the water. The eatery consists of a simple room with an outdoor deck for enjoying good summer weather. The menu includes cakes and pastries, along with soups and sandwiches. For dinner, you can choose between fresh fish of the day and a lamb fillet with roasted potatoes, vegetables, and pepper sauce. For starters, there's a choice of salmon or soup of the day.

STEKKABÓL GUESTHOUSE

Stekkar; tel. 354/864-9675; www.stekkabol.net; rooms from 23,000ISK

Stekkaból Guesthouse is a cute countryside guesthouse run by a husband and wife who aim to make you feel at home. The rooms are on the small side, but they're tidy, and free Wi-Fi is included. The guesthouse is in a picturesque spot on the fjord, making it a perfect spot to spend the night. Breakfast is included in the price of the room.

★ FOSSHOTEL WESTFJORDS

Aðalstræti 100; tel. 354/456-2004; www.islandshotel.is; Apr.-Oct.; rooms from 28,000ISK

Fosshotel Westfjords is one of the nicest outposts of Iceland's Fosshotel chain. The lobby and rooms have an earthy, natural feel with warm hues and lots of wood accents. The beds are quite comfortable. Rooms are larger than average and have free Wi-Fi, private bathrooms, and flat-screen TVs. Meals are served in the cozy in-house **restaurant** (6pm-10pm daily Apr.-Oct.; entrées from 2,200ISK), which specializes in fish. Entrées are light and fresh, and the chefs have a classic sensibility. Expect cod, salmon, lobster, and other fish, as well as meat and a couple of vegetarian options.

HOTEL WEST

Aðalstræti 62; tel. 354/456-5020; www.hotelwest.is; rooms from 31,200ISK

Hotel West offers single, double, and superior rooms, all with private bathrooms. Rooms are clean and sparsely decorated, but many have views over the fjord. The hotel is close to the grocery store and pharmacy and is a short drive from the Látrabjarg cliffs, where you can go puffin-watching.

Information and Services

TOURIST INFORMATION CENTER

Aðalstræti 62; tel. 354/456-5006; 10am-4pm

The tourist information center is in the Westfjords Adventures office in the center of town. You can book tours and pick up pamphlets and hiking maps for the region, and access the Internet.

Getting There

Patreksfjörður is a 2.5-hour, 130-kilometer (81-mi) drive southwest of **Þingeyri** via an unpaved stretch of **Route 60** and unpaved **Route 62.** It is recommended to have a 4WD rental car.

LÁTRABJARG PENINSULA

The Látrabjarg Peninsula is in the northwest fjord region near Patreksfjörður and has dramatic sea cliffs and an abundance of bird species, making it a paradise for bird lovers. From June through August, the cliffs around the peninsula are home to numerous puffins, gulls, and kittiwakes.

Sports and Recreation

★ BIRD-WATCHING

Látrabjarg cliffs, short walk from parking area

Látrabjarg is one of the best bird-watching spots in West Iceland, as millions of seabirds gather to nest here each season. Puffins are a common sight in the summer months—you can see the adorable, bright-beaked birds May-August. You can also see fulmars, razorbills, and guillemots along the cliffs May-August.

The colossal rock formations of the **Látrabjarg cliffs** jut out of the earth at interesting angles, and the layered basalt forms intricate crevices that host nests. Trails allow you to access the cliffs by foot; stay on marked paths. Always be respectful of the area and be mindful where you step to avoid nests. The height of the cliffs is humbling, with some reaching up to 441 meters (1,447 ft). The

Látrabjarg cliffs

cliffs offer some of the most scenic views on the peninsula.

If you trek the cliffs by foot, you will want to have a pair of binoculars on hand to get a closer look. It's best to park your vehicle at the end of **Route 612** and walk east toward the cliffs.

RAUÐISANDUR

Route 614

Rauðisandur is a secluded beach with golden-red sand and gorgeous views of the Látrabjarg area. Snæfellsjökull looms in the background. Take a walk along the shore and be on the lookout for seals bobbing in the water. **Route 614,** an unpaved road, takes you to the beach.

Food and Accommodations

HOTEL BREIÐAVÍK

Breiðavík/Látrabjarg; tel. 354/456-1575; www.breidavik.is; rooms from 33,000ISK

Hotel Breiðavík is just 12 kilometers (7 mi) away from the Látrabjarg cliffs and offers darling accommodations for your stay. Double rooms look a little dated, with bright carpet and old-fashioned linens, but the beds are comfortable, and some rooms with private bathrooms are available. All rooms have access to Wi-Fi, kitchen facilities, and a washing machine. The staff are warm and welcoming, and the breakfast is hearty. For budget travelers, there are sleeping bag rooms as well as camping, but be sure to call ahead for availability. The in-house **restaurant** (5pm-10pm daily; entrées from 2,800ISK) specializes in fish and lamb, but has other options. The salmon is fresh, seasoned perfectly, and highly recommended.

HÓTEL LÁTRABJARG

Fagrihvammur; tel. 354/419-2810; www.hotellatrabjarg.com; rooms from 35,000ISK

Hótel Látrabjarg offers larger-than-average rooms with killer views from gigantic windows. Rooms are bright with standard beds (some are carpeted), and all rooms have simple furnishings ranging from two-seat couches to armchairs. Breakfast is included in the price of the room.

Getting There

You have one option to get to Látrabjarg: **Route 612,** which can be rough on your rental car because it's unpaved. Beware of steep drops and do not dream of exceeding the speed limit. Be safe. Látrabjarg is 59 kilometers (37 mi) southwest from **Patreksfjörður.**

North Iceland

There's a lot to explore in North Iceland, and Akureyri is the center of it all.

Iceland's second most populous city, Akureyri has a thriving art scene, gorgeous gardens, and restaurants that rival Reykjavík's. The harbor serves as a port for large cruise ships, with views of the country's highest peaks and longest fjord.

Akureyri is a perfect place to base yourself when exploring the north. The open terrain from Akureyri to Siglufjörður, the northernmost town in Iceland, treats visitors to traditional churches, wondrous waterfalls, and a dreamy seaside.

Farther west is Northwest Iceland. This region comprises sparsely populated farm country. In fact, depending on the time of year, you

Highlights

Look for ★ to find recommended sights, activities, dining, and lodging.

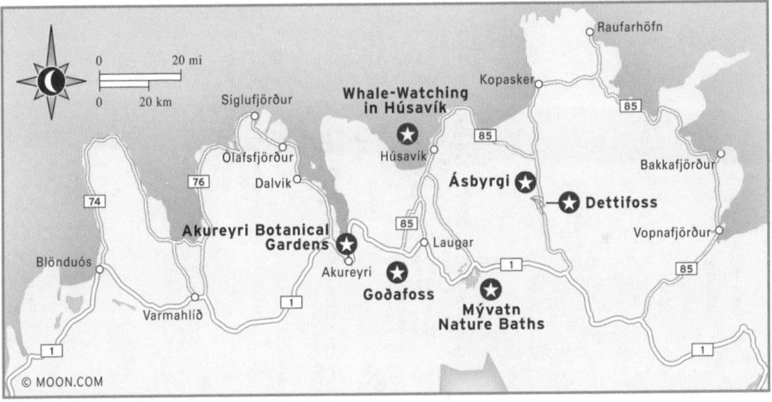

★ **Akureyri Botanical Gardens:** The northernmost botanical garden in the world has an eclectic collection of native and international flora (page 200).

★ **Goðafoss:** Witness the thundering Waterfall of the Gods, a spectacular sight any time of year (page 211).

★ **Mývatn Nature Baths:** Just try to resist taking a dip in the soothing, heated waters of Mývatn (page 213).

★ **Whale-Watching in Húsavík:** The unofficial whale-watching capital of Iceland offers a chance to view as many as 12 species of these gentle giants (page 222).

★ **Ásbyrgi:** This gigantic canyon features cool rock formations, looping walking paths, lush greenery, birds—and tons of photo opportunities (page 224).

★ **Dettifoss:** The largest waterfall on the island, and the most powerful in Europe, is 100 meters (328 ft) wide and 45 meters (148 ft) high (page 225).

North Iceland

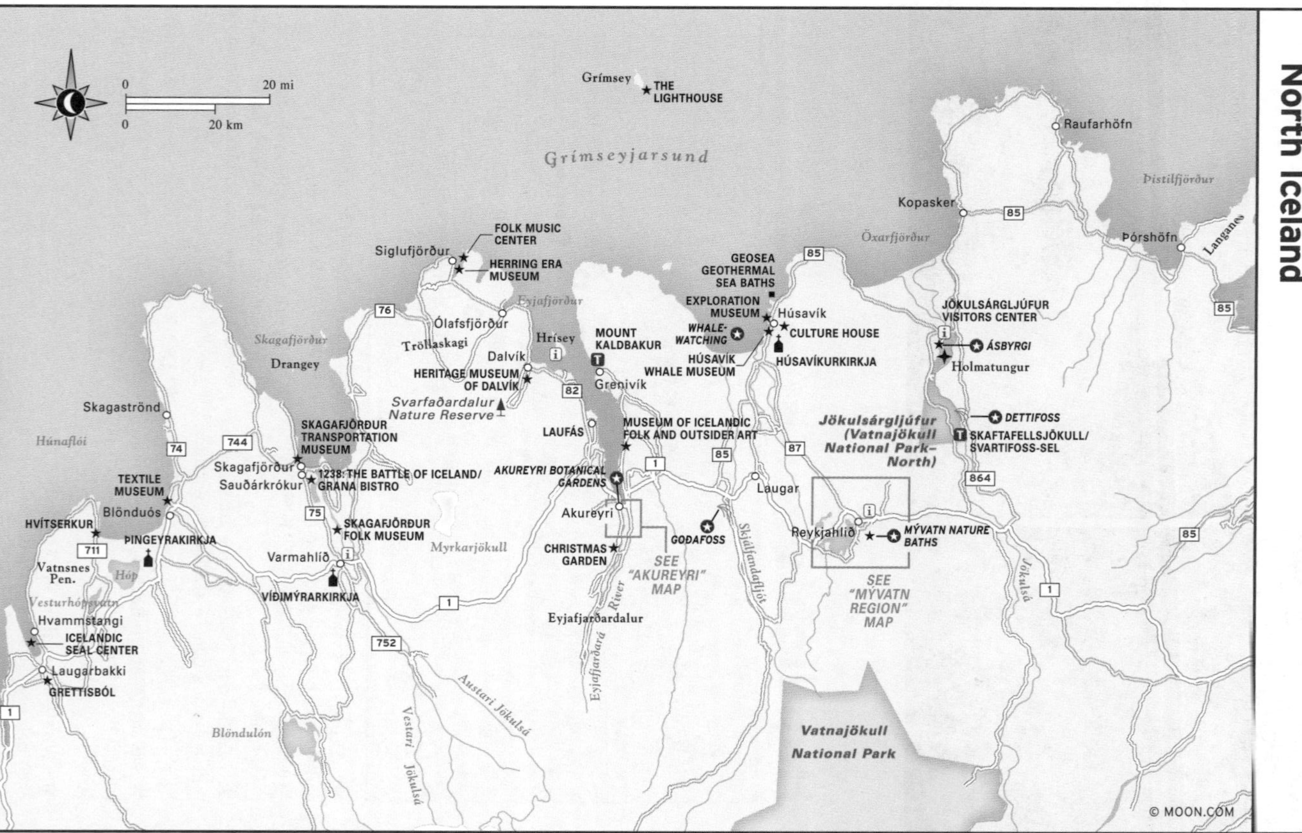

North Iceland Tourist Routes

THE ARCTIC COAST WAY

North Iceland's newest tourist route, the Arctic Coast Way, debuted in June 2019. The well-supported route spans 900 kilometers (560 mi), leading travelers on a journey among 21 towns and villages close to the Arctic Circle. Nine days is recommended for the full route, best traveled from the west in the town of **Hvammstangi** to the northeast in **Þórshöfn.** Along the way you will see spectacular landscapes of mountains, steep cliffs, charming fishing villages, glacial river deltas, and crossings to islands like **Grímsey** and **Hrísey.**

This scenic route includes some of the most beautiful towns in the north, like **Siglufjörður,** with its picturesque harbor, and charming **Húsavík,** known for its plentiful whale-watching opportunities. Other striking attractions along the way include the enormous canyon **Ásbyrgi,** which offers numerous walking paths, interesting rock formations, and waterfalls; and the mighty **Hvítserkur** rock formation, one of the most photographed sights in the northwest. The basalt rock stack resembles a rhinoceros jutting out of the sea.

Arctic Sea coast

You don't have to spend nine days following the route if time is an issue; you can explore sections of the Arctic Coast Way during your trip. For more information on the route, visit **www.arcticcoastway.is/en.**

THE DIAMOND CIRCLE

The Diamond Circle is a spectacular tourist route in northeast Iceland that spans 250 kilometers (155 mi). The route, which includes five main destinations, is best enjoyed over two days, as you will want to spend some time exploring the sights. The first stop on the Diamond Circle is the magnificent **Goðafoss,** followed by the lush landscapes of **Lake Mývatn.** Next is the powerful **Dettifoss** waterfall, followed by the horseshoe-shaped **Ásbyrgi canyon.** The last stop is the charming town of **Húsavík,** where you can go whale-watching and stop by the quirky Eurovision museum. The roads connecting the sights are well-maintained, and the stops range from 35-62 kilometers (21-38 mi) apart.

may see more seals, birds, horses, and whales than people in areas like Húnaflói and Skagafjörður.

Heading from Akureyri toward eastern Iceland, stops include Krafla's steamy lava fields, Lake Mývatn's lush lands, and the majestic Dettifoss waterfall. In the summer, birders and geology buffs will want to stretch the drive out an extra couple of days.

From waterfalls and hiking trails to the best skiing on the island, the north has plenty to keep you busy.

PLANNING YOUR TIME

North Iceland is a huge chunk of land (for Iceland), but it's quite easy to split into manageable sections, using a major town as a home base and doing day trips from there.

Previous: GeoSea baths; Akureyri Botanical Gardens; Góðafoss.

Akureyri, Húsavík, and **Mývatn** are the largest and most frequented destinations for tourists, with museums, outdoor activities, and historical sites to visit.

If you're traveling the **Ring Road** clockwise, Northwest Iceland would be your first destination after visiting the Westfjords. The northwest offers some of the most exquisite scenery on the island in its small towns and counties, including **Hvammstangi, Blönduós,** and **Skagafjörður.** Akureyri is a great base while visiting this area.

Akureyri rivals Reykjavík for the center of artistic life in Iceland. Plan to spend as much time as possible up here, with at least one day each in Mývatn and Húsavík and two days in Akureyri—three days if you want to include a trip to **Grímsey.**

When driving in the north, it's important to take the **weather** into consideration. Some roads are impassable in the **winter.** It's possible to see much of North Iceland by sticking to the Ring Road, which is the best-maintained road in the region. However, always be sure to check the road conditions and weather forecast before heading out in a car.

Itinerary Ideas

THREE DAYS IN THE NORTH

Day 1: Akureyri

1 Spend the morning exploring the center of town, strolling the harbor area and visiting the **Akureyri Botanical Gardens.**

2 Get a taste of the region's culture at the **Nonnahús** museum.

3 Go for a swim at one of the best swimming pools in the north, the **Akureyri Swimming Pool.**

4 Order a traditional lamb soup at **Kaffi Ilmur,** followed by some tasty local ice cream at Brynjar.

5 Get in your rental car and drive to the impressive waterfall **Dettifoss.**

6 After driving back to Akureyri, enjoy an elegant dinner at **Strikið,** opting for a lamb or fish entrée.

7 Spend the night at the modern and centrally located **Hotel Akureyri.**

Day 2: Whale-Watching in Húsavík

1 From Akureyri, drive to Húsavik on Route 1. Take a whale-watching tour from the harbor with **Gentle Giants.**

2 Have lunch by the harbor at **Salka Restaurant,** which serves up fantastic pizzas.

3 Walk along the harbor, photograph the Húsavik church, and make your way to the **Húsavík Whale Museum.**

4 Have a delicious seafood meal at the memorable **Naustið.**

5 Spend the night at the comfortable and central **Fosshotel Húsavík.**

Itinerary Ideas

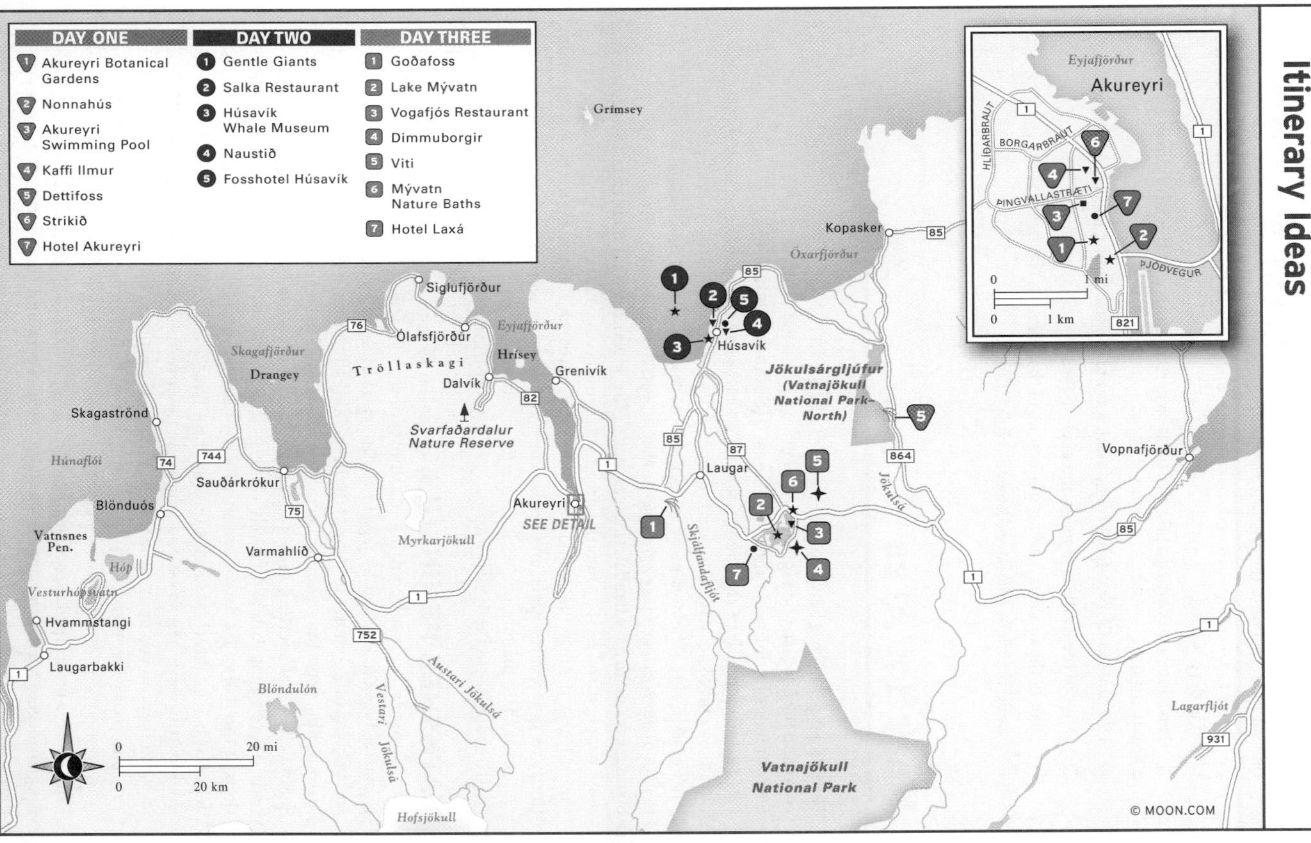

Day 3: Hiking and Relaxing Around Mývatn

1 From Húsavik, make your way to the Mývatn area on Route 1. Before reaching Mývatn, make a small detour to the gigantic waterfall **Goðafoss.**

2 Drive to **Lake Mývatn** and soak in the scenery, which is lush in summer and snow-kissed in deep winter.

3 Have lunch at **Vogafjós Restaurant,** where you can visit the farm's cows and have a hearty meal.

4 Continue to **Dimmuborgir** and walk around the fascinating lava landscapes.

5 Drive to the Krafla lava fields and explore the **Viti** explosion crater.

6 Soak in the soothing geothermal waters of the **Mývatn Nature Baths.**

7 Spend the night and have dinner at **Hotel Láxa.**

Húnaflói Area

Húnaflói is a large bay between the Strandir coast and the Skagaströnd region. It is about 50 kilometers (31 mi) wide and 100 kilometers (62 mi) long, with the small towns of Blönduós and Skagaströnd located on the bay's eastern side. The northwest is steeped in saga history, as legendary hero Grettir the Strong was said to have lived in the area, but most people travel to the Húnaflói area for the charming fishing villages and the opportunity to spot whales, seals, and birds. The region is lush in the summer, with a majestic coastline similar to the Westfjords.

VATNSNES PENINSULA

The Vatnsnes Peninsula, jutting out into Húnaflói Bay and marked by jagged rocks and bobbing hills, is home to some of the best seal-watching opportunities in the north, with a good chance of spotting harbor and gray seals. There's a museum with lovely exhibitions at the **Icelandic Seal Center,** which does research on local seal species; outside of this, spotting seals here is really a matter of luck, but they can pop up anywhere along the Vatnsnes coast. **Hvammstangi** is the largest town on the peninsula and a good base. **Route 711,** a gravel road accessible from the Ring Road, goes to Hvammstangi and around the peninsula.

Sights

ICELANDIC SEAL CENTER

(Selasetur Íslands)

Brekkugata 2, Hvammstangi; tel. 354/451-2345; www.selasetur.is; 10am-5pm daily May 15-Sept. 15, 11am-3pm Mon.-Fri. Sept. 16-Sept. 30; adults 1,100ISK, children under 15 free

The Icelandic Seal Center is as cute as it sounds, if you like seals. There is a serious research component to the facility, but the museum section captures these lovable, adorable creatures perfectly. Most of the exhibitions are geared toward children, and topics include the seals of the North Atlantic and the Arctic, the importance of seals in Icelandic culture and tradition, seal biology (with skeletons on display), and the evolution of seal hunting on the island. There are also documentaries on Icelandic seals in English. The main seals the center works with are harbor, harp, bearded, gray, hooded, and ringed seals. (There's also the odd walrus that comes ashore in Iceland from Greenland—the seal center is contacted in that event.) The staff has information on the best sites for seal-watching opportunities, and a small shop (hours variable; check website) sells souvenirs and light meals. For independent travelers, it is possible to go to the popular seal-watching spots without a tour guide, but the company **Selasigling** also offers seal-watching tours from the Hyammstangi harbor.

GRETTISBÓL

Laugarbakki; tel. 354/451-0050; www.visithunathing.is/en

Grettisból, Grettir's Lair, is an outdoor area and cultural center dedicated to the great saga hero Grettir "the Strong" Ásmundsson from *Grettir's Saga*. One of the most infamous outlaws of the sagas, Grettir was born on the farm Bjarg, which is only 7 kilometers (4.3 mi) south of this cultural center. There is a Viking garden at Grettisból, and from the road you will see a big Viking sword sculpture. In the summer months (June-Aug.), a market in the house sells Viking-related wares, such as figurines, artwork, and woolen goods. The center is open year-round, and if you're a fan of the sagas, this should be on your itinerary. At the annual **Grettistak** festival, held at Grettisból in August, locals have a strongman competition in the spirit of Grettir.

MERCHANT MUSEUM
(Bardúsa-Verslunarminjasafn)

Brekkugata 4, Hvammstangi; tel. 354/451-2747; 10am-6pm daily May 1-Oct. 20, open rest of year by request; free

A small museum in Hvammstangi housed in the remains of an early-20th-century shop, the Merchant Museum today keeps all the old goods that were key to society in the town, such as fishing equipment, kitchen utensils, and other home goods. The museum also sells Icelandic-made handcrafts.

HVÍTSERKUR

Húnaflói Bay, GPS coordinates: N 65.6062, W 20.6351

Hvítserkur is one of the most photographed sights in Northwest Iceland. The stone structure, which stands 15 meters (49 ft) tall, is said to resemble a rhinoceros. The basalt rock stack juts out of Húnaflói Bay and serves as a nesting area for a variety of bird species, including seagulls and fulmar. The best way to view Hvítserkur is along the eastern shore of the Vatnsnes Peninsula.

Seal-Watching

SELASIGLING

Höfðabraut 13; tel. 354/897-9900; adults 8,500ISK, children 7-15 4,500ISK, children 6 and under free

This tour company offers 1.5-hour seal-watching tours from the Hvammstangi

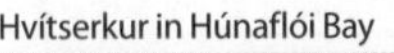

Hvítserkur in Húnaflói Bay

harbor, departing at 10am, 1pm, and 4pm daily from May 15-September 30.

Entertainment and Events

THE GREAT SEAL COUNT

www.selasetur.is/en

The great seal count is an annual event every July or August in which locals and tourists volunteer their time to count seals during low tide four hours per day. The count takes place along Vatnsnes Peninsula, and the count is vital in determining the health of the seal population off the coasts of Iceland.

Food and Accommodations

SJAVARBORG RESTAURANT

Strandgata 1; tel. 354/451-3131; www.sjavarborg-restaurant.is; lunch 11:30am-1:30pm daily, dinner 5pm-9pm daily; entrées from 2,550ISK

This popular eatery is located close to the town harbor. The building was originally a slaughterhouse, and then a freezing plant, before becoming the restaurant it is today. Its interior is a modern mix of concrete and wood with rustic driftwood accents. The menu is simple, with burgers, fish, and soup for lunch, and fish, steaks, burgers, sandwiches, pasta, and salads for dinner.

ÓSAR HOSTEL

Vatnsnesvegur; tel. 354/451-2678; www.hostel.is; rooms from 16,000ISK

Ósar Hostel is just 20 minutes from the Ring Road, making this a popular choice in the area for budget travelers making the trek around the island. Dorm rooms are adequate but nothing to write home about. It's open February 1-December 1.

DÆLI GUESTHOUSE

Víðidalur; tel. 354/451-2566; www.daeli.is; rooms from 18,000ISK

Dæli Guesthouse has larger-than-average rooms, some wood-paneled, that are simple and smart. The 14 rooms have private bathrooms, TVs, and free Wi-Fi, and guests have access to a sauna, a hot tub, mini golf, a playground, and a café. A kitchen is available to prepare meals, and guests have access to a barbecue grill.

HOTEL HVAMMSTANGI

Norðurbraut 1; tel. 354/855-1303; rooms from 28,000ISK

Hotel Hvammstangi is a guesthouse about 6 kilometers (3.7 mi) from the highway and in the middle of some great seal-watching spots. Rooms are small but neat and tastefully decorated. Each room has a private bathroom, there is a shared TV lounge with complimentary coffee and tea, and guests have access to free Wi-Fi. The town's public swimming pool, with hot tub and steam bath, is across the street from the hotel, and admission is free for guests.

Getting There

By car, Hvammstangi is 190 kilometers (118 mi) north of **Reykjavík** on **Route 1** and 200 kilometers (124 mi) west of **Akureyri.**

BLÖNDUÓS

Blönduós is a tiny town that was built around a bridge over the Blanda River (Blönduós means "mouth of the river Blanda" in Icelandic). Home to just a few shops, private homes, and guesthouses, the town is a small spot that has a few attractions. If you are traveling on the Ring Road and have some time, think about visiting the Textile Museum and the local church, which is steeped in history.

Sights

TEXTILE MUSEUM (Heimilisiðnaðarsafnið)

Árbraut 29; tel. 354/452-4067; www.textile.is; 10am-5pm daily June 1-Aug. 31; adults 1,500ISK, children under 16 free

This quaint museum is for fiber enthusiasts. On display are local crafts, Icelandic national costumes, looms of different sizes, and wonderful woolen products. The gift shop has a collection of cute wares, including wool for knitting projects and classically patterned Icelandic sweaters.

ÞINGEYRAKIRKJA

Austur-Húnavatnssýsla; tel. 354/895-4473; 10am-5pm daily June 1-Aug. 31, open by request rest of year; 500ISK

Þingeyrakirkja, Þingeyrar church, offers one of the most beautiful panoramic views in all of North Iceland, overlooking Húnafjörður bay. Þingeyrakirkja was built out of stone in Romanesque style and was officially consecrated in 1877. The land surrounding the church was the site of Iceland's first monastery, which was founded in 1133. An important place from the time of early settlement, Þingeyrakirkja is mentioned in the saga literature as a regional assembly site. Next to the church is a large circular structure, which is believed to be a judgment circle; it is listed as a heritage site. In the summer, tourists can enter the church and have a look.

Horse Riding

GALSI HORSE RIDING

Arnargerði 33; tel. 354/659-1523; www.steinnes.is

This small, family-run business offers tours for beginners and experienced riders. For an introduction to the Icelandic horse, Galsi offers a 20-minute lesson on how to properly saddle and sit on one. The course costs 3,500ISK per person. Galsi also offers an easy 1.5-hour ride in the scenic surroundings of Blönduós for 8,000ISK. Advanced riders can opt for a four-hour tour for 18,000ISK.

Food and Accommodations

B&S RESTAURANT

Nordurlandsvegur 4; tel. 354/453-5060; www.bogs.is; 11am-9pm daily; entrées from 2,890ISK

B&S Restaurant is housed in a bright orange building in the heart of town. The menu is full of comfort food like burgers, pizza, and sandwiches, as well as meat and fish dishes. It's also family friendly, with an extensive children's menu.

GLADHEIMAR COTTAGES

Brautarhvammi; tel. 354/820-1300; www.gladheimar.is; cottages from 22,410ISK

Gladheimar Cottages offers 20 self-contained cottages year-round that include private bathrooms, a patio, a hot tub, access to a barbecue grill, and proximity to the town's swimming pool. The cottages aren't luxurious, but they're clean, convenient, and won't break the bank for family accommodation.

HOTEL BLANDA

Aðalgata 6; 354/898-1832; www.hotelblanda.is; rooms from 27,000ISK

This family-run guesthouse is located in a quaint house in the heart of town. Hotel Blanda offers 19 rooms ranging from singles to family rooms. All rooms feature simple, modern decor with TVs and private bathrooms. Breakfast is included.

Getting There

Blönduós is 58 kilometers (36 mi), 45 minutes, northeast of **Hvammstangi** on **Route 1.**

Skagafjörður

With sloping mountains, a beautiful coastline, and chunks of glacial ice dotting the fjord, Skagafjörður's landscape is heavenly. Skagafjörður is often described as horse country, and that's very true. Horse farms and horse tour operators abound here—it's the only county in Iceland where horses outnumber humans.

Skagafjörður is just 40 kilometers (25 mi) long and 15 kilometers (9 mi) wide, with the towns of Sauðárkrókur and Varmahlíð the main areas for tourism. Here, farms reign supreme and all residents are involved in agriculture in one form or another. Tourism has picked up in recent years, and there are a few museums, some historical sites, and plenty of outdoor activities to keep visitors entertained.

VARMAHLÍÐ

Tourists don't typically travel to the town of Varmahlíð, but rather through it, as it's close to where **Route 1** passes through the area. There's a historic church to check out, but those who stick around for a few hours usually have booked a river-rafting or horse tour. The town has defined itself as a place for **adventure activities** over the past few years.

Sights

VÍÐIMÝRARKIRKJA

GPS coordinates N 65.5389, W 19.4710; tel. 354/453-5095; noon-6pm daily June 1-Aug. 31; 1,000ISK

Just outside Varmahlíð lies Víðimýrarkirkja, one of the last remaining preserved **turf churches** in Iceland. Turf houses are representative of a very old building method. Víðimýri Church, which features a frame made from driftwood, was built in 1834 and has turf walls but timber gables both back and front. At the beginning of the 20th century, the church's fate was uncertain, but the National Museum of Iceland became responsible for its renovation and maintenance. The church still holds Sunday services at 11am, and tourists are welcome to attend.

Sports and Recreation

HESTASPORT

Vegamót; tel. 354/453-8383; www.riding.is; 1-hour tours 8,500ISK, 2-hour tours 12,000ISK

Skagafjörður is horse country. Hestasport offers riding tours year-round on scenic paths along the region. The staff clearly has a passion for horses, and guides are well informed, patient, and excited to take you to some hidden gems in the area. Options range from one-hour to full-day tours, and the staff has all the equipment you need for your excursion—helmets, rain clothes, and all other necessary gear.

BAKKAFLÖT RAFTING

560 Varmahlíð; tel. 354/453-8245; www.bakkaflot.is; 3-4-hour tour 15,200ISK

Bakkaflöt Rafting has been offering river-rafting tours for more than 30 years on the Austari Jökulsá river and the Vestari Jökulsá river, which are fed by the Hofsjökull glacier. Five levels of rafting classes range from easy to very demanding, based on an individual's level of experience. Tours are available May-October.

Bakkaflöt is 37 kilometers (23 mi) from Sauðárkrókur, about 300 kilometers (186 mi) from Reykjavík, and about 100 kilometers (62 mi) from Akureyri. Once you arrive in Varmahlið along **Route 1,** take **Route 752** and follow that for 10 kilometers (6.2 mi).

VARMAHLÍÐ SWIMMING POOL

560 Varmahlíð; tel. 354/455-6020; 7am-9pm Mon.-Fri., 10am-5pm Sat.-Sun. June 1-Aug. 25, 8am-9pm Mon.-Thurs., 8am-2pm Fri., 10am-4pm Sat. Aug. 26.-May 31; 1,050ISK

The Varmahlíð Swimming Pool has two sections—one that is 12.5 by 25 meters (41 by 82 ft) for adults, and a children's pool that's 12.5 by 8 meters (41 by 25 ft). The children's pool is extremely popular among local families, and the slide is a favorite with kids. For adults, there are hot tubs and a sauna in the sports hall that's connected to the pool area.

Food and Accommodations

HÓTEL VARMAHLÍÐ

tel. 354/453-8170; www.hotelvarmahlid.is; rooms from 26,500ISK

Located near Route 1, Hótel Varmahlíð is the only hotel in the area, and it's a lovely place to stay. The 19 rooms are cozy and modern, with private bathrooms, TVs, free Wi-Fi, and gorgeous photographs of the area by locals adorning the walls. It is a comfortable spot with hospitable employees and an in-house restaurant serving yummy dishes. A breakfast buffet is included in the price of the room, and lunch and dinner menus focus on local ingredients found in the region, such as lightly salted cod heads, horse fillets, and tasty rhubarb cobbler made from local farm products. The **restaurant** is open 7:30am-10pm daily, and entrées start at 3,800ISK.

Information and Services

TOURIST INFORMATION OFFICE

tel. 354/455-6161; www.visitskagafjordur.is; 1pm-7pm daily June 1-Aug. 31

In the center of the village, the Skagafjörður tourist information office has pamphlets about the region, Internet access, maps, and the ability to book tours.

Getting There

Varmahlíð is 286 kilometers (178 mi) northeast of **Reykjavík** on **Route 1** and 93 kilometers (58 mi) west of **Akureyri** on Route 1.

SAUÐÁRKRÓKUR

Sauðárkrókur is Skagafjörður's largest town, but don't let that fool you—this is a village of fewer than 3,000 people. The name means "sheep's corner" in Icelandic, but that's a bit misleading, as this remains more of a fishing town than a sheep-farming town. To learn about the region, stop by the Skagafjörður Folk Museum.

Sights

SKAGAFJÖRÐUR FOLK MUSEUM

(Byggðasafn Skagfirðinga)

GPS coordinates N 65.6104, W 19.5036; tel. 354/453-6173; www.glaumbaer.is; 10am-4pm Mon.-Fri. Apr. 1-May 19, 10am-6pm daily May 20-Sept. 20, 10am-4pm Mon.-Fri. Sept. 21-Oct. 20, open by request rest of year; adults 1,700ISK, children under 17 free

The Skagafjörður Folk Museum is an extensive exhibition that includes 13 buildings, each of which had its own function, ranging from a kitchen to a sleeping room. According to the sagas, the first known inhabitants of the Glaumbær farm lived there in the 11th century.

The main event is the farmhouse, **Glaumbær,** built circa 1879. It was constructed from stones, turf, and timber, and the structure has been maintained incredibly well. The estate provided little rock suitable for building purposes, but there was plenty of good turf, so the walls of the farmhouse contain relatively little rock: Builders made do with what they had.

Also on the museum grounds are two 19th-century timber houses, **Áshús** and **Gilsstofa,** that are typical of the homes built in the area at that time. Áshús contains exhibitions about the region and houses the museum's administrative offices. In Gilsstofa, there are offices, an information center, and a souvenir shop.

The current iteration of **Glaumbær church** was built in 1926. Earlier churches at Glaumbær had been built of wood, and most of them were covered with turf for protection against the elements. However, the last wooden church was blown down in a storm. The church that currently stands is a more modern structure with a concrete base and wood over it.

The **Heritage House** showcases exhibitions that highlight four 20th-century tradesmen's workshops. Also on permanent display are objects from the private collections of novelist Guðrún from Lundur (1887-1975), composer Eyþór Stefánsson (1901-1999), and artist Jóhannes Geir Jónsson (1927-2003). Guðrún's books are still read widely today in Iceland, and Eyþór's songs are sung regularly around the country. Jóhannes Geir's paintings show saga scenes of life in the 13th century.

From the **Ring Road,** head north on **Route 75** to reach the Folk Museum.

SKAGAFJÖRÐUR TRANSPORTATION MUSEUM (Samgönguminjasafn Skagafjarðar)

Storagerdi; tel. 354/455-6161; www.visitskagafjordur.is; 11am-6pm daily mid-June-Aug.; 800ISK

This is a great place to spend a little time inside if the weather is bad, admiring the large collection of classic vehicles under one roof. The makes and models of automobiles vary widely, and there's also some farm machinery on display dating back to the middle of the last century. Car fans will be pleased.

1238: THE BATTLE OF ICELAND

Aðalgata 21; tel. 354/588-1238; www.1238.is; 11am-4pm Mon.-Thurs., 11am-5pm Fri., 11am-4pm Sat.; adults 3,450ISK, children 6-13 2,400ISK, 2 adults and 2 children 8,900ISK

The newly opened museum 1238: The Battle of Iceland uses virtual reality technology to transport guests back to the Viking age. The museum focuses on one of the most violent eras in Iceland's history, the Sturlung Era (1220-1264), when numerous battles took place. Virtual reality headsets make it seem like you are in the middle of it all.

Sports and Recreation

SAUÐÁRKRÓKUR SWIMMING POOL

Skagfirðingabraut; tel. 354/453-5226; 6:50am-9pm Mon.-Fri., 10am-5pm Sat.-Sun. June 1-Aug. 31, 6:50am-8:30pm Mon.-Fri., 10am-4pm Sat.-Sun. Sept.-May; 1,050ISK

The Sauðárkrókur Swimming Pool is a 25-meter (82-ft) outdoor pool with hot tubs, a sauna, and sun beds.

HLÍÐARENDI GOLF COURSE

Route 75; tel. 354/453-5075; www.gss.is; greens fees 4,500ISK

The Hlíðarendi Golf Course is the longest nine-hole golf course in Iceland. It is located in picturesque country surroundings backdropped by mountains. Reserve a tee time in advance. The facility is open year-round, but call ahead for opening hours because they change frequently.

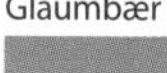

Glaumbær

Food

HARD WOK CAFÉ

Aðalgata 8; tel. 354/453-5355; 11:45am-9:30pm daily; entrées from 2,590ISK

Hard Wok Café is an interesting Asian/pizza fusion restaurant that seems out of place in a small town in Iceland, but it works. The food is surprising, with choices including fish and chips, stir-fry dishes, hamburgers, pizza, and Asian-inspired sandwiches. The restaurant is a favorite among locals.

GRANA BISTRO

Aðalgata 21; tel. 354/588-1238; 11:30am-4pm Mon.-Wed., 11:30am-10pm Thurs.-Sun.; entrées from 2,800ISK

This lovely casual bistro offers lunch specials like chicken salad, mushroom soup, and baked cod dishes. There's also pizza on the menu as well as shellfish soup, Korean-style chicken wings, and the fish of the day, served with seasonal vegetables.

KK RESTAURANT

Aðalgata 16; tel. 354/453-6454; www.kkrestaurant.is; 6pm-9pm Tues.-Sat.; entrées from 2,990ISK

KK Restaurant is in an attractive building on the main street of town that dates back to 1887. Today, it's a modern, comfortable restaurant that serves casual food like burgers and pizza, and appetizers like mozzarella sticks and onion rings. It also serves meat and fish dishes, including pan-fried arctic char, roasted lobster tails, and lamb fillet.

Accommodations

MIKLIGARÐUR GUESTHOUSE

Kirkjutorg 3; tel. 354/453-6880; www.arctichotels.is; rooms from 16,560ISK

This guesthouse does not get points for style—the decor is dated and the rooms are small and a bit sad—but the rooms are clean and the staff is accommodating. Guests have access to shared bathroom facilities, free Wi-Fi, and free parking, and a tasty breakfast is included in the room price.

HÓTEL TINDASTÓLL

Lindargata 3; tel. 354/453-5002; www.arctichotels.is; rooms from 25,760ISK

Hótel Tindastóll occupies two adjacent buildings. The original, a green house with a traditional look, has the distinction of being the oldest hotel in Iceland. It opened in 1884 and has undergone a number of renovations. The rooms are cozy, tastefully decorated, and have the feeling of home. In 2012, the second building opened, and its rooms are spacious, bright, and modern with flat-screen TVs, free Wi-Fi, and private bathrooms. Breakfast is included.

HÓTEL MIKLIGARÐUR

Skagfirðingabraut 24; tel. 354/453-6330; www.arctichotels.is; rooms from 27,000ISK

Hótel Mikligarður offers 65 small rooms with private bathrooms, and not much else. There aren't a lot of amenities, but the location is convenient and it makes for an adequate short stay. Free Wi-Fi is available, and breakfast is included.

Getting There

By car, take **Route 75,** which is paved, from the **Ring Road.** Sauðárkrókur is about 25 minutes or 25 kilometers (16 mi) north of **Varmahlíð.**

DRANGEY

Drangey is a small, rocky island, dotted with moss and grass, in the middle of Skagafjörður. Its steep cliffs jut almost 200 meters (656 ft) out of the sea. The island is home to pure natural beauty and thriving birdlife. Drangey is a favorite nesting spot for puffins and guillemots, along with razor-billed auks, ravens, gyrfalcons, and other seabirds.

Other than the secluded beauty and birdlife, Drangey is known for its inclusion in several sagas. Grettir Ásmundarson was said to have lived on the island for nearly three years with his brother Illugi. Grettir swam to Reykir (a farm) from Drangey to get equipment to make a fire, a pretty daring journey considering the water temperature.

Getting There

During the summer months you can reach the island by boat from the **Sauðárkrókur marina. Drangey Tours** (tel. 354/821-0090; www.drangey.net) operates daily boat trips (11am June-mid-Aug.; adults 13,900ISK, children 7-14 7,500ISK, children 6 and under free). The excursion takes about four hours, and it's a wonderful way to spend the day. Be sure to check the schedule, as it may change due to weather. It is not necessary to book in advance.

Tröllaskagi

Tröllaskagi (Troll Peninsula), which lies between the fjords Skagafjörður and Eyjafjorður, has a gorgeous mountainous landscape, with some peaks reaching more than 1,400 meters (4,594 ft) above sea level. Several deep valleys throughout the peninsula were created by glaciers and rivers. Tröllaskagi offers opportunities for outdoor activities, including hiking and whale-watching.

DALVÍK

Dalvík is a small fishing town perhaps best known to tourists as the gateway to **Grímsey** and **Hrísey** islands, as the ferry to those places departs from the **Dalvík harbor.** But it's also a great spot for hikers up for the challenge of navigating the hilly and mountainous landscape around the town. Every year in late June or early July, there is a **"hiking week"** in Dalvík, during which groups get together and hike with a guide.

Sights

SVARFAÐARDALUR NATURE RESERVE

Route 805

In a valley just west of town, the Svarfaðardalur Nature Reserve is about 8 square kilometers (3 sq mi) of wetlands on the banks of the Svarfaðardalsá. The unspoiled environment is a breeding ground for a number of bird species, including great northern divers and harlequin ducks. Watch where you walk to avoid nests, and wear rubber boots in wet weather.

HERITAGE MUSEUM OF DALVÍK (Byggðasafnið Dalvík)

Hvoli við Karlsrauðatorg; tel. 354/460-4928; www.dalvikurbyggd.is; 10am-5pm daily June 1-Aug. 30, open by request in winter; 1,000ISK

The Heritage Museum of Dalvík has an extensive collection of photographs and objects, including tools and home furnishings, that relate to the life and work of Dalvík's residents over the years. A natural history collection contains mounts of Icelandic mammals and birds, along with eggs, rocks, shells, and grass/moss. Other exhibits relate to renowned individuals that hail from the area, ranging from politicians to artists. The collection is vast and a bit quirky.

Hiking

Though the hike up Bæjarfjall is relatively easy and can be walked unguided, most of the other hikes around Tröllaskagi are more challenging and require a guide. (Unfortunately, at the time of writing, the one company that had Dalvík hikes had not yet opened again after COVID-19).

BÆJARFJALL

Distance: *9 km (5 mi) round-trip*
Hiking Time: *3 hours*
Information and Maps: *www.northiceland.is*
Trailhead: *Dalvík church*

This easy hike starts from the Dalvík church, where you will find a marked gravel road that leads to the mountain Bæjarfjall. During the beginning of the hike you will have beautiful views of a trickling stream and vast gorge that opens into a valley. As you continue up, you will have a clear view over Dalvík, if the weather cooperates. You will reach an altitude of 744 meters (2,440 ft) during this trek. After enjoying some time at the top, you follow the path back down.

Sports and Recreation

THE BEER SPA

(Bjórböðin)

Ægisgata 31; tel. 354/414-2828; www.bjorbodin.is; 11am-9pm daily; 11,900ISK, couples bath 19,900ISK

The Beer Spa is an exciting development in North Iceland, owned and operated by local brewery Kaldi, which offers brewery tours daily (www.bruggsmidjan.is). The Beer Spa features seven spa tubs (maximum two people) made from kambala wood that are full of beer for a relaxing soak. Once you arrive at the facility, a staff member welcomes you, explains the soaking process, provides you with a towel, and shows you to the locker room.

After you secure your belongings and change into a bathing suit, you'll be shown to your bath in a private room. Guests have 25 minutes to soak in the beer bath, and then you head to a relaxation room for another 25 minutes. There are also two outside hot tubs requiring a separate entry fee (2,000ISK, free if you are taking a beer bath) that can hold 8-10 people. It's recommended you not shower for at least four hours afterward so that your skin reaps the benefits of the therapeutic bath. It's also recommended you book your reservation in advance online.

At the 75-seat **restaurant** (entrées from 3,090ISK), enjoy a meal or a beer inside or, if the weather is nice, outside on a lovely patio that overlooks the mountainous landscape. It's a casual eatery with a friendly staff, and the menu includes burgers, sandwiches, steaks, fish, and small dishes. The Kaldi burger is the winner, topped with bacon, cheese, caramelized onions, and tomatoes. There's a kids' menu as well.

The Beer Spa is located 12 kilometers (7 mi) southeast of Dalvík via **Routes 82** and **808,** both of which are paved.

ARCTIC SEA TOURS

tel. 354/771-7600; www.arcticseatours.is; daily; 15,990ISK per person

Arctic Sea Tours operates a three-hour whale-watching tour where you have a 98 percent chance of seeing whales or dolphins, according to the company. You might see white-beaked dolphins, minke whales, harbor porpoises, and, if you're lucky, a humpback whale or an enormous blue whale. At the end of the tour, you will have an opportunity to do some fishing, and the fresh catches (most likely cod) will be grilled back on land for all to enjoy. The tours leave from Dalvík harbor year-round.

DALVÍK SWIMMING POOL

Svarfaðarbraut 34; tel. 354/466-3233; 6:15am-8pm Mon.-Fri., 9am-5pm Sat.-Sun.; 950ISK

The Dalvík Swimming Pool is close to the town's campsite, so expect a crowd in the summer months. The facility has an outdoor pool, hot tubs, a children's pool, waterslide, sauna, and gym.

ARNARHOLT GOLF COURSE

Arnarholt Svarfaðardal; tel. 354/466-1204; year-round; greens fees 5,000ISK

Just 7 kilometers (4.3 mi) outside Dalvík is the Arnarholt Golf Course, a nine-hole course said to have been built on a 9th-century burial ground. If that doesn't spook you away, you'll find a course that is well maintained, and carts, clubs, and equipment are available to rent. Be sure to call ahead for a tee time. An on-site **restaurant** is open 1pm-9pm daily.

Festivals and Events

HIKING WEEK

www.dalvikurbyggd.is; late June/early July

Dalvík is quite hilly, and locals love to hike. Every summer, locals and tourists gather for a "hiking week," featuring nine different guided hikes over nine days during which hikers explore the mountains along Tröllaskagi. Hikes range between 2-10 hours and vary in difficulty from leisurely walks along the Dalvík harbor to steep mountain climbs. Pay in advance to join the hikes (check out their website for more information); shorter hikes cost 1,500ISK and longer hikes are 3,000ISK.

Food and Accommodations

GREGOR'S PUB

Goðabraut 3; tel. 354/847-8846; 6pm-10pm daily; entrées from 2,000ISK

Gregor's Pub offers a great casual dining experience ranging from soup to tender lamb fillets. The menu also includes hamburgers, sandwiches, and pizza. At night it transforms into a bar where locals gather to grab a pint and catch up.

HOTEL DALVÍK

Skíðabraut 18; tel. 354/466-3395; www.hoteldalvik.com; double rooms from 13,000ISK, 32,000ISK for bungalows

Hotel Dalvík has 30 clean and average-size rooms with standard beds, private bathrooms, and free Wi-Fi. The rooms have a bit of a 1980s feel to them, with red carpeting and gold accents. In addition to double rooms, Hotel Dalvík offers bungalows and a junior suite. An on-site restaurant serves breakfast (included in the price of the room), and guests have access to free parking.

YTRI-VÍK LODGE

Árskógsströnd; tel. 354/466-1982; www.heyiceland.is; cottages from 26,000ISK

Ytri-Vík Lodge offers cottages that range from accommodations for two people up to a three-story house for a large group. The cottages are made from wood and have fully equipped kitchens, roomy sleeping spaces, and all the comforts of home. The cottages all have decks, which have glorious views of the sea with mountains looming in the background. It's a gorgeous scene to enjoy while sipping your morning coffee.

DALVÍK CAMPGROUND

Sundlaug Dalvíkur; tel. 354/460-4940; 1,250ISK

The Dalvík Campground is close to the town's swimming pool. The facility is pretty basic, with an adequate cooking area and warm showers. The campground, which accommodates tents and RVs (with hookups), is open June-August. In addition to the pool, there is a nice playground nearby, as well as a soccer field and a basketball court. Electricity is 1,000ISK per vehicle.

Information and Services

BERG MENNINGARHUS CULTURAL CENTER

Goðabraut; tel. 354/846-4908; info@dalvikurbyggd.is; 10am-5pm Mon.-Fri., 1pm-5pm Sat.

The tourist information center is based inside the Berg Menningarhus Cultural Center and offers Internet access, pamphlets about the region, maps, and information about local sights.

Getting There

BY CAR

Dalvík is 34 kilometers (21 mi) southeast of **Siglufjörður** on **Route 82,** which is paved; 18 kilometers (11 mi) south of **Ólafsfjörður** on Route 82; and 42 kilometers (26 mi) south of **Akureyri,** also on Route 82.

BY BOAT

The ferry **Sæfari** (www.saefari.is) provides daily trips from **Dalvík Harbor** to the islands of **Grímsey** (about 3.5 hours away) and **Hrísey** (a short 30 minutes away). Check the website for the latest timetable, as it tends to change.

HRÍSEY

Hrísey was established as a herring station and today is a major tourist draw. Known as the "pearl of Eyjafjörður," the island, which is 35 kilometers (22 mi) north of Akureyri, has a lot of appeal for **bird-watching** enthusiasts. Hrísey is 7.5 kilometers (4.6 mi) long and 2.4 kilometers (1.4 mi) wide, and about 200 people call it home. Its population soars during the summer months when ferries full of tourists come to shore.

Outside of the beautiful nature the attractions are minimal, but tractor rides on a hay wagon are quite popular, and there's a small exhibition on shark hunting. The **tractor rides** (tel. 354/695-0077; 1,300ISK, children are free) are about 40 minutes long and take visitors around the island. Budget one full day for the island.

Sights

THE HOUSE OF SHARK-JÖRUNDUR (Jörundur Hús)

Norðurvegur 3; tel. 354/695-0077; www.hrisey.net; 1pm-5pm daily June-Aug.; 1,000ISK

This small museum houses objects related to shark hunting. The house was owned and built by Jörundur Jónsson, called Shark-Jörundur, in 1885, using timber from Norwegian ships that had run ashore on Hrísey. In 1917 the house was moved down the hill to its current site, but a statue of Jörundur is erected where the house originally stood.

BIRD-WATCHING

About 40 bird species nest in Hrísey, and its populations thrive because hunting and egg collection are strictly prohibited and there are no predators (such as mice, mink, or foxes) on the island. Hrísey is known for having the densest population of ptarmigans in Iceland during the nesting season. The **southern part** of the island has the best bird-watching opportunities along the edges.

Festivals and Events

HRÍSEY FAMILY FESTIVAL

www.hrisey.is; July; free

A family festival is held on the island every year, on a weekend in July. The festivities include music, tractor rides around the island, food vendors, and a bonfire at night. For the kids, there's a playground, clowns, and sandcastle-building at the beach. The festival is free and open to everyone.

Food and Accommodations

Lodging options on the island are very limited. Many visitors opt to day-trip to Hrísey from Akureyri or Dalvík.

VERBUÐIN 66

Sjávargata 2; tel. 354/467-1166; www.hrisey.is; entrées from 2,200ISK

This casual eatery is your only chance to get a bite to eat when visiting Hrísey. The food is good, and you can't go wrong with an order of fish and chips or a bacon burger and fries. There are also chicken wings, tandoori chicken salad, and vegan burgers on the menu.

HRÍSEY CAMPGROUND

tel. 354/461-2255; June-Aug.; 1,500ISK

The Hrísey Campground is small with adequate facilities. It's conveniently located next to the swimming pool. The campsite, which is in an open field, has showers, hot and cold water, and restrooms. The location in the center of town and close to the sea is lovely, but it can get quite chilly. Be sure to have appropriate gear for cold temperatures.

Information and Services

TOURIST INFORMATION OFFICE

Norðurvegur 3; tel. 354/695-0077; hrisey@hrisey.net; www.hrisey.is; noon-5pm daily June-Aug.

The tourist information office is open daily June-August, and you can book tours, buy tickets for the ferry, and get maps and information about the island.

Getting There

The ferry **Sævar** (tel. 354/695-5544; www.hrisey.is) sails between the island and the nearby village of **Árskógssandur**, just a few kilometers east of Dalvík. Sævar sails nine times daily June 1-August 31, and a round-trip fare costs 3,400ISK for adults or 1,700ISK for children 12-15. The ferry trip takes less than 30 minutes and is subject to weather conditions. Be sure to call ahead for current departure times, as they tend to change often due to stormy weather.

SIGLUFJÖRÐUR

Just a one-hour drive from Akureyri, secluded Siglufjörður is the northernmost town in all of Iceland. It's easy to fall in love with this beautiful harbor town. Siglufjörður's marina is home to much of the activity in the village, with bustling restaurants and a few town-specific museums focusing on the herring industry and the local music scene. For much of the year, the town of less than 2,000 is quiet, as it endures a sometimes-punishing winter with wind that feels like it's cutting right through you. That said, skiers are attracted to the region, and there are a couple of trails to enjoy. In the summer, however, the town comes alive with exhibitions, concerts, and packed coffeehouses and restaurants.

Sights

Buying a ticket to the Herring Era Museum also grants you entry into the **Folk Music Center;** the **Icelandic Poetry Center** (Túngötu 5; tel. 354/865-6543; noon-4pm daily), which houses numerous books of poetry and hosts events in Icelandic; and the **Old Slipway** (Snorragata 10; tel. 354/467-1604; 10am-6pm daily), a boatyard that includes an exhibition on the 200-year history of boatbuilding in the town.

HERRING ERA MUSEUM (Síldarminjasafn Íslands)

Snorragata 10; tel. 354/467-1604; www.sild.is; 10am-6pm daily June-Aug., 1pm-5pm daily May and Sept., by appointment rest of the year; 1,800ISK

The Herring Era Museum is one of the most well-presented museums in Iceland. Yes, it's educational and it's about fish, but it's anything but boring. The main exhibition is based in a large red building named Róaldsbrakki, a former Norwegian salting station that was built in 1907. Inside are interactive exhibits of photographs and film clips showing how fish was processed and salted, which was the source of the town's livelihood for generations. There's a boat inside, along with a lot of fishing gear and equipment. It's clear that great care went into creating this museum. If you're in town, this is definitely worth a visit.

FOLK MUSIC CENTER (Þjóðlagasetrið Siglufjörður)

Norðurgata 1; tel. 354/467-2300; www.folkmusik.is; noon-6pm daily June-Aug., by request rest of year; 800ISK

The Folk Music Center is a charming two-floor museum set in what once was the private home of folklorist Reverend Bjarni Þorsteinsson (1861-1938). The museum showcases Bjarni's collection of classic Icelandic folk songs, along with interesting instruments, photographs, and film clips. You have the opportunity to listen to music that includes genres like hymns, the traditional chanting style called *rimur,* and nursery rhymes.

Festivals and Events

HERRING FESTIVAL

www.hatid.is; first weekend in August

The Herring Festival, which is held the first weekend in August, is a fun event for locals and tourists alike. Guests can enjoy music, theatrical performances, a huge herring buffet, and fireworks in the evening.

Sports and Recreation

SIGLUFJÖRÐUR SKIING CENTER

Tjarnargata 14; tel. 354/467-2120; 10am-4pm Mon. and Thurs.-Sun., 3pm-7pm Tues.-Wed. in winter; 4,000ISK

Iceland is not known for skiing, but there are a few ski areas in the north, with the Siglufjörður Skiing Center being the best. Three lifts carry skiers up to the slopes, with the highest lift measuring 530 meters (1,728 ft) in length with a vertical rise of about 180 meters (591 ft). The top of the lift is over 650 meters (2,133 ft). The scenery is breathtaking. All the equipment you need is available to rent, and there are instructors on-site. Snowboarding and cross-country skiing are also possible. It's typically open November-April, but that can change due to weather; be sure to call ahead.

1: Dalvík **2:** Herring Era Museum **3:** Siglufjörður harbor

1

2

3

SIGLUFJÖRÐUR SWIMMING POOL

Hvanneyrarbraut 52; tel. 354/467-1352; 6:30am-7pm Mon.-Fri., 10am-6pm Sat.-Sun. June 7-Aug. 31, 6:30am-7:45pm Mon.-Fri., 2pm-6pm Sat., 10am-2pm Sun. Sept. 1-June 6; 850ISK

The Siglufjörður Swimming Pool is a delightful place to spend a couple of hours when the weather is frightful. You will find a lot of locals and their children enjoying the pool. The facility includes an indoor pool and a large hot tub outside.

Food

KAFFI RAUÐKA

Gránugata 19; tel. 354/467-1550; www.kaffiraudka.is; 11am-10pm daily; snacks from 800ISK

Kaffi Rauðka is hands down the town's best place to hang out in the summer. The outdoor seating area is filled with tourists and locals sipping coffee drinks or cocktails or enjoying light meals. Inside, the two levels are decorated in a rustic theme with lots of wood and loads of comfort. The bright red building is hard to miss.

TORGIÐ

Aðalgata 32; tel. 354/467-2323; www.torgid.net/en; lunch buffet noon-2pm Mon.-Fri., dinner 6pm-9pm Thurs.-Sun.; entrées from 2,100ISK

Torgið is the best option for families, or for just grabbing a quick bite to eat before heading out to explore the surroundings. Tourist-friendly fare on the menu includes hamburgers, sandwiches, and pizza, as well as some seafood options.

HARBOR HOUSE CAFÉ

Gránugata 5b; tel. 354/659-1394; www.harborhouse.is; lunch noon-2pm, dinner 6pm-10pm daily; entrées from 2,490ISK

This small harborside café sells light meals and coffee for lunch and delectable seafood dishes for dinner. The seafood soup with mussels, shrimp, and lobster is memorable. The café is small and cozy, and the staff is very friendly. You will see a local or two with their laptop and a cup of coffee or tourists curling up with a book to get out of the rain.

SEGULL 67 BRUGGHÚS

Vetrarbraut 8-10; tel. 354/863-2120; www.segull67.is; noon-8pm daily

A newly opened family-owned microbrewery situated in the heart of town, Segull 67 Brugghús is housed in a converted fish factory. The brewery offers tours including a beer tasting for 2,500ISK per person. Call ahead for the tour schedule.

Accommodations

★ SIGLUNES GUESTHOUSE

Laekjargata 10; tel. 354/467-1222; www.hotelsiglunes.is; rooms from 19,855ISK

Siglunes Guesthouse is the hippest place to stay in the north, and it attracts a lot of young travelers. The interior is darling, with vintage wood furniture and cool rugs, art, and wallpaper. Ten rooms have private bathrooms. An old-fashioned piano and fireplace are in the lobby area, and it's a great place to relax after a day of exploring the sights. Rooms are larger than average, with comfy beds and an antique flavor to the decor. Breakfast is included in the room price, and the in-house restaurant and bar is quite popular.

THE HERRING HOUSE GUESTHOUSE

Hlíðarvegur 1; tel. 354/868-4200; www.theherringhouse.com; rooms from 22,000ISK

This charming guesthouse offers four rooms and is just a two-minute walk to the center of town. The guesthouse has a lovely garden and a terrace with sweeping views of the mountainous scenery. Rooms are spacious with minimal decor, and there are shared bathroom facilities and free Wi-Fi during your stay.

SIGLÓ HÓTEL

Snorragata 3; tel. 354/461-7730; www.siglohotel.is; rooms from 33,900ISK

Sigló Hótel is a beautiful property along the harbor and close to major town attractions. Rooms, ranging from doubles to suites, are all bright and airy with private bathrooms. All rooms have a window seat overlooking the town, free Wi-Fi, a TV, and comfortable furniture. Breakfast is included in the price.

SIGLUFJÖRÐUR CAMPGROUND

Gránugata 24; tel. 354/663-5560; mid-May-mid-Sept.; 1,400ISK

The Siglufjörður Campground is near the center of town, close to the harbor and with beautiful mountain views. It has a cooking area and hot showers. The campsite is in an open field with little shelter and welcomes tent campers as well as RVs. The main museums and restaurants are all within walking distance. Electricity costs 1,200ISK and washing machines are available for 900ISK per wash.

Getting There

Getting to Siglufjörður is a trying exercise at times. From Akureyi, **Route 82** and **Route 76,** both paved, connect to Siglufjörður, if the weather is cooperating. This region can have heavy snowfall and it is always best to frequently check road conditions at www.road.is. The trip takes about 1 hour 15 minutes.

A **tunnel** links **Siglufjörður, Olafsfjörður,** and **Dalvík.** Driving through the one-lane, two-way tunnel can be heart-stopping, with cars turning into pockets on the side to let the driver going the opposite way pass by. **Ólafsfjörður** is 17 kilometers (11 mi) southeast of Siglufjörður on Route 76.

Grímsey

About 40 kilometers (25 mi) off the coast of Iceland, Grímsey is a windswept and secluded island, about five square kilometers (3 sq mi) in area, that is as striking in beauty as it is difficult to reach.

Just 100 people reside in Grímsey, and those who remain come from hardy stock, battling arctic temperatures and isolation. Fishers brave the elements, including frost and storms and waves that could reach 15 meters (49 ft) high. It's not an easy life.

Tourists come to explore the tiny island, bird-watch, and experience 24 hours of daylight in the height of the summer. Night does not reach Grímsey until late July, when the sun sets around midnight, only to rise a short time later. The island can be explored in one day.

SIGHTS

The Cliffs

East side of island

The cliffs on the east side of the island tower 60-100 meters (197-328 ft). In the old days, the basalt cliffs served as a major source of food, as locals collected eggs along the rifts. It was a tenuous task: A rope would be lowered 60 meters down from the edge of the cliff while the individual collected eggs. There was a great risk that the rope would break or a large rock could break off, hitting and killing the climber. Today, the egg collection practice is safer and more modern, but the cliffs are a reminder of the past and their importance to the island's sustenance. They're also interesting formations and serve as a great backdrop when photographing birds.

The Lighthouse

Southeast corner of island

Bright yellow and close to the cliff's edge, Grímsey's lighthouse is one of the most significant buildings on the island. It was built in 1937 and is situated on the southeast corner of the island. It was originally operated manually with a gas lamp that had to be turned on and off by hand. Today, the lighthouse is automatic and still plays an important role in directing boat traffic along the coast. Although the lighthouse itself is closed to the public, it's a popular place for photos, capturing birdlife and the cliffs in the background.

Crossing the Arctic Circle

Want to witness the **midnight sun?** That's when the sun remains above the horizon for a full 24 hours during the summer solstice on June 20 or 21. There's only one place you can experience this phenomenon in Iceland: where the Arctic Circle crosses the country's northernmost point, on Grímsey. (If you'd prefer nearly 24 hours of darkness, there's always **polar night,** on December 21.)

A small **symbolic bridge** crossing the Arctic Circle can be found at 66°33'N, north of Grímsey's airport terminal and next to Guesthouse Básar. Beside the bridge is a pole showing the distance to many well-known cities in the world, including London and New York.

Tourists who make the pilgrimage can buy evidence of their trip in the form of a **diploma** in the local gift store **Gallerí Sól** (Sólberg 611; tel. 354/467-3190; gullsol@visir.is), which is open Monday, Wednesday, and Friday during the summer months (June-Aug.). You can also reserve your diploma at Gallerí Sól by phone or email. Diplomas cost 1,000ISK. Those who come to Grímsey on a tour receive a diploma free of charge.

FESTIVALS AND EVENTS

SUMMER SOLSTICE FESTIVAL

www.visitakureyri.is/en; June; free

The summer solstice brings nearly 24 hours of complete daylight to Iceland, and locals on Grímsey celebrate every June. The festival includes live music, markets, guided walks, a family scavenger hunt, and a seafood buffet. The festival is free, except for the seafood buffet, and is open to everyone.

GRÍMSEY DAY

www.grimsey.is; June

Grímsey Day is an annual festival that takes place at the beginning of June each year over three days. It focuses on old traditions from Grímsey, like collecting eggs from the cliffs, as well as enjoying seasonal local food, music, and art.

SPORTS AND RECREATION

Bird-Watching

Grímsey is one of the best spots in North Iceland for bird-watchers interested in seabirds. The high season for birding is from **April,** when birds migrate to the island to nest, to **August,** when birds depart the island for warmer weather. Bird-watchers will have a chance to see arctic terns, black-legged kittiwakes, northern fulmars, razorbills, common guillemots, black guillemots, and murres. You can also see white wagtails, northern wheatears, and snow buntings.

The main attractions, however, are the adorable **Atlantic puffins,** as Grímsey is home to one of the largest colonies in Iceland. The birds, with their bright beaks and big personalities, are a delight to watch nesting and gliding along the cliffs. Please be aware of eggs and be careful not to disturb nesting areas during the spring. Grímsey is a small island and the best bird-watching spots are the cliffs that line the island.

Pools and Hot Springs

GRÍMSEY ISLAND THERMAL POOL

tel. 354/467-3155; 8pm-9:30pm Mon.-Wed., 2pm-4pm Sat.; 1,050ISK

The Grímsey Island Thermal Pool is situated near the airport and is a quiet spot to take a dip. You likely won't find crowds here, and the hours change often. For current hours, inquire at the tourist information office or at your guesthouse.

FOOD AND ACCOMMODATIONS

GUESTHOUSE GULLSÓL

Sólbergi; 354/467-3190; www.gullsol.is; rooms from 13,000ISK

Guesthouse Gullsól offers four single rooms and two doubles in a charming wood house, one of the oldest structures on the island. Rooms are small, but clean and neat, and it's the closest guesthouse to the main population area. Guests share bathroom facilities and have access to a fully equipped kitchen to prepare meals. It's open year-round.

GUESTHOUSE BÁSAR

tel. 354/467-3103; www.gistiheimilibasar.is; rooms from 20,000ISK

Guesthouse Básar, next to the small airport, is an eight-room guesthouse just steps from the Arctic Circle. Literally. Rooms are simple and neat, and amenities include a common TV lounge and a fully equipped kitchen. Breakfast is included, and lunch and dinner can be requested as well. The guesthouse is open year-round.

INFORMATION AND SERVICES

A few years ago, the towns of Grímsey, Hrísey, and Akureyri voted to become a municipality overseen by Akureyri. Tourist information and ferry fares and schedules for all three towns can be found at the **tourist information center** at Hof concert hall by the harbor in Akureyri.

Safety

Weather can be your greatest enemy on the island, with unexpected wind gusts and horizontal rain. All children under the age of 14 must wear a life jacket when in the harbor area, whether they are playing, walking, or about to board a ferry. It is island law. The ferry staff provides life jackets at the harbor.

GETTING THERE

By Boat

Sæfari (tel. 354/853-2211; www.samskip.is) operates ferry service between **Dalvík** and Grímsey five times a week in the summer and four times a week in the winter. It takes about three hours each way, and the ferry holds 108 people. Book in advance in the summer months; tickets can be purchased at the **tourist information office** at Hof concert hall in Akureyri (tel. 354/450-1050; info@visitakureyri.is). A round-trip fare is 8,000ISK. Departure times from Dalvík in the summer are Monday, Tuesday, Wednesday, Friday, and Sunday at 9am; the ferry returns from Grímsey at 8pm. Check the website for

an Atlantic puffin colony on the cliffs of Grímsey

up-to-date departure information. Schedules can vary due to weather.

By Air

The flight from **Akureyri** to Grímsey is one of the most beautiful 30-minute airplane rides you will ever take. The jaw-dropping views of the landscape make the trip feel a tad too short. The landing is not for the faint of heart, as the small plane has to land on a miniscule strip of grass on an island that looks like a rock in the middle of the ocean. During the summer (June-August), **Norlandair** (www.norlandair.is) provides frequent flights to Grímsey (the airport is within walking distance from town) from Akureyri (Urðargil 15) for about 30,000ISK round-trip. For current departure timetables and precise ticket prices, check Norlandair's website.

Akureyri

TOP EXPERIENCE

Akureyri is commonly referred to as Iceland's "second city," a moniker many of the town's 18,000 residents find amusing given its small size. Akureyri has its own personality, and it looks and feels quite different from Reykjavík, more low-key and relaxed than the capital city. There are gorgeous gardens to explore, charming museums, paddleboats littering the fjord in the summer months, and a booming art scene.

Akureyri has a tighter community than Reykjavík, and there is a lot of support for local artists. Painters, sculptors, and craftspeople occupy numerous private studios. The museums reflect the rich cultural landscape of the town, displaying varied works from some of the region's most important artists.

Akureyri also boasts delicious restaurants and first-rate hotels, and its concert hall, Hof, is a must-see for architecture enthusiasts. Akureyri is a perfect place to base yourself while exploring the Tröllaskagi Peninsula and Eyjafjörður, Iceland's longest fjord at 60 kilometers (37.2 mi).

Many tourists choose Akureyri as their home base when exploring the north, opting to spend nights in the town while booking day tours or putting some miles on their rental car to places like Húsavík and Mývatn.

Akureyri has gotten more traffic in recent years as a popular stop for cruise ships, and word is spreading about this charming, beautiful town. It's also surprisingly easy to get to. If you have the time, spend at least a couple of days here.

SIGHTS

★ Akureyri Botanical Gardens (Lystigarður Akureyrar)

Eyrarlandsholt; tel. 354/462-7487; www.lystigardur.akureyri.is; 8am-10pm Mon.-Fri., 9am-10pm Sat.-Sun. June 1-Sept. 30; free

The Akureyri Botanical Gardens are gorgeous and well kept; it's hard to find a better place in the city to take a stroll. The attraction is treasured by locals, and they're thrilled to share the beauty and tranquility with tourists. Known as one of the northernmost botanical gardens in the world, the public park opened in 1912, and flowers and plants made their debut in the park in 1957. Thousands of types of native and international flora can be found in the garden beds and nursery. While roaming the gardens during the summer, you'll see arctic poppy flowers, northern marsh violets, bilberry bushes, frog orchids, and hundreds of other species. The caretakers are always introducing new species to keep the collection fresh and eclectic. You'll also find walking paths, bridges, and a fountain in the gardens.

Akureyri

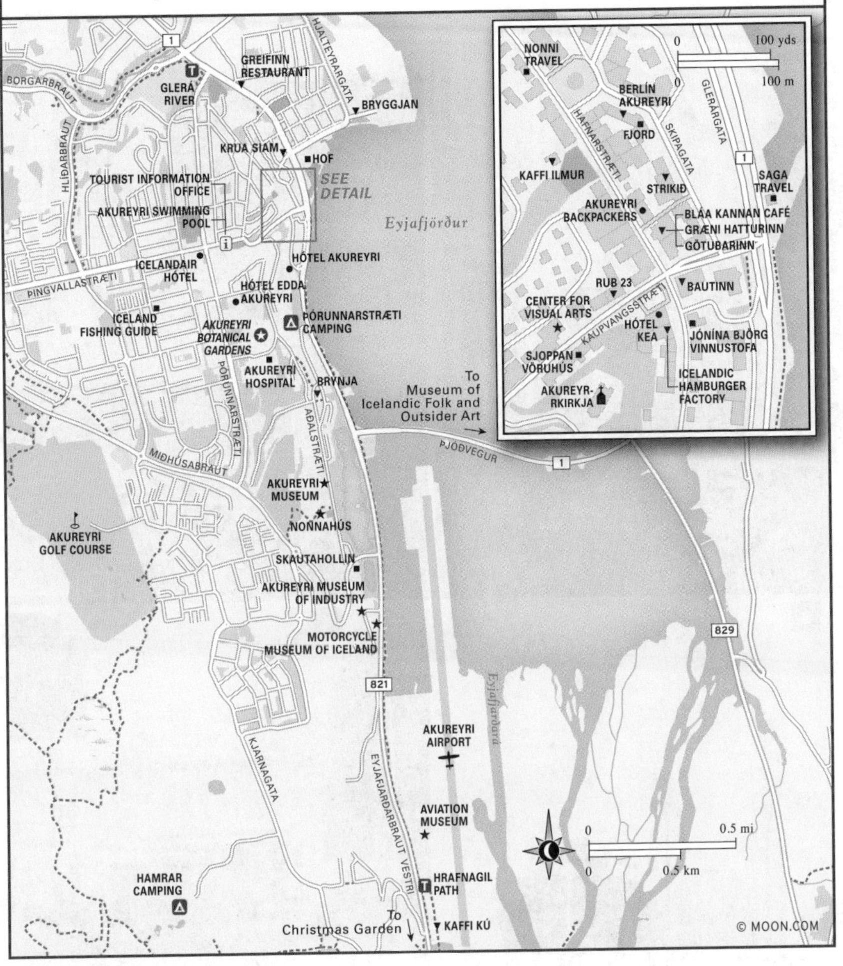

Akureyrarkirkja

Eyrarlandsvegur; tel. 354/462-7700; www.akureyrarkirkja.is; 10am-4pm Mon.-Sat., 4pm-7pm Sun. June 15-Aug. 15; free

The Akureyrarkirkja, the Akureyri Church, is in the center of the city, rising above it on a hill. The steep steps up to the grounds, with the church towering above, make for a great photo opportunity. The church was designed by state architect Guðjón Samúelsson, who delivered a design that is unique and Icelandic, with stark white walls, wood pews, and a lot of windows. While the outside is beautiful, the interior is exquisite, complete with a 3,200-pipe organ and a large central window that once belonged to Coventry Cathedral in England. The church, which was completed in 1940, is open to the public in the summer. The **Sunday service** is at 11am year-round, and tourists are more than welcome to join. Please note that the church is closed to tourists during funerals or other ceremonies.

1
2
KETILH
3
4

Center for Visual Arts
(Sjónlistamiðstöðin)

Kaupvangsstræti 12; tel. 354/461-2610; www.listasafn.akureyri.is

The Center for Visual Arts comprises three art museums in three separate buildings. The first, the **Akureyri Art Museum (Listasafnið á Akureyri)** (noon-5pm daily; 1,900ISK), hosts exhibitions in a variety of media, including landscape and portrait paintings, sculpture, photography, and other visual arts. The exhibitions focus on contemporary art. New exhibitions are revealed every eight weeks or so. The second building is the gallery **Kettle House (Ketilhús),** which serves as a space for local concerts and meetings, as well as art- and design-related events. Exhibitions in Kettle House are by invitation only and can include everything from painting exhibitions to performance art. The third building, **Melting Pot (Deiglan),** across the street from the Akureyri Art Museum, is devoted to young artists, giving them a platform to express and show their work.

Akureyri Museum
(Minjasafnið á Akureyri)

Aðalstræti 58; tel. 354/462-4162; www.minjasafnid.is; 11am-5pm daily; 2,000ISK

The Akureyri Museum has historical exhibitions including displays that feature nautical maps, 19th-century photography, and artifacts from everyday life in the settlement era. The exhibits also detail the region's geological background and its role in saga stories. The museum grounds have a beautiful garden.

Nonnahús

Aðalstræti 54; tel. 354/462-3555; www.minjasafnid.is/en; 10am-5pm daily June 1-Sept. 1, 10am-5pm Thurs.-Sun. Sept. 2-Oct. 1; adults 1,800ISK, children 17 and under free

Nonnahús, or Nonni's House, is a museum in the childhood home of Jesuit priest and children's author Jón Sveinsson (1857-1944). The house gets its name from Jón's nickname, Nonni, and it's one of the oldest structures in the town. The house was built in 1850, and it looks like a nondescript black wooden house from the outside. Inside, however, you get a sense of the life and work of one of Akureyri's most treasured sons. On the ground floor, there is a collection of Jón's books, from about 40 different countries where his works were published. Upstairs, you can get a look at his bedroom and some personal artifacts. A little **gift shop** sells his books in various languages.

1: Akureyri **2:** Akureyri Art Museum
3: Akureyrarkirkja **4:** Kaffi Ilmur

Akureyri Museum of Industry
(Iðnaðarsafnið á Akureyri)

Krókeyri; tel. 354/462-3600; www.idnadarsafnid.is; 10am-5pm daily June 1-Aug. 31, 1pm-4pm Fri.-Sun. Sept 1.-May 31; 1,500ISK

The Akureyri Museum of Industry displays relics from Iceland's industries, such as agriculture, fishing, and construction, throughout the years. Exhibitions include products, machinery, and photos of people hard at work in the region. It's a quaint museum with a passionate curator, but you can skip this if time is an issue.

Motorcycle Museum of Iceland
(Mótorhjólasafnið)

Krókeyri 2; tel. 354/866-3500; www.motorhjolasafn.is; noon-6pm daily June 1-Aug. 31, 3pm-7pm Sat. only Sept. 1-May 31; 1,000ISK adults, children 13 and under free

A small museum founded in the memory of local biker Heidar Johannsson, this museum has about 50 bikes on display, as well as photographs, objects, and gear related to Iceland's 100-year history of motorbikes.

Aviation Museum
(Flugsafn Íslands)

Akureyri Airport; tel. 354/461-4400; www.flugsafn.is/en; 1pm-4pm Sat., by request rest of week; 1,500ISK

This small museum located at a hangar at the airport is dedicated to the planes and pilots who have flown the windy skies over

Iceland. On display are a flying ambulance and Iceland's first gliders, as well as some relics from World War II, when U.S. and British troops occupied Iceland. There are lots of photographs and some accounts from pilots.

Christmas Garden (Jólagarðurinn)

tel. 354/463-1433; 10am-6pm daily June-Aug., noon-6pm daily Sept.-Dec., 2pm-6pm daily Jan.-May; free

If you're a fan of Christmas, do not miss the Christmas Garden, just a 10-minute drive from downtown Akureyri. The bright red house, which resembles a gingerbread house, has an astounding number of Christmas decorations, ranging from traditional to Icelandic-themed wares featuring the Yule Lads (Christmas elves). You can pick up a locally made trinket and buy some Christmas-themed candy, or just enjoy the jolly atmosphere. A garden outside offers benches, local art, and a tiny place to buy waffles and coffee. It's a cute space.

The Christmas Garden is about 10 kilometers (6 mi) south of downtown Akureyri on Route 821.

Museum of Icelandic Folk and Outsider Art (Safnasafnið)

Svalbarðsstrond; tel. 354/461-4066; www.safnasafnid.is/english; 10am-5pm daily May 15-Aug. 31; 1,000ISK

For something a little different, try the Museum of Icelandic Folk and Outsider Art, one of those quirky museums that doesn't get the attention it deserves. The museum is the only institution on the island that collects and displays outsider art. It houses 5,000 works from local artists, as well as a library and research facility. You will find paintings, sculptures, drawings, models, books, dolls, tools, and toys. Every year there are about 15 new exhibitions on display, delighting locals and surprising tourists with art you won't see anywhere else on the island. The museum is 12 kilometers (7.5 mi) north of Akureyri on Route 1.

SPORTS AND RECREATION

Fishing

ICELAND FISHING GUIDE

tel. 354/660-1642; www.icelandfishingguide.com; tours from 40,000ISK

Iceland Fishing Guide provides guided fishing tours to lakes and rivers around Akureyri. You'll have a chance at reeling in salmon, trout, and arctic char, among other fish. The tours, available April-September, are suitable for beginners as well as experienced anglers; choose from day tours or longer trips. Licenses needed for the tour are arranged in advance.

Hiking

While Akureyri is known as more of an urban playground, similar to Reykjavík, there are some hiking opportunities on the outskirts of town, namely around **Eyjafjarðardalur,** a wide valley surrounding the Eyjafjarðará River. To get information on trails and pick up maps, visit the **tourist information center** at Hof. Most hikes are moderate in difficulty.

HRAFNAGIL PATH

Distance: *18-km (11-mi) loop*
Hiking Time: *4-hour loop*
Information and Maps: *www.visitakureyri.is/en*
Trailhead: *Akureyri airport*

Starting from the parking lot at Akureyri Airport, the Hrafnagil path is a lovely, easy walk on a paved, flat surface, where you'll see locals walking, cycling, and enjoying some fresh air. Sights along the way include Kjarnaskógur forest, thick with small trees, and a local school and swimming pool.

GLERÁ RIVER

Distance: *5.4-km (3-mi) loop*
Hiking Time: *1-hour loop*
Information and Maps: *www.visitakureyri.is/en*
Trailhead: *Glerátorg mall parking area*

The lower part of the river Glerá is a perfect place for quick hike. The trail, which is a combination of gravel and asphalt, starts along the rippling river and its canyon, before you pass the old Akureyri power plant and the town reservoir. As you continue, you will come upon a small wooded area with small trees and a residential region. After the school, you turn right and meet up with the river Glerá again, making your way back to the parking area. It's a great route to get a sense of the nature that surrounds Akureyri.

Ice-Skating

SKAUTAHOLLIN

Naustavegi 1; tel. 354/461-2440; www.sasport.is; 1pm-4pm and 7pm-9pm Fri., 1pm-5pm Sat., 1pm-4pm Sun. Sept.-May; 900ISK

Skautahollin is a delightful skating hall chock-full of local families. If the weather is bad outside, visit the hall, rent a pair of skates, and join the fun.

Skiing

HLÍÐARFJALL

tel. 354/462-2280; www.hlidarfjall.is; Nov.-Apr.; day pass for adults 5,800ISK, children 6-17 1,700ISK

The Hlíðarfjall ski area is just a few minutes outside of town and offers more than a dozen well-kept trails. If you're dying to ski on a glacier, this is your chance. Bear in mind that the trails are 1,000 meters (3,280 ft) at the highest, so don't expect major vertical drops. A shuttle bus can pick you up at the tourist information office for 1,500ISK round-trip if you don't have a rental car. Other activities include snowboarding and cross-country skiing. You can rent all the equipment you need at the ski area. The season is November-April. Check the website for hours, as they tend to change due to weather.

Pools and Hot Springs

AKUREYRI SWIMMING POOL

Þingvallastræti; tel. 354/461-4455; 6:45am-9pm Mon.-Fri., 8am-9pm Sat., 8am-7:30pm Sun.; 1,050ISK

If you're going to visit one swimming pool in North Iceland, the Akureyri Swimming Pool should be it. The fantastic facilities include two outdoor pools, children's pools and play areas, waterslides, a sauna, and a steam room. The pool is in the center of town and well-maintained, drawing both locals and tourists. Rain or shine, this is a great spot to relax and spend some time.

Golf

AKUREYRI GOLF COURSE

Jadar; tel. 354/462-2974; greens fees 6,000ISK

Akureyri Golf Course is a wildly popular 18-hole facility that has the distinction of being the northernmost course in the world. The par-71 course loops around broad ridges and is quite scenic, with towering mountains in the background. Club and gear rentals are available on-site. Be sure to call ahead for a tee time. The course also plays host to the Arctic Open, held during the summer solstice. It's open year-round, but call ahead for opening hours because the schedule is changeable.

Tours

SAGA TRAVEL

Kaupvangsstræti 4; tel. 354/558-8888; www.sagatravel.is

Saga Travel is an Akureyri-based company that offers day tours from Akureyri and Mývatn, including horse-riding, lava cave visits, super-Jeep tours, sightseeing by bus, and hiking excursions. Day tours start from 19,900ISK.

NONNI TRAVEL

Brekkugata 5; tel. 354/461-1841; www.nonnitravel.is

Another Akureyri-based tour company is Nonni Travel, which offers day tours in North Iceland to sites like Goðafoss, Dettifoss, Grímsey, and Lake Mývatn. Day tours start at 11,000ISK.

ENTERTAINMENT AND EVENTS

HOF

Strandgata 12; tel. 354/450-1000; www.menningarhus.is

Hof is the striking building by the harbor

that is home to Akureyri's big concert performances, including rock concerts, symphonies, and everything in between. Hof, which opened in 2010, also houses the restaurant 1862 Nordic Bistro and the main tourist information office. Even if you're not going to attend a concert, or pick up brochures at the tourist office, architecture buffs will want to visit this building for its unique round concrete design. The interior is amazing, with modern curved wood accents intertwined with metal. It's open 8am-10pm daily, or later when there is a performance.

SHOPPING

Akureyri has ample shopping opportunities, offering everything from handmade Icelandic sweaters to home decor to pieces of fine art by local artists. If you are interested in art and handcrafts, Akureyri is a great place to spend some krona.

JÓNÍNA BJÖRG VINNUSTOFA

Hafnarstræti 90; www.joninabjorg.com; hours vary

Jónina Björg Helgadóttir is a visual artist working in graphic arts and paintings. She maintains a small studio in the heart of Akureyri where her work is on display and for sale. Her work can be described as figurative and inspired by Salvador Dalí. Her opening hours vary, but she can be reached at jonina@joninabjorg.com to arrange a time to visit.

SJOPPAN VÖRUHÚS

Kaupvangsstræti 21; tel. 354/864-0710; www.sjoppanvoruhus.is; noon-5pm daily

Sjoppan Vöruhús is a fun design shop that carriers local Icelandic design wares as well as goods from abroad. Here, you can find art prints, letterpress cards, wooden birds, jewelry, candles, and knitted goods. The store is a family-run business, and great care is put into the store selection.

FJORD

Skipagata 6; tel. 354/467-2007; www.fjordhome.is; 11am-5pm Mon.-Fri., noon-5pm Sat.

Fjord is a design shop that opened in Akureyri in 2019, offering ethical and sustainable small-batch products. At Fjord you can find candles, wool blankets, books, jewelry, and pillows. The wares are from designers from Iceland and abroad.

FOOD

Icelandic

KAFFI ILMUR

Hafnarstræti; tel. 354/571-6444; www.kaffiilmur.is; 8am-11pm daily; entrées from 2,190ISK

Kaffi Ilmur is a delightful little café off the main street in town. You'll find soups, sandwiches, salads, snacks, and fresh pastries, along with a great cup of coffee. Situated in a two-story house perched on a small hill, it's a lovely, quiet spot to have a light meal in the heart of downtown Akureyri. The buffet includes hot dishes, a salad bar, soup of the day, and fresh homemade bread. Kaffi Ilmur is especially great to visit during the summer when the large patio is filled with people enjoying meals and drinks, overlooking the town.

Seafood

★ RUB 23

Kaupvangsstræti 6; tel. 354/462-2223; www.rub23.is; 11:30am-10pm Mon.-Fri., 5:30pm-10pm Sat.-Sun.; entrées from 4,990ISK

Rub 23 is your best bet if you're looking for fresh and eclectic fish dishes. The restaurant, which also serves scrumptious sushi, specializes in cod, arctic char, blue ling, and salmon with a choice of "rubs," including citrus rosemary, Indian, sweet mango chili, Texas barbecue, and Asian fusion, among others. Meat dishes include lamb, chicken, beef, and minke whale with your choice of rub. Dinner for two, with drinks, can be pricey, but if you want a taste, the lunch menu (available on weekdays from 11am-2pm) is glorious as well.

Casual

BERLÍN AKUREYRI

Skipagata 4; tel. 354/772-5061; www.berlinakureyri.is; 9am-3pm daily; entrées from 1,350ISK

Berlín Akureyri fills an important gap in

town: brunch. The coffee shop offers breakfast, brunch, and lunch daily. A favorite among locals, you will find classics like bacon and eggs, pancakes, and waffles, plus smoothies, salads, and a vegan burger.

GREIFINN RESTAURANT

Gléragata 20; tel. 354/460-1600; www.greifinn.is; 11:30am-10pm daily; entrées from 2,690ISK

Greifinn Restaurant feels like the Icelandic version of TGI Friday's. There are mozzarella sticks, hamburgers, nachos, soups, sandwiches, burritos, and even pizza. It's casual, family friendly, and quick, with no surprises.

ICELANDIC HAMBURGER FACTORY (Íslenska Hamborgarafabrikkan)

Hafnarstræti 87-89; tel. 354/460-2000; www.fabrikkan.is; 5pm-9pm Sun.-Thurs., 5pm-10pm Fri.-Sat.; 2,699ISK

Icelandic Hamburger Factory is the best spot to grab a hamburger in Akureyri. The family-friendly joint offers 120-gram (4-oz) hamburgers on a square bun, ranging from traditional beef burgers to more exotic whale-meat burgers. There's something for every meat-eater here. The "surf and turf burger" is a sight to behold, with a beef patty, tiger prawns, Japanese seaweed, cheese, red onions, lettuce, tomatoes, and a garlic-cheese sauce. Other options include a barbecue burger, a lamb burger, and a Mexican-inspired salsa burger.

BAUTINN

Hafnarstræti 92; tel. 354/462-1818; www.bautinn.is; 11am-9:30pm Sun.-Thurs., noon-10pm Fri.-Sat.; entrées from 3,990ISK

At this typical casual eatery with plenty of tourist-friendly fare, you will find hamburgers, pasta, pizza, sandwiches, and soup on the menu, as well as more traditional Icelandic cuisine such as lamb, horse, whale, and beef steaks and an array of fish dishes. This is a popular place for locals as well as large tourist groups. The service is friendly and accommodating.

STRIKIÐ

Skipagata 14; tel. 354/462-7100; www.strikid.is; 11:30am-10pm Mon.-Thurs., 11:30am-11pm Fri.-Sat., 5pm-10pm Sun.; entrées from 4,990ISK

Strikið does a nice job with lamb and fish dishes, some more traditional, others with a Middle Eastern and Italian flair. The restaurant occupies one of the highest buildings in Akureyri, offering fantastic views of the town. There's a lovely four-course menu (7,990ISK) available that incorporates fresh, local ingredients including fish and meat. If you're after some fine dining that doesn't break the bank (by Iceland standards), this is a good option.

Asian

KRUA SIAM

Strandgata 13; tel. 354/466-3800; www.kruasiam.is; 11:30am-1:30pm and 5pm-9:30pm Mon.-Fri., 5pm-9:30pm Sat.-Sun.; entrées from 2,470ISK

Krua Siam has all the main dishes you'd expect at a Thai restaurant, without many surprises. The mainstays are here, including spring rolls, pad thai, and beef and curry with coconut milk. The lamb and fish are fresh, local, and divine.

Mediterranean

BRYGGJAN

Strandgata 49; tel. 354/440-6600; www.bryggjan.is; 11:30am-9pm daily; entrées from 4,190ISK

Bryggjan is known for its perfect pizzas in just about any combination of ingredients you could imagine. You can go the traditional route with a ham and pepperoni pizza, or more exotic with a shrimp, tuna, onion, and tomato pie. If you're not up for pizza, there are soups, sandwiches, and starters, such as mozzarella sticks and nachos.

Cafés

BLÁA KANNAN CAFÉ

Hafnarstræti 96; tel. 354/461-4600; 9am-11pm daily; 1,800ISK

Bláa Kannan Café is a charming café housed in a bright blue building on the main street, one of the oldest structures in the city. The interior is quaint and cozy, and the friendly staff serves freshly baked bread, pastries, soups, and sandwiches. It tends to get crowded during lunchtime, when fresh soup is served with bread and butter. In summer, locals and tourists sip drinks and soak up the sun at the outdoor tables. The central location and simple, good food make this place a winner.

KAFFI KÚ

Garður farm; tel. 354/867-3826; www.kaffiku.is; 11am-6pm Mon.-Fri., noon-6pm Sat.-Sun.; 2,750ISK

Kaffi Kú (Café Cow) is a fun experience for everyone from solo travelers to families. The café is housed in a cowshed, and guests can order light meals, coffee, and cakes while overlooking the cows from a glass partition. It's located on a farm just 10 kilometers (6 mi) south of Akureyri, about a 10-minute drive via Routes 1 and 829.

Ice Cream

BRYNJA

Aðalstræti 3; tel. 354/462-4478; noon-11pm daily; from 900ISK

Ice cream is serious business in Iceland, and the holy grail is Brynja. Icelanders are known to enjoy ice cream in any type of weather, and Brynja has been supplying locals with delicious creamy concoctions since 1942. In the summer, it's common to see a line outside the shop. In short, the ice cream is fantastic. Try a scoop or two.

BARS AND NIGHTLIFE

GÖTUBARINN

Hafnarstræti 96; tel. 354/462-4747; 7pm-1am Sun.-Thurs., 5pm-2am Fri.-Sat.

Götubarinn is a wildly popular bar that has a great selection of beers and wines. It's situated in the city center in a nondescript green building, but the inside is warm, friendly, and crowded.

GRÆNI HATTURINN

Hafnarstræti 96; tel. 354/461-4646; 8pm-3am Fri.-Sat.

Græni Hatturinn, which means "The Green Hat," is a centrally located bar that features live music and DJs. The crowd tends to be on the younger side, and it can get very loud and crowded on weekends. The opening hours vary depending on special events. Check local listings for concerts and events during the week.

ACCOMMODATIONS

Under 10,000ISK

ÞÓRUNNARSTRÆTI CAMPING

Hafnarstræti 49; tel. 354/462-3379; May-Sept.; 1,800ISK

Þórunnarstræti Camping is in an ideal location right next to the town's swimming pool and a stone's throw from shops, restaurants, and museums. The facilities are good, with hot showers and a decent cooking area. Electricity is available for 1,100ISK and washing machines for 500ISK per wash. Tent and RV campers are welcome.

HAMRAR CAMPING

Kjarnaskógur; tel. 354/461-2264; May-Sept.; 1,800ISK

Hamrar Camping is a little outside the city center, but it's larger than Þórunnarstræti and slightly less crowded. The facilities are similar, with hot showers and an adequate cooking area. Both tent and RV campers are welcome. Hookups are available.

10,000-20,000ISK

HÓTEL EDDA AKUREYRI

Þórunnarstræti; tel. 354/444-4900; www.icelandairhotels.com; June 10-Aug. 12; rooms from 15,000ISK

Hótel Edda Akureyri offers 204 rooms during the summer. The rest of the year, the hotel serves as accommodations for university students. For hotel guests, the digs are comfortable, with private bathrooms for 132 of the rooms (the rest have shared facilities), free Wi-Fi, and clean, minimalist decor. The rooms with private bathrooms are large with comfortable beds. The remaining no-frills rooms are small but clean and comfortable. A breakfast buffet is also available (adults

2,450ISK, children 6-12 1,225ISK, children 5 and under free).

AKUREYRI BACKPACKERS

Hafnarstræti 98; tel. 354/571-9050; www.akureyribackpackers.com; dorm room from 5,000ISK, private rooms from 19,000ISK

Akureyri Backpackers caters to the 20-something traveler looking for a fun atmosphere and a clean place to stay. Rooms range from privates to dormitory-style accommodations. It's a good opportunity to meet fellow travelers. The hostel's bar tends to get packed, and its restaurant frequented by young guests. Tourist information services are top-notch; there's a desk for booking tours, buying bus and flight tickets, and renting cars. A common cooking area allows you to prepare your own meals, and laundry facilities are available. Recommended for young travelers.

HÓTEL AKUREYRI

Hafnarstræti 67; tel. 354/462-5600; www.hotel-akureyri.is; rooms from 19,000ISK

Hótel Akureyri is a posh boutique hotel close to the city center. The exterior looks quaint and old-fashioned, but the inside reveals modern and tastefully decorated rooms with standard beds, private bathrooms, free Wi-Fi, and free parking. For an extra fee, you can request a room with a beautiful ocean view. A standard breakfast buffet is included in the room price.

Over 20,000 ISK

HÓTEL KEA

Hafnarstræti 87-89; tel. 354/460-2000; www.keahotels.is; rooms from 28,000ISK

Hótel Kea has modern amenities and first-class service. The 104-room hotel, which is a stone's throw from the Akureyri Church, features an elegant interior. Spacious rooms offer hardwood floors, big, comfortable beds, free Wi-Fi, satellite television, and private bathrooms. Some of the luxury stems from 24-hour room service and same-day dry-cleaning services. The hotel restaurant serves a hearty breakfast that's included in the room price.

★ ICELANDAIR HÓTEL AKUREYRI

Þingvallastræti 23; tel. 354/518-1000; www.icelandairhotels.com; rooms from 30,000ISK

Icelandair Hótel Akureyri is one of Icelandair Hótels' latest additions and one of the loveliest hotels in the north. The 99-room hotel is beautiful, with art and design accents touching every corner of the property. The lobby is rustic and Nordic chic with sheep and reindeer skins adorning gorgeous wood furniture. Rooms range from standard twins to family rooms and suites, and the clientele ranges from business travelers in town for a night to families staying multiple days. The hotel restaurant also doesn't disappoint; fresh and local ingredients go beyond traditional lamb and fish dishes. Breakfast is included in the room price.

INFORMATION AND SERVICES

TOURIST INFORMATION OFFICE

Geislagata 9; tel. 354/460-1000; www.visitakureyri.is; 10am-5pm daily

The tourist information office is based in Akureyri's city hall. It has pamphlets on tours and seasonal events, along with a gift shop that sells unique Icelandic wares.

Medical Services

If you have a medical emergency, dial 112 for help.

AKUREYRI HOSPITAL

Eyrarlandsvegi; tel. 354/463-0100; www.sak.is

North Iceland's largest hospital provides general and specialized health care services and emergency care.

AKUREYRI PHARMACY (Akureyrarapótek)

Kaupangur; tel. 354/460-9999; www.akureyrarapotek.is; 9am-6pm Mon.-Fri., 10am-4pm Sat., noon-4pm Sun.

Akureyri Pharmacy (Akureyrarapótek) is close to the swimming pool and camping area.

GETTING THERE

By Air

AKUREYRI AIRPORT

Urðargil 15; tel. 354/424-4000

Akureyri Airport sits at the base of Eyjafjörður, just 3 kilometers (1.8 mi) from the city center, and is a quite small commuter airport. Icelandair operates daily flights from **Reykjavík City Airport,** which take about 45 minutes. The flight offers spectacular views of the landscape when the weather is clear. Check flight schedules and book tickets at **Icelandair** (www.icelandair.com; starts at 18,000ISK each way).

Taxis to the airport can be hired at **Hof,** along the harbor, or arranged by your hotel or guesthouse. It's a 30-minute walk or a 5-minute drive from downtown. Taxis are available at the airport.

By Car

By car, Akureyri is 391 kilometers (243 mi) from **Reykjavík** on **Route 1.** In good weather, it will take you about five hours. Always check weather and road conditions at www.road.is before setting out on your road trip.

Parking in Akureyri is considered a sport by some. If you are a local with a personal parking space, you're in the clear. Tourists, however, must be mindful of where they park and how long they have left the car. To deal with the limited parking spaces, the town has instituted a system where you must retrieve a small cardboard clock that has movable hands from the tourist information center or local gas stations. Before you leave your car in a designated parking area, move the hands of the clock to show the current time and display it clearly on the dashboard. Most spaces allow for two-hour parking, but make sure. Also, parking attendants closely monitor the clocks, and if you are past the time, or the attendant cannot see the clock, you will be issued a fine of 15,000ISK.

By Bus

The **Strætó** 57 bus (www.straeto.is) leaves **Mjodd bus station** in **Reykjavík** a few times a week, reaching downtown Akureyri in about eight hours for 10,780ISK. Check the website for details.

By Boat

Arriving to Akureyri by sea is becoming more common, as cruise ships are increasingly adding Akureyri as a port of call. Most cruise ships dock at **Strandgata,** a few steps from downtown Akureyri.

GETTING AROUND

By Bus

Akureyri is small and walkable, but local town buses are free of charge. The **yellow buses** run 6:25am-11pm on weekdays and noon-6pm on weekends and holidays. Get a schedule from your hotel or guesthouse or from www.straeto.is.

By Taxi

BSO (Strandgata; tel. 354/461-1010; www.bso.is) is the only cab company in Akureyri, and it provides service 24 hours a day. It's possible to get taxis that can take up to eight people, as well as special cars for people with disabilities. Akureyri is a small town, but expect to pay 2,000-3,000ISK for a short ride.

Around Akureyri

LAUFÁS

tel. 354/463-3196; www.visitakureyri.is; 9am-5pm daily June 1-Aug. 31; 1,800ISK

Laufás is an ancient farm estate that gives a peek inside what life was like in the region as far back as the settlement era, complete with turf-covered houses that you can enter. The farm is even mentioned in historical records soon after the settlement of Iceland (874-930). The church on the property was built in 1865 and contains a pulpit dating from 1698, and the rectory dates from 1853. There have been numerous churches built, and then rebuilt, at the site over the centuries. It's a lovely place to spend a couple of hours, soak in the scenery, and reflect on what farm living looked like in the 19th century. There's a café in the service center, along with a small souvenir shop.

Getting There

The farm is 30 kilometers (19 mi) north of Akureyri and can be reached by **Route 83.**

TOP EXPERIENCE

★ GOÐAFOSS

In a country full of spectacular waterfalls, what sets Goðafoss apart is the sheer width of the tumbling falls. White water surges over the rim, thundering down and crashing into rocks and water. The water of the Skjálfandafljót River falls from a height of 12 meters (40 ft) over a width of 30 meters (98 ft). Curved like a horseshoe, with a rock that splits Goðafoss in two, it's quite a show to watch the waters surge over the rocky ridge. Plan to spend some time here, walking along the perimeter, snapping photos, and taking in the beauty. You can walk along the perimeter, on the rocks, but take care if the temperature drops as it can be slippery and there are no barriers at the falls. Along with Dettifoss, Goðafoss is the most visited waterfall in north Iceland.

Goðafoss, which means "waterfall of the gods," derives its name from Iceland's long history with Christianity. In AD 1000, lawyer Þorgeir Þorkelsson made Christianity the official religion of Iceland. After his conversion, Þorgeir threw his statues of the Norse gods into the waterfall. The name Goðafoss was born.

Getting There

Goðafoss is located just off **Route 1,** 50 kilometers (31 mi) east of **Akureyri** and 49 kilometers (30 mi) west of **Reykjahlíð.** It's 46 kilometers (29 mi) from **Húsavík** via **Route 85** and then **Route 845.**

HIKING MOUNT KALDBAKUR

Distance: *2.2 km (1.4 mi) round-trip*
Hiking Time: *1 hour round-trip*
Information and Maps: *www.visitakureyri.is*
Trailhead: *Several routes up the mountain, see map at tourist information office*

Fewer than 400 people call **Grenivík** home, but the small, close-knit village is a popular place to stop to take some photos of the stunning fjord and mountainous landscape or to climb **Mount Kaldbakur,** which stands at 1,167 meters (3,829 ft). Hikers rave about the view from the top, where on clear days you can get a glimpse of Hrísey Island. For hiking routes, stop by the **tourist information office** at Hof by the harbor in Akureyri (tel. 354/460-1199; www.visitakureyri.is).

Kaldbakur Tours (tel. 354/837-3770; www.kaldbaksferdir.com) offers snowcat and sledding tours January-May, starting at 9,000ISK, 4,500ISK for children 6-12, and free for children under 6.

Getting There

Grenivík is 38 kilometers (23 mi) north of **Akureyri** via **Route 83.**

1

2

Mývatn Region

Mývatn is one of the most popular tourist destinations in the northeast. Visitors are lured by gorgeous hiking trails, rich birdlife, activities along Lake Mývatn, and the soothing Mývatn Nature Baths. The region has been shaped over time by punishing volcanic eruptions. It's a place to soak in the rugged landscape, with its vast lava fields, gigantic craters, soaring mountains, and, of course, the 36.5-square-kilometer (14.1-sq-mi) lake that is home to scores of bird and fish species.

The Mývatn region is perfect for independent travelers who prefer to roam on their own time. Jump into a rental car and discover everything from the charming town of Reykjahlíð on the northeastern shore of Lake Mývatn, to roaring waterfalls, volcanic craters, and black lava rock pillars. Alternatively, you can go bird-watching, whale-watching, or on Jeep tours.

SIGHTS

★ Mývatn Nature Baths (Jarðböðin)

tel. 354/464-4411; www.myvatnnaturebaths.is; noon-10pm daily; adults 5,700ISK, children 13-15 2,700ISK, children 12 and under free (accompanied by parent)

Despite obvious comparisons to the Blue Lagoon, the Mývatn Nature Baths, 3 kilometers (1.9 mi) east of Reykjahlíð, have their own unique personality and atmosphere. There's more room to wade and fewer people in the locker rooms, and the steam baths are far from full.

The bathing experience is heavenly, soothing your skin and relaxing every inch of your body. The views of the landscape are striking, with the volcanic crater of Hverfjall and the edge of Lake Mývatn in the background.

The milky-blue water, which stands at 36°C (96.8°F), comes from the National Power Company's borehole in Bjarnaflag. The water temperature reaches a scorching 130°C (266°F) when it arrives to the basin next to the lagoon, but it cools significantly before filtering into the glorious human-made hot spring. Overall, the basin and lagoon hold about 2.5 million liters (660,000 gallons) of water.

The bottom of the lagoon is covered by gravel and sand, and it contains a large amount of minerals. Because of its chemical composition, vegetation and bacteria are not a problem. There is some sulfur in the water, which is beneficial for skin problems such as eczema and psoriasis, as well as respiratory issues. However, it's not a good idea to wear silver or brass jewelry in the water, as the pieces can be damaged by the sulfur.

Café Kvika (noon-9pm daily; snacks from 600ISK) serves light, healthy meals overlooking the lagoon, with a menu including soup, sandwiches, pastries, and a salad bar. Beer and wine are available for purchase, and you're allowed to bring drinks to the lagoon, provided you have a wristband.

From Akureyri, the Nature Baths are about 87 kilometers (54 mi) east on the **Ring Road,** about 1 hour 15 minutes.

Skútustaðagígar

From Route 1, drive across the bridge over Laxá and drive east on Route 848 for about 5 km (3 mi)

Skútustaðagígar pseudo craters are an interesting geological phenomenon in which the craters were formed by gas explosions, when hot lava from volcanic eruptions flowed over the wet, cool marshy area. The craters are a popular site for bird-watchers and are protected as a natural wetland conservation area. The craters formed when steam became trapped under the lava, leading to extreme pressure which resulted in explosions, about 2,300 years ago.

1: Laufás **2:** Goðafoss

Mývatn Region

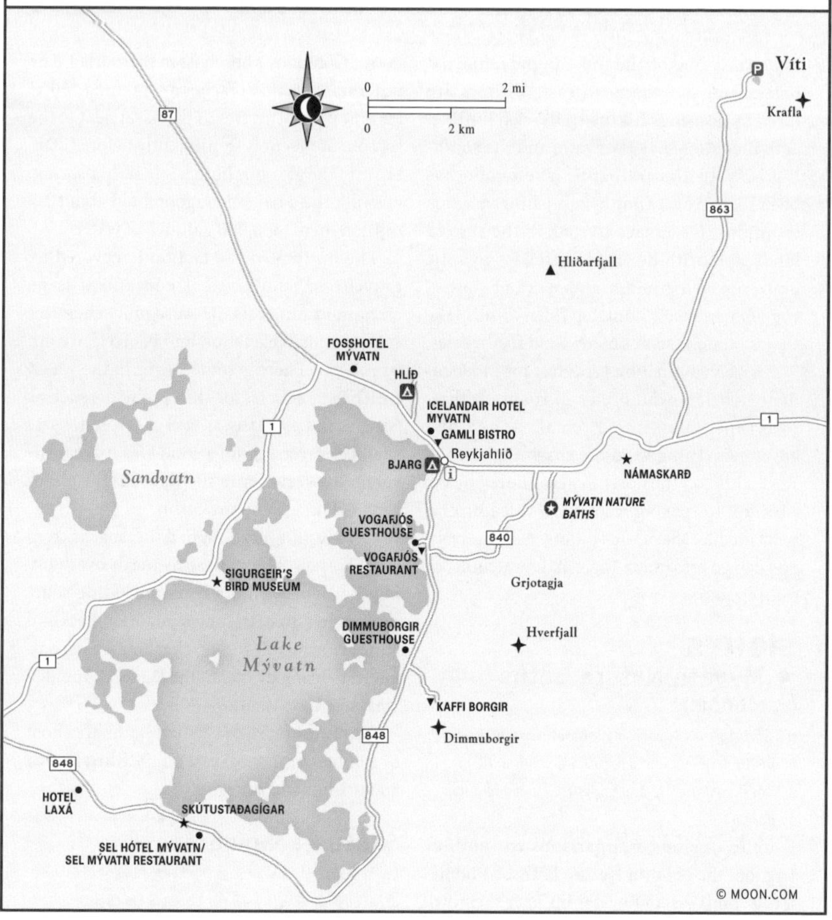

Dimmuborgir

Route 87

Dimmuborgir, which means “dark cities” or “dark castles,” comprises interesting rock formations jutting out of the ground, resembling a fort guarding an ancient city. The black lava pillars were born from a collapsed lava tube created by a large volcanic eruption more than 2,000 years ago. Scientists say that lava pooled over a small lake in the region, and as it crossed wet land the water started to boil; the vapor emitting from the lava then formed pillars, some of which reach several meters in height. There’s a popular photo opportunity in the structure known as Kirkjan (the Church), which is a curved lava tube resembling a steeple. While it’s tempting to scale many of the structures, climbing is strictly prohibited.

To get there, head south from **Húsavík,** turning onto **Route 87;** keep straight once you reach the first junction at Lake Mývatn and then follow it around the eastern edge. It is about a 45-minute drive from Húsavík.

Hverfjall

GPS coordinates N 65.6061, W 16.8751, car park 15 km (9 mi) east of Mývatn off of Route 848

Hverfjall (or Hverfell, depending on which Icelander you ask) is the largest tephra crater in the Mývatn region. Tephra craters are created from volcanic debris. The crater is striking because it's almost a perfect circle, and considering its size, 140 meters (5,511 ft) deep and 1 kilometer (0.6 mi) across, it's quite impressive. Scientists have said that the crater was formed after repeated eruptions over 2,500 years ago. There are two walking paths around the rim, one on the north side and one on the south, and it takes about 15 minutes to climb. It gives you a good view of the landscape.

Take **Route 1** to get to Hverfjall. It's 15 kilometers (9 mi) east of **Mývatn** off of **Route 848,** about a 20-minute drive.

Krafla

car park is 24 km (15 mi) northeast of Mývatn off of Route 1

The Krafla lava fields are home to **Víti** (Hell), one of the best-known craters in Iceland. Víti is huge, about 300 meters (984 ft) in diameter, exposing interesting formations that resulted from lava flows and hydrologic forces. The crater was formed during a massive volcanic eruption in 1724. The eruption continued for five years, and Víti's bubbling cauldron of mud boiled for more than a century after that. The area is another reminder of how active this island has been, and continues to be, with spectacular eruptions continually reshaping the land. Today you can visit this region to get a glimpse of the crater, hike around the area, and take in the very much alive hot springs and mud pools.

Krafla is 24 kilometers (15 mi) northeast of **Mývatn** off of **Route 1,** about a 25-minute drive. Víti is situated near Krafla, and a paved road leads up to it from Route 1. The **car park** area is right next to the rim; you should allow at least an hour for walking around the rim.

Námaskarð

15 km (9 mi) northeast of Lake Mývatn on Route 1

Námaskarð is a big draw for tourists because of its sheer otherworldly atmosphere. The yellow and brown colors of the clay, along with the gray mud pools, make it look like a movie scene from another planet. A short path loops around the region; be sure to stay on it for safety reasons, as the mud pools can reach temperatures of 100°C (212°F). The area is secluded and the smell of sulfur can be a bit much for some, but it's worth a visit.

Námaskarð is 15 kilometers (9 mi) northeast of **Lake Mývatn** on **Route 1.**

Sigurgeir's Bird Museum (Fuglasafn Sigurgeirs)

GPS coordinates N 65.6288, W 16.9951, Ytri-Neslond; tel. 354/464-4477; www.fuglasafn.is; noon-5pm daily June 1-Aug. 31, 2pm-4pm daily Sept. 1-May 14; adults 1,800ISK, children 7-14 1,000ISK, children 6 and under free

Iceland's largest privately owned mounted bird collection is at the farm Ytri-Neslond near Lake Mývatn. The museum features about 180 species of birds and more than 300 birds in total, ranging from goldeneye ducks to puffins. The birds are in glass displays, and they are labeled with information about the species. An on-site café serves coffee and snacks. Binoculars are available to use for bird-watching outside the museum. The museum was created in honor of Mývatn resident Sigurgeir Stefansson, who had a passion for birds and died tragically in an accident in 1999 at the age of 37.

Take **Route 1** to reach the bird museum, which is on the north side of the lake.

SPORTS AND RECREATION

Bird-Watching

All of Iceland has been established as a birdwatcher's paradise, but Mývatn gets particular props for hosting a few species not found in much of the island, namely the duck species—gadwall, shoveler, and common scoter. In the bay of **Neslandavík,** you can see large flocks

1

2

The Mysterious Marimo of Mývatn

A rare form of algae is disappearing from Lake Mývatn. The algae, called marimo (which means "water plant ball" in Japanese), is a round spongy moss that collects on the bottom of lakes. It exists only in this part of Iceland and parts of Japan, Scotland, and Estonia.

Iceland's marimo can be found in water that is about 2 meters (7 ft) deep, and they grow at most to 12 centimeters (5 inches) in diameter. The marimo in Mývatn was discovered in 1978. You can see the moss gently roll back and forth in the waves. The lake balls are a curiosity, as they can grow only in very specific conditions with the right amount of sediment, certain light conditions, and lake current. Perhaps most curious, for non-scientists, is the Icelandic translation: Lake balls are called kúluskítur, which means "ball of shit" in Icelandic. The numbers of marimo have been declining, and scientists are unsure as to why.

of greater scaup, Eurasian wigeon, and tufted duck species, as well as common pochard and ring-necked ducks. The **Laxa River** is a popular spot for locals to bring binoculars and a pair of boots to walk along the perimeter in search of harlequin ducks. Other waterbirds that are common to the area include the red-breasted merganser, whooper swan, and great northern diver. Short-eared owls are seen rarely. Keep your eyes peeled.

The best season for bird-watching is from the beginning of May to the middle of August, as that's the high nesting season, but some species, such as geese, remain in the autumn. Remember that the lake is a protected area, and some regions are off-limits to cars. Stop by the **tourist information office** in Reykjahlíð (Hraunvegi 8; tel. 354/464-4390; www.visitmyvatn.is) for maps and tips on where to catch certain species, and always remember to be careful of nests.

Jeep Tours

SEL HÓTEL MÝVATN

tel. 354/464-4164; www.myvatn.is/en; tours 26,0000ISK per person

Sel Hótel Mývatn offers action-packed super-Jeep tours year-round, from riding on mountain tracks in the summer to navigating on top of fresh winter snow. Tours take you to the rock formations of Dimmuborgir, the crater at Hverfjall, and some hidden places that the local tour guide knows well. It's a great option to get out and explore nature with an experienced guide who has all the safety equipment needed to handle any difficult weather conditions. Tours are about three hours.

FOOD

GAMLI BISTRO (Gamli Baerinn)

Mývatnssveit; tel. 354/464-4170; www.myvatnhotel.is; 11am-8pm daily; entrées from 2,350ISK

This cozy countryside café offers soups, sandwiches, burgers, coffee, and cakes. Try the hearty Icelandic meat soup.

KAFFI BORGIR

tel. 354/662-4748; www.kaffiborgir.is; 10am-8pm daily; entrées from 2,450ISK

Kaffi Borgir is conveniently situated near the Mývatn Nature Baths and Dimmuborgir, which means this place can get crowded in the summer months. It's a cafeteria-style café that serves hot meals like lamb or fish, coffee, and pastries. It's good for a quick bite to eat.

SEL MÝVATN RESTAURANT

Skútustaðir, Mývatn; tel. 354/464-4164; www.myvatn.is; noon-2pm and 6pm-9pm daily summer, 6pm-9pm daily winter; entrées from 2,990ISK

Sel Mývatn Restaurant, at Sel Hótel Mývatn, is your best bet for a traditional Icelandic dinner buffet featuring island delicacies, such as smoked trout and marinated salmon, and more exotic dishes, such as shark, blood

1: Mývatn Nature Baths **2:** Námaskarð

pudding, smoked lamb, liver pudding, and sheep's head jelly. But if you're not after something so exotic, don't fret, because there are plenty of fish and lamb dishes on the menu.

VOGAFJÓS RESTAURANT

Vogar; tel. 354/464-3800; www.vogafjosfarmresort.is/en; 11am-10pm daily summer, 10am-9:30pm daily winter; dinner entrées from 3,750ISK

This is a cute and quirky eatery based in a dairy barn on a family farm. While enjoying your meal of sandwiches, salads, or hot food, you can watch dairy cows get milked from the other side of a glass partition (milkings are at 7am and 6pm). Many of the ingredients are locally sourced, including the beef; the hamburger you order will literally be farm-to-table. And try the fresh mozzarella. The entire experience is worthwhile, from the cows to the quality food to the beautiful landscapes you see from the café's huge windows.

ACCOMMODATIONS

Camping

There are a couple of camping opportunities around Mývatn, but it's important to note that they become quite full during the summer months.

BJARG

tel. 354/464-4240; May-Sept.; 1,700ISK

The Bjarg campsite is situated perfectly, right next to the lakeshore of Lake Mývatn near Reykjahlíð. It's close to shops, the tourist information office, and excellent hiking trails. The facilities are top-notch, with laundry facilities, a cooking area to prepare meals, hot showers, and a place to rent bicycles. It's in an open field with no shelter. Tents and RVs are welcome.

HLÍÐ

tel. 354/464-4103; www.myvatnaccommodations.is; 2,000ISK

Hlíð is a campsite that includes cottages for rent. The camping section is on the northern shore of Lake Mývatn, and it's a short five-minute walk to the grocery store and tourist information office. It's in an open field with no shelter, in a pretty space close to the lake. It has an adequate cooking area, warm showers, and an area for tents and RVs. There are laundry facilities on-site. Two-bedroom cottages cost 40,000ISK per night and are available June-early September.

10,000-30,000ISK

DIMMUBORGIR GUESTHOUSE

Geiteyjarströnd 1, Mývatn; tel. 354/464-4210; www.dimmuborgir.is; rooms from 23,000ISK

Dimmuborgir Guesthouse offers eight double rooms with private bathrooms, as well as nine cottages. Rooms are bright and clean with simple furnishings and free Wi-Fi. A living room has a television. Cottages are roomy and wood-paneled, and half have private bathrooms. The owners are warm and friendly and have a long tradition of smoking trout in a nearby smokehouse that they love to show guests. Breakfast is included.

ICELANDAIR HÓTEL MÝVATN

Kísilvegur, Reykjahlíð; tel. 354/444-4000; www.icelandairhotels.com; rooms from 27,000ISK

Icelandair Hótel Mývatn is a smart and modern hotel with 59 spacious rooms, killer views, and accommodating staff. Rooms have big comfy beds and huge windows overlooking gorgeous scenery. The hotel **restaurant** serves up a delicious breakfast that is included in the room price. The dinner menu has all the lamb and fish dishes you'd expect.

Over 30,000ISK

VOGAFJOS GUESTHOUSE

Vogafjós Vegur, Mývatn; tel. 354/464-3800; www.vogafjosfarmresort.is; rooms from 31,000ISK

Vogafjós Guesthouse has been owned and operated by the same family for more than a century. With spectacular views of mountains and lava fields, the guesthouse offers 26 rooms. All have private bathrooms, and breakfast is included.

FOSSHOTEL MÝVATN

Grímsstaðir; tel. 354/453-0000; www.islandhotel.is; rooms from 32,000ISK

Fosshotel Mývatn opened its doors in July 2017, adding 92 rooms to the popular region. The exterior blends into the surrounding nature thanks to its turf roof, muted colors, and wood design. Rooms are bright and spacious, with modern furnishings and wood floors. Options range from standard doubles to suites with access to an outdoor hot tub. Breakfast is included in the rate of the room.

★ HOTEL LAXÁ

Olnbogaás; tel. 354/464-1900; www.hotellaxa.is; rooms from 35,000ISK

Hotel Laxá is a stylish addition to Mývatn. The 80-room hotel is modern, convenient to the major attractions in the region, and gets high points for service. During the winter months, guests can request northern lights "wake-up calls" if the natural phenomenon makes an appearance. Rooms are spacious, with large windows, wood furnishings, and modern accents. There is also an in-house restaurant and bistro bar for lighter fare.

SEL HÓTEL MÝVATN

Skútustaðir, Mývatn; tel. 354/464-4164; www.myvatn.is; rooms from 36,000ISK

Sel Hótel Mývatn is halfway between modern and quaint. The hotel's exterior is a gray block structure that looks fairly new, while the rooms boast vintage furniture, dainty linens, and all the comforts of home. The in-house restaurant does a fantastic Icelandic dinner buffet.

INFORMATION AND SERVICES

TOURIST INFORMATION CENTER

Hraunvegi 8, Reykjahlíð; tel. 354/464-4460; www.visitmyvatn.is; 8am-6pm daily June-Sept.

Mývatn's tourist information center offers Internet access, pamphlets about the region, and the chance to book local tours.

GETTING THERE

It's best to have a **car** to explore the region or to book a **tour** from **Akureyri.**

By car, Lake Mývatn is 92 kilometers (57 mi) east of Akureyri on **Route 1.** The town of **Reykjahlíð** connects to paved **Route 848,** which follows Lake Mývatn's northern edge. The lake's perimeter is about 40 kilometers (25 mi).

Húsavík

Húsavík has transformed itself from a placid small town with little appeal to the outside world to a must-see destination for tourists interested in some of the best **whale-watching** opportunities on the island. Húsavík is home to fewer than 3,000 full-time residents, but in the summer the numbers spike dramatically as Icelanders from other towns, tourists coming in on bus tours, and independent travelers converge on Húsavík's harbor. The main draw for tourists is, of course, whale-watching tours, but the charm of the small town, with its tasty restaurants and classic Icelandic hospitality, makes this a destination to consider even if you're not up for a boat tour.

Húsavík was in the spotlight in 2020 for a very different, funny reason: The movie *Eurovision Song Contest: The Story of Fire Saga* was filmed in the town. Locals loved hosting Will Ferrell, Rachel McAdams, Pierce Brosnan, and the crew during the shoot and were inspired to open a Eurovision Museum in 2021.

SIGHTS

Húsavík Whale Museum (Hvalasafnið á Húsavík)

Hafnarstétt 1; tel. 354/414-2800; www.hvalasafn.is/en; 9am-6pm daily June-Sept., 9am-4pm daily Oct.-Nov., by appointment rest of the year; adults

2,000ISK, children 17 and under free (must be accompanied by an adult)

The Húsavík Whale Museum is a comprehensive museum on Iceland's most famous marine mammals. The exhibits have been developed and maintained with great care, and the curator clearly has a passion for whales. The museum, which is housed in a huge building that used to be a slaughterhouse, provides information on the whale species that inhabit the waters off Iceland's coasts as well as whale ecology and conservation. There are 10 different whale skeletons to check out, as well as a sperm whale jawbone that is the size of a car. It's incredible to stand next to it. Short films available in English teach about whales, and a library has a large selection of marine books. If you visit only one museum in Húsavík, this should be it.

Eurovision Song Contest Exhibition

Laugarbrekka 26; tel. 354/848-7600; www.husavikhotel.com/eurovision; open daily 4pm-10pm; free

Housed in the Húsavík Cape Hotel, the Eurovision exhibition was created after the Will Ferrell movie *Eurovision Song Contest: The Story of Fire Saga* was filmed in Húsavík. The exhibition collection includes items from Icelandic Eurovision participants as well as costumes and props from the *Story of Fire Saga* movie. This is a fun, kitchsy stop in the small town, and Eurovision fans will love it.

Exploration Museum

(Könnunarsögusafnið)

Höfði 24; tel. 354/463-3399; www.explorationmuseum.com; 11am-4pm May 1-Sept. 30, open by request rest of year; free

The Exploration Museum focuses on various types of exploration, from Vikings coming to Iceland to Americans landing on the moon. Maps and photographs are on display, and documentaries about Apollo astronauts training in Húsavík before missions are available in English. It may not sound like it makes sense, but the exhibits work, doing a nice job of tying Viking captains, arctic explorers, and astronauts together.

Culture House at Húsavík

(Safnahúsið á Húsavík)

Stóragarði 17; tel. 354/464-1860; www.husmus.is; 10am-6pm Mon.-Fri., 1pm-5pm Sat.-Sun. June 1-Aug. 31, 10am-5pm Mon.-Fri., 10am-3pm Sat. Sept. 1-May 31; 1,500ISK

The Culture House at Húsavík features two fantastic exhibitions that provide a window into life in Húsavík over the ages. The first exhibit has a maritime theme and includes a number of boats, many of which were built in Húsavík. Other displays include fishing equipment, tools used for seal and shark hunting, and photos and documentaries in English. The second exhibit focuses on daily life and natural history in the region. Here you can view homemade objects and crafts and learn about subsistence farming. Regional archives and a library are on-site.

Húsavíkurkirkja

9am-11am and 3pm-5pm daily June-Aug.; free

Located close to the harbor, the Húsavíkurkirkja is one of the town's most significant landmarks. Built in 1907, the Húsavík Church stands 26 meters (85 ft) high and has a white exterior with reddish-brown trim and a dark green steeple/roof. The interior features strong wood beams, beautiful windows, and red-cushioned pews. Icelandic state architect Rögnvaldur Ólafsson designed the church, and all of the wood used to construct it was imported from Norway. The painting behind the altar is revered by town locals. Icelandic artist Sveinn Thórarinsson was commissioned to portray the resurrection of Lazarus for the church. His work incorporated Iceland's landscape, including the mountains and mist of Dettifoss.

1: Húsavíkurkirkja **2:** a whale in Húsavík

1
2
KNÖRRINN

SPORTS AND RECREATION

★ Whale-Watching

If you leave Húsavík without getting on a whale-watching boat to view the gentle giants up close, you're missing out. The main whale-watching season runs from the middle of May to the end of October, but the high season is June and July. That time frame is your best chance to see as many as 12 species of whales, with the most common being minke and humpback whales. If you're lucky, you'll spot fin whales, orcas, and blue whales. You can always count on sighting dolphins, as they love to hang out close to the bay. Many of the guides are passionate about whales and love sharing stories about up-close-and-personal encounters.

Three main companies offer whale-watching tours. Each company operates boats of different sizes and all have stellar reputations for ethical environmental practices. The tours are about three hours and depart daily.

- **Gentle Giants** (tel. 354/464-1500; www.gentlegiants.is; adults 10,790ISK, children 7-15 4,490ISK, children 6 and under free), April 1-November 30
- **North Sailing** (tel. 354/464-7272; www.northsailing.is; adults 10,990ISK, children 7-15 4,000ISK, children 6 and under free), March 1-October 14
- **Salka** (tel. 354/464-3999; www.salkawhale-watching.is; adults 10,500ISK, children 7-15 4,200ISK, children 6 and under free), mid-May-mid-September

Bring your camera, plus a pair of binoculars if you're inclined, and dress warmly, even in the summer. The tours do venture out into the open ocean and sea conditions vary according to the weather; it can get very wet and windy. Bring a hat, gloves, scarf, and layers, including a waterproof layer.

Pools and Hot Springs

GEOSEA GEOTHERMAL SEA BATHS

Vitaslóð 1; tel. 354/464-1210; www.geosea.is/en; noon-10pm daily Sept. 1-May 31, 11am-11pm daily June 1-Aug. 31; adults 4,900ISK, children 6-16 2,200ISK, children 5 and younger free

Húsavík's newest swimming facility is the GeoSea Geothermal Sea Baths. The baths, located along the coast of Húsavík, harness naturally heated geothermal water from Húsavikurhöfði, and bathers enjoy the water at a temperature of 38-39°C (102-104°F). The concrete structure has a curvy shape, and an inner ledge allows guests to sit comfortably in the water. There is a **restaurant** on-site that serves soups, sandwiches, pastries, and juices as well as beer and wine.

HÚSAVÍK SWIMMING POOL

Héðinsbraut; tel. 354/464-1144; 6:45am-9pm Mon.-Fri., 10am-5pm Sat.-Sun.; 950ISK

The Húsavík Swimming Pool is close to the campsite, which means it can get pretty crowded in the summer. Besides the pool, a couple of hot tubs also draw a crowd.

FOOD

SALKA RESTAURANT

Garðarsbraut 4; tel. 354/464-2551; 11:30am-10pm daily; entrées from 2,800ISK

Salka Restaurant is a harborside eatery that is owned by a whale-watching company. The food is good but predictable, though the pizzas are quite nice. There are also soups, sandwiches, hamburgers, and fish and lamb dishes on the menu. The restaurant is proudly whale friendly, so whale meat is not an option.

★ NAUSTIÐ

Naustagarður 2; tel. 354/464-1520; noon-10pm daily; entrées from 2,800ISK

Naustið is known for its seafood. The restaurant uses fresh ingredients and local fish including cod, salmon, and blue ling. An outdoor eating area is delightful in good weather, and local musicians often play concerts. The interior is rustic, with wood-paneled walls and seafaring-related artwork.

GAMLÍ BAUKUR

Hafnarstett 9; tel. 354/464-2442; www.gamlibaukur.is; 11:30am-11pm daily; entrées from 2,900ISK

Gamlí Baukur is a unique restaurant built from driftwood found along the coastline of Húsavík. The rustic vibe continues inside, with large tables and photos of the town's fishing history adorning the walls. The food is hearty, and the fish and lamb dishes hit the spot. The meat soup is also divine. The casual ambience of the restaurant carries over to the evening, when it transforms into a concert venue for local and visiting Icelandic acts. The combination of good music and good beer is hard to beat.

ACCOMMODATIONS

Under 10,000ISK

HÚSAVÍK CAMPGROUND

Héðinsbraut; tel. 354/845-0705; May 15-Sept. 30; 1,600ISK

The Húsavík Campground regularly receives kudos. It's a well-maintained, large, and efficient facility that is wildly popular in June and July. The kitchen area is great and the showers are steaming hot. The campground, which is close to the center of town, is situated in an open field with no shelter. Tents and RVs are welcome. Electricity is available for 800ISK per day.

10,000-30,000ISK

HÚSAVÍK GUESTHOUSE

Laugarbrekka 16; tel. 354/463-3399; www.husavikguesthouse.is; rooms from 19,000ISK

Húsavík Guesthouse is a family-run guesthouse with options ranging from singles to family rooms. The atmosphere looks and feels very much like you're staying in a comfortable, well-loved home. There's art on the walls, jam-packed bookshelves with everything from novels to travel guides, and comfortable guest rooms. Guests share bathroom facilities, and breakfast is included.

ÁRBÓL GUESTHOUSE

Ásgarðsvegur 2; tel. 354/464-2220; www.arbol.is; rooms from 20,250ISK

Árból Guesthouse is a quaint guesthouse close to the center of town. Some of the rooms have the look of a wood-paneled hunting lodge, while others look like you're staying at your grandmother's house. The rooms (singles, doubles, triples, and family rooms) are clean and comfortable and a bit larger than average. All rooms share bathroom facilities, and breakfast is included.

HÚSAVÍK CAPE HOTEL

Laugarbrekka 26; tel. 354/463-3399; www.husavikhotel.com; rooms from 26,000ISK

Húsavík Cape Hotel is housed in a historic 1950 building that was owned by the Húsavík Fishing Company. In 2012 it was transformed into a smart and rustic hotel, complete with standard beds, hardwood floors, and simple furnishings. Guests have access to free Wi-Fi, and breakfast is included.

FOSSHOTEL HÚSAVÍK

Ketilsbraut 22; tel. 354/464-1220; www.islandshotel.is; rooms from 27,000ISK

Fosshotel Húsavík is a 70-room hotel, with 44 standard rooms and 26 superior rooms with king-size beds, satellite TV, and private bathrooms. The hotel is decorated in nautical accents, and superior rooms have a fun and fresh whale theme to the decor. The hotel's bar and restaurant is appropriately called Moby Dick, serving fresh fish and other traditional Icelandic cuisine. Guests have access to free Wi-Fi and free parking, and breakfast is included.

INFORMATION AND SERVICES

TOURIST INFORMATION OFFICE

Hafnarstett 1; tel. 354/464-4300; www.visithusavik.is; 10am-4pm daily June-Sept.

The tourist office is close to the harbor and offers Internet access, pamphlets about the region, and tour bookings.

GETTING THERE

By Car

By car, Húsavík is 90 kilometers (56 mi) northeast of **Akureyri** via paved **Route 85,** and it's 56 kilometers (35 mi) north of **Mývatn** on **Route 87,** which is also paved.

By Air

HÚSAVIK AIRPORT

10 km (6 mi) southwest of town; tel. 354/424-4000

Húsavík Airport is 10 kilometers (6 mi) south of the center of Húsavík. **Eagle Air** (tel. 354/562-4200; www.eagleair.is) offers 10 flights a week from **Reykjavík.** It's about a 45-minute flight and costs about 25,000ISK each way.

Jökulsárgljúfur (Vatnajökull National Park–North)

Jökulsárgljúfur National Park was established in 1973 and became part of Vatnajökull National Park in 2008, forming the largest national park in Europe. Jökulsárgljúfur is the northern division of Vatnajökull National Park. Within it are some of North Iceland's most visited sites, including Dettifoss and Ásbyrgi. Several well-maintained hiking trails travel along the perimeter of waterfalls, rivers, and canyons. Many tourists stop at Dettifoss to photograph the powerful waterfall, but the park has other treasures that are worthy of a longer visit; the mountainous landscape is breathtaking. Try to spend at least one day in this area.

Note that hikers must register with the park office at Ásbyrgi before they set out on their journey. Safety first.

SIGHTS

★ Ásbyrgi

Route 85

Ásbyrgi (Shelter of the Gods) is an enormous canyon full of interesting rock formations, lush grass, well-maintained walking paths, thriving birdlife, and several bodies of water, including rivers and waterfalls. The horseshoe-shaped canyon measures roughly 3.5 kilometers (2.2 mi) in length and 1.1 kilometers (0.7 mi) across.

Scientists have said that Ásbyrgi was most likely formed by glacial flooding of the Jökulsá á Fjöllum River after the last ice age, and additional flooding some 3,000 years ago. However, Icelandic folklore has a different explanation for the canyon's unique shape: It has been nicknamed Sleipnir's Footprint, after the legend that the canyon was formed when Odin's eight-legged horse, Sleipnir, touched one of its feet to the ground, creating the depressions. Folklore also stipulates that the canyon is the central meeting point of the huldufólk (hidden people) who live among the cliffs.

Tourists make the trek to Ásbyrgi to take in the steep rock formations and enjoy a **hike.** In some spots hikers have to be careful in navigating the rocks. Be sure to wear proper footwear and take caution over any slippery-looking patches. One easy hike, which is about one kilometer (0.6 mi) and takes 30-60 minutes, starts at the **car park** at Ásbyrgi and leads to a platform at a small pond named **Botnstjörn.** Along the way are lots of trees, shrubbery, and rock formations. A lovely view over the pond takes in ducks and other birds and offers vistas of the western side of the canyon.

Ásbyrgi is 65 kilometers (40 mi) south of **Húsavík.** To reach the **visitors center** (Gljúfrastofa; tel. 354/470-7100) in Ásbyrgi from Húsavík, take paved **Route 85.**

Hólmatungur

Route 85

Hólmatungur is an area on the western side of the canyon of the glacial **Jökulsá river** that has breathtaking basalt column formations, along with choppy streams and the wondrous waterfall **Rettarfoss.** It's a beautiful spot that offers scenic views and wonderful photo ops.

To reach Hólmatungur from **Ásbyrgi**

and **Route 85,** head south on **Route 862,** which is on the west side of the **Jökulsá.** Route 862 is a gravel road between Route 85 and **Dettifoss.** (Heading south of Dettifoss to Route 1, the road is paved.) Hólmantungur lies along this unpaved stretch. The gravel road is passable for normal vehicles, but it's closed during wintertime and does not open until late **May** or early **June.**

TOP EXPERIENCE

★ Dettifoss

Route 862

Dettifoss, which means "tumble falls," is the largest waterfall on the island, and the most powerful in Europe, with an average flow of 200 cubic meters (70 tons) of water per second. During an especially rainy day, the flow can reach 500 cubic meters (176 tons) per second. This force is not because of the fall's height, but its width. Spanning 100 meters (329 ft) wide and 45 meters (148 ft) high, Dettifoss is gigantic. The grayish color of the water comes from sand and rocks that get picked up along the way.

Because of the waterfall's size and sheer beauty, plan to spend at least a couple of hours here to take it all in. There are several viewing platforms. This is an open, slippery spot with lots of steps and minimal guardrails; be careful. If you're visiting on a windy day, expect to get hit with spray—but that's part of the fun, to really experience the falls. It's also common to see a rainbow or two depending on the weather.

Tour companies include Dettifoss as part of the **"Diamond Circle,"** a popular route around the Mývatn region and Húsavík, based in Akureyri. For a day tour, check out **Reykjavík Excursions** (tel. 354/580-5400; www.re.is).

Dettifoss is 28 kilometers (17 mi) south of **Ásbyrgi.** From Ásbyrgi and **Route 85,** head south on **Route 862** on the west side of the river **Jökulsá.** Route 862 is a gravel road between Route 85 and Dettifoss. (Heading south of Dettifoss to **Route 1,** the road is paved.) The gravel road is passable for normal vehicles, but it's closed during wintertime and does not open until late **May** or early **June.**

HIKING

Vatnajökull National Park is a lovely place for hiking in the summer as there are many marked trails. Hiking maps for the park are available in the visitor centers and

Dettifoss

Visiting Vatnajökull National Park

Dettifoss, Vatnajökull National Park

Vatnajökull National Park (www.vatnajokulsthjodgardur.is), which was named a UNESCO World Heritage site in 2019, is huge, covering 13 percent of the island and 13,700 square kilometers (5,290 sq mi), and is the largest national park in western Europe.

Jökulsárgljúfur National Park and **Skaftafell National Park** were combined with **Vatnajökull glacier** in 2008 to form Vatnajökull National Park. Jökulsárgljúfur and Skaftafell are now considered the northern and southern divisions of the park.

Vatnajökull National Park has several **visitors centers;** some of the main ones are listed here.

- **Jökulsárgljúfur visitors center** (Ásbyrgi; tel. 354/465-2195; www.ust.is; 11am-3pm daily) is the best gateway to the **northern part** of the park and blockbuster sights like the Ásbyrgi canyon and Dettifoss.
- **Snæfellsstofa visitors center** (Skriðuklaustur; tel. 354/470-0840; 9am-3pm daily June 1-Aug. 31, 10am-4pm daily Sept., open by request in winter) serves as a gateway to the **eastern part** of the park and Mount Snæfell (page 242).
- **Skaftafell visitors center** (Skaftafellsvegur, 785 Öræfi; tel. 354/470-8300; www.vatnajokulsthjodgardur.is; 10am-4pm daily Jan.-May, 8am-7pm daily June-Aug., 9am-7pm daily Sept., 10am-5pm daily Oct.-Dec.) serves as both a national park office and visitors center near the **southern entrance** to the park.

There are no roads in the national park except for the tracks leading up to private farms. Wardens operate in the park, assisted by park rangers during the summer months (June-Aug.). Visitors are encouraged to seek information and advice from park staff, who can teach visitors about the area and its history, ecology, and geology. There are a variety of hikes throughout the park and everyone should be able to find a suitable outing.

information offices. It is not recommended to embark on solo hikes in the winter months.

SVARTIFOSS-SEL

Distance: *5.5 km (3.4 mi) round-trip*
Hiking Time: *2 hours round-trip*
Information and Maps: *www.vatnajokulsthjodgardur.is/en*
Trailhead: *Skaftafell visitors center*

Starting from the Skaftafell visitors center, you'll cross through the campground, following the signs along the trail until you reach a viewpoint above Svartifoss, revealing a spectacular view of water thrashing against basalt columns before falling below. In the summer months, the bright green moss against the black basalt rocks is stunning. After spending some time at the viewpoint, continue down to the ravine, cross a small bridge and scale the basalt rock steps, and continue on the trail. You will walk toward the old turf house at Sel, which is an interesting look at how life was in Iceland in the old days. This is an easy hike on a relatively flat trail.

SKAFTAFELLSJÖKULL

Distance: *3.7-km (2.2-mi) loop*
Hiking Time: *1.5-hour loop*
Information and Maps: *www.vatnajokulsthjodgardur.is/en*
Trailhead: *Skaftafell visitors center*

This easy hike, which follows a paved trail, begins at the Skaftafell visitors center. Along the way, you will see an open, vast landscape with few trees and a looming glacier ahead of you. The trail leads to the impressive glacier, Skaftafellsjökull. You can get a close look of the glacier, but be sure to follow safety warnings explained on a sign at the end of the trail. Under no circumstances should you walk on a glacier without a guide. Enjoy the glacier safely, marveling at the colors and shapes of the ice.

ACCOMMODATIONS

ÁSBYRGI CAMPGROUND

tel. 354/470-7100; mid-May-Sept.; 1,500ISK

You won't find any hotels or guesthouses within the park limits; the only option for overnight guests is the Ásbyrgi campground. The site, which is situated in an open field, is open from mid-May through September and allows for 350 tents as well as RVs (with hookups). There are adequate cooking facilities, hot showers, and a small shop that sells some food and hiking gear. Bring all the food, water, and supplies you need with you.

INFORMATION AND SERVICES

TOURIST INFORMATION CENTER

tel. 354/465-2195; www.ust.is; 11am-3pm daily

The national park's tourist information center is based at Ásbyrgi and is open year-round.

GETTING THERE AND AROUND

It's best to have a car to explore the park. Keep in mind that while Jökulsárgljúfur is open year-round, the roads beyond **Ásbyrgi,** including **Route 862,** are closed during wintertime and do not open until late **May** or early **June.**

East Iceland and the Eastfjords

East Iceland is where you find some actual "ice," including Vatnajökull glacier, a giant white spot on the map that is truly breathtaking in person. You can drive or hike right up to the glacier's edge in Skaftafell.

In the summer, it can be crowded with fellow travelers, but there are plenty of detours to take to avoid the hordes. Lacking infrastructure and people, the east is one of the most remote parts of the island, and travel can be difficult in winter.

One of the least visited destinations in Iceland is one you should keep on your radar: the Eastfjords. If you're looking for remote, unspoiled beauty, it's here. The Ring Road weaves through the fjords, where you will see gorgeous mountains, charming fishing villages, and

Highlights

Look for ★ to find recommended sights, activities, dining, and lodging.

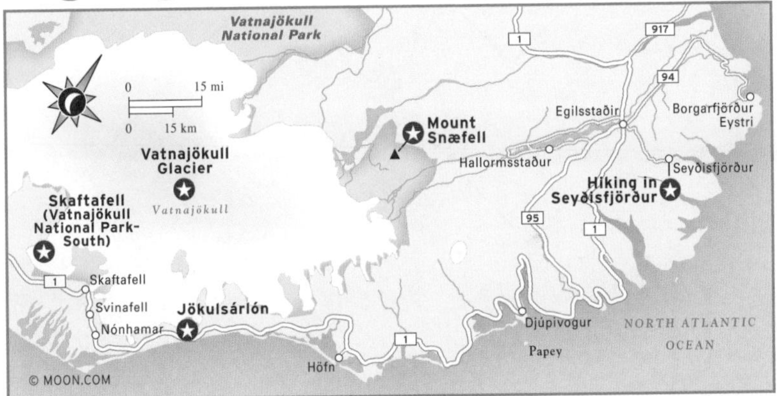

★ **Mount Snæfell:** It's only a moderate hike to the top of Iceland's highest mountain, where views span from the highlands to Vatnajökull and all the way out to sea (page 241).

★ **Hiking in Seyðisfjörður:** This tiny town of fewer than 1,000 residents offers a variety of hiking gems for hikers of all levels (page 246).

★ **Vatnajökull Glacier:** Covering about 8 percent of the country, this is the biggest glacier in Europe—and under the ice cap are still-active volcanoes (page 258).

★ **Jökulsárlón:** At the Glacier Lagoon, the deepest lake in Iceland, huge blocks of ice constantly break off a glacier and float on the surface (page 260).

★ **Skaftafell (Vatnajökull National Park–South):** One of East Iceland's most beautiful places has striking white glaciers set against a backdrop of green fields and black sands (page 260).

East Iceland and the Eastfjords

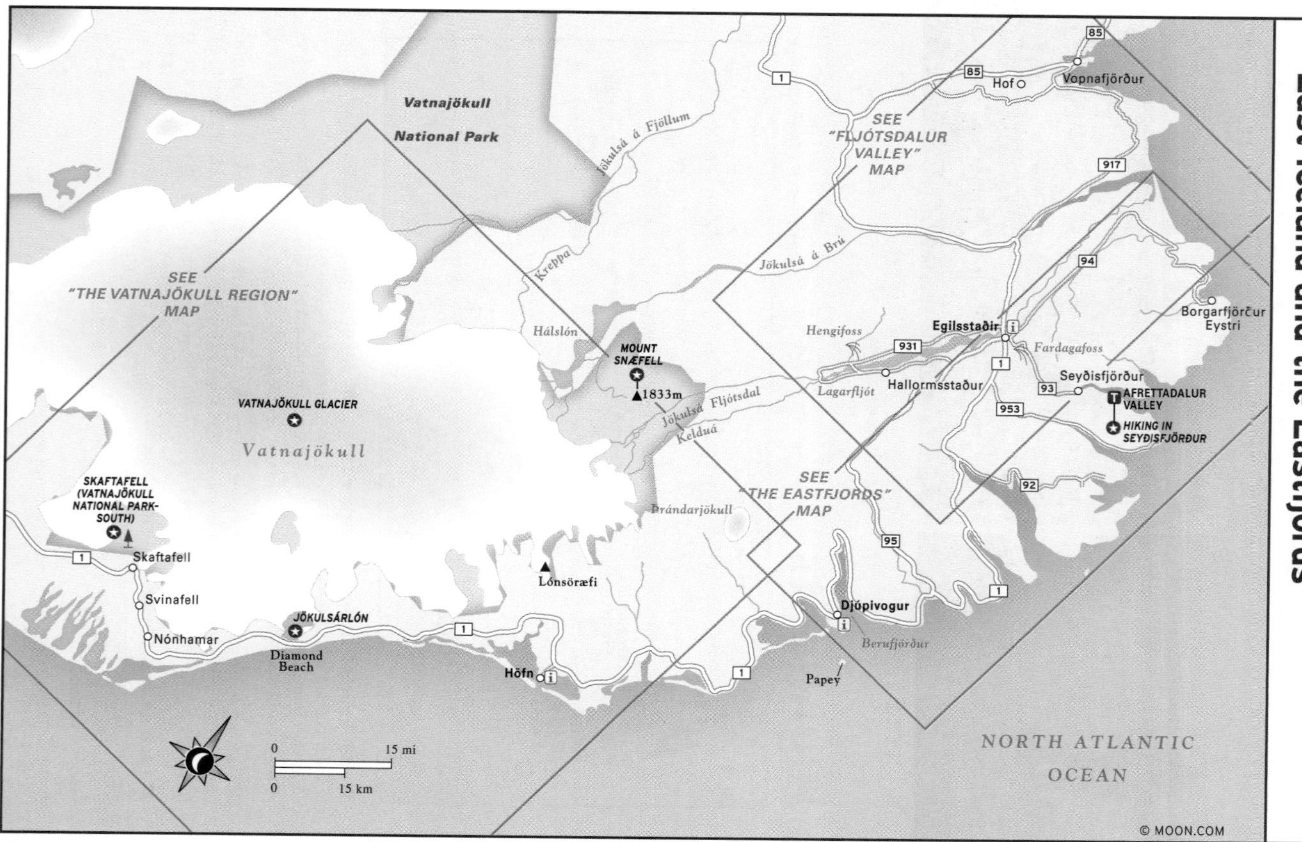

thriving wildlife. It's not easy to get around the region (you need a car), but it's worth the costs and trouble.

The east is also home to one of the most active volcanic areas on the island, and Vatnajökull National Park deserves at least one day of its own. Navigating the glacier (with a guide and proper equipment) is one of those unforgettable, bucket-list excursions.

East Iceland is often overlooked, but it has some of the most pristine, untouched nature in Iceland. If you can spare a couple of days, spend some time hiking and photographing the Eastfjords. Even during the high season, there's a good chance you won't bump into many other tourists. The east can be your own private treasure.

PLANNING YOUR TIME

East Iceland is not conducive to tight schedules, as weather can be unpredictable. It's best to visit in the **late spring, summer,** or **early autumn.** Winter travel to and around the area is challenging. The wind and snow can make travel here difficult at best, dangerous at worst. Monitor weather conditions closely and check to see if roads have been closed.

The **Ring Road (Route 1)** takes you through the east, and most people choose either **Egilsstaðir** or **Seyðisfjörður** as a base. Both towns are complete with guesthouses, restaurants, bus stations, and airports. Some guesthouses and restaurants operate only June-August. Seyðisfjörður is the best option for an extended stay in the Eastfjords.

The east is a paradise for hikers, as there are numerous places to roam and experience the pristine nature of the region with few fellow travelers nearby. The east is sparsely populated and many tourists drive past the region to get from Höfn to Mývatn. Dedicate three days to enjoy the natural wonders such as **Jökulsárlón** and **Svartifoss** and to also have some time to hike.

Itinerary Ideas

THREE DAYS IN EAST ICELAND

Day 1: Scenic Skaftafell and Vatnajökull National Park

Pack a **lunch** today, as restaurant options are scarce and you have an active day.

1 First, visit **Skaftafellsstofa Visitor Center** for maps and an orientation of the region.

2 From the visitors center, you can take a quick, mile-long hike to **Svartifoss** waterfall and photograph the unique basalt columns surrounding the falls.

3 Call ahead to Icelandic Mountain Guides to arrange for a glacier hike on the **Svinafellsjökull** glacier tongue.

4 After a busy day of hiking, have dinner and spend the night at **Hótel Skaftafell.**

Day 2: Exploring Jökulsárlón and Höfn

1 Start the day with a drive to **Fjallsárlón,** a small glacier lagoon, where you can walk along the calm shore and take photos.

Previous: Seyðisfjörður; Skaftafell; Glacier Lagoon ice in Vatnajökull National Park.

Itinerary Ideas

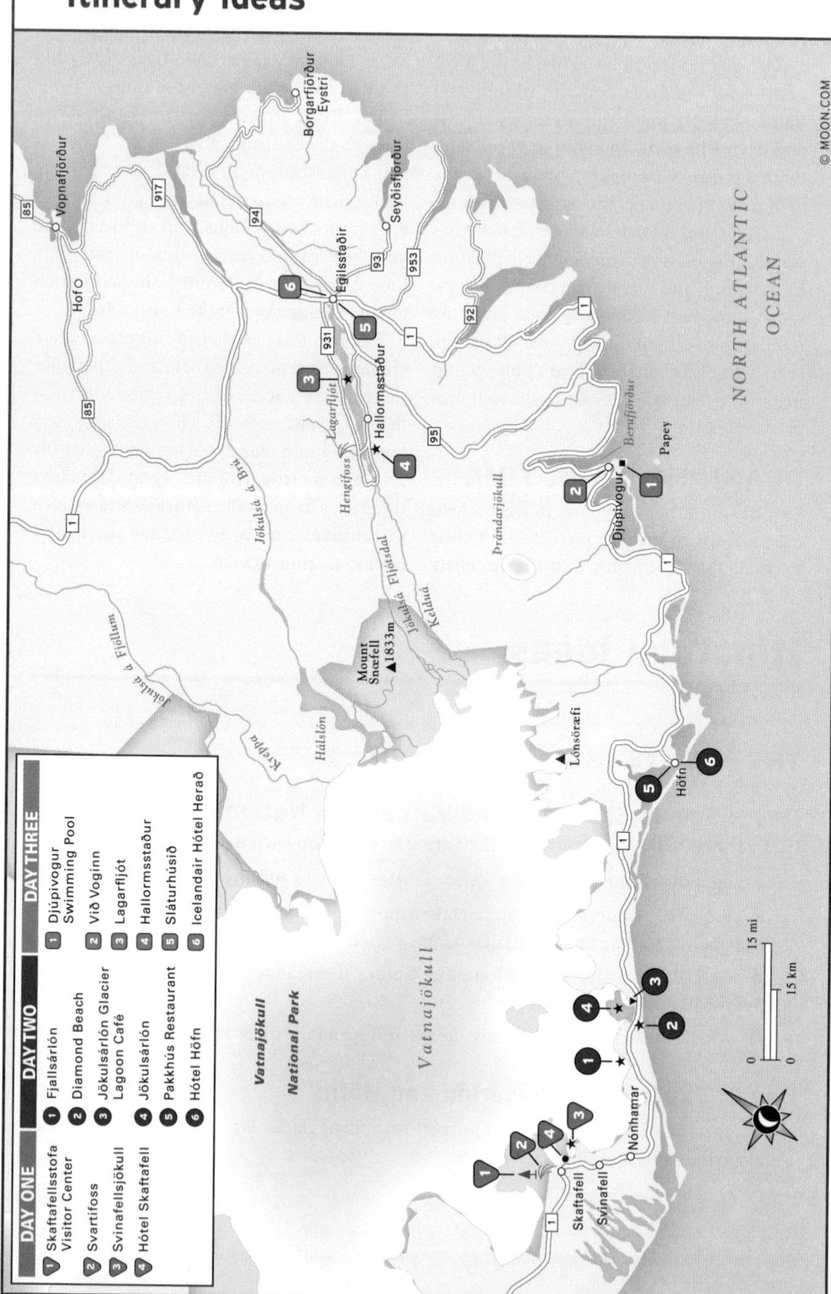

2 Get back in your car for a 10-minute drive to the **Diamond Beach,** where polished pieces of ice lie atop the rich black sands, resembling diamonds.

3 Have lunch at the **Jökulsárlón Glacier Lagoon café** before walking along the shore, admiring the icebergs.

4 Take a guided boat tour on **Jökulsárlón** with Glacier Lagoon to get up close to the mammoth icebergs bobbing in the lagoon.

5 Drive to Höfn and explore the harbor area before having dinner at **Pakkhús Restaurant.**

6 Spend the night at **Hótel Höfn.**

Day 3: The Charming Eastfjords

1 Make your way farther east to the beautiful town of Djúpivogur and explore the harbor area before relaxing at the **Djúpivogur swimming pool.**

2 Stop by **Við Voginn** in Djúpivogur for lunch.

3 Continue north to walk along **Lagarfljót,** Iceland's own Loch Ness.

4 Roam around the largest forested area in Iceland, **Hallormsstaður.**

5 Drive to Egilsstaðir and visit **Sláturhúsið,** a cultural center with art exhibitions.

6 Have dinner and spend the night at **Icelandair Hótel Herað.**

Vopnafjörður

Vopnafjörður (Weapon Fjord) is full of picturesque mountains, pure waterfalls, and historic farms. It's one of the best spots to get a glimpse of orcas. It's pretty, steeped in medieval history, and home to gorgeous wildlife.

The history of the town, also called Vopnafjörður, dates back 1,100 years. The bay was first settled by Viking seafarers from Norway. Foreign merchants frequently sailed to Vopnafjörður in the early modern age, and a settlement gradually formed on the peninsula where the village of Vopnafjörður now stands. It became one of Iceland's major commercial harbors in the 18th and 19th centuries. In the last half century, the fishing industry has grown considerably, and is today the largest business sector in the area.

The town has also had an impact on literature: *Independent People,* the epic Icelandic novel by Nobel Prize winner Halldór Laxness, was said to have been inspired by life in the highlands around Vopnafjörður.

SIGHTS

Bustarfell

off Route 85 about 20 km (12 mi) south of Vopnafjörður; tel. 354/855-4511; www.visitvopnafjordur.com; 10am-5pm daily June 1-Sept. 20; 1,100ISK

The old farm of Bustarfell is one of the best-preserved of the traditional Icelandic turf houses. The museum offers a great opportunity to see how people's ways of living have changed through the centuries. The foundations of the current house are from 1770, but the house has undergone alterations over the years. The rooms are authentically furnished in the style of centuries past. The museum covers life from the 18th century to the mid-20th century. The **café** is a good spot to enjoy coffee, light meals, and yummy pastries as well as exhibitions from local artists.

East Iceland Emigration Center (Vesturfaramiðstöð Austurlands)

Kaupvangur 2; tel. 354/473-1200; www.visitvopnafjordur.com; 10am-5pm Mon., Thurs., and Sat. June 1-Sept. 20, 10am-5pm Mon. and Thurs. Sept. 21 May 31; free

The East Iceland Emigration Center is dedicated to the period of 1875-1914, when many residents emigrated from the region after the great Askja eruption of 1875 displaced hundreds. The center is focused on the history of the region and renewing contact with emigrants' descendants. There are documents and photos on display.

Múlastofa Cultural Center

Hafnarbyggð 4a; tel. 354/473-1331; www.visitvopnafjordur.com; 10am-10pm daily June 1-Aug. 25; 600ISK

This small exhibition is dedicated to local brothers Jón Múli Árnason and Jónas Árnason. Both were writers, singers, and musicians who grew up in Vopnafjörður, and their father managed the general store between 1917-1924. On display are photographs, videos, and interactive exhibits where guests can listen to the brothers speak, sing, and perform plays.

Fuglabjarganes

Strandhafnarvegur, off Route 85

Fuglabjarganes is a prominent cliff that juts out on the northern coast of the town. You can get a good look at it from a marked walking path from the unpaved **Strandhafnarvegur road,** which is along the **Fugla River.** The scenery is beautiful, with white sand beaches, stone walls, towering cliffs, and impressive rock caverns and pillars.

SPORTS AND RECREATION

Bird-Watching

Vopnafjörður is a bird-watcher's dream. You can see a mix of seabirds, waterfowl, waders, passerines, and raptors. A couple of the best spots to see birds are the **Tangi Peninsula** north of Vopnafjörður, which is a beautiful and remote place to watch seabirds, and the area around the **Nypslon estuary,** which provides habitat for various duck species. The region can be reached from **Route 85** and is signposted.

Fishing

There are several fishing opportunities, through tours, within a few minutes' drive of Vopnafjörður.

HOFSA RIVER

92 km (57 mi) from Égilsstaðir via Route 917

The Hofsa River is just a 15-minute drive east from Vopnafjörður, and the stretch of the river open to angling encompasses 30 kilometers (19 mi) in a wide valley. Salmon season runs **July 1-September 20. Permits** are needed and must be secured in advance. For details on permits, visit the region's website (www.vopnafjordur.com/activities/angling).

SELA RIVER

100 km (62 mi) from Egilsstaðir via Route 917

The Sela River is a 10-minute drive north from Vopnafjörður and has long been one of the most popular of Icelandic salmon rivers. Fishing is fly only, and the river has a catch-and-release system in place. **Guides,** like Anglers (www.anglers.is), are available.

VESTURDALSA RIVER

92 km (57 mi) from Égilsstaðir via Route 917

Fifteen minutes south of Vopnafjörður, the Vesturdalsa River originates from the runoff of **Lake Arnarvatn** in the highlands above Vopnafjörður, flows 34 kilometers (21 mi) to the lowlands, and empties into **Nypslon estuary.** The fishing area reaches 27 kilometers (17 mi) up to a waterfall not accessible to salmon. A catch-and-release policy is in effect.

Hiking

Vopnafjörður offers several hiking routes that vary from easy to challenging. Beginners will find a wide range of mapped routes and marked trails that offer scenic views of the whole of Vopnafjörður—the **bay,** the **Tangi Peninsula,** inland areas, and mountains. For maps and detailed trail information, visit the

tourist information center, and always be sure to check the weather forecast and report your itinerary.

GLJUFURSA RIVER HIKE

Distance: *6 km (34 mi) round-trip*
Hiking Time: *3 hours round-trip*
Information and Maps: *Vopnafjörður tourist information center*
Trailhead: *Small walking path from parking lot off Route 917*

An easy route that is popular among locals is around **Drangsnes Peninsula** to the towering waterfalls at the Gljufursa River. The out-and-back hike is accessible via Routes 85 and 917, about 3 kilometers (2 mi) south of town.

KROSSAVÍK MOUNTAIN HIKE

Distance: *2.2 km (1.4 mi) round-trip*
Hiking Time: *1 hour round-trip*
Information and Maps: *Vopnafjörður tourist information center*
Trailhead: *Walking path from Route 917*

More experienced hikers looking for a challenging trail should hike to the top of Krossavík mountain, which reaches 1,080 meters (3,543 ft). The mountain stands opposite the village on the other side of the bay, and the trailhead is accessible via Route 917.

Pools and Hot Springs

SELÁRLAUG

3.5 km (7.2 mi) from Route 85; tel. 354/473-1499; 10am-10pm daily May 1-Aug. 29, 2pm-7pm Mon.-Fri., noon-4pm Sat.-Sun. Aug. 30-Apr. 30; 950ISK

The local swimming pool is called Selárlaug, where you will find locals taking a dip and socializing with friends and family. The facility has a large sun deck, patio chairs, and hot pots.

FOOD

CAFE HJALEIGAN

tel. 354/855-4511; www.visitvopnafjordur.com; 10am-5pm daily June 1-Sept. 15; snacks from 1,000ISK

Cafe Hjaleigan is the café at Bustarfell museum off Route 85, about 20 kilometers (12 mi) south from Vopnafjörður. It serves coffee, soft drinks, and light meals such as sandwiches, as well as pastries.

OLLASJOPPA

Kolbeinsgata 35; tel. 354/473-1803; 10am-10pm daily; entrées from 1,800ISK

Ollasjoppa is a tiny café that offers quick fare including pizza, hamburgers, sandwiches, and pitas, along with hot dishes with lamb, fish, and chicken.

ACCOMMODATIONS

SIREKSSTADIR FARM COTTAGES

Sireksstadir; tel. 354/848-2174; www.sireksstadir.is; rooms from 14,000ISK

Sireksstadir Farm Cottages offers two cottages for families or groups that can accommodate 4-6 people, as well as seven double rooms in their guesthouse. The cottages are cozy and have a large deck and a barbecue grill. Guests are invited to observe farm activities, and the rooms are available year-round. The staff are friendly, welcoming, and inclusive.

HOTEL TANGI

Hafnarbyggð 17; tel. 354/473-1203; www.visitvopnafjordur.com; rooms from 15,000ISK

Hotel Tangi is a standard countryside hotel with 17 rooms, a restaurant, and a bar. The exterior of the block building isn't much to look at, but the inside is comfortable, with standard beds and IKEA-like furniture. There are single and double rooms, some with shared bathroom facilities.

INFORMATION AND SERVICES

VOPNAFJÖRÐUR TOURIST INFORMATION OFFICE

Hafnarbyggð 4a; tel. 354/473-1331; www.vopnafjordur.is; 10am-5pm Mon.-Fri., noon-4pm Sat.-Sun.

The main tourist information office is housed in a huge yellow building in the center of town. It has brochures and maps about the region, as well as a small food store to stock up on essentials if you're staying at a self-catering guesthouse or farm.

GETTING THERE

By Car

By car, the paved **Route 85** connects Vopnafjörður with **Bakkafjörður,** a small fishing village 34 kilometers (21 mi) south of Vopnafjörður. **Route 1,** in the south, connects to **Egilsstaðir** (75 minutes). For the most scenic route, take unpaved **Route 917** over the mountains. Vopnafjörður is 212 kilometers (132 mi) from **Akureyri,** about 2.5 hours on Route 1.

By Plane

VOPNAFJÖRÐUR AIRPORT

tel. 354/424-4000

There are flights from the northern town of **Akureyri** to Vopnafjörður Airport, which is situated at the bottom of the fjord. Daily flights are about 45 minutes. One-way flights cost about 9,000ISK.

Fljótsdalur Valley

Fljótsdalur Valley encompasses the towns of Egilsstaðir and Fellabær, which form the largest urban center in East Iceland. The region supports a strong rural community that stretches from Biskupsháls in the west and Héraðsflói, a bay in the north, to the mountain ranges surrounding the central eastern fjords in the east and Vatnajökull and Öxi in the south. While Egilsstaðir is the largest town in the region, nature takes center stage in the valley: The region is home to Mount Snæfell, the highest mountain in Iceland.

EGILSSTAÐIR

Egilsstaðir is considered the unofficial capital of East Iceland, but it still has fewer than 3,000 residents. The quaint town earned its name based on a reference to the nearby farm Egil's stead, which appears in saga stories. The community developed and grew after Iceland gained independence from Denmark in 1944. That said, the town today remains sparsely populated, but the harbor welcomes thousands of visitors who come to Iceland via ferry from mainland Europe.

Sights

EAST ICELAND HERITAGE MUSEUM (Minjasafn Austurlands)

Laufskógar 1; tel. 354/471-1412; www.minjasafn.is/english; 10am-6pm daily June 1-Aug. 31, 11am-4pm Tues.-Fri. Sept.1-May 31; adults 1,500ISK, 17 and under free

The East Iceland Heritage Museum showcases how life was lived in the region over the last 200 years. The main exhibition features objects including clothing, food, and tools, as well as items used for hunting, crafts, food production, and hobbies. You can also enter a room of a 19th-century farmhouse that was moved from the countryside into the museum. The display depicts a small bedroom/living room, with sparse furnishings. It's an interesting view into what life was like in this remote part of Iceland—a hardscrabble, difficult existence.

SLÁTURHÚSIÐ

Kaupvangur 9; tel. 354/897-9479; www.slaturhusid.is; 11am-4pm Tues.-Fri., 1pm-4pm Sat.; free

The Sláturhúsið has injected some much-needed culture into Egilsstaðir. Founded in 2006, the Slaughterhouse Culture Center is home to theater and dance productions as well as workshops, performances, lectures, and exhibitions. An artist residency available to locals and visitors provides studio space in exchange for tuition. The concrete building is cold and nondescript, but one might expect that from an old slaughterhouse.

Sports and Recreation

SANDFELLSSKÓGUR HORSEBACK RIDING

17 km south of Egilsstaðir on Route 1; tel. 354/471-2420; www.visitegilsstadir.is/en

Fljótsdalur Valley

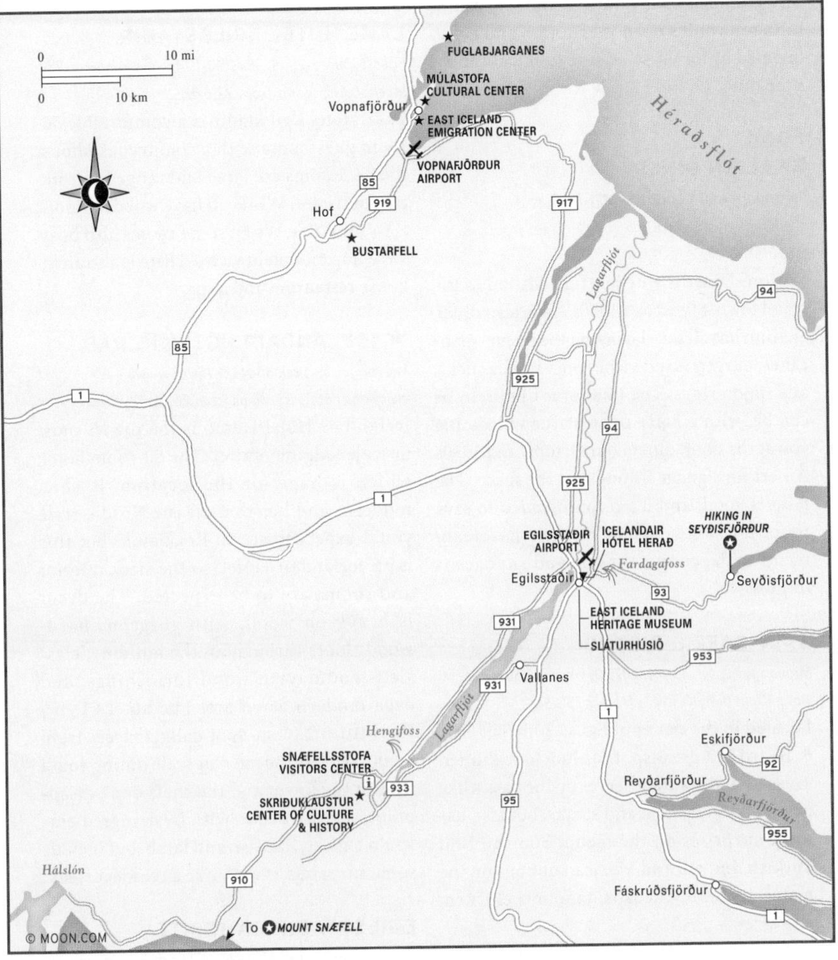

Those interested in a horse-riding tour have a great option with the travel service at Sandfellsskógur, which also offers horse rentals. Beautiful trails wind through the forest and traverse hills and valleys. You can rent a horse for 1-4 hours, and there's even a midnight summer tour. Horse tours are available June 1-September 15 and cost 8,000ISK for a one-hour rental.

EGILSSTAÐIR SWIMMING POOL

Tjarnarbraut 26; tel. 354/470-0777; 6:30am-9:30pm Mon.-Fri., 10am-6pm Sat.-Sun.; 1,000ISK

The Egilsstaðir Swimming Pool is one of the nicest in the region, with a 50-meter (164-ft) heated pool, waterslides for kids, hot tubs, and a fitness center.

EKKJUFELL GOLF COURSE

Fellabær; tel. 354/894-0604; greens fees 2,500ISK

The Ekkjufell Golf Course is the sole course in the town. It's open year-round and is frequented by locals, so be sure to call ahead for a tee time.

Food

SKÁLINN DINER

Fagradalsbraut 13; tel. 354/471-1899; www.skalinndiner.is; 8am-10pm daily; entrées from 2,100ISK

Skálinn Diner is a delightful addition to the small town. Styled as a 1950s American diner, Skálinn has all the classics on the menu—pancakes, burgers, sandwiches, mozzarella sticks, and onion rings. The interior is as kitschy as can be, with a Betty Boop statue welcoming you at the door, diner countertops, and 1950s American signage throughout the space. The food is good, and it's recommended to save room for some dessert, as their ice cream menu with scoops, shakes, and sundaes is impressive.

SALT CAFÉ & BISTRO

Miðvangur 2; tel. 354/471-1700; www.saltbistro.is; 11am-10pm daily; entrées from 2,750ISK

Located in the center of Egilsstaðir, Salt Café & Bistro is a great spot for lunch or dinner. The casual restaurant serves up the basics like pizzas, burgers, fish, and steaks, but also has some surprises on the menu. You can find Turkish, Indian, and Mexican options on the menu, including kebabs, tandoori chicken, and tacos.

Accommodations

HÚSEY

Hróastunga; tel. 354/471-3010; www.huseyfarm.is/en; beds 5,300ISK, single room 7,000ISK, 2-person private room 11,100ISK

Húsey is a 20-bed youth hostel that was converted from an old farmhouse. It's in an isolated part of the village, and there are great opportunities to spot seals and hike remote paths. The hostel has a common kitchen available for preparing your own meals. Sheets are available for a fee, and there is a barbecue on-site. There are private rooms available as well.

LAKE HOTEL EGILSSTAÐIR

Egilsstöðum 1-2; tel. 354/471-1114; www.english.lakehotel.is; rooms from 23,670ISK

Lake Hotel Egilsstaðir is a comfortable 50-room guesthouse with a country farmhouse theme. Rooms are large and range from singles to triples. While all have wooden floors, a TV, and free Wi-Fi, some rooms also boast sweeping mountain views. There is also an in-house restaurant and a spa.

★ ICELANDAIR HÓTEL HERAÐ

Miðvangur 5-7; tel. 354/471-1500; www.icelandairhotels.is; rooms from 26,000ISK

Icelandair Hótel Herað is the town's most upscale lodging option. The 60-room hotel, which is huge for the location, is chic, modern, and has that classic Nordic style you'd expect to see in Reykjavík. But this is an Icelandair Hótel, so the sleek interior and rooms are to be expected. The decor is heavy on wood, with gorgeous hardwood floors throughout the building, classic Scandinavian wood furnishings, and even modern wood art. The hotel's **Lyng Restaurant** (6pm-9pm daily; entrées from 4,000ISK) has the most upscale dining you'll find in the town, and the chefs don't disappoint, serving dishes with fresh ingredients you'd expect, like fish and lamb, but include some surprises as well, like a reindeer steak.

EGILSSTAÐIR CAMPSITE

Kaupvangur 10; tel. 354/470-0750; open year-round; 2,000ISK per person, children under 12 free

The Egilsstaðir Campsite can be quite busy in the summer. The campsite is close to town, and amenities include hot showers and adequate cooking facilities. There are areas for tents and RVs with hookups and the cost for electricity is 1,000ISK for 24 hours. The campsite is situated in an open field with trees along the perimeter. You must book and pay online in advance to camp at www.campegilsstadir.is.

Iceland's Loch Ness Monster

Scotland has the Loch Ness monster, and Iceland has **Lagarfljótsormur,** a huge worm-like monster said to call **Lagarfljót** home. People have reported spotting the monster inside the freshwater, glacier-fed lake, which is about 30 kilometers (19 mi) long, as well as outside the body of water. It is said to have many humps and slither in a slow fashion. The tale is part of Icelandic folklore, and locals have a sense of humor about "sightings." If you do happen to see the monster, make sure you report it to the local **heritage museum** in Egilsstaðir.

Information and Services

TOURIST INFORMATION CENTER

Kaupvangur 17; tel. 354/470-0750; www.east.is; 7am-11pm daily June-Aug., 9am-6pm Mon.-Fri. and 8am-11pm Sat.-Sun. Sept., 8:30am-12:30pm Mon.-Fri. Oct.-May

Egilsstaðir's tourist information center is the largest and most comprehensive in the region, and one of the largest in the country. You will find hiking maps, basic travel supplies, a café and souvenir shop, Internet access, and a booking center for an array of tours. The site is also home to the bus station and the local campsite.

Getting There

By car, **Route 1** connects Egilsstaðir with the North Iceland town **Akureyri,** which is 3.5 hours and 266 kilometers (165 mi) away. Egilsstaðir is 128 kilometers (79.5 mi) from **Vopnafjörður,** about 1.5 hours.

EGILSSTAÐIR AIRPORT

tel. 354/424-4000

Egilsstaðir Airport is in the heart of town, and there are daily flights by **Icelandair (www.icelandair.com)** from Reykjavík's domestic airport. Flights take about one hour and cost around 16,000ISK each way.

AROUND EGILSSTAÐIR

Egilsstaðir is situated along a beautiful glacial lake called **Lagarfljót** that stretches 35 kilometers (21.7 mi) long and offers numerous opportunities for hiking and outdoor recreation.

Hallormsstaður

20-minute drive on Route 931

You've probably noticed that trees are a rare sight in Iceland. Hallormsstaður has the distinction of being the largest forest in the country, though it would be considered small by other standards. It stretches along Lagarfljót and a small cove; it's beautiful to roam among native birch trees that have survived inclement weather and found a way to thrive. There are also scores of imported species, including willow and rowan.

Hallormsstaður is 23 kilometers (14 mi) southwest of Egilsstaðir on **Route 1** and **Route 931,** which is unpaved, about a 20-minute drive.

Hengifoss

Car park off of Route 931

After roaming Iceland's largest forest, take a walk to the opposite side of the lake and look at the towering 120-meter (394-ft) waterfall Hengifoss. The landscape reveals a layer of basalt above ancient tree trunks. Have your camera ready.

Hengifoss is 34 kilometers (21 mi) from Egilsstaðir on **Route 931,** a gravel road. For a close look you can stop at the designated **car park** off of Route 931 and walk uphill about 2.5 kilometers (1.6 mi) to the waterfall.

Fardagafoss

Route 93

Fardagafoss is a waterfall that weaves up the Fjardarheiði mountain, flowing over a rocky ridge. It's about 5 kilometers (3 mi) from Egilsstaðir on **Route 93.** There is a small

1
2
3

parking lot, and the waterfall is a short walk from the road.

★ MOUNT SNÆFELL

Mount Snæfell (Snow Mountain) is the highest mountain, excluding glaciers, in Iceland. Despite towering 1,833 meters (6,013 ft), it's fairly easy to scale.

Sights

SKRIÐUKLAUSTUR CENTER OF CULTURE & HISTORY

Skriðuklaustur; tel. 354/471-2990; www.skriduklaustur.is/en; 10am-6pm daily June 1-Aug. 31, 11am-5pm daily May and Sept., noon-4pm daily Apr. and Oct., open by request Nov.-Mar.; adults 1,100ISK, children under 16 free

The Skriðuklaustur Center of Culture & History is an impressive historical site that includes the ruins of a 16th-century monastery as well as the home of the celebrated novelist Gunnar Gunnarsson, the author of *Af Borgslægtens Historie (Guest the One-Eyed),* the first Icelandic book made into a movie. Gunnar's home was built in 1939 and was donated to the state by the writer in 1948. You can view photographs and objects that belonged to Gunnar Gunnarsson, and the building also serves as a cultural center where various events and exhibitions are held throughout the year.

Hiking

MOUNT SNÆFELL SUMMIT HIKE

Distance: *8 km (5 mi) round-trip*
Hiking Time: *12 hours round-trip*
Information and Maps: *Snæfellsstofa visitors center*
Trailhead: *Snæfellsskáli Mountain Hut, GPS N 64.8042, W 15.6418*

A well-kept trail begins at the base of the mountain and continues to the top. Hiking groups start at the mountain hut **Snæfellsskáli.** The dormant volcano offers spectacular views over the highlands, down Fljótsdalur valley, and of Vatnajökull glacier. You can see rivers, canyons, and valleys—and you may even catch a glimpse of a reindeer herd. Climbing doesn't get better.

The moderate hike is about 8 kilometers (5 mi) and takes about 12 hours. The top of the mountain is snowcapped all year long. Bring good boots and waterproof gear, alert people of your travel plans, and monitor the weather closely. If conditions are not good, do not attempt a climb.

HIKING FROM MOUNT SNÆFELL TO LÓNSÖRÆFI

Distance: *55 km (34 mi) one-way*
Hiking Time: *4 days one-way*
Information and Maps: *Snæfellsstofa visitors center*
Trailhead: *Snæfellsskáli Mountain Hut, GPS N 64.8042, W 15.6418; tel. 354/575-8400*

The trek from Mount Snæfell to Lónsöræfi, an isolated wildlife preserve in a raw part of the east, is growing in popularity. The landscape is rocky and angular, with sweeping hills and vast valleys. Colors are muted, and the atmosphere is serene. Along the trek, hikers see glaciers, waterfalls, and cliffs. The hike, which starts at the **Snæfellsskáli mountain hut,** is about 55 kilometers (34 mi) and takes four days, with 6-8 hours of walking per day. The maximum elevation is 250 meters (870 ft). It's challenging and for experienced hikers only—recent years have seen many search-and-rescue operations deployed in this isolated region in the name of stranded hikers.

The landscape is striking but unforgiving, with strong winds and remnants of sub-glacial eruptions of the past. It's a beautiful patch of land, but be sure to monitor the weather closely before your hike, and keep in mind that there are not a lot of guesthouses or eateries nearby. You will feel like you're on your own, because in much of the area, you are—birds here outnumber humans by the thousands. Bird enthusiasts looking for a glimpse of whimbrels will love Lónsöræfi. The brown and white waders with curved bills can be seen year-round.

The only road into the Lónsöræfi reserve

1: Hengifoss 2: Lagarfljót lake 3: Mount Snæfell

is the **F980,** a rough gravel road off of Route 1 that ends after 25 kilometers (16 mi) at Illikambur. As it's only drivable for super Jeeps (which are huge and outfitted for rugged terrain) and experienced drivers, please do not attempt to take a compact car or SUV on the trip. There is a river crossing along the way, and you will get stuck.

Reindeer Tour

TRAVEL EAST

tel. 354/471-3060; www.traveleasticeland.is; 31,900ISK per person

Spotting reindeer while exploring East Iceland is up to chance, but local experts can make it happen. Travel East is a small tourism company that offers a variety of tours in the region, including a reindeer safari. The four-hour tour is led by a local guide experienced in tracking these majestic beasts. Tours run October 1-June 30. Sightings tend to be best during the winter months as the herd migrates deep into the valleys.

Accommodations

SNÆFELLSSKÁLI MOUNTAIN HUT

tel. 354/842-4367; 6,000ISK

The mountain hut offers basic amenities including beds, bathrooms, and cooking facilities that can sleep 40 people. The whole area is open only in the summer.

Information and Services

SNÆFELLSSTOFA VISITORS CENTER

Skriðuklaustur; tel. 354/470-0840; 10am-3pm daily May and Sept.-Oct., 10am-5pm daily June-Aug., open by request in winter

The Snæfellsstofa visitors center is the information center for the east area of Vatnajökull National Park. The visitors center houses a fascinating exhibition on the area, the glacier, and local flora and fauna. Snæfell is one of the most visited destinations within the national park, and the center gives you a preview into the vast region. The center's souvenir shop focuses on local products, including woolen goods and food products.

Getting There

To get to the base, take unpaved **Route 910** to **Route F909.** The journey from Egilsstaðir takes about 1.5 hours and is 93 kilometers (58 mi). Getting here requires a rugged **four-wheel drive,** as the roads are at best challenging and at worst treacherous. Don't try to make it in a compact rental car or you'll wind up stranded.

The Eastfjords

The Eastfjords are some of the most remote and unspoiled parts of Iceland. In all, there are 14 fjords, each with its own charm and tiny population. There are waterfalls among small fishing villages, and unique museums lure tourists off the Ring Road. If you're on an extended trip to Iceland, you should make time to explore this wonderful land where wildlife greatly outnumbers humans.

BORGARFJÖRÐUR EYSTRI

This fjord is a prime destination for hiking, as there are numerous well-maintained trails, gorgeous mountains, and deserted bays. The big draw is the spectacular scenery that you don't have to share with hordes of tourists, unlike in other parts of the country.

Sights

ÁLFABORG

Route 94; GPS N 65.3119, W 13.4832

Álfaborg, or "fjord of Borg," is a 30-meter (98-ft) rocky hill known in folklore as the home of the queen of Iceland's hidden people. Many locals are amused by this history and happily relay stories of elves that have been passed down through the years. Álfaborg is a legally protected natural site, and a fun "elf rock" to photograph and climb upon. It can be found off of Route 94, a few kilometers south of town.

Bird-Watching

Birdlife thrives in the area. About 8,000 pairs of puffins nest every summer in Borgarfjörður Eystri from mid-April to mid-August. Other common bird species nesting there are fulmars, kittiwakes, and eider ducks. An observation platform at the marina connects to a small islet that puffins love, giving you a close-up view from about two meters away. The region is a photographer's dream; the birds are plentiful and the scenery breathtaking. The marina in the center of the village is the best place to spot puffins and kittiwakes.

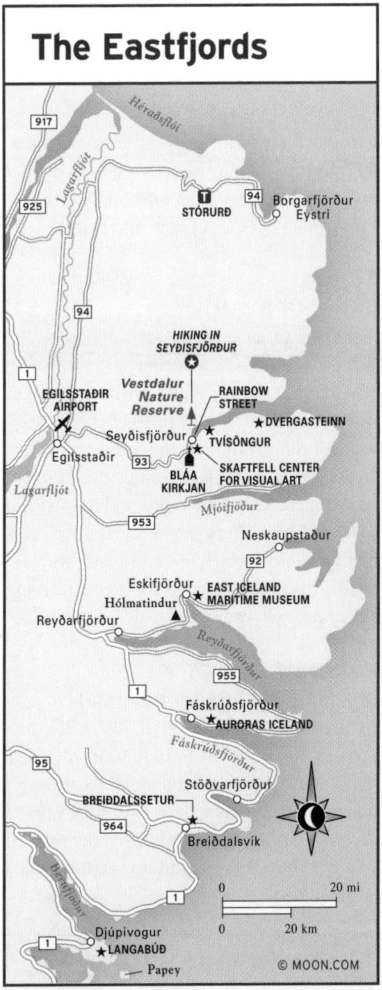

The Eastfjords

Hiking

Borgarfjörður Eystri is home to numerous well-maintained hiking trails and has earned the nickname "Paradise of the Hiker." There are 27 day routes in the region where hikers can see black-sand beaches, towering mountains, ancient farm ruins, and colorful hills and valleys. The region is also known for its exceptional hiking facilities, including **lodges** and **restrooms** at certain points. A **hiking map** is for sale at local tourism businesses as well as the information center in **Egilsstaðir.** The hikes vary in degree of difficulty and length, so be sure to consult the maps closely.

STÓRURÐ

Distance: *14 km (8.6 mi) round-trip*
Hiking Time: *7 hours*
Information and Maps: *www.east.is*
Trailhead: *Álfheimar Guesthouse*

Hiking to Stórurð (the Giant Boulders) is a moderate hike that lies below the towering Dyrfjöll mountain. This hike takes you along an ancient boulder region that was likely created by a powerful landslide during the ice age. Along the way, on a marked path, you will see placid valleys, small ponds, and an incredibly rocky terrain. The hike hits an elevation of 400-700 meters (1,300-2,300 ft).

Food and Accommodations

BLÁBJÖRG GUESTHOUSE

Gamla Frystihusið; tel. 354/846-0085; www.blabjorg.is; rooms from 17,000ISK

Blábjörg Guesthouse offers 11 rooms in an unexpected building: a renovated fish processing factory. Rooms are bright and cozy, and six rooms have beautiful seaside views. Amenities include a common kitchen and dining room, shared bathroom facilities, and free Wi-Fi

The Hidden People

You may have heard the adage that the majority of Icelanders believe in elves, but it's not that simple. In Icelandic folklore, the hidden people (Huldufólk) are supernatural beings that live in Iceland's wild spaces. You won't find many Icelanders that believe that actual elves walk among the population, but you may hear of tales passed down through generations, for instance a particular stone near a farm that is significant to a family. Below are some sites connected to the Huldufólk.

- **Ásbyrgi:** This giant glacial canyon in Jökulsárgljúfur National Park (the northern part of Vanajökull National Park) is thought to be a central meeting point for the hidden people (page 224).
- **Álfaborg:** Near Borgarfjörður Eystri, some believe this hill to be the home of the queen of the Huldufólk (page 242).
- **Dvergasteinn:** Not far from the tiny town of Seyðisfjörður, folklore holds that this stone is home to dwarves (page 246).

throughout the building. The ground floor features a spa and wellness center with hot tubs and saunas.

ALFHEIMAR GUESTHOUSE

Brekkubær; tel. 354/861-3677; www.alfheimar.com; rooms from 23,00ISK

Alfheimar Guesthouse is a remote 32-room guesthouse situated near a puffin colony. The hosts, a husband and wife, are inviting, making you feel like you're staying with friends. Rooms are spacious and have the comforts of home. The free Wi-Fi is surprisingly strong for the region, and the in-house **restaurant** (7am-8pm daily; entrées from 3,500ISK) has some delicious options. A breakfast buffet is included in the price of the room.

Getting There

Borgarfjörður Eystri is 70 kilometers (43 mi) north of **Egilsstaðir. Route 94,** a paved road, connects to Egilsstaðir, which is about an hour away from the fjord.

SEYÐISFJÖRÐUR

Seyðisfjörður gets a lot of traffic for a tiny town of fewer than 1,000 residents. This is due to the harbor, which acts as the main ferry terminal for passengers to and from continental Europe. You may be arriving as a point of necessity, but the darling town has lots of reasons to stay a couple of days and explore.

Sights

BLÁA KIRKJAN

Hafnargata 44; tel. 354/470-2308; www.blaakirkjan.is

The Bláa Kirkjan, or Blue Church, is a quaint wooden structure built in 1922 that hosts a series of concerts during the summer months. Genres range from classical music to choral to jazz. Concerts are held in July and August and cost 3,000ISK. Check the website for the summer schedule. If you like traditional churches, be sure to check it out, but if you're not seeing a concert here, you can skip it.

RAINBOW STREET

(Seyðisfjörður Regnbogagata)

At the end of Bláa Kirkjan you will come across one of the most photographed places in East Iceland, the rainbow-painted street. It was meant to be a temporary summer project several years ago, but locals loved the painted street, so it has stayed and it remains a tourist attraction.

1: horses grazing in the Eastfjords **2:** the Bláa Kirkjan

1
2

TVÍSÖNGUR

walking path from Hafnargata 47

Tvísöngur is a "sound sculpture" by German artist Lukas Kühne that is situated on a mountainside in Seyðisfjörður. The concrete structure consists of five interconnected domes of different sizes ranging 2-4 meters (7-14 ft). Each dome has its own unique resonance that corresponds to a tone in the Icelandic musical tradition of five-tone harmony, and the dome works as a natural amplifier to that tone. Guests can experience an acoustic sensation that can be explored and experimented with. The site's remoteness and serenity offer a perfect setting for playing music or singing—alone, in harmony, or even for an audience.

Tvísöngur is accessed by a gravel walking path that starts across from the **Brimberg Fish Factory** (Hafnargata 47). It takes 15-20 minutes and is a moderately difficult walk. Make sure you have good shoes.

SKAFTFELL CENTER FOR VISUAL ART (Myndlistarmiðstöð Austurlands)

Austurvegur 42; tel. 354/472-1632; www.skaftfell.is; noon-6pm Mon.-Fri., 4pm-6pm Sat.-Sun.; free

The Skaftfell Center for Visual Art works hard to bring contemporary art exhibitions to a predominantly rural area—and it succeeds. The center hosts exhibitions by local and visiting artists as well as a permanent exhibition of contemporary art featuring Icelandic and international artists. You can take a private tour for 2,500ISK (maximum five guests).

DVERGASTEINN

Vesturgata 12

Dvergasteinn, or Dwarf Boulder, was once the site of a church, with the namesake boulder behind it. The church moved, but the boulder remained, and folklore enthusiasts say the stone is inhabited by dwarves, or "hidden people."

★ Hiking

Seyðisfjörður has quite a few trails to choose from, ranging from easy to more challenging. Hiking maps are available at the town's **tourist information center.**

VESTDALSEYRI NATURE RESERVE HIKE

Distance: *4 km (2 mi) round-trip*
Hiking Time: *2.5 hours round-trip*
Information and Maps: *Seyðisfjörður tourist information center*
Trailhead: *Vestdalseyri entrance off of Route 951*

The Vestdalseyri Nature Reserve, about one kilometer (0.6 mi) north of town, is a valley known for its many **waterfalls** and rich birdlife. It's a beautiful place to roam and take in the mountain scenery. It contains an easy hike that is one of the most popular trails in Seyðisfjörður. You can start at the Vestdalseyri entrance and follow the trail. After passing a few glorious waterfalls, you will arrive at a small lake, **Vestdalsvatn,** which remains frozen most of the year.

SKALANES NATURE RESERVE HIKE

Distance: *9 km (6 mi) round-trip*
Hiking Time: *2.5 hours round-trip*
Information and Maps: *Seyðisfjörður tourist information center*
Trailhead: *Parking area by the Austdalsa River*

For an easy lowland hike, start from the parking area by the **Austdalsa River** and head to the nature reserve Skalanes, where there is a **guesthouse** and **museum.** This hike includes views of the gorgeous **Skalanesbjarg bird cliffs,** where you can see nesting eider ducks May-July. Please be mindful of nests and eggs and be careful where you step along the way.

AFRETTADALUR VALLEY HIKE

Distance: *17 km (11 mi) round-trip*
Hiking Time: *8 hours round-trip*
Information and Maps: *Seyðisfjörður tourist information center*
Trailhead: *Austdalsa parking area, 17 km (11 mi) east of Seyðisfjörður*

A more challenging trail starts from Skalanes and goes up along the edge of the cliffs to the **Skollaskard pass,** which is steep. You continue on into a valley, Afrettadalur. The landscape is breathtaking, but be careful to monitor weather conditions. The hike has an elevation gain of 643 meters (2,109 ft).

BRIMNES HIKE

Distance: *5.5 km (3.4 mi) round-trip*
Hiking Time: *2 hours round-trip*
Information and Maps: *Seyðisfjörður tourist information center*
Trailhead: *Selsstadir farm, which is signposted, about 10 km (6 mi) from the center of town*

The hike through Brimnes is another gem of a trek. Brimnes is on the north shore of Seyðisfjörður and was for centuries one of the major fishing villages in East Iceland. Start at the Selsstadir farm, which is signposted, 10 kilometers (6 miles) from the center of town, where you'll find ruins of old buildings and a small orange lighthouse. A walk out to Brimnes in good weather with good visibility is memorable. Be sure to have your camera ready. This is a moderately difficult hike.

BREKKA SETTLEMENT HIKE

Distance: *24 km (15 mi) round-trip*
Hiking Time: *14 hours round-trip*
Information and Maps: *Seyðisfjörður tourist information center*
Trailhead: *Austdalsa parking area, 17 km (11 mi) east of Seyðisfjörður*

Experienced climbers with endurance should check out the historical trail that leads from the Austdalsa parking area up past the abandoned farmstead Austdalur. It's extremely important to follow the trail posts down into the Brekkugja opening, and to be careful when crossing the snowbanks above it, before continuing down the Brekkudalur valley to the Brekka settlement, a historic village. The highest elevation reached is 781 meters (2,562 ft), and the trail has some steep climbs. This is typically done as a long day hike in the summer, strictly in June-August while monitoring weather conditions.

Other Sports and Recreation

STAFDALUR SKI AREA

tel. 354/898-2798; www.stafdalur.is; Dec.-May; lift tickets 1,600ISK Tues.-Fri., 2,800ISK Sat.-Sun. and holidays

The Stafdalur Ski Area is 9 kilometers (6 mi) southwest from Seyðisfjörður and has a 1,000-meter (3,280-ft) ski lift, as well as a lift for children. Cross-country skiing and snowmobiling are possible from the ski area; there is excellent access for snowmobiles from the ski area to magnificent mountains, deserted fjords, and the famous Dyrfjoll mountains. Rentals are available for skis, boots, poles, and snowboards.

SUNDHÖLL SEYÐISFJARÐAR SWIMMING POOL

Suðurgata 5; tel. 354/470-2340; 7am-10am and 3pm-8pm Mon.-Fri., 11am-2pm Sat.; 1,000ISK

The town swimming pool, Sundhöll Seyðisfjarðar, is small, but it's frequented by locals and their children. If the weather is bad, a dip in one of the hot tubs is divine.

Food

SKAFTFELL BISTRO

Austurvegur 42; tel. 354/472-1633; www.skaftfell.is; noon-10pm daily; entrées from 2,500ISK

Skaftfell Bistro is a cool spot to grab a bite to eat. It's decorated with works by the artist Dieter Roth, and has shelves of art books to check out while you dine. Sandwiches, pizza, pastries, and soup are on offer.

KAFFI LÁRA EL GRILLO BAR

Norðugata 3; tel. 354/472-1703; www.elgrillobar.com; 11:30am-1:30am Mon.-Thurs., 11:30am-3:30am Fri.-Sat., 12:30pm-1:30am Sun.; entrées from 2,600ISK

Kaffi Lára El Grillo Bar is a relaxed café in town where you can have a cup of coffee, watch a soccer game, and dine outside when the weather is nice. You can buy coffee, cakes, soups, sandwiches, and other light meals. At night, the place turns into the local bar, and locals gather to drink a few pints and listen to music.

★ NORÐ AUSTUR

Norðurgata 2; tel. 354/787-4000; www.nordaustur.is; 5pm-10pm Wed.-Sun.; maki rolls from 2,700ISK

You might not expect to find excellent sushi in a tiny Iceland town, but Norð Austur delivers. Trained sushi chefs use fresh fish caught by local fishers to create delectable maki rolls with salmon, cherry-wood smoked Icelandic char, and cod. There are also numerous small plates on the menu including arctic char tartar, soba salad, and ceviche. The restaurant is open Wed.-Sun. 5pm-10pm and is an excellent spot to have dinner.

Accommodations

HAFALDAN SEYÐISFJÖRÐUR HOSTEL

Suðurgata 8; tel. 354/611-4410; www.hafaldan.is; rooms from 13,000ISK, dormitory beds from 5,000ISK

Hafaldan Seyðisfjörður Hostel offers rooms in two buildings. Halfaldan Harbor Hostel is on the north side of the fjord, just two minutes from the town center, offering twin, double, and four-bed rooms, all with shared bathroom and kitchen facilities. The second location, Hafaldan Hospital Hostel, occupies a historic former hospital building. It offers private double rooms as well as double, twin, and dormitory rooms with shared facilities. In both locations, the dining and living rooms are lively and great places to meet fellow travelers. Rooms aren't pretty, but they are clean and adequate. The guests tend to be young budget travelers.

HÓTEL SNÆFELL

Austurvegur 3; tel. 354/472-1277; www.hotelaldan.com; rooms from 15,000ISK

Hótel Snæfell is operated by the same owners as Hótel Aldan. This guesthouse is based in a large three-story wooden house and offers 12 rooms. The rooms are bright and spacious and feature comfortable beds, but they lack the charm of rooms at Hótel Aldan. Guests have access to free Wi-Fi, a private bathroom with a shower, a small television, and laundry service. Breakfast is included.

SEYÐISFJÖRÐUR GUESTHOUSE

Hafnargata 4; tel. 354/898-6242; www.seydisfjordurguesthouse.is; rooms from 22,080ISK

Seyðisfjörður Guesthouse offers double and family rooms in the heart of Seyðisfjörður. Rooms are bare bones with beds and a little table, but they are large and clean. Guests have access to shared bathroom facilities, a communal kitchen, laundry room, and garden.

★ HÓTEL ALDAN

Norðurgata 2; tel. 354/472-1277; www.hotelaldan.is; rooms from 29,900ISK

Hótel Aldan is an adorable guesthouse that features seven double rooms and two triples with vintage furniture, antique lamps, and modern amenities, including Wi-Fi, minibars, private bathrooms with showers, TV and DVD players, and laundry service. Rooms are tasteful, charming, and Icelandic chic, with wood furnishings, muted colors, and minimalist design. Breakfast is included in the room rate, and the hotel is open year-round.

SEYÐISFJÖRÐUR CAMPSITE

Ránargata 1; tel. 354/792-0070; May 1-Sept. 30; 2,000ISK per adult, children under 14 free

You have the option to camp close to the town center at the Seyðisfjörður Campsite, in a facility that has showers, hot and cold running water, and shared kitchen facilities. There's also a free Internet connection. The campsite accommodates tents and RVs, and hookups are available. Washing machines are available for 700ISK, tumble dryers for 700ISK, and showers for 100ISK per 2 minutes.

Information and Services

SEYÐISFJÖRÐUR TOURIST INFORMATION CENTER

Ferjuleiru 1; tel. 354/472-1551; 8am-4pm daily

The tourist information center is at the ferry terminal by the harbor. You can find brochures about the region, ferry timetables and rates, hiking maps, road maps, and stamps. There's also free Wi-Fi, and a small café serves coffee, soft drinks, and snacks.

Getting There

Seyðisfjörður is 27 kilometers (17 mi) east of **Egilsstaðir,** the nearest hub. By car, **Route 93,** which is paved, is your only option to get to Seyðisfjörður.

Smyril Line (tel. +298/345900; www.smyrilline.com) operates a ferry from **Denmark** to the **Faroe Islands** to Iceland, with weekly departures from Hirtshals, Denmark. The trip from Denmark to Iceland is approximately 47 hours and costs about 224,000ISK round-trip for two people with a vehicle. For more information, check the rates and schedule online.

ESKIFJÖRÐUR

Eskifjörður is a small, single-road village that was established as a base of operations for Norwegian fishermen. Today, it's a quiet town of about 1,000 residents with a couple of guesthouses that draw tourists in the summer months. A few scenic hiking paths offer splendid views of the landscape and local birdlife.

Sights

EAST ICELAND MARITIME MUSEUM (Sjóminjasafn Austurlands)

Strandgata 39b; tel. 354/470-9063; 1pm-5pm daily June 1-Aug. 31, open by request Sept.-May; 1,000ISK

The East Iceland Maritime Museum pays tribute to the town's rich fishing history with exhibits of items relating to fishing and seafaring, as well as artifacts of local trade, industry, and medicine from times past. The collection is housed in a black wooden building that was built in 1816, called **Gamlabúð.**

Hiking

MOUNT HOLMATINDUR

Distance: *10 km (6 mi) round-trip*
Hiking Time: *8 hours round-trip*
Information and Maps: *www.east.is*
Trailhead: *Signpost 3.5 km (2.2 mi) east of town, off of Route 92*

Locals take pride in Mount Holmatindur, which stands 985 meters (3,231 ft) high and towers over the fjord opposite the town. The trek to the top, which has fantastic views of the east, can be challenging; those who make it can sign a logbook declaring their achievement. Because the trailhead is situated near paved **Route 92** just 3.5 kilometers (2.2 mi) east from the center of town, it's quite easy to get to the mountain. Check the weather forecast before you head out, bring the proper gear, and alert your hotel of your plans.

Other Sports and Recreation

ESKIFJÖRÐUR SWIMMING POOL

tel. 354/476-1218; 6am-9pm Mon.-Fri., 10am-6pm Sat.-Sun. June-Aug., 6am-8pm Mon.-Fri., 1pm-6pm Sat.-Sun. Apr.-May and Sept.-Oct.; adults 950ISK, children 6-17 250ISK

The Eskifjörður Swimming Pool features an outdoor 25-meter (83-ft) pool, a children's pool with three waterslides, two hot tubs, a sauna, and a fitness center.

BYGGÐARHOLT GOLF COURSE

Strandgata 71a; tel. 354/892-4622; year-round; greens fees 3,000ISK

The Byggðarholt golf course is a nine-hole course with yardage markers, a putting green, chipping green, and practice bunker area.

ODDSSKARÐ SKI REGION

tel. 354/476-1465; www.east.is/en; 2pm-8pm Mon.-Fri., 10am-4pm Sat.-Sun. during winter

Oddsskarð is the largest skiing region in East Iceland, with three lifts, a ski lodge for 40 people, and tracks for cross-country skiing. Skis and snowboards are available to rent.

Food and Accommodations

MJOEYRI GUESTHOUSE

Strandgata 120; tel. 354/477-1247; www.mjoeyri.is; rooms from 21,000ISK, cottages from 37,000ISK

Mjoeyri Guesthouse offers two types of accommodations: standard rooms at the guesthouse and five self-catering cottages. Cottages are equipped with a kitchen, a dining room, one bedroom, and a balcony with a beautiful view of the landscape. Rooms are no-frills with standard beds and basic furnishings. The owners are friendly and accommodating. There's a daily breakfast buffet from 8am-10am for 2,100ISK per person.

HOTEL ESKIFJÖRÐUR

Strandgata 47; tel. 354/476-0099; www.hoteleskifjordur.is; 26,900ISK

Hotel Eskifjörður is situated in the center of town, offering spacious rooms with impressive views of the Holmatindur mountains. Rooms are tidy with minimalist decor, and the front desk can arrange a number of activities in the area, including horse riding, boating, hiking, and history tours.

Getting There

Eskifjörður is 73 kilometers (45 mi) south of **Seyðisfjörður** on **Route 92.** Be sure to check the weather forecast before you head out; the road, though paved, can be challenging—even dangerous—during wet weather.

NESKAUPSTAÐUR

Fifty years ago, Neskaupstaður was only accessible by sea, making it the most remote and untouched spot in the Eastfjords. However, a tunnel was built that connected the town with Eskifjörður via paved **Route 92.** There still isn't a lot to do here, but there are a few museums to visit if you want to make a quick stop before continuing on the Ring Road.

Sights

MUSEUM HOUSE (Safnahúsið)

Miðstræti 1; tel. 354/470-9063; www.fjardabyggd.is; 1pm-5pm daily June 1-Aug. 31; 1,000ISK

The Museum House (Safnahúsið) is home to three museums. The **Museum of Natural History** will be a winner if you're traveling with children, as a special exhibition allows them to touch different animals. There are also displays of Icelandic mammals, birds, insects, and shellfish, as well as exhibitions on stones and flora found in East Iceland. The **Josafat Hinriksson Maritime Museum** showcases relics relating to ironwork, fishing, boatbuilding, and the way in which people lived in East Iceland in the old days. The town's art museum, the **Tryggvi Olafsson Art Collection,** is dedicated to the works of local artist Tryggvi, who was born in the town in 1940. He is one of East Iceland's most revered contemporary artists. Tryggvi's bright, colorful paintings mix abstract art with wildlife and landscape themes.

RAUÐUBJÖRG LOOKOUT POINT

Route 92

Rauðubjörg, which means "red cliffs," is a great example of the varied landscape of East Iceland. While the cliffs are predominantly red, you can see hues ranging from brown to white, and it's a striking sight against the bright blue sea. You'll find a lookout point where you can safely pull off the road just south of Neskaupstaður via paved Route 92.

Hiking

PÁSKAHELLIR (EASTER CAVE)

Distance: *2 km (1.2 mi) round-trip*
Hiking Time: *20-30 minutes round-trip*
Information and Maps: *www.east.is*
Trailhead: *Entrance of the Neskaupstaður Nature Reserve*

Páskahellir (Easter cave) is a small cave located within the Neskaupstaður Nature Reserve; the village has been a protected nature reserve since the 1970s. Inside the cave you will see pillow lava and tunnels as well as holes that were likely formed by prehistoric trees. It's an interesting look at the geology of Iceland.

Food and Accommodations

NESBÆR KAFFIHÚS

Egilsbraut 5; tel. 354/477-1115; 9am-6pm Mon.-Fri., 10am-5pm Sat.; entrées from 1,990ISK

Located in the center of town, Nesbær Kaffihús is a cozy coffeehouse popular among locals and tourists for lunch. The menu features crepes, sandwiches, salads, and soup.

HILDIBRAND HOTEL

Hafnarbraut 2; tel. 354/477-1950; www.hildibrandhotel.com; rooms from 25,000ISK, apartments from 36,000ISK

This guesthouse offers nine double rooms and 15 self-catering apartments. While the guesthouse rooms are a little on the Spartan side, the apartments are spacious, with full-size kitchens, large sofas, flat-screen TVs, and ocean views.

Getting There

Neskaupstaður is 72 kilometers (45 mi) southeast of **Egilsstaðir** on **Route 92.** Check the weather forecast before you head out, as the road, though paved, can be challenging—even dangerous—during wet weather.

FÁSKRÚÐSFJÖRÐUR

Fáskrúðsfjörður is a small village of fewer than 500 people nestled on a long fjord of the same name. It's the most "French" part of Iceland. The village was originally a base for more than 5,000 French fishermen who came every year to fish the Icelandic waters. Some settled here in the late 19th century. The village had a hospital, chapel, and cemetery that were built by the French settlers, and both the buildings and the history remain, as the streets of Fáskrúðsfjörður are marked in both Icelandic and French.

Sights

FRENCH FISHERMEN IN ICELAND

Hafnargata 12; tel. 354/475-1170; 10am-6pm daily June 1-Aug. 31, by appointment in winter; 1,000ISK

This aptly named museum does a great job of describing the history of the town and the importance of the impact of the French, and it even has a delightful and popular little café that sells coffee, cakes, and light meals.

AURORAS ICELAND

Hafnargata 7; tel. 354/783-9500; www.auroras.is; 12:30pm-5pm daily June 15-Aug. 15, open by request rest of the year; adults 1,000ISK, children 13-15 800ISK, childen 12 and under free

Auroras Iceland is an unexpected treat in this small village. The gallery offers a photo exhibition of northern lights that were captured above the fjord. Guests can see large photos of the natural phenomenon along with time-lapse videos of northern lights dancing and flickering in the sky.

Festivals and Events

FRENCH DAYS

www.franskirdagar.com; July

If you visit during the last weekend in July, you can join in with the French Days festival, which celebrates the town's history with French-inspired food and flags.

Food and Accommodations

CAFÉ SUMARLÍNA

Búðavegur 59; tel. 354/475-1575; www.sumarlina.is; 11am-10pm Mon.-Fri., noon-10pm Sat.-Sun.; entrées from 2,650ISK

Café Sumarlína occupies a cute white house in the center of town. The atmosphere is warm and inviting, and the staff is the same. The menu features pizzas, burgers, lamb and fish entrées, and quite a few French-inspired dishes, like crepes and baguette sandwiches.

FOSSHOTEL EASTFJORDS

Hafnargata 11-14; tel. 354/470-4070; www.islandshotel.is; rooms from 32,000ISK

Fosshotel Eastfjords is a 47-room hotel with French-inspired decor, paying homage to the history of the town. It offers standard, superior, single, and triple rooms with hardwood floors, muted wallpaper, quality linens, and simple furniture. It has an in-house French-inspired **bar and restaurant** (6:30am-9pm daily; dinner entrées from 3,890ISK), free parking, and free Wi-Fi. Breakfast is included in the price of the room.

Getting There

Fáskrúðsfjörður is 50 kilometers (31 mi) south of **Egilsstaðir** on **Route 92.** Be sure to check the weather forecast before you head out because the road, though paved, can be challenging and dangerous during wet weather.

STÖDVARFJÖRÐUR

Stöðvarfjörður is another minuscule village in the Eastfjords that has strikingly beautiful nature to explore, including rocky terrain, mountains, and a gorgeous shoreline.

Sights

PETRA'S STONE & MINERAL COLLECTION (Steinasafn Petru Stöðvarfirði)

Fjarðarbraut 21; tel. 354/475-8834; www.steinapetra.is; 10am-5pm daily June 1-Aug. 31, by appointment rest of the year; adults 1,500ISK, children 13 and under free

Petra's Stone & Mineral Collection is a stunning private collection of more than 1,000 stones that are cut and polished, revealing crystals and other beautiful facets. The owner started amassing stones in 1976, and the collection includes lava, crystals, basalt, pearls, granite, opals, and amethysts.

SAXA

Route 96

Saxa, a sea geyser, is an interesting natural phenomenon where the waves crash into a rocky crevice and shoot high into the air, creating water "eruptions." The name Saxa is derived from the kelp and seaweed that are saxað (chopped) inside the crevices and then hurled into the air with the waves. The sea geyser is a cool sight and unique to the area.

Food and Accommodations

SAXA GUESTHOUSE

Fjarðarbraut 41; tel. 354/511-3055; saxa@saxa.is; rooms from 22,100ISK

SAXA Guesthouse is close to the harbor in the heart of the town. Its 14 rooms are bright and minimalist. A common lounge has a TV and a terrace to enjoy in good weather. Breakfast is included. The in-house **café** (7am-9pm daily; entrées from 2,700ISK) is open for breakfast, lunch, and dinner and offers soups, salads, sandwiches, and lamb and fish meals.

Getting There

Stöðvarfjörður is 73 kilometers (45 mi) southeast of **Egilsstaðir** on **Route 92.** Be sure to check the weather forecast before you head out; the road, though paved, can be dangerous during wet weather.

BREIÐDALSVÍK

Breiðdalsvík is a blip of a town with fewer than 150 residents. There's not much going on here, but a couple of guesthouses serve those who need a break from the Ring Road.

Sights

BREIÐDALSSETUR

Gamla Kaupfélagið; tel. 354/525-5210; noon-4pm daily June 1-Aug. 31, limited hours in winter; free

Breiðdalssetur is a small museum that houses exhibitions about the geology of East Iceland and a couple of the scientists that worked in the region, George Walker and Stefán Einarsson. The museum contains minerals and stones as well as photos and geological information.

Food and Accommodations

THE OLD GENERAL STORE

Sólvellir 25; tel. 354/475-6670; www.breiddalsvik.is; 7am-9pm daily

The Old General Store is a quaint café and shop that retains the charm of its history. Built in 1956, it has its original wood shelves and displays some old product tins of brands that were popular in Iceland during the 1950s and 1960s. It's also a great spot to grab a cup of coffee and slice of cake or pick up some necessities for your journey.

EYJAR FISHING LODGE

Eyjar; tel. 354/567-5204; rooms from 15,000ISK

Eyjar Fishing Lodge has the look and feel of an authentic fishing lodge, with some luxury amenities. Its eight rooms come with heated floors and free Wi-Fi, and are decorated with lots of wood and fish-inspired art. The lodge also has a common lounge, hot tub, and sauna.

HÓTEL BLÁFELL

Solvellir 14; tel. 354/475-6770; www.breiddalsvik.is; rooms from 28,000ISK

Hótel Bláfell is a darling 34-room country hotel offering singles, doubles, and family rooms that range from simple modern decor to wood-paneled, rustic chic. All rooms have private bathrooms, free Wi-Fi, and standard beds. The hotel also has a sauna, lounge with fireplace, and library with interesting books and even board games. The **restaurant** (7am-9pm daily; entrées from 4,200ISK) does a nice take on classic fish and lamb dishes, but the menu doesn't have any surprises.

Getting There

Breiðdalsvík is 83 kilometers (52 mi) southeast of **Egilsstaðir** on **Route 95.** Check the weather forecast before you head out because wet weather could make the road challenging—even dangerous.

DJÚPIVOGUR

Djúpivogur, a town of fewer than 500 people, has a history of fishing and trading dating to 1589. A picturesque landscape is the backdrop to countless hiking trails, free to roam and explore. The 1,069-meter (3,507-ft) **Mount Búlandstindur** looms over the town, dominating the terrain. A few museums are aimed at tourists looking to spend time indoors.

Sights

LANGABÚÐ

Búð 1; tel. 354/478-8220; www.langabud.is; 10am-6pm daily May 2-Oct. 1, open by appointment rest of the year; 500ISK

Langabúð is the oldest building in the town, dating back to 1790, and it houses a heritage museum as well as an exhibition dedicated to a local sculptor. The folk museum contains an eclectic collection of pieces integral to the town's history, including fishing equipment such as whale harpoons as well as antique parts that belonged to early wagons. The collection may seem like there isn't a strong theme, but that's part of the charm, a mishmash of town history. As for the art portion of the building, artist **Ríkarður Jónsson** (1888-1974) was known as the founder of a national folk-art movement in Iceland. Classic themes of work and family are depicted in his portraiture and wood sculpture, and the museum houses many of his wood carvings and the tools he used in his work.

BIRD AND MINERAL MUSEUM (Fuglavefur Djupavogs)

Bakka 1; tel. 354/478-8928; www.djupivogur.is; 10am-6pm daily in summer, open by appointment in winter; 500ISK

The Bird and Mineral Museum holds about 130 species of stuffed birds, along with nests and eggs. There are also photos and books about birdlife and Icelandic minerals. The focus may seem random, but the curators have taken great care to unify the bird and mineral collections under one roof.

Hiking and Bird-Watching

Hiking the serene and well-kept trails around the flat Bulandsnes Peninsula is a must for bird-watchers. Most of the birds nesting in Iceland can be seen on or around Bulandsnes during the migration period in the summer, with the places of greatest interest being the lakes **Breidivogur** and **Fyluvogur.** In this area, you can see tufted ducks and pintails, as well as less common species like red-throated divers and black-tailed godwits.

BULANDSNES PENINSULA HIKE

Distance: *5-10 km (3-6 mi)*
Time: *2-4 hours*
Information and Maps: *Tourist Information Center*
Trailhead: *Bondarvarða cairn, east of Djúpivogur*

There are two different routes. If you opt for the shorter route, it's easier and approximately 5 kilometers (3 mi), which takes about two hours. If you opt for the shorter route, you must turn on **Ulfseyjarsund** (a fork) and continue to the **airstrip,** then continue to the lakes Breidivogur and Fyluvogur and back to where you started.

If you choose the longer route, you have to turn near Ulfseyjarsund, go to the airstrip, and from there hike to **Ulfsey beach.** At the southwest tip of Ulfsey, there is a sign, and from there you can choose whether to view Ulfsey, **Hvaley, or Sandey,** a trio of islets that are now connected to the mainland. Then you go back the same way from the sign in Ulfsey, to the airstrip and then to the

1

2

lakes Breidivogur and Fyluvogur and back to Bondavarða.

Pools and Hot Springs

DJÚPIVOGUR SWIMMING POOL

Varða 6; tel. 354/478-8999; 7am-8:30pm Mon.-Fri., 11am-3pm Sat.; 1,050ISK

On a rainy day, the Djúpivogur Swimming Pool is a great option. In the winter, you will see locals and their children taking a dip in the heated pool or one of the hot tubs, but the summer sees a lot of tourist traffic.

Food and Accommodations

LANGABÚÐ

Búð 1; tel. 354/478-8220; 10am-6pm daily May 2-Oct. 1; snacks from 800ISK

Langabúð is a tiny café that serves pastries, coffee, and light meals that hit the spot. The cakes are hard to resist, and the ingredients for the soups and sandwiches are local and fresh.

VIÐ VOGINN

Vogaland 2; tel. 354/478-8860; www.vidvoginn.is; entrées from 2,600ISK

Við Voginn is a great spot to stop after a long drive for a lunch or a snack. The small café offers options like burgers, fish and chips, cakes, and coffee. Open for lunch and dinner, Við Voginn is open daily 11am-8pm.

BERUNES HOSTEL

Berufjörður; tel. 354/869-7227; www.berunes.is; Apr. 16-Oct. 31; rooms from 14,800ISK

This charming converted farmhouse just outside of Djúpivogur offers rooms that accommodate 1-4 people as well as five self-contained cottages that can house 2-5 people. Rooms are small but comfortable, and some of them remind you of a guesthouse out of the 1970s. Berunes serves meals in a building next to the hostel. **Gestastofa Café** serves breakfast year-round (7am-10am daily), and a three-course dinner is served in July and August (6pm-9pm daily).

★ HÓTEL FRAMTÍÐ

Vogalandi 4; tel. 354/478-8887; www.hotelframtid.com; rooms from 25,950ISK

Hótel Framtíð is the place to go if you want to stay in town. This is the only close option. The 42-room hotel has wood-paneled rooms that remind you of a hunting lodge, standard beds, and simple furnishings. Its **Framtíð Restaurant** (call ahead because opening hours vary; entrées from 5,320ISK) features entrées including roast lamb fillets with fresh vegetables and potatoes, and grilled lobster tails. Desserts are scrumptious, including whipped skyr with cream and mixed berries and apple cake with fresh cream. Group menus are available for parties of 10 or more.

DJÚPIVOGUR CAMPGROUND

tel. 354/478-8887; May 1-Sept. 30; 1,750ISK per person, children 14 and under free

The Djúpivogur Campground is conveniently situated close to Hótel Framtíð, which is where you pay the camping fees. At the height of the summer season (July), the site is littered with vans and campers, but it can feel like a little community, and it's fun to meet fellow travelers. The facilities are decent, with an indoor cooking area and steaming-hot showers (300ISK). The campground is in an open field, and there is room for tents and RVs, with hookups available. Electricity is available for 1,050ISK and washing machines for 1,050ISK per 90 minutes.

Information and Services

TOURIST INFORMATION CENTER

Bakka 3; tel. 354/478-8220; www.djupivogur.is; 9am-5pm Mon.-Fri., noon-4pm Sat.-Sun. May 15-Sept. 15

The tourist information center offers hiking maps, brochures about the region, and Internet access.

Getting There

Djúpivogur is 86 kilometers (53 mi) south of **Egilsstaðir** on **Route 1.**

1: Mount Holmatindur **2:** Langabúð

The Vatnajökull Region

In the Vatnajökull region, Iceland earns its "fire and ice" reputation. You'll see the glacier descend into black sands and hot streams erupt from frozen banks of ice.

The region is easy to access, as there are frequent flights and buses between Reykjavík and Höfn. For flights, check out **Eagle Air** (www.eagleair.is), and for buses, try **Strætó** (www.straeto.is) and **Reykjavík Excursions** (www.re.is). Höfn is the best gateway to the region and the perfect town in which to base yourself.

HÖFN

Höfn, which means "harbor," is the gateway to Vatnajökull glacier, and guesthouses and cafés accommodate the growing number of tourists to the region. There are roughly 2,000 residents of Höfn, which makes it quite a sleepy town, but it comes alive in the summer, when legions of tourists from around the world gear up to scale the glacier. The town has a few small museums, including a spectacular one dedicated to the looming Vatnajökull.

Sights

FOLK MUSEUM
(Gamlabúð)

Heppuvegur 1; tel. 354/470-8330; 9am-5pm daily Oct. 1-Apr. 30, 9am-6pm daily May 1-May 31, 9am-7pm daily June 1-Aug. 31, 9am-6pm daily Sept. 1-Sept. 30; free

The Folk Museum has a small collection of artifacts that shows what life was like in one of the most isolated parts of the country from the 19th century on. You will find objects related to the old ways of farming, including antique tractors and cars. The museum is small, and free, but don't feel bad if you miss it.

HORNAFJÖRÐUR ART MUSEUM
(Listasafn Hornafjarðar)

Hafnarbraut 27; tel. 354/470-8057; 9am-3pm Mon.-Fri., 1pm-5pm Sat.-Sun. June 1-Sept. 30, 9am-3pm Mon.-Fri. and by request rest of year; free

The Hornafjörður Art Museum displays the work of celebrated local artist Svavar Gudnason, who had a strong connection to his hometown of Höfn and the Vatnajökull region. Svavar was born in Höfn in 1909 and spent his youth there before moving to Reykjavík in 1928. He had been introduced to landscape painting at an early age, and his work depicts the natural surroundings in Southeast Iceland, portraying the sea, glaciers, lakes, and mountains. In the winter months, works from other artists are displayed alongside those of Svavar.

Bird-Watching

Bird-watchers must head to **Ósland,** a conservation area in the south of Höfn that was once an island but is now connected to the mainland (you can reach it by walking from the harbor in Höfn). Arctic terns are a common sight during their nesting season, which takes place early in the summer, and there are walking trails along the perimeter of a pond they frequent.

Located on the hill **Óslandshæð** is a memorial to fishermen lost at sea and an information board about the surrounding natural area, including details on the flora and fauna.

Other Sports and Recreation

HÖFN SWIMMING POOL

Víkurbraut 9; tel. 354/470-8477; 6:45am-9pm Mon.-Fri., 10am-7pm Sat.-Sun. May 15-Sept. 30, 6:45am-9pm Mon.-Fri., 10am-5pm Sat.-Sun. Oct. 1-May 14; 1,000ISK

The local Höfn Swimming Pool isn't as spectacular as some of the other pools in the region, but it's a nice spot for a dip when taking a break from hiking and touring.

SILFURNESVÖLLUR

Dalbraut; tel. 354/478-2197; greens fees 4,000ISK

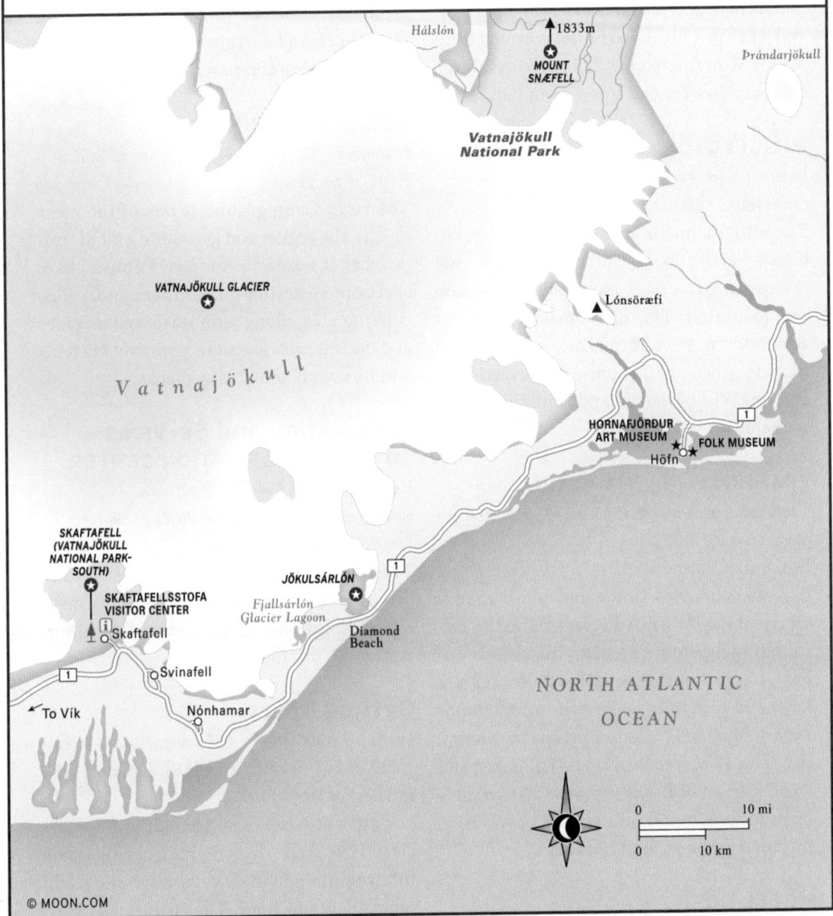

The Silfurnesvöllur golf course is on the outskirts of Höfn. It is a well-kept nine-hole course open year-round that stretches along the shore with a breathtaking view over Vatnajökull glacier and its mountain ridge.

Food

PAKKHÚS RESTAURANT

Krosseyjarvegi 3; tel. 354/478-2280; www.pakkhus.is; entrées from 4,400ISK

Pakkhús is a lovely restaurant that overlooks the Höfn harbor, next to the tourist information center. The fresh langoustines are to die for, but there are many options for those that don't enjoy seafood, including lamb, beef, pork, and duck entrées. There is also a vegetarian option.

Accommodations

HÓTEL EDDA HÖFN

Ránarsloð 3; tel. 354/444-4850; www.hoteledda.is; mid-May-Sept. 30; rooms from 23,000ISK

Hótel Edda Höfn is a chain hotel offering 36 rooms that are spacious and bright, but devoid of character. But the amenities are good, and each room has a private bathroom. Guests have access to free Wi-Fi and parking, and a yummy breakfast buffet is available for 2,450ISK per person, 1,225ISK for children 6-12, and free for children five and under.

MILK FACTORY GUESTHOUSE

Dalbraut 2; tel. 354/478-8900; www.milkfactory.is; rooms from 27,000ISK

The Milk Factory is a newly renovated guesthouse that overlooks Vatnajökull glacier and is close to attractions including Jökulsárlón and Skaftafell. The 17 rooms are spacious and modern, yet minimalistic in decor, and include private bathrooms, flat-screen TVs, and free Wi-Fi. Doubles and family rooms are available.

FOSSHOTEL VATNAJÖKULL

Lindarbakki; tel. 354/478-2555; www.islandshotel.is; rooms from 29,000ISK

Fosshotel Vatnajökull is a 66-room hotel that offers doubles, suites, and family rooms. Overlooking Vatnajökull glacier and the surrounding mountain scenery, the view is unbeatable in Southeast Iceland. Rooms are large and tastefully decorated in contemporary design, and include a private bathroom, flat-screen TV, free Wi-Fi, a coffee maker, and small refrigerator. The in-house restaurant is open for lunch and dinner, and breakfast is included in the price of the room.

HÓTEL HÖFN

Víkurbraut 20; tel. 354/478-1240; www.hotelhofn.is; rooms from 40,000ISK

Hótel Höfn is a 68-room hotel that looks and feels like a chain hotel designed for business travelers. The rooms are sparsely furnished with standard beds, hardwood floors, flat-screen TVs, and free Wi-Fi. The in-house restaurant serves classic Icelandic cuisine ranging from fresh fish to lamb dishes. There are a couple of vegetarian options. The **restaurant** (6pm-10pm daily; 3,990ISK) has an eclectic menu. There are a few dishes serving lobster caught by local fishermen, and you can't go wrong with any—though the chili-and-garlic-roasted lobster tails in particular are divine. Other menu options include sushi, lamb, beef, and shrimp options; pizza; vegetarian entrées; and pasta.

HÖFN CAMPGROUND

Hafnarbraut 52; tel. 354/478-1606; Apr. 15-Sept. 30; 2,000ISK per person

The Höfn Campground is one of the nicer ones in the region and gets quite a bit of traffic when it's open in summer. Campers have access to steaming-hot showers and a nice cooking area, along with washing machines and the Internet. The site accommodates tents and RVs, with hookups available.

Information and Services

TOURIST INFORMATION CENTER

Heppuvegur 1; tel. 354/470-8330; www.visitvatnajokull.is; 9am-6pm daily May 1-Sept. 30, 9am-5pm daily Oct 1.-Apr. 30

The tourist information center has tourist brochures about the region and hiking maps as well as Internet access and booking information for day tours.

Getting There

Höfn is on **Route 1,** 187 kilometers (116 mi) south of **Egilsstaðir** and 451 kilometers (280 mi) east of **Reykjavík.**

Eagle Air (tel. 354/562-4200; www.eagleair.is) operates daily flights from Reykjavík for around 26,000ISK each way. The flight takes about one hour. The airport is about 5 kilometers (3 mi) north of town.

★ VATNAJÖKULL GLACIER

Vatnajökull (Water Glacier) is a cool spot to visit—quite literally, as it's Iceland's remaining piece of the last ice age. Vatnajökull features miles of white, pure ice, intertwined with blue and smoky hues in interesting shapes formed by compression. It's a wide-open space, sitting

1: Höfn **2:** arctic tern **3:** lobster dinner in Höfn
4: Vatnajökull glacier

1
2
3
4

on top of active volcanoes. You will experience whipping winds, sky-high elevations, and cold temperatures.

Vatnajökull has the distinction of being the largest glacier in Europe and the third largest in the world (after glaciers in Greenland and Antarctica). It spans 8,805 square kilometers (3,400 sq mi), which covers about 8 percent of the country, and the average thickness is 400 meters (1,312 ft).

Of the volcanoes, the most active are the systems near **Mount Grímsfjall** (1,719 m/5,640 ft), and at **Grímsvötn** (1,725 m/5,659 ft). **Mount Barðarbunga** (2,009 m/6,591 ft) awakened in 2014 and is another volcanic fissure. **Mount Kverkfjöll** (1,929 m/6,329 ft) and **Mount Hvannadalshnjúkur** (2,110 m/6,923 ft) also lie beneath the glacier.

Vatnajökull's vast, rugged terrain is a large draw for hikers and climbers from around the world, but be sure you come prepared. Bring the necessary gear, monitor weather conditions, and alert people of your whereabouts.

Arctic Adventures (tel. 354/562-7000; https://adventures.is) offers ice cave and super Jeep tours. The 5.5-hour Glacier Explorer tour is a guided glacier hike that is available year-round for 15,490ISK.

TOP EXPERIENCE

★ JÖKULSÁRLÓN

Jökulsárlón (Glacier Lagoon) is a spectacular sight that begs to be photographed. Chunks of ice are scattered about, walls of ice jut from the sea, and icebergs of various sizes float on the water. Huge blocks of ice constantly break off the Breiðamerkurjökull glacier into the lagoon, which, though not very wide, is up to 250 meters (821 ft) deep—the deepest lake in Iceland—and then slowly move toward a river mouth and the Atlantic Ocean.

Jökulsárlón is a popular destination throughout the year, but it's quite crowded during the height of the summer season (July-Aug.). Even without a tour, plan to spend a couple of hours here to wander around and take in the beauty.

Fjallsárlón Glacier Lagoon is a smaller lagoon situated close to Jökulsárlón Glacier Lagoon. Zodiac boat tours let you get up close to the towering, jagged icebergs.

Diamond Beach

off Route 1

You can also venture to the river mouth and nearby **Diamond Beach.** Chunks of ice sometimes wash ashore, and are scattered about like giant diamonds against a backdrop of black sand. The scene is spectacular any time of year, but truly magical when the sun is shining.

Tours

GLACIER LAGOON

Jökulsárlón Ehf; tel. 354/478-2222; www.icelagoon.is; 10am-5pm daily May and Oct., 9am-7pm daily June-Sept.; 5,900ISK

If you'd like a closer look at the icebergs, Glacier Lagoon offers tours on amphibious boats May-October. During the excursion, you sail among the huge icebergs, get to taste the 1,000-year-old ice, and, if you're lucky, see seals bobbing in the lagoon. The tour lasts about 40 minutes and includes an English-speaking guide who explains the geology of the lagoon. Tours are weather-dependent, so be sure to call ahead. Zodiac boat tours are available for 10,500ISK.

Getting There

Jökulsárlón is close to **Route 1,** 80 kilometers (50 mi) west of **Höfn** and 377 kilometers (234 mi) east of **Reykjavík,** about five hours.

★ SKAFTAFELL (VATNAJÖKULL NATIONAL PARK–SOUTH)

Skaftafell is one of East Iceland's most beautiful places, where visitors are treated to striking white glaciers against a backdrop of green fields and black sands. Skaftafell

1: Jökulsárlón, Glacier Lagoon **2:** Svartifoss waterfall

1
2

Glacial Floods

When Grímsvötn volcano erupted underneath Vatnajökull in 1996, the world watched in fascination as lava flowed from fissures and ash launched thousands of feet into the air. But another phenomenon captured the attention of millions—**jökulhlaup,** which is Icelandic for "glacial floods." A glacial flood occurs when water dammed by a sub-glacial lake is released, triggered by volcanic eruptions. Glacial lakes can hold millions to hundreds of millions of cubic meters of water and can wreak havoc on surrounding areas when released.

Locals still talk about the 1996 eruption, and you have a chance to relive it through a film shown at the **Skaftafell visitors center.**

and Jökulsárgljúfur National Parks, along with Vatnajökull glacier, combined in 2008 to become Vatnajökull National Park. Skaftafell is the southern division of the park. For more information on the park, see page 226.

A common draw for many tourists are the black-sand beaches, which are a result of glaciers grinding down the bedrock. They're particularly striking on clear days with the snowcapped mountains and blue skies in the background. Much of the black sand is carried to the sea by glacial rivers, the waves and winds shaping the sand into complex formations. In the westernmost part of the Vatnajökull region is 1,000-square-kilometer (386-sq-mi) **Skeiðarársandur,** which is the largest black glacier sand area in the world. It can be accessed by Route 1.

Tours

Tourism companies offer everything from ice walks to Jeep tours.

ICELANDIC MOUNTAIN GUIDES

tel. 354/587-9999; www.mountainguides.is

Icelandic Mountain Guides offers a year-round guided walking tour on the **Svínafellsjökull** glacier tongue in Skaftafell. The 2.5-hour tour costs 9,300ISK.

Waterfalls

HUNDAFOSS

1.5 km (0.9 mi) uphill from the visitors center, on the way to Svartifoss

Hundafoss (Hound Falls) was named after the many dogs that were swept over the edge during floods. Be prepared to take a lot of pictures here. The falls are gorgeous in all seasons. In the summer, the rocky terrain behind the falls is surrounded by beautiful greenery. The drop is steep and the roar is soothing.

ÞJÓFAFOSS

viewing point 4 km (2 mi) northwest from Route 26

Þjófafoss (Thieves' Falls) is a smaller waterfall set against a backdrop of lava fields.

SVARTIFOSS

about 1.5 km (0.9 mi) from the Skaftafell visitors center

Ahead is the more spectacular Svartifoss (Black Falls) waterfall, where thundering white water cascades over striking black basalt rock columns. Svartifoss cannot be seen from the road, but it is just 1.5 kilometers (0.9 mi) from the **Skaftafell visitors center,** and the trail is clearly marked. The **hike** is easy, and it may be a surprise that you're going uphill; the view from above will alert you. The hike is about 90 minutes round-trip at a leisurely pace.

You can either return the same way or cross the river by Svartifoss and return from there. That route gives you a closer look at **Þjófafoss.**

Hiking

NÚPSSTAÐARSKÓGAR TO SKAFTAFELL HIKE

Distance: *60 km (37 mi)*

Hiking Time: *5 days*
Information and Maps: *www.east.is*
Trailhead: *Bottom of the valley of Núpsstaðarskógar*

Hiking from Núpsstaðarskógar, a valley rich with birch trees and rivers, to Skaftafell is an ideal five-day backpack trip that gives you a great slice of the beautiful east. The hike is a challenging one, clocking in at 60 kilometers (38 mi), and reaching an altitude of 800 meters (2,625 ft) with an ascent of 450 meters (1,475 ft). Most people start the hike at the bottom of the valley of Núpsstaðarskógar, and average 6-7 hours of walking a day. Along the way, hikers are rewarded with numerous waterfalls, steep canyons, a glacier lagoon, towering mountains, and a glorious birch forest. The hike is strenuous and only safe in the summer, but it's worth it.

Food and Accommodations

Bringing your own food is your best option here. Your only close option is the restaurant at **Hótel Skaftafell.**

HÓTEL SKAFTAFELL

Skaftafelli 2 Freysnesi; tel. 354/478-1945; www.hotelskaftafell.is; rooms from 31,000ISK

Hótel Skaftafell is a 63-room hotel that looks a bit rustic, but it's comfortable and close to the national park. Rooms are standard with private bathrooms and classic countryside decor. A standard breakfast is included. The restaurant (8am-9pm daily; 3,700ISK) serves breakfast, lunch, and dinner, including traditional lamb and fish dishes as well as a few vegetarian options. The huge banquet room tends to fill up with busloads of tourists.

SKAFTAFELL CAMPGROUND

tel. 354/470-8300; open year-round; adults 1,500ISK per night, children 13-17 900ISK, children under 13 free

If you want to stay inside the park, the Skaftafell Campground is your only option. The campground is next to the entrance gate to the park; vehicle entry is allowed 7:30am-11pm. Visitors should register prior to camping. The facilities are great, but keep in mind that there is a distance between the facilities and where you set up camp. The campground offers hot showers and bathrooms (bring flip-flops; it can get pretty dirty during the height of camping season). Visitors can stock up on food and basic supplies at the visitors center, but it is advisable to bring what you need with you. The visitors center is also where you pay the camping fees. The open field accommodates about 400 tents, and there is a section for RVs with the option to pay for electricity.

Information and Services

SKAFTAFELLSSTOFA VISITOR CENTER

Skaftafellsvegur; tel. 354/478-1627; www.vatnajokulsthjodgardur.is; 10am-6pm daily Nov.-Feb., 9am-6pm daily Mar.-May and Sept.-Oct., 8am-7pm daily June-Aug.

The national park office, which is near the entrance to the park, also serves as the visitors center. Here, you will find information, maps, and someone on hand to answer all your questions about the history and geology of the region.

Getting There

Skaftafell is on the **Ring Road,** Route 1, about 330 kilometers (205 mi) east of **Reykjavík** and 130 kilometers (81 mi) west of **Höfn.**

The Highlands

Dramatic and wild, Iceland's uninhabited interior is home to an otherworldly landscape that must be seen to be believed.

It's cut by endless wind and marked by vast expanses of ice and desert. This is the most distinctive and unforgiving landscape on the island, complete with lava fields and volcanoes. The country's largest glaciers—Vatnajökull, Langjökull, and Hofsjökull—form the region's backdrop.

The isolation seems romantic to some, especially travelers seeking a relatively tourist-free area. But the highlands are not for those seeking lush greenery and gorgeous ocean views in the background. Largely devoid of plant life, the highlands are essentially a desert, but starkly

Highlights

Look for ★ to find recommended sights, activities, dining, and lodging.

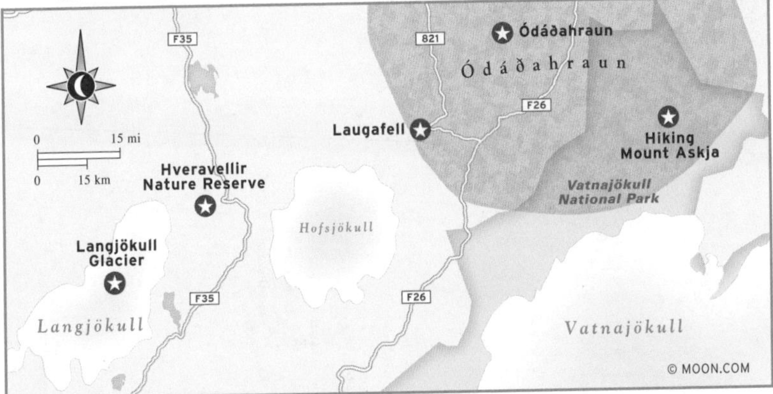

★ **Ódáðahraun:** See unusual lava and sand formations shaped by eruptions on the largest lava field in Iceland—which is actually considered an arctic desert (page 268).

★ **Laugafell:** This popular geothermal hot spot is a desert oasis in an isolated stretch of the highlands (page 268).

★ **Hiking Mount Askja:** A can't-miss adventure, hiking this volcano offers sensational views (page 269).

★ **Langjökull Glacier:** Iceland's second-largest glacier, this mammoth ice cap beckons (page 272).

★ **Hveravellir Nature Reserve:** Soak in a hot spring and camp overnight in one of Europe's last great wilderness spots (page 272).

The Highlands

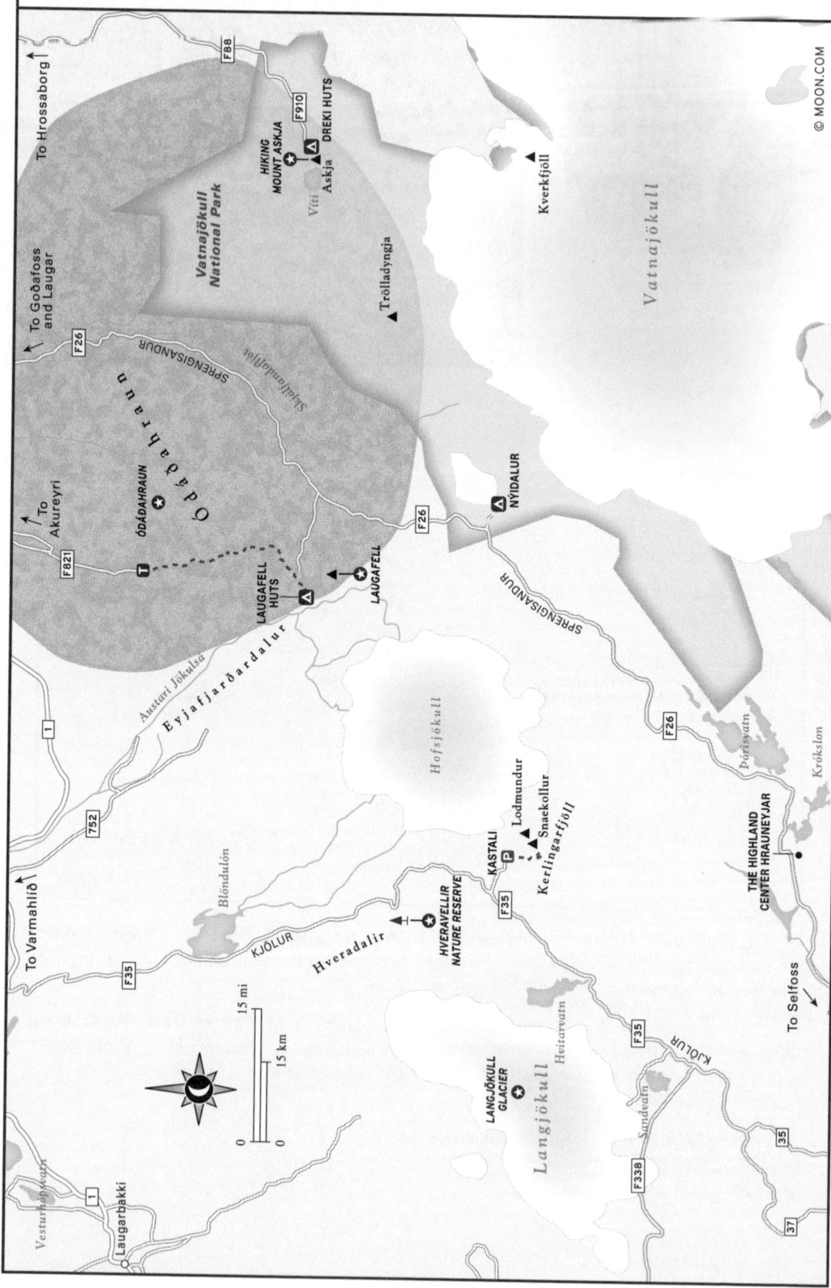

beautiful. If you are an avid hiker, informed and prepared, and looking to explore something different in Iceland, this region may be for you.

PLANNING YOUR TIME

Planning a trip to the highlands depends very much on what you want to see and do. For a peek at the interior without the burden of driving, take a **day tour** to see glaciers, volcanoes, and the landscape. Most companies offering tours to the highlands are based in Reykjavík. Other travelers like to plan **multiday hikes** throughout the interior. If you are keen on a lengthy hike, be sure to plan thoroughly, bring adequate gear and supplies, and take proper safety precautions.

Travelers have far fewer choices for accommodations (mainly huts) and food, and they must stay abreast of the weather forecast throughout the day, as the weather can change quickly. Be prepared for anything in the highlands, and make sure to book your accommodations ahead of time.

SAFETY

Navigating the highlands should not be taken lightly. The roads are rough, the wind is punishing, and the weather can be unpredictable—it can snow any day of the year. Pay close attention to road closures, and if a road calls for a **super Jeep** (a huge Jeep with gigantic tires outfitted to handle rough terrain), heed the warning. If you attempt the ride in a smaller car or city SUV, you will likely damage your rental vehicle. The best plan is to discuss your itinerary with the rental company and see if a super Jeep is necessary. Do not guess; a mistake will be costly. Also, be sure to **fill up your tank** before heading out, because there are no full-service gas stations in the highlands.

If you are planning a **hike,** be sure to wear **appropriate windproof clothing,** bring an adequate amount of **water** and **food,** and alert people of your trip itinerary. You can, and should, **register your trip** at www.safetravel.is. Bring maps, a **GPS device,** and a **compass,** and know where all the **emergency huts** are located on your route. Be prepared for anything, and don't underestimate Iceland's weather; always check for **weather alerts** before setting off on any hike. If you find yourself in an emergency, dial the **emergency number 112.**

GETTING AROUND

The highlands are a seasonal destination, and that season is short. Snow could fall any day of the year. If you are planning a trip in the summer, you may still face road closures due to a late snowfall or possible volcanic activity. Roads to the interior are typically only open **mid-June-August,** but check for closures before you head out. For up-to-date conditions, visit the **Icelandic Road and Coastal Administration** website at www.road.is.

When it comes to **car rentals,** don't skimp on your vehicle choice if you are planning to drive to the region. You're required to drive an **F-road-approved four-wheel-drive vehicle** in the highlands, which have many unpaved, rough roads and other challenges. Many different insurance options are offered on car rentals, and be mindful that driving the Ring Road is very different from driving in the highlands, where there can be sandstorms and wind damage, so pick the right insurance for the region you plan to travel to. Fill up with gas before you leave and take gas cans.

TOURS

Don't want to worry about renting a car and navigating the highlands on your own? These tour companies offer everything from day trips to multiday tours.

ARCTIC ADVENTURES

tel. 354/562-7000; www.adventures.is

Arctic Adventures is a Reykjavík-based

Previous: the volcanic landscape of the highlands; a super Jeep at Langjökull glacier; flowers growing in Askja's lava field.

company that operates a June-September three-day hiking tour where you start off by exploring the Westman Islands before hiking along Fjaðrárgljúfur, a deep canyon, Laki, a series of craters, and Lakagígar, a volcanic fissure. You then continue to the rugged landscapes of the Landamannalaugar, which is located in the Fjallabak Nature Reserve in the highlands. The tour (119,990ISK) includes hiking, sightseeing, and Landmannalaugar facility fees. Guests are picked up and dropped off in Reykjavík. The tour also includes two nights of accommodation with a private bathroom and breakfast.

ICELANDIC MOUNTAIN GUIDES

tel. 354/587-9999; www.mountainguides.is

Icelandic Mountain Guides runs a five-day hiking tour from June-September to Laugavegur trail in the highlands. You will board a bus in Reykjavík at 7am that will take you through the mountain tracks, where you will see the mighty Hekla volcano as well as other volcanoes and mountains before arriving in Landmannalaugar in the early afternoon. Tour participants will hike 4-7 hours per day, ranging 12-17 kilometers (7.5-10.5 mi). The package costs 234,900ISK.

Route F26 (Sprengisandur)

Black lava, gigantic boulders, and towering mountains await you along Sprengisandur. Tourists travel to this region to check out what is essentially an arctic desert. It's dry and barren, with its water trapped in the glaciers. Iceland's summer is warm enough for significant melting.

SIGHTS

Trölladyngja

Route F910, GPS coordinates N 64.8931, W 17.2547

Trölladyngja (Troll's Volcano) is the largest shield volcano, a domed volcano that is comprised of fluid lava flows, in the country, and connects the Grimsvötn and Bárðarbunga central volcanoes. Mount Trölladyngja (1,468 m/4,816 ft) is still active and only viewable from the road. It's 10 kilometers (6 mi) in diameter with a 100-meter (328-ft) crater on top. Lava flowed from it in all directions, especially to the north and west. The Gæsavötn Route F910 passes through the north of it.

★ Ódáðahraun

Route F88

Ódáðahraun (Crime Lava Field) is not only the largest lava field in Iceland, it's the largest desert in Europe, spanning more than 6,000 square kilometers (2,317 sq mi). Black, brown, and gray colors dominate the landscape. Visitors to the area will see endless sand, vast expanses of lava, and interesting geological formations caused by volcanic activity over the centuries. The lava shapes range from flat and smooth to rough and jagged. The region garnered its name, "crime lava," based on lore that numerous criminals hid out in the area trying to elude the authorities. The wind blows strongly, and there always seems to be a chill in the air. The isolation can be overwhelming—it's an eerie place to visit, though great for roaming and taking photos. Route F88 takes you to Ódáðahraun.

★ Laugafell

Route F821, GPS coordinates N 65.0278, W 18.3319

Laugafell (Bath Mountain) is situated northeast of the **Hofsjökull glacier,** about 20 kilometers (12 mi) southwest from the end of the **Eyjafjarðardalur valley.** It's a special place in the vast barren stretch of the highlands, with the spectacular 879-meter (2,883-ft) mountain adjacent to a geothermal hot spot. Two **hot springs** (free) open to visitors are in the northwestern portion of the mountain, and patches of grass and plants among the bubbling pools make it a desert oasis. It is important to have a good map for this region to find the hot springs and trails. Three **mountain huts** (www.fi.is; rooms from 17,000ISK) are open during the summer; they have cooking facilities, and guests can access a geothermal nature pool. Laugafell and the region are accessible by **Route F821.**

Askja

Route F88

Askja is a caldera in the remote, awe-inspiring Dyngjufjöll Mountains. Essentially huge volcanic craters, calderas are formed by collapsing land after a volcanic eruption. At 1,519 meters (4,983 ft), Askja emerges from the **Ódáðahraun lava field,** and the terrain is quite rocky. **Víti** is a tremendous pale blue lake-filled crater that emerged after the great eruption of the Askja volcano in 1875. It's possible to take a dip in the water, which reaches a temperature of about 30°C (86°F).

Askja is one of the most popular destinations in the highlands. There are two **mountain huts** (the Dreki huts, www.ffa.is) on **Route F88,** about 100 kilometers (62 mi) from the Ring Road. From there, it's an 8-kilometer (5-mi) drive up into the Askja caldera. It is a **walk** of about 2.5 kilometers (1.5 mi) from the **car park** to Víti. Keep in mind that the roads are usually only open for about three months, from late June until September. Depending on the weather, the open period could be longer or shorter.

Kverkfjöll

Route F910 to Route F902, GPS N 64.7475, W 16.6315

Reaching 1,764 meters (5,787 ft), the Kverkfjöll volcano includes two calderas that are filled with ice. The area is striking for its range of colors, with a deep black background that gives way to gorgeous blues and icy white. The main attractions are the **ice caves** that were created by hot springs, slowly melting the ice into interesting shapes. Stay safe, however, and please observe the caves from the outside; you never know when the ice mass could give way. To get to Kverkfjöll, take **Route F910** southeast to **Route F902.**

SPORTS AND RECREATION

★ Hiking Askja

Distance: *11.5 km (7.1 mi) round-trip*

Hiking Time: *2 hours round-trip*

Information and Maps: *www.visiticeland.is*

Trailhead: *Parking lot (N 65.0140, W 16.4500), which can be reached by Route 1 to Route F88*

Passionate hikers will want to walk the rim of Askja. It offers some slopes and ultra-rocky terrain along with spectacular views of lava fields, mountains, and the mighty **Víti crater.** It's about a 30-minute moderate hike, 2.5 kilometers (1.5 mi) one-way, from the **car park** up to the caldera. The landscape is punishing, and devoid of vegetation, but the muted colors of brown and gray are striking against spots of snow and the blue water in the crater. The highest point in Askja is 1,516 meters (4,973 ft). The rim is about 6.5 kilometers (4 mi) around, which takes about an hour to walk. If you are not planning to hike the rim, you can just explore near the car park. To reach the car park, take **Route 1** to **Route F88.**

While the trail is well maintained, the main challenge is weather. If the forecast calls for wind, it's best to skip the planned hike. Do not underestimate the power of Iceland's wind, especially in the highlands.

FOOD AND ACCOMMODATIONS

Make sure to book your accommodation ahead of time.

THE HIGHLAND CENTER HRAUNEYJAR

Route F26; tel. 354/487-7782; www.thehighlandcenter.is; open year-round; rooms from 38,000ISK

The Highland Center Hrauneyjar offers 99 rooms ranging from doubles with shared bathroom facilities to double rooms with private bathrooms and free Wi-Fi. There are also triple rooms available as well as sleeping bag accommodation for a cheaper price. The GPS coordinates are N 64.1964, W 19.2655. Rooms are sparsely decorated with a bed, desk, and

1
2
3
4

Navigating the Arctic Desert Safely

Every year there are tourists that arrive in the highlands looking for a once-in-a-lifetime adventure but find themselves unprepared. Safety needs to be your top priority. Some tourists need to be rescued, and then there are those who don't make it out alive. Do not underestimate the weather in Iceland, even in the summer as there can be brutal winds mixed with wet weather any time of year. Keep these things in mind—some may seem like common sense, but they're still important to note.

- A **car approved for F roads** is required in the highlands, and if the trail calls for a **super Jeep,** take heed.
- **Check the weather and road conditions.** Before you head out on your journey, visit www.en.vedur.is for the latest weather information and www.road.is for road conditions.
- **Have enough gas for your trip.** Gas stations are few and far between in the highlands.
- **Dress the part.** Make sure you have waterproof layers, warm clothing, and sturdy footwear.
- **Bring adequate food and water.** Don't count on buying food along the journey.
- Have **maps,** a **compass,** and a **charged mobile phone** on hand.
- If you find yourself in trouble, the **emergency number** in Iceland is **112.**

small table. It's not luxury, but it's the only option other than mountain huts. Along with the guesthouse, Hrauneyjar has a **restaurant** (7am-8pm daily) open year-round, a **gas station,** and a tourist shop that offers food, maps, and fishing permits. It's a good idea to stop here to pick up essentials (like food, water, and gas) even if you don't plan to stay at the guesthouse.

NÝIDALUR

tel. 354/860-3334; www.fi.is; July-Aug.; 9,500ISK, tent camping outside 2,000ISK

There are mountain huts along the valley Nýidalur that sleep 79 people total; each hut usually sleeps around 20 people. The GPS coordinates are N 64.7355, W 18.0725. The area can be reached by Route F26. The huts have cooking facilities, toilets, and hot showers. It costs 9,500ISK per night to stay inside the huts, and 2,000ISK for tent camping outside in an open field. Shower use costs 500ISK. The huts are open July-August.

1: lava formations at Ódáðahraun **2:** the Víti crater on Mount Askja **3:** the Dreki huts at Drekagil gorge **4:** glacier caves at Kverkfjöll

LAUGAFELL HUTS

GPS N 65.0269, W 18.3321; tel. 354/833-5687; www.ffa.is; open summer; 8,000ISK

The Laugafell huts are located about 15 kilometers (9 mi) northeast of Hofsjökull glacier and 20 kilometers (12 mi) southwest from the end of the Eyjafjarðardalur valley. The huts can be reached by Route F752 or F881 from Route F26 or by F821. Accommodations are basic, with gas available for cooking and restrooms near the swimming pool. It costs 8,000ISK to stay the night, and showers cost an additional 500ISK. The huts are open only during the summer months.

DREKI HUTS

GPS N 65.0417, W 16.5948; tel. 354/462-2720; www.ffa.is, www.nat.is; open summer; 9,000ISK

The mountain huts closest to Askja are at Drekagil gorge. The Dreki huts can be reached by Route F88 from the Ring Road east of Lake Mývatn or by Route F910 from Route F26. There are two residential huts on the site that can accommodate 60 people. The huts have gas available for cooking and there are toilets and shower facilities. The Dreki huts are an ideal base for those interested in exploring the Askja caldera, which is an 8-kilometer (5-mi) drive from the huts. It costs 9,000ISK to stay the night. Showers cost an additional 500ISK. The huts are open only during the summer months.

GETTING THERE AND AROUND

By F-Road-Approved 4WD Vehicle

Route F26 is not for the faint of heart. It cannot be emphasized enough that you must have a proper vehicle to navigate this road—an **F-road-approved four-wheel drive.** Weather is cruel to this road, and there are rivers to ford, large uneven sections, gravel, and potholes. The 200-kilometer (124-mi) route roams from **Mount Hekla** in the south to the glorious waterfall **Goðafoss** in the north. The route is not a year-round destination, and the road typically opens at the **end of June.** It could open later if the region had a particularly harsh winter with a lot of snowfall. To check road closures and the opening date, visit the **Icelandic Road and Coastal Administration** website (www.road.is).

Another important detail to keep in mind is that the only **gas station** along Route F26 is at **Hrauneyjar.** Be prepared and fill up before your journey. Also make sure you have all **food, water,** and **supplies** that you need. Depending on where you are staying the day before, you can stock up in Reykjavík before you head out, or at a town in the south.

Tours

To get to the region by bus, check out the schedule of **Reykjavik Excursions** (tel. 354/562-1011; www.re.is), which offers trips June-October. The 12-hour round trip costs 9,900ISK and the tour departs from **Reykjavík.** You can also purchase a bus pass that allows you to hop off and on the bus. It is necessary to book in advance.

Route F35 (Kjölur)

For a less treacherous route to the highlands, Route F35 is your best bet. The majority of the route is flat and can be accessible up until **October** (depending on the weather, of course). As elsewhere in the highlands, an **F-road-approved four-wheel drive** vehicle is required. Be safe, monitor weather reports, and be aware of road conditions.

Route F35 runs along the east side of Langjökull, between it and **Hofsjökull.** From **Reykjavík,** you head east on **Route 1.** Before you reach the town of **Selfoss,** turn left on F35 and continue past **Gullfoss** for about 37 kilometers (23 mi).

SIGHTS

★ Langjökull Glacier

Route F35

At 952 square kilometers (368 sq mi), Langjökull (Long Glacier) is the second-largest ice cap in Iceland after Vatnajökull. The ice is quite thick, up to 580 meters (1,900 ft) deep. The highest point of the ice cap is about 1,450 meters (4,757 ft) above sea level. The rocky terrain and snowy patches are vast and haunting.

★ Hveravellir Nature Reserve

Route F35; tel. 354/452-4200; www.hveravellir.is

Situated in the western highlands, the Hveravellir Nature Reserve is one of the last great wilderness spots in Europe. It's about 90 kilometers (56 mi) north of **Gullfoss** on **Route F35.** Hveravellir is a natural geothermal hot spot with smoking fumaroles and bubbling water holes, and it's a special experience to see geothermal energy at work. It's also a popular place to hike.

1: Langjökull glacier **2:** Hveravellir Nature Reserve

1

2

There are private rooms in one of two **huts**, called the New Hut (28,800ISK per room, linens and breakfast included), **dormitories** (8,000ISK per person), and a **campsite** (1,900ISK per person) available within the reserve. One bathing-friendly, waist-deep **pool** is situated close to the mountain huts, and it's a safe place to take a dip.

Kerlingarfjöll

GPS N 64.6834, W 19.2999, Route F35; tel. 354/664-7000; www.kerlingarfjoll.is

The mountain range Kerlingarfjöll (Women's Mountains) shows all the characteristics of a matured caldera, including volcanic formations and geothermal hot spots. In short, this is a geology buff's dream. The towering peaks were created by eruptions from a large caldera lying under the mountains; while the caldera is still considered active, it has been silent for tens of thousands of years. Visitors will see steep slopes and pointy peaks dotted with ice, leading into a hotbed of geothermal activity. While the earth steams below, aboveground it's quiet and desolate.

Accommodations are available at **Kerlingarfjöll**, which has **double rooms** (38,800ISK), **private cabins** (58,080ISK), a **campsite** for tents (2,000ISK), and **dorms** (7,680ISK per person). The breakfast buffet is 2,500ISK per person. At the end of the 2021 season, the owners announced that they were planning to embark on extensive renovations, closing the facilities until July 2022.

To get to Kerlingarfjöll from **Gullfoss,** drive north on **F35.** For 15 kilometers (9 mi) the road is asphalt, and the remaining 38-kilometer (24-mi) section is gravel.

Hofsjökull Glacier

GPS N 64.8167, W 18.8167, east of Vatnajokull, between Vididalur and Hofsdalur

Hofsjökull (Temple Glacier) is the third-largest glacier in Iceland after Vatnajökull and Langjökull. It is situated in the western highlands, north of the mountain range **Kerlingarfjöll.** The glacier covers an area of 925 square kilometers (357 sq mi), reaching 1,765 meters (5,790 ft) at the top. It's vast and can be quite windy. Also, visitors will have to be careful of huge crevasses in the ice.

HIKING

Hikers have many choices for roaming the interior. These popular options vary in scenery and degree of difficulty.

Hveradalir

GPS N 64.6453, W 19.2825

Hiking the geothermal area Hveradalir (Hot Springs Valley) is wildly popular, and for good reason. The valley offers views of mountains, vast expanses of desert-like earth marked by steam vents (reminding visitors that the land is very much alive), and hot springs. Hveradalir is accessible off **Route 1.**

NEÐRI-HVERADALIR HIKE

Distance: *3-km (2-mi) loop*
Hiking Time: *3-hour loop*
Information and Maps: *www.visiticeland.is*
Trailhead: *Neðri-Hveradalir car park*

A moderate hike begins at the car park by Neðri-Hveradalir (Lower Hveradalir) and takes you through the geothermal area Hveradalir, where ice and fire meet. The route is a 3-kilometer (2-mi) loop and takes about three hours. Hikers will view the stark white glacial landscape and see the steam rise out of the ground near the numerous hot springs. Muted colors of brown and black in a desert-like landscape give way to pockets of stark white snow in some regions and lush green vegetation in others. Every few meters you'll want to stop and take in the views, and everything seems to warrant a photo.

ÁSGARÐSÁ RIVER HIKE

Distance: *11.2-km (7-mi) loop*
Hiking Time: *5-hour loop*
Information and Maps: *www.visiticeland.is*
Trailhead: *Keis parking lot*

For a longer, more demanding hike, start at the car park called Keis, toward the bottom of Hveradalir, where you follow the Ásgarðsá River for 4.5 kilometers (2.8 mi). The hike is

Crossing a River

When driving in the highlands you will likely come across a river or two. They can range from small creeks to large rivers that vary in depth. Below are a few tips that you should keep in mind when you arrive at a river crossing.

- Never cross a river unless you are **100 percent confident** of how to do it. If you are unsure or uncomfortable crossing, wait for another vehicle to cross first.
- Look for the best place to ford, where it is most **shallow.**
- Note that rivers tend to have less volume **earlier in the day.**
- Wade into the river with two or three other people, clasping arms, to **gauge the depth** of the river.

an 11.2-kilometer (7-mi) loop. Being so close to the river, you will see vegetation, which is a rare sight in much of the highlands. During the hike, there will be points where you have to cross water, so dress accordingly. Hikers will pass hills and geothermal hot spots as the river twists and turns. Overall, it's a five-hour hike and moderately difficult.

Kerlingarfjöll

Distance: *7-km (4-mi) loop*
Hiking Time: *6-hour loop*
Information and Maps: *www.visiticeland.is*
Trailhead: *Kastali parking lot*

For a more difficult walk, start at the car park called Kastali and continue to 1,432-meter (4,698-ft) Mount Lodmundur, then to the highest peak of Kerlingarfjöll, Mount Snækollur, at 1,460 meters (4,790 ft). The trail is rocky and there are quite a few slopes, but the payoff is the gorgeous views of the barren landscape below and mountains in the distance. It's one of the best overviews of the highlands. This is a 7-kilometer (4-mi) hike, in a loop, which takes about six hours.

GETTING THERE AND AROUND

By F-Road-Approved 4WD Vehicle

The 200-kilometer (124-mi) Kjölur route (Route F35) begins near the picturesque waterfall **Gullfoss** in the south and extends to **Blönduós** in the northwest. This route is not a year-round destination: The road typically opens the **middle of June,** but it could be later if the winter was harsh. The road closes in **September,** but how early in September depends on the weather. You need an **F-road-approved four-wheel-drive vehicle** for the journey. Be sure to gas up before you head to the highlands, as there are no gas stations in the region. It's best to get supplies in Reykjavík or a large town in the south. Depending on the duration of your trip, it might be necessary to bring **gas cans.**

TOP EXPERIENCE

Ring Road Road Trip

The Ring Road (Route 1) encircles Iceland, connecting many of the most popular attractions. Paved for most of its 1,332-kilometer (828-mi) length, the Ring Road is the most accessible route around the country. Driving along, you'll encounter breathtaking landscapes ranging from towering mountains to barren lava fields to glaciers looming in the distance.

The Ring Road is popular for a reason: The loop is a convenient way to see the best of Iceland's nature, starting with the most popular attractions in the south to lesser-known gems around the island. For travelers who have at least 10 days, driving the Ring Road is ideal, the best use of time to see as much as possible without backtracking to one or two bases.

Highlights

Look for ★ to find recommended sights, activities, dining, and lodging.

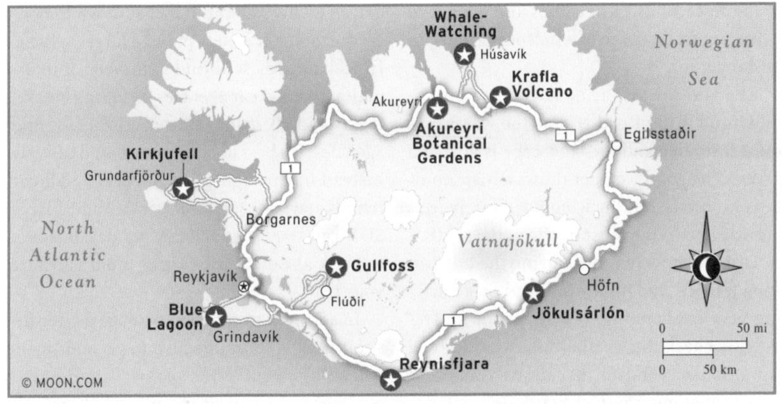

★ **Blue Lagoon:** The famous Blue Lagoon lives up to the hype as a place to relax after your flight to the island (page 282).

★ **Gullfoss:** If you see one waterfall in Iceland, let it be this spectacular example along the Golden Circle route (page 283).

★ **Reynisfjara:** Explore one of Iceland's most beautiful glacial black-sand beaches (page 284).

★ **Jökulsárlón:** Stand in awe of this icy, otherworldly glacial lake (page 286).

★ **Krafla Volcano:** Get up close to one of Iceland's powerful volcanoes (page 287).

★ **Whale-Watching in Húsavik:** Tiny Húsavík has earned its reputation as the whale-watching capital of the island (page 288).

★ **Akureyri Botanical Gardens:** The "capital" of the North is rightfully proud of its pretty, eclectic botanical gardens (page 290).

★ **Kirkjufell:** This conical mountain is one of the most striking sights in Iceland (page 291).

The suggested itinerary, which includes the Snæfellsnes Peninsula, can be supplemented with the many other different options in the destination chapters. Some of the can't-miss sites include the Golden Circle attractions, Seljalandsfoss and Skógafoss waterfalls in the south, Skaftafell and Jókulsárlón in the east, the Mývatn area and Akureyri in the north, and Snæfellsnes in the west. For activities, it's highly recommended to take a whale-watching tour in Húsavík and take a boat tour among the icebergs at Jókulsárlón.

Planning the Drive

SEASONAL CONSIDERATIONS AND ROAD CONDITIONS

Plan your trip on the Ring Road in the **summer (June-August)** and the shoulder months **(May and September).** Iceland's weather is known for being notoriously changeable and this, of course, impacts a Ring Road drive. Sunny skies can give way to fog in seconds, rain comes and goes, and drivers must be aware of windspeeds that can be dangerous.

The **summer** is the most popular time to undergo a Ring Road trip as the weather is most favorable and the landscape is lush and green. The good weather draws a high number of tourists, but the Ring Road rarely feels crowded, with the most traffic in the south.

Despite snow removal during the **winter,** snowfall, ice, and high winds can make driving very challenging. It's important to frequently check the weather forecast and road conditions as windstorms can strike any time of year, making driving hazardous.

Keep in mind that it's always necessary to check **road conditions** before you head out in your car. Weather changes rapidly in Iceland, and you do not want to be unprepared. You should check weather and road conditions at the beginning of each day before hitting the road. Important websites to look at include **www.road.is** and **www.vedur.is.**

RENTING YOUR CAR

For a summer road trip, a **2WD** car will be adequate, though having a **4WD** vehicle wouldn't hurt. In the winter, you will want a car with **studded tires** for potentially icy roads. You should only rent a campervan in the summer months, when campsites are open.

For regular cars, the Ring Road can be driven in any size car. It comes down to preference: Some travelers prefer a larger vehicle. In Iceland, you will find a number of international rental car agencies including **Hertz, Avis,** and **Budget,** as well as local rental agencies. It's best to book your rental directly instead of through third parties. Small car rentals start at 15,000ISK per day and a large SUV can start at 40,000ISK per day. It is best to book ahead, at least three months before your trip.

In addition to collision damage waiver insurance, it is recommended to get additional **gravel protection insurance,** and possibly sand and ash insurance as well. When collecting your car, you should **take photos of existing damage** to the vehicle, and make sure you understand your rental agreement and insurance policy. Check lights and tires, and make sure there's a **spare tire. GPS devices** can be rented through your car rental agency for a small fee. It's always a good idea to have **paper maps** just in case, too.

Previous: the Ring Road; the Blue Lagoon; walkway near Selfoss on the Golden Circle.

WHAT TO PACK

Packing for a road trip can seem daunting, so here is a handy guide.

- **Paper maps,** which can be purchased at gas stations or tourist information centers (GPS optional)
- **Reusable water bottle**
- **Snacks** for the car
- **Sturdy walking shoes** or boots with good tread
- Layers and **waterproof outerwear**
- **Bathing suit** for swimming pools and hot springs
- **Mobile phone, chargers,** and **adapters**

GETTING GAS

Gas stations are located around the Ring Road, but there are pockets where they become scarce, namely between **Vík** in the south and **Mývatn** in the north. It's a good idea to **fully fill your tank** when you have the opportunity.

For a medium-size car, it costs about 10,000ISK to fill up a tank with petrol. At the time of writing, petrol costs about 260ISK per liter and diesel costs 230ISK per liter. You can check up-to-date gas prices at www.gsmbensin.is.

Unmanned gas stations are popular in rural areas. You must have a **4-digit PIN** for your credit card to fill up at these gas stations. If you don't have a card with a PIN, contact your bank ahead of your visit.

ENVIRONMENTALLY FRIENDLY TRAVEL

Here are some tips for making your Ring Road trip more environmentally friendly:

- Drink the tap water instead of buying bottles of water in shops. Iceland has some of the cleanest water on the planet.
- Protect the land by never driving off-road.
- Be sure to camp within campsites.
- Make sure you recycle.

Unfortunately, Iceland's current infrastructure does not make it feasible to rent an electric car for this road trip. Charging stations are few and far between in many areas of the island.

DRIVING LAWS

There are a few rules travelers should be aware of when driving the Ring Road.

- **Off-road driving is strictly prohibited** and there are **hefty fines** from authorities.
- All passengers in a vehicle must **wear a seat belt.**
- **Talking on a mobile phone** while driving is prohibited.
- **Driving under the influence** is illegal and fines start at 100,000ISK.
- Drivers must **use headlights at all times,** even in bright daylight.

Speed Limits

Speeding **fines** are high, and can be collected through the rental car company, which will have an imprint of your credit card. Fines can range from 30,000ISK to 200,000ISK. There are **speed cameras** along the Ring Road. The speed limits are:

- 90 km/h (56 mph) on paved roads (like the Ring Road)
- 80 km/h (50 mph) on gravel roads
- 50 km/h (31 mph) or less in residential areas

CELL PHONE SERVICE

Iceland has surprisingly good cell phone service across the island, even in the highlands. You can purchase **SIM cards** at Keflavik airport, as well as shops around the country. The three main cell phone providers in Iceland are **Vodafone, Siminn,** and **Nova.** Always make sure your mobile phone is **fully charged.** In case of an emergency, the national emergency number is **112.**

Ring Road Road Trip

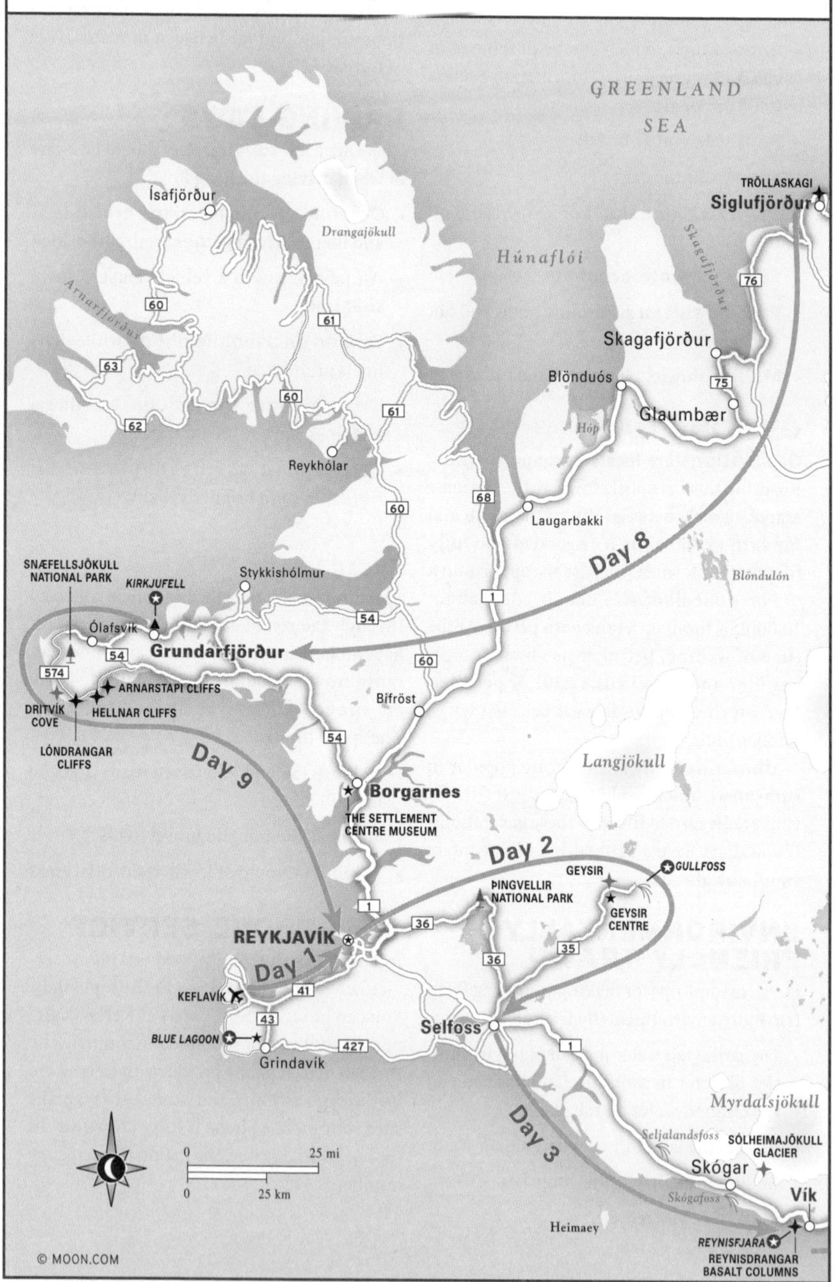

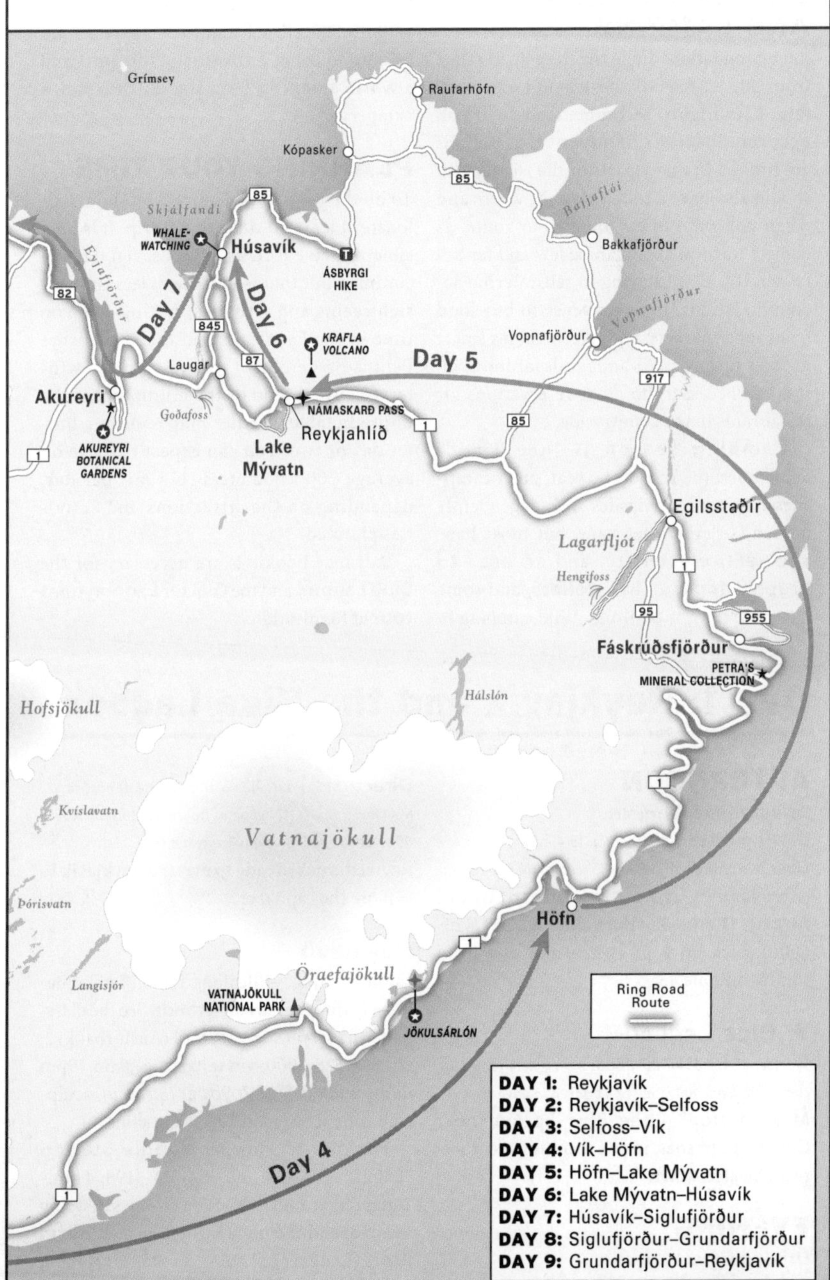
Grímsey
Raufarhöfn
Kópasker
85
Skjálfandi
Bakkafjörður
Þistilfjörður
WHALE-WATCHING
Húsavík
ÁSBYRGI HIKE
Eyjafjörður
82
Day 7
Day 6
845
KRAFLA VOLCANO
Vopnafjörður
Laugar
87
Day 5
917
Akureyri
NÁMASKARÐ PASS
Goðafoss
Reykjahlíð
1
Lake Mývatn
AKUREYRI BOTANICAL GARDENS
Egilsstaðir
Lagarfljót
Hengifoss
95
955
Fáskrúðsfjörður
PETRA'S MINERAL COLLECTION
Hálslón
Hofsjökull
Kvíslavatn
Vatnajökull
Þórisvatn
Höfn
Öraefajökull
Langisjór
VATNAJÖKULL NATIONAL PARK
JÖKULSÁRLÓN
Ring Road Route
Day 4
DAY 1: Reykjavík
DAY 2: Reykjavík–Selfoss
DAY 3: Selfoss–Vík
DAY 4: Vík–Höfn
DAY 5: Höfn–Lake Mývatn
DAY 6: Lake Mývatn–Húsavík
DAY 7: Húsavík–Siglufjörður
DAY 8: Siglufjörður–Grundarfjörður
DAY 9: Grundarfjörður–Reykjavík

FOOD, ACOMMODATIONS, AND CAMPING

Accommodations along the Ring Road range from budget-friendly hostels to luxury hotels. It is highly recommended to **book accommodations in advance,** as options are limited in many parts of the island. You should also have a rough plan for where and when you want to eat along your route, as choices in rural areas can be few and far between. If you are staying in self-catering accommodations, it makes sense to buy food from supermarkets, and in general it's smart to stock up on snacks and meals for the road. It is not necessary to make reservations for restaurants in the countryside.

Camping season is June 1-mid-September; the rest of the year, most campsites are closed. Campsites are independently owned, so amenities vary, but most have **showers, electricity,** and an **area to prepare food;** all have **toilets,** and some have **washing machines.** Wild camping in Iceland is against the law (without permission from the landowner). A campsite can range 1,200-2,500ISK per night. Campers should be sure to bring a **three-season tent** and a **warm sleeping bag;** you can also park a campervan.

PLANNING YOUR TIME

To do the Ring Road justice, you should allocate at least **10 days** to the trip. It is possible to drive it in as few as seven days in summer, but that would mean less time for sightseeing and activities, cutting down on time in the Eastfjords and the Snæfellsnes Peninsula detour in the west. In the winter, 10 days should be the minimum, as the unpredictable weather may require a buffer day or two. You can expect to drive on average 200 kilometers (124 mi) per day, depending on the attractions and activities planned.

Advance bookings are necessary for the **Blue Lagoon** and the **Glacier Lagoon boat tour** at Jökulsárlón.

Day 1: Reykjavík and the Blue Lagoon

AFTERNOON

Driving time: *25 minutes*
Driving distance: *21.5 km (13.4 mi)*
Directions: *Route 41 to Route 43 south to the Blue Lagoon*

After landing at **Keflavík International Airport** (Keflavíkurflugvöllur; tel. 354/425-6000), pick up your **rental car** and head south on Route 43.

★ Blue Lagoon

Svartsengi; tel. 354/420-8800; www.bluelagoon.com; 9am-9pm daily, must be booked in advance

Make a stop at the Blue Lagoon near Grindavík to soak in the soothing, geothermally heated water.

EVENING

Driving time: *50 minutes*
Driving distance: *49 km (30 mi)*
Directions: *Route 43 north to Route 41 east to Reykjavik; Route 41 becomes Route 40; turn on Route 49 west to get to Reykjavík city center*

Revived, you're ready to drive to Reykjavík to explore the capital city.

Reykjavík

In the evening, walk along **Tjörnin** pond before visiting the harbor, **Grandi.** See the glass-paneled **Harpa concert hall** (Austurbakki 2; tel. 354/528-5000; www.harpa.is; 9am-10pm daily) and the ***Sun Voyager*** *(Sæbraut)* sculpture, which resembles a Viking ship.

For dinner, stop by **Noodle Station** (Laugavegur 103; tel. 354/551-3198; 11am-10pm daily; 1,880ISK) for a cheap, satisfying meal. Spend the night at well-located **Hótel Frón** (Laugavegur 22A; tel. 354/511-4666; www.hotelfron.is; rooms from 25,000ISK).

DAY 1 INDEX

Day 2: The Golden Circle

MORNING

Driving time: *50 minutes*

Driving distance: *48 km (30 mi)*

Directions: *Route 49 east turns into Route 1 (the Ring Road); Route 1 to Route 36 east to Þingvellir National Park*

From Reykjavík, set off on a tour of the Golden Circle, a trio of must-see sights.

Þingvellir National Park

Þingvellir National Park is a geological wonder and also the birthplace of democracy in Iceland. The **Þingvellir Interpretive Center** (tel. 354/482-2660; www.thingvellir.is; 9am-8pm daily June-Aug., 9am-5pm daily Sept.-Apr.; free, parking 750ISK) gives a great overview of the national park's history and geographical significance, along with maps for hiking trails. Spend 1-2 hours roaming this UNESCO World Heritage site's main sights, including **Almannagjá** (All Man's Gorge) and **Lögberg** (Law Rock).

AFTERNOON

Driving time: *1 hour*

Driving distance: *70 km (73 mi)*

Directions: *Route 36 to Routes 365, 37, and 35 northeast to Geysir and Gullfoss*

Geysir

Heading east, Route 36 turns into Route 365, through a roundabout to Route 37 to the geothermal area of Geysir, about a 50-minute drive. The famous Geysir hasn't erupted since 2005, but nearby **Strokkur** erupts every 5-7 minutes. Eat lunch in the **Geysir Center cafeteria** (Biskupstungnabraut; tel. 354/519-6020; www.geysircenter.com; 10am-8pm daily), where you can also shop for souvenirs.

★ Gullfoss

After lunch, head 10 minutes east on Route 35 to the famous Gullfoss, where white water thrashes down two tiers.

EVENING

Driving time: *1 hour*

Driving distance: *72 km (45 mi)*

Directions: *Route 35 southwest to Route 1 southeast to Selfoss*

Selfoss

After a day of sightseeing, drive to Selfoss, the largest town in South Iceland, where you will have dinner and spend the night at **Hotel South Coast** (Eyrarvegur 11-13; tel. 354/464-1113; www.hotelsouthcoast.is; rooms from 33,000ISK).

DAY 2 INDEX

Day 3: The South Coast

MORNING

Driving time: *1.5 hours*
Driving distance: *100 km (62 mi)*
Directions: *Route 1 east to Route 249 north to Seljalandsfoss; Route 1 east to Skógafoss*

Seljalandsfoss

From Selfoss, drive along the spectacular south coast on Route 1, with your first stop at Seljalandsfoss, a beautiful waterfall about an hour east. Turn left on **Þórsmerkurvegur (Route 249),** where a car park for Seljalandsfoss is clearly signed. At Seljalandsfoss, you can actually walk behind the falls on a footpath at the base of the waterfall. Explore and snap some photos for about an hour.

Skógafoss

After visiting Seljalandsfoss, continue on Route 1 east for another 30 minutes to Skógafoss. Turn left on Skógar, then left again on Skógafoss, where you'll see the car park for the massive 60-meter (197-ft) waterfall in the village of **Skógar.**

AFTERNOON AND EVENING

Driving time: *45 min*
Driving distance: *46 km (29 mi)*
Directions: *Route 1 east to Route 215 south to Reynisfjara; Route 1 east to Vík*

★ Reynisfjara

Next, head to Reynisfjara beach near the village of Vík. This is about a 30-minute drive east, turning right toward the coast on **Reynishverfisvegur (Route 215).** This is perhaps the most famous black-sand beach in Iceland, due to its unique **basalt columns.**

Vík

Backtrack to Route 1 and head east to the tiny town of Vík. Have a snack at the darling **Skool Beans** (Klettsvegur; tel. 354/830-0079; www.skoolbeans.com; 9am-5pm daily). After lunch, take a fun one-hour zipline tour with **True Adventure** (Suðurvíkurvegur 5; tel. 354/698-8890; www.trueadventure.is; 14,900ISK), headquartered just on the other side of the Ring Road, a 12-minute walk or 2-minute drive.

Have dinner at **Suður-Vík Restaurant and Café** (Suðurvikurvegur 1; tel. 354/487-1515; noon-10pm daily; entrées from 3,900ISK), right next to True Adventure. Add some much-needed variety to your diet in Iceland with their perfectly spiced Thai dishes. Spend the night at spacious, contemporary **Hotel Kría** (Sléttuvegur 12-14; tel. 354/416-2100; www.hotelkria.is; rooms from 41,000ISK).

DAY 3 INDEX

1: Blue Lagoon **2:** downtown Reykjavík
3: Reynisfjara **4:** Gullfoss

1
2
Gleðigata
3
4

Day 4: The Glacial East

MORNING

Driving time: *2 hours*
Driving distance: *140 km (86 mi)*
Directions: *Route 1 east to Vatnajökull National Park*

Vatnajökull National Park

Get ready to see some icebergs today, as you drive the Ring Road to Vatnajökull National Park, which is just under two hours east of Vík on Route 1. Turn left on Skaftafellsvegur, which turns into Hæðavegur.

Vatnajökull National Park is the home of Europe's largest ice cap, specifically **Skaftafell,** the southern part of Vatnajökull, which used to be its own national park. Stop by **Skaftafellsoffa** (Skaftafellsvegur; tel. 354/478-1627; www.vatnajokulsthjodgardur.is; 10am-6pm daily Nov.-Feb., 9am-6pm daily Mar.-May and Sept.-Oct., 8am-7pm daily June-Aug.), the national park office, for information about the many footpaths and hiking trails in the region. Plan to spend the morning here hiking and taking in some of the park's many vistas and waterfalls.

AFTERNOON

Driving time: *1 hour*
Driving distance: *58 km (36 mi)*
Directions: *Route 1 east to Jökulsárlón*

★ Jökulsárlón

Continue on Route 1 for about an hour to Jökulsárlón, a glacial lagoon, where you will see huge chunks of ice floating in the water and, if you're lucky, a curious seal or two. Take a 40-minute boat tour of the lagoon, which you should book in advance, with **Glacier Lagoon** (Jökulsárlón Ehf; tel. 354/478-2222; www.icelagoon.is; 10am-5pm daily May and Oct., 9am-7pm daily June-Sept.; 5,900ISK) to get close to icebergs and even get a chance to taste the ice.

EVENING

Driving time: *1 hour*
Driving distance: *80 km (40 mi)*
Directions: *Route 1 east to Route 99 South to Höfn*

Höfn

Drive another hour on Route 1 to the sleepy town of Höfn, gateway for tourists seeking to visit the glacier, where you can have a fantastic lobster dinner at **Þakkhús** (Krosseyjarvegi 3; tel. 354/478-2280; www.pakkhus.is; entrées from 4,400ISK) and spend the night in the brightly decorated **Hótel Höfn** (Víkurbraut 20; tel. 354/478-1240; www.hotelhofn.is; rooms from 40,000ISK).

DAY 4 INDEX

- Skaftafell, Vatnajökull National Park, page 260
- Jökulsárlón, page 260
- Höfn, page 256

Day 5: The Eastfjords to Mývatn

MORNING

Driving time: *3 hours*

Driving distance: *211 km (131 mi)*

Directions: *Route 1 north to Stöðvarfjörður and Route 955 to Fáskrúðsfjörður*

Petra's Mineral Collection

Fjarðarbraut 21, Stöðvarfjörður; tel. 354/475-8834; www.steinapetra.is; 10am-5pm daily June 1-Aug. 31, by appointment rest of the year; 1,500ISK

Today's long drive takes you north to the spectacular Eastfjords, dotted with small fishing villages and quirky attractions. About 2.5 hours in, make a stop at Petra's Mineral Collection, right off the Ring Road in **Stöðvarfjörður,** to check out an enormous collection of geodes, minerals, and found objects.

Fáskrúðsfjörður

It's just over 25 minutes to the unique town of Fáskrúðsfjörður, distinguished by its French influence. Have lunch at **Café Sumarlína** (Búðavegur 59; tel. 354/475-1575; www.sumarlina.is; 11am-10pm Mon.-Fri., noon-10pm Sat.-Sun., entrées from 2,650ISK).

AFTERNOON

Driving time: *3 hours*

Driving distance: *257 km (159 mi)*

Directions: *Route 1 north to Egilsstaðir and west to Krafla turnoff and Námaskarð*

Lagarfljót

Continue about an hour north on Route 1 to **Egilsstaðir** and the long and narrow lake Lagarfljót. Get out of the car to stretch your legs and take a look at the dramatic lake.

★ Krafla

Drive another two hours northwest toward **Lake Mývatn**, turning off the Ring Road just before the lake to visit the huge, 300-meter (984-ft) crater of the Krafla volcano. A paved road leads up to the lava fields, where you can hike to hot springs and mud pools.

Námaskarð

Less than 2 kilometers (0.9 mi) west of the turnoff for Krafla on Route 1 is the sulfurous, multicolored Námaskarð pass (15 km/9 mi northeast of Mývatn on Route 1). A short walking path encircles the mud pools.

EVENING

Driving time: *25 minutes*

Driving distance: *20 km (12 mi)*

Directions: *Route 1 west to Lake Mývatn area; Route 848 south to Vogafjós Restaurant and Hotel Laxá*

Lake Mývatn

MÝVATN NATURE BATHS

tel. 354/464-4411; www.myvatnnaturebaths.is; noon-10pm daily, 5,700ISK

Back on Route 1, head west toward Lake Mývatn for 1.7 kilometers (1 mi), then make a left at the turnoff for Mývatn Nature Baths, where you can have a relaxing evening soak.

VOGAFJÓS RESTAURANT

Vogar; tel. 354/464-3800; www.vogafjos.is; 11am-10pm daily summer, 10am-9:30pm daily winter; dinner entrées from 3,750ISK

For dinner, continue west on Route 1 and turn south on Route 848 to head to **Vogar.** Dine at cute, quirky Vogafjós Restaurant.

HOTEL LAXÁ

Olnbogaás; tel. 354/464-1900; www.hotellaxa.is; rooms from 35,000ISK

After dinner, head south on Route 848 to go halfway around the lake, about 16 kilometers (10 mi) from the restaurant. Spend the night at Hotel Laxá, a modern hotel that offers huge windows in rooms that overlook the wonders of Mývatn.

DAY 5 INDEX

Day 6: Detour to Húsavík

MORNING

Driving time: *45 minutes*
Driving distance: *62 km (38 mi)*
Directions: *Route 1 along west side of Lake Mývatn to Route 845 and Route 85 north to Húsavík*

★ Whale-Watching

From Lake Mývatn, take a 45-minute detour off Route 1 to Route 87, then Route 85 to **Húsavík,** a placid seaside town known for its spectacular whale-watching. Take a morning cruise with **Gentle Giants** (tel. 354/464-1500; www.gentlegiants.is; adults 10,790ISK, children 7-15 4,490ISK, children 6 and under free; 3-hour tour) to get a glimpse of the giant sea mammals. Afterward, stroll along the **harbor** and have lunch at **Salka Restaurant** (Garðarsbraut 4; tel. 354/464-2551; 11:30am-10pm daily; entrées from 2,800ISK).

AFTERNOON

Driving time: *50 minutes*
Driving distance: *62 km (39 mi)*
Directions: *Route 85 east to Ásbyrgi turnoff*

Ásbyrgi

From Húsavík, drive east for 50 minutes on Route 85 to Ásbyrgi, a horseshoe-shaped gorge with towering rock walls. Follow the 1-kilometer (0.6-mi) **footpath** starting from the parking lot; it takes 30-60 minutes depending on how often you pause to soak in the natural beauty of the region. At the bottom of the canyon you can see small lakes, thick trees, and interesting rock formations.

EVENING

Driving time: *50 minutes*
Driving distance: *62 km (39 mi)*
Directions: *Route 85 west to Húsavík*

Húsavík

Back in Húsavík, have dinner at **Gamlí Baukur** (Hafnarstett 9; tel. 354/464-2442; www.gamlibaukur.is; 11:30am-11pm daily; entrées from 2,900ISK), and stay at **Fosshotel Húsavík** (Ketilsbraut 22; tel. 354/464-1220; www.islandshotel.is; rooms from 27,000ISK).

DAY 6 INDEX

1: kayaking on Jökulsárlón Glacier Lagoon
2: Húsavík, known for whale-watching **3:** Mývatn Nature Baths in winter

1

2

3

Day 7: The North

MORNING

Driving time: *1.5 hours*

Driving distance: *83 km (52 mi)*

Directions: *Route 85 south to Route 845 south to Route 1 south to Goðafoss; Route 1 west to Akureyri*

Goðafoss

Drive 40 minutes south on Route 85 to Route 845 and finally back to the Ring Road and get ready to see the "waterfall of the Gods": Goðafoss, one of the most beautiful waterfalls on the island. Spend a couple of hours roaming the area and soaking in the views.

Akureyri

From Goðafoss, hop back on Route 1 for 30 minutes, heading west to Akureyri, the charming unofficial capital of North Iceland.

★ AKUREYRI BOTANICAL GARDENS

Eyrarlandsholt; tel. 354/462-7487; www.lystigardur.akureyri.is; 8am-10pm Mon.-Fri., 9am-10pm Sat.-Sun. June-Sept.; free

Be sure to visit the Akureyri Botanical Gardens, one of the northernmost botanical gardens in the world. The gorgeous grounds boast native and international species alike.

CITY CENTER

Make your way to the city center (a few minutes' drive or a 10-minute walk from the Botanical Gardens) to check out the **Akureyrarkirkja** church (Eyrarlandsvegur; tel. 354/462-7700; www.akureyrarkirkja.is; 10am-4pm Mon.-Sat., 4pm-7pm Sun. June 15-Aug. 15; free) and have lunch at **Berlín Akureyri** (Skipagata 4; tel. 354/772-5061; entrées from 1,350ISK).

AFTERNOON AND EVENING

Driving time: *1 hour*

Driving distance: *78 km (48 mi)*

Directions: *Route 82 north turns into Route 76 to Siglufjörður*

Tröllaskagi Peninsula

From Akureyri, set off for a drive north on Route 82 along the western side of Tröllaskagi Peninsula. You'll be following **Eyafjördur,** Iceland's longest fjord, so the scenery boasts breathtaking views of mountains and jagged cliffs.

Siglufjörður

After just over an hour, you'll reach the pretty town of Siglufjörður. Check out the **harbor** area and visit the fascinating **Herring Era Museum** (Snorragata 10; tel. 354/467-1604; www.sild.is; 10am-6pm daily June-Aug., 1pm-5pm daily May and Sept., by appointment rest of the year; 1,800ISK). The **Folk Music Center** (Norðurgata 1; tel. 354/467-2300; www.folkmusik.is; noon-6pm daily June-Aug., by request rest of year; 800ISK) is also worth a stop.

Have dinner at the unmissable **Kaffi Raudka** (Gránugata 19; tel. 354/467-1550; www.kaffiraudka.is; 11am-10pm daily; entrées from 2,500ISK) on the harbor and spend the night at hip **Siglunes Guesthouse** (Laekjargata 10; tel. 354/467-1222; www.hotel-siglunes.is; rooms from 19,855ISK).

DAY 7 INDEX

Day 8: Driving to Snæfellsnes

The long journey to the Snæfellsnes Peninsula will take nearly the entire day.

MORNING

Driving time: *1.5 hours*

Driving distance: *107 km (66 mi)*

Directions: *Route 76 west and south to Route 75 west to Skagafjörður*

Skagafjörður

Take Route 76 out of Siglufjörður—this entails heading north at first, but ultimately you'll be going south and west toward the Snæfellsnes Peninsula. Stop in Skagafjörður, a region known for its large number of horses, along the way. Take a break from driving with a visit to the **Skagafjörður Folk Museum** (tel. 354/453-6173; www.glaumbaer.is; 10am-4pm Mon.-Fri. Apr 1.-May 19, 9am-6pm daily May 20-Sept. 20, 10am-4pm daily Sept. 21-Oct. 20, open by request rest of year; adults 1,700ISK, children under 17 free), where you can learn about the turf houses Icelanders used to call home.

AFTERNOON AND EVENING

Driving time: *4 hours*

Driving distance: *285 km (177 mi)*

Directions: *Route 1 west to Route 54 west to Route 56 north to Route 54 west to Kirkjufell*

★ Kirkjufell

Route 54 is a semi-elliptical road that runs around the Snæfellsnes Peninsula. Since you will be approaching from the south, you will hit the peninsula on the southern stretch of Route 54, then cut across to the northern stretch to check out the beautiful mountain of Kirkjufell near **Grundarfjörður.** Kirkjufell is popular with photographers in Iceland thanks to its unique shape. When viewed from the south, the mountain looks very thin, coming to a point at the top, resembling a fin. Wander the picturesque beaches around the mountain and take pictures of it from every angle.

Grundarfjörður

After a full day of driving, head to **Grundarfjörður Swimming Pool** (Borgarbraut 19; tel. 354/430-8564; 7am-9pm Mon.-Fri., 10am-6pm Sat.-Sun.; 900ISK) for a relaxing soak and mingling with the locals of the tiny town of Grundarfjörður. Then head to **Kirkjufell Hotel** (Nesvegur 8; tel. 354/438-6893; www.kirkjufellhotel.is; rooms from 25,000ISK), where the in-house **restaurant** (breakfast 7am-10am, dinner 5pm-9pm daily; entrées from 2,800ISK) has a reputation for excellent seafood.

DAY 8 INDEX

1

2

Day 9: Snæfellsjökull National Park and Borgarnes

MORNING

Driving time: *1 hour*

Driving distance: *52 km (32 mi)*

Directions: *Route 54 west to Route 574 west to Snæfellsjökull National Park*

Snæfellsjökull National Park

This morning, drive on Route 54 to Route 574 around Snæfellsjökull National Park. From Grundarfjörður, the most direct route is to take the northern stretch of Route 54 to Route 574 and approach the park from the north. Some of the more picturesque landmarks are on the southern end of the park: **Dritvík Cove** and **Lóndrangar Cliffs,** as well as **Hellnar** and **Arnarstapi Cliffs,** known for their rich birdlife. These sites are all within minutes of each other, so plan to spend the entire morning driving short distances, wandering footpaths, and enjoying the vistas of this beautiful national park, with Snæfellsjökull glacier looming in the background.

AFTERNOON

Driving time: *1.5 hours*

Driving distance: *134 km (83 mi)*

Directions: *Route 54 east to Borgarnes*

Borgarnes

On your way back to Reykjavík, make a stop at the lovely town of Borgarnes. Have a pizza lunch at **La Colina** (Hrafnaklettur 1b; tel. 354/437-0110; noon-9pm daily; entrées from 2,100ISK) and visit **The Settlement Center** museum (Brákarbraut 13-15; tel. 354/437-1600; www.landnam.is/eng; 10am-5pm daily; adults 2,500ISK, students/seniors 1,900ISK, children under 14 free), where you can learn about the sagas, Iceland's rich literary and historical tales.

EVENING

Driving time: *1 hour*

Driving distance: *76 km (47 mi)*

Directions: *Route 1 south to Route 49 west to Reykjavík*

Reykjavík

Back on the Ring Road, drive to Reykjavík. Spend a low-key evening in the city. For sweeping panoramic city views, visit either the church tower of **Hallgrímskirkja** (Hallgrímstorg; tel. 354/510-1000; www.hallgrimskirkja.is; 10am-5pm daily) or **Perlan (The Pearl)** (Öskjuhlíð; tel. 354/562-0200; www.perlan.is); a small fee is charged to access viewing decks at both sites.

Do as the locals do, and enjoy a relaxing swim at the pool **Laugarsdalaug** (Sundlaugavegur 30; tel. 354/411-5100; 6:30am-10pm Mon.-Fri., 8am-10pm Sat.-Sun.; 1,000ISK). Afterward, head to **Fish Market** (Aðlstræti 12; tel. 354/578-8877; www.fiskmarkadurinn.is; 5:30pm-10:30pm daily; entrées from 4,990ISK) for dinner, then to **Hotel Frón** (Laugavegur 22A; tel. 354/511-4666; www.hotelfron.is; rooms from 27,000ISK) for the night.

DAY 9 INDEX

1: Botanical Gardens in Akureyri **2:** Grundarfjörður

Last Day

REYKJAVÍK

Spend as much time in Reykjavík as possible before heading back to Keflavík for your flight. If you only have time for a quick coffee, check out Reykjavík's oldest coffeehouse, **Mokka** (Skólavörðustígur 3A; tel. 354/552-1174; www.mokka.is; 9am-6:30pm daily; 500ISK), or pick up one of the city's famous hot dogs at ★ **Bæjarins Beztu Pylsur** (Tryggvatagata 1; tel. 354/511-1566; www.bbp.is; 10am-12:30am Sun.-Thurs., 10am-1am Fri.-Sat.; 450ISK).

KEFLAVÍK INTERNATIONAL AIRPORT

Driving time: *50 minutes*

Driving distance: *49 km (30 mi)*

Directions: *Route 41 west to Reykjavik*

Drive back to **Keflavík** to drop off your rental car and catch your flight back home. Congratulations on completing your Ring Road road trip!

LAST DAY INDEX

Bæjarins Beztu Pylsur

Background

The Landscape

GEOGRAPHY

Iceland is the westernmost European country, situated in the North Atlantic between North America and Europe. Iceland is east of Greenland and south of the Arctic Circle, atop the northern Mid-Atlantic Ridge. It lies 859 kilometers (534 mi) from Scotland and 4,200 kilometers (2,610 mi) from New York City. The area of Iceland is 103,022 square kilometers (39,777 sq mi), and a frequent comparison among Icelandic tour guides is that Iceland is roughly the size of the U.S. state Kentucky.

Geology

Iceland is a volcanic island constantly in flux, with magma breaking through fissures and periodic eruptions that redesign the rocky landscape. Iceland's land is made up of igneous rock, most of which is basalt, which forms from cooling magma. Most of Iceland's mountains were formed with basalt that has been carved by water and ice erosion. Some of the most well-known mountains in Iceland are Esja, Hekla, Snæfellsjökull, and Öræfajökull. Earthquakes are a common occurrence, but large tremors are rarely felt.

VOLCANOES

The three most active volcanoes on the island are Katla, Hekla, and Eyjafjallajökull. Eyjafjallajökull erupted in 2010, grounding air travel in Europe for days thanks to a large ash cloud. Most of Iceland's eruptions are small, and it's rare that they cause travel disruptions. Residents have learned to adapt to eruptions, and most volcanoes are away from residential areas.

More often than not, volcanic eruptions are actually a growing source of tourism for the country. Local travel companies offer helicopter, Jeep, and airplane tours when an eruption occurs. Most of Iceland's volcanic eruptions, such as the 2021 Fagradalsfjall eruption, are fissure vents, where lava seeps out of the cracks in the earth's crust. Fagradalsfjall produced fountains of lava shooting out of the earth, delighting photographers and keeping volcanologists busy. The main threat was from toxins in the air, and those close to the region were asked to stay indoors and turn up their heating if they were sensitive to air quality.

Air

When there isn't an eruption, Iceland's air is some of the cleanest and purest you will experience, as pollution is low and the Gulf Stream produces a strong, steady wind that blows toxins away. The main source of pollution on the island is from industry, mainly aluminum smelters.

Water

Like the air, Iceland's water is remarkably pure. There's clean, tasty drinking water on tap and geothermally heated water that fills swimming pools and provides hot water in homes. Snow can fall in any month of the year, but large snowfalls are uncommon in the Reykjavík area, at least during the last couple of decades. Ice covers about 11 percent of the country, mostly in the form of Iceland's largest glaciers: Vatnajökull, Hofsjökull, Langjökull, and Mýrdalsjökull. Melting ice from the glaciers and snowmelt form the rivers. Some of the major rivers include Krossá, Hvítá, Hofsá, and Lagarfljót.

Iceland's water is at the center of some of the country's tourist attractions. The human-made Blue Lagoon near Grindavík allows visitors to bathe in geothermally heated water, which soothes and heals the skin. Locals and tourists enjoy hot springs throughout the country, and spectacular waterfalls with roaring water tumble over basalt rock and earth. The largest and most visited waterfalls in Iceland are Gullfoss, Dettifoss, Goðafoss, Seljalandsfoss, and Skógafoss.

Climate

Iceland isn't as cold as you may think. The Gulf Stream swirls along the western and southern coasts and works to moderate Iceland's climate. But "moderate" doesn't mean "calm." The Gulf Stream is responsible for Iceland's frequent weather changes—as in lots of wind and rain.

The biggest challenge of the climate is the unpredictability. The "summer" tourist season runs from the end of May to the beginning of September, and during that time, the climate ranges from rainy May days to the midnight sun in July to the possibility of snow in parts of the country in September. The winter

Previous: horses grazing in southern Iceland.

Average Temperatures in Reykjavík

- **January:** -0.6°C / 30.9°F
- **February:** 0.7°C / 33.3°F
- **March:** 2.2°C / 36°F
- **April:** 5.2°C / 41.4°F
- **May:** 6°C / 42.8°F
- **June:** 10.7°C / 51.3°
- **July:** 12.8°C / 55°F
- **August:** 11°C / 51.8°F
- **September:** 7.9°C / 46.4°F
- **October:** 5.8°C / 42.4°F
- **November:** 3.1°C / 37.6°F
- **December:** 1.3°C / 34.3°F

climate brings colder temperatures, dark days, whipping winds, and the possibility of seeing the northern lights on clear nights.

The climate is similar around the island, with the exception of the highlands, which become inaccessible from mid-September to early June. The roads to the highlands are closed in this season due to heavy snow conditions.

Weather

Weather in Iceland is not casual conversation, but serious business. Weather forecasts are frequent but largely hit or miss. The weather can change rapidly, from calm winds and sunny skies to rain, snow, sleet, and back again, all in the same hour. It's unpredictable, exhilarating, and confusing for many tourists, but Icelanders have learned to adapt and go with the flow. As a result, plans tend to be loose for locals, whether it's for meeting friends for coffee or going for a job interview. If the weather acts up, Icelanders understand.

Some of the most extreme weather you could experience on this island is wind—the type of wind in winter that could knock you off your feet. If the weather forecast is showing strong winds, especially in the countryside, alter your plans accordingly. Do not underestimate the wind and be sure to heed any storm advisories. Be safe, smart, and prepared. The changing conditions are part of the experience of traveling to Iceland, and the key is being prepared with layers of clothing, proper footwear, and waterproof outerwear.

Daylight

Due to Iceland's proximity to the Arctic Circle, the island has almost endless daylight during the summer months from the midnight sun. The long days, about 20-22 hours of daylight in June and July, are magical, but it's a good idea to bring a sleep mask as some travelers find it difficult to sleep. The winter, however, has the opposite challenges. Days are much shorter, with just 4-5 hours of daylight in December. While this can be great for northern lights viewing, it limits your time seeing attractions.

Northern Lights

The biggest winter attraction in Iceland is the aurora borealis (northern lights). People travel from around the world to catch a glimpse of the green, white, blue, and red lights dancing in the night sky. There's something very special about bundling up in your warmest winter gear, trekking outside main towns to avoid bright lights, and hunting for northern lights. The natural phenomenon is caused by solar winds, which blow electronic particles into molecules of atmospheric gases, causing an emission of bright light. The best time to see northern lights is from September to March, and there are forecasts predicting visibility on the **national weather website** (www.vedur.is). When the forecast is favorable, it's best to drive (or take a tour bus) to a dark area and look up. Northern lights tours are offered by **Reykjavík Excursions** (www.re.is).

PLANTS

Don't be fooled by photos of the vast, barren lava fields; there is in fact life thriving on

Iceland's land. The most common plants in Iceland are the hundreds of species of moss found throughout the country, clinging to rocks, basalt columns, and the earth. It's common to find Icelandic moss, maritime sunburst lichen, dulse, rockweed, and several species of algae in Iceland. Visitors will notice the lack of trees throughout Iceland, but that wasn't always the case. The lack of trees is due to a combination of Vikings using the trees to build their homes and boats, and as fuel. Additionally, volcanic eruptions and lava flows have led to deforestation, as well as sheep contributing to soil erosion.

Iceland has an abundance of rhubarb plants and bilberry shrubs (which Icelanders refer to as blueberries). Berry-picking season runs from late July to early August, but the season can be delayed if the winter was particularly bad.

As for flowers, the pale-pink glacier poppy is the country's national flower, and other common flowers are sea mayweed, alpine bartsia, meadow buttercup, and arctic poppy. Others include wood cranesbill, oysterplant, purple lupine, and bluegrass.

ANIMALS

Iceland may not be known for its land mammals—other than sheep, cows, horses, reindeer, and the arctic fox—but animals in the ocean and sky are varied and ample. Sheep, cows, and horses can be found in every region of the island, but reindeer are only found in East Iceland. There are no reptiles or amphibians on the island.

Fish

Fish are the lifeblood of Iceland: They sustain its inhabitants and serve as the country's biggest trade resource. The waters surrounding Iceland support cod, haddock, catfish, mussels, halibut, plaice, lumpfish, monkfish, skate, and Greenland shark. Native to Icelandic river waters are salmon, trout, and arctic char.

Sunrise and Sunset in Reykjavík

- **January 1:** 11:19am - 3:45pm
- **February 5:** 9:55am - 5:30pm
- **March 5:** 8:21am - 6:59pm
- **April 1:** 6:42am - 8:23pm
- **May 5:** 4:39am - 10:12pm
- **June 5:** 3:15am - 11:39pm
- **June 21:** 2:54am - 12:05am
- **July 1:** 3:07am - 11:55pm
- **August 5:** 4:50am - 10:14pm
- **September 5:** 6:16am - 8:36pm
- **October 1:** 7:37am - 6:57pm
- **November 5:** 9:24am - 4:58pm
- **December 3:** 10:51am - 3:44pm
- **December 21:** 11:22am - 3:30pm

Seals

Several species of seals call Iceland home, with harbor seals and gray seals being the most common. There are seal-watching sites in the north of Iceland; at Hvammstangi, there's a seal center that's a museum, point of information, and seal-watching enterprise. Harbor seals are more common to spot because they spend more time on land, whereas gray seals prefer the ocean. Harp, ringed, hooded, and bearded seals are also spotted in Iceland, but these are rarer.

Whales

Whale-watching is a spectacular way to spend an afternoon in Iceland, and there are several species to see, depending on where in Iceland you set out on your excursion. High season for whales around Iceland is May to October, and 14 species of cetaceans have been seen off the coasts of the island: blue, fin, minke, pilot, humpback, sei, orca, sperm, bottlenose, beluga, and narwhal whales, as well as white-beaked dolphins, white-sided dolphins, and harbor porpoises. The best places for whale-watching are Reykjavík in the south, Snæfellsnes in the west, and Húsavík and Akureyri in the north.

Birds

Bird-watchers are delighted when they visit, as there are more than 300 species of birds in Iceland. The island is a stopover for birds migrating between North America and Europe, and common species are ravens, eider ducks, arctic terns, Iceland gulls, white gulls, black-headed gulls, skuas, white-tailed eagles, gannets, fulmars, kittiwakes, and oystercatchers.

The bird that has become synonymous with Iceland is the adorable puffin, with its black and white body, bright orange feet, and colorful red, blue, and orange beak. Puffins are remarkable swimmers and divers, able to dive underwater and surface with as many as 10 small fish in their beaks in under a minute. While exceptional in water, puffins are clumsy in flight and are known for their uneven landings on land. It's part of their charm. Millions of puffins call Iceland home, although their numbers have dwindled over the years. It's possible to see puffins during the summer in areas including the Westman Islands, Grímsey, and the Látrabjarg cliffs in the Westfjords. Puffins are not aggressive, and if you get too close, they will fly away.

History

SETTLEMENT

Iceland has the distinction of being the last country in Europe to be settled. The country has had impeccable record-keeping, and for that reason, it's known that the first permanent resident in Iceland was Ingólfur Arnarson, who built a farm in Reykjavík in the year 874. The earliest settlers were emigrants from Norway who opposed the king, Harald, due to a blood feud, and they wanted to make a new life in a new land. The Norwegians brought along their slaves from Ireland and Scotland, which means Icelanders are a blend of Norse and Celtic stock.

As word got out about the new land, within a few decades most of the coastline was claimed, with farms and fishing stations popping up. A government wasn't formed until 930, when the Alþing (parliament) was created, but in the meantime the new settlers determined that each farmstead should have a self-appointed chief. Once the Alþing was established in Þingvellir, a legislative body was elected.

CONVERSION TO CHRISTIANITY

Christianity came to Iceland, some say, by force. By the 10th century, the island faced mounting political pressure from the king of Norway, Olaf Tryggvason, to convert to Christianity or face the consequences, meaning war. As the end of the first millennium grew near, many prominent Icelanders had accepted the new faith.

By the year 1000, the Alþing was divided into two religious groups: modern Christians and pagans. The two groups were steadfast in their beliefs, and a civil war seemed likely. The law speaker, Þorgeir Þorkelsson, was called upon for a decision. (The law speaker was appointed to office and was required to recite the law during parliamentary meetings.) Þorgeir decided that Iceland would be a Christian country, but that pagans could still celebrate their rituals in the privacy of their farms. Þorgeir was baptized in Þingvellir, and Christianity became the law of the land. Christian churches were built, a bishop was established in 1056, and the majority of today's religious Icelanders are Christian.

Historical Timeline

874	Ingólfur Arnarson, Iceland's first permanent settler, builds a farm in Reykjavík
930	Alþing (parliament) is established at Þingvellir
1000	Law speaker Þorgeir Þorkelsson decrees Iceland a Christian country
1380	Iceland becomes part of the Kalmar Union, making it effectively a colony of Denmark
1602	Danish government forbids Iceland to trade with countries other than Denmark
1904	Hannes Hafstein becomes the first Minister of Icelandic Affairs
1915	Iceland creates its own flag
1918	Iceland becomes a sovereign state from Denmark
1941	25,000 British troops leave military base near Keflavík, replaced by 40,000 American troops
1944	Referendum confirms Icelandic independence from Denmark
1949	Iceland joins NATO
1980	Vigdís Finnbogadóttir is elected president, the first woman in the world to become an elected head of state
1994	Iceland joins the European Economic Area
2008	Iceland's three major banks fail in the midst of the global financial crisis
2017	Iceland surpasses 2 million visitors a year
2021	Fagradalsfjall volcano erupts in Geldingadlir in the Reykjanes Peninsula

DANISH RULE

Iceland remained under Norwegian kingship rule until 1380, when the death of Olav IV put an end to the Norwegian male royal line. Norway (and by extension, Iceland) became part of the Kalmar Union, along with Denmark and Sweden, with Denmark as the dominant nation. At this time, Iceland effectively became a colony of Denmark, with the king owning the land and the church's money. Iceland's government now answered to Denmark and did so for the next several hundred years.

Iceland was still very much centered on fishing and farming, and it was quite isolated from the dealings in mainland Europe. In 1602, the Danish government, which was pursuing mercantilist policies, decreed that Iceland was forbidden to trade with countries other than Denmark. The Danish trade monopoly would remain in effect until 1786.

INDEPENDENCE

Iceland began inching toward independence when it was granted a Minister of Icelandic Affairs in 1904, who would be based in Reykjavík. Hannes Hafstein was the first to serve in the minister position, and his place in Iceland's history is prominent. During this time, Iceland became more autonomous, building up Reykjavík's harbor, founding the University of Iceland, and eventually creating its own flag in 1915.

Over the next couple of decades, Iceland was taking more control of its affairs, and when World War II started, there was an economic opportunity for the island. Iceland was invited to join the Allied war effort by Great Britain, but Iceland's government refused, declaring its neutrality. Britain pushed for Iceland's cooperation, but ultimately British naval forces arrived in Iceland, began building a base near Keflavík, and occupied the country for its proximity to North America. In all, 25,000 British soldiers occupied Iceland, which created a significant number of jobs for Icelanders. The British left in 1941, but more than 40,000 American troops replaced them, continuing the economic win for Iceland. There were jobs, opportunity, an American radio station, and lots of money flowing into the tiny island nation.

Denmark took a step back from Iceland's affairs during World War II, and Icelanders eventually held a referendum on its independence. Almost 99 percent of the population voted in the referendum, 97 percent of which voted for independence. On June 17, 1944, Iceland became totally independent of Denmark. American troops maintained the Keflavík NATO base until 2006.

MODERN-DAY ICELAND

An independent Iceland plodded along, building up its fishing resources, investing in infrastructure, and looking toward the future. During years of rule by the center-right Independence Party, banks were deregulated in the early 2000s and Iceland's financial sector began taking off at a rapid pace. Iceland was being lauded for its financial acumen, but it all imploded in 2008, when the country's three major banks failed, sending Iceland into one of the deepest financial crises seen in modern Europe.

In the years since, tourism helped Iceland recover. People from around the world have become aware of and infatuated with Iceland for its raw nature, volcanic eruptions, and culture.

Government and Economy

GOVERNMENT

Iceland's democracy dates back to the year 930, when the Alþing (parliament) was formed, but its modern constitution was signed on June 17, 1944, when Iceland achieved independence from Denmark. The Alþing, which consists of 63 seats, meets four days a week near Austurvöllur in the center of Reykjavík. Nine judges make up the High Court of Iceland and are appointed by the president. Iceland's president serves more of a ceremonial role, while the prime minister holds most of the executive powers. Other high-level cabinet positions are the Minister of Finance and Minister of Foreign Affairs.

Political Parties

Iceland's political parties number in double digits, with 11 parties running for seats in the 2021 election. However, in the Alþing, eight parties hold seats: the Independence Party, the Progressive Party, the Social Democratic Alliance, the Left-Green Movement, the Pirate Party, the Center Party, the People's Party, and the Reform Party.

The Left-Green Movement (Vinstri Græn) is a left-wing party while the Independence Party (Sjálfstæðisflokkurinn) is a center-right party that was formed in 1929 after a merger of the Conservative and Liberal parties. The current prime minister, Katrín Jakobsdóttir, who worked in media before getting into politics, has served as leader of the party since 2013. The Independence Party was in power in the years leading up to the economic collapse of 2008. It was voted out of the majority in 2009 but regained seats, and power, in 2013. The Social Democratic Alliance, Left-Green Movement, and Pirate Party are the more liberal political parties on the island. Iceland's sitting president, Guðni Th. Jóhannesson, who took office in 2016 and was re-elected in 2020, is a historian and former docent at the University of Iceland. Guðni is unaffiliated with any political party. He replaced Ólafur Ragnar Grímsson, who served five terms.

Elections

Iceland holds parliamentary elections every four years. The country has a multi-party system, which means they must form coalition governments. Iceland also elects a head of state every four years.

Defense

Iceland does not have a military, but is a member of NATO and hosted British and American troops in Keflavík during and after World War II. American troops remained in Iceland, on the NATO base, until 2006. Iceland's Coast Guard oversees crisis management and protection along the coasts of Iceland and has been known to participate in daring rescues at sea. The Icelandic police force consists of fewer than 1,000 officers, who maintain the peace. The crime rate is exceptionally low in Iceland, and police officers do not carry handguns.

ECONOMY

Iceland's economy is perhaps best known to tourists for taking a dive during the 2008 financial crisis. The island's economy has rebounded from the collapse, with tourism playing a significant role in this recovery. Alternative energy helps, too.

Banking Crisis

In early 2008, Iceland's currency began floundering compared to the euro, and that was the first international signal that there was deep trouble lurking in Iceland's financial sector. By the autumn, all three of Iceland's major banks had failed, lifting the veil on Iceland's house of cards. Following the collapse, unemployment soared, pension funds shrank, and inflation skyrocketed to more than 70 percent. Loans taken out in foreign currency became unmanageable to thousands of Icelanders, credit lines were cut off, and capital controls were put in place that restricted how much money Icelanders could move out of the country. It was dire. The IMF made an emergency loan of $2.1 billion in November 2008.

Tourism

An increase in tourism helped Iceland recover from its 2008 economic collapse. The island became more affordable to visit and the news about the country's economic troubles made headlines around the world, shining a light on Iceland. By 2017, more than two million tourists visited Iceland a year, a sharp contrast from the 50,000 a year in the early 2000s. In fact, tourism is now the country's second-biggest revenue source after fish. Tourism comprises 10 percent of Iceland's GDP, and more than two million tourists visited Iceland in 2018. Most of Iceland's tourists come from the United States, China, Great Britain, the Nordic countries, Germany, France, and Switzerland. The issue going forward is how to keep tourism sustainable and protect Iceland's land from too much traffic.

Fishing

It's no secret that fish are the lifeblood of Iceland. They nourish its residents and are Iceland's number one export. Iceland's biggest trading partners are within the European Union, which is interesting because the reason to oppose joining the EU, for many, is for Iceland to maintain complete control of its fishing stock. Cod is the most common fish export.

Energy

One of the perks of living on a volcanic island is having a hotbed of geothermal energy. About 98 percent of the island's energy comes from geothermal and hydroelectric sources, which means low costs and low pollution. The pollution that does inhabit Iceland's airspace stems from an increasing number of aluminum smelters that have popped up in the last couple of decades. Foreign aluminum providers look to Iceland for its cheap energy and vast open land. The smelters do create jobs and revenue for the country, but it's a trade-off that many Icelanders remain unhappy about.

Currency

Iceland maintains its own currency, as it is

not a member of the European Union. The Icelandic króna has a small circulation and is pegged to the euro. The notes are 500, 1,000, 5,000, and 10,000. Following the financial crisis, inflation soared more than 70 percent, and Iceland's currency took a hit. The uncertainty was a maddening time for many Icelanders. Inflation is still high, and exchange rates rise and fall. Capital controls were created in 2008 that limit how much money Icelanders can move out of the country, but they were lifted in 2017.

People and Culture

POPULATION

About 360,000 people call Iceland home, and more than two-thirds live in the capital city, Reykjavík, and its suburbs. Outside of Reykjavík, Hafnarfjörður, and Kopavogur, the most populated towns in Iceland include Keflavík and Selfoss in the south, Akureyri in the north, Akranes and Borgarnes in the west, and Höfn and Egilsstaðir in the east. About 90 percent of the island population is composed of native Icelanders, but the foreign-born population continues to grow with the inflow of migrant workers and refugees.

Native Icelanders have a genetic makeup that combines Gaelic and Norse heritage, and many Icelanders consider themselves Nordic instead of Scandinavian. Social lives center on family, as Icelanders tend to be a close-knit bunch. It often seems like all Icelandic people either know one another, or have friends in common.

LANGUAGE

The official language of Iceland is Icelandic, which is considered a Germanic language. Icelanders like to think of their language as poetic and musical, and maintaining their tongue is an important part of Icelandic culture. Most Icelanders speak English and are happy to converse with tourists in English, but they enjoy when foreign tourists give the language a go, even just a few words. The closest language to Icelandic is Faroese, which roughly 50,000 people speak, and the other close language spoken by a larger group is Norwegian. Many Icelanders can understand Norwegian, Swedish, and Danish due to some similarities. Learning Icelandic is a challenge for many foreigners because of the complex grammar and accent.

ICELANDIC NAMES

Iceland has a strident naming committee that must approve names parents wish to give their newborns, in the spirit of maintaining Icelandic culture. For that reason, you will find a lot of common first names, including Bjorn, Jón, Ólafur, Guðmundur, and Magnús for males, and Guðrun, Sara, and Anna for females. Very few Icelanders have surnames; instead, Iceland follows a patronymic system in which children are given their father's first name followed by -son or -dottir. If a man named Einar has a son named Johannes and a daughter named Anna, their names will be Johannes Einarsson and Anna Einarsdottir.

RELIGION

Icelanders have an interesting relationship with religion. Most of the country identifies as Lutheran (about 60 percent), but most Icelanders aren't known to attend church regularly or be very vocal about their religious beliefs. While the majority of the country identifies as Christian, Iceland is considered a progressive nation. There is no separation of church and state in Iceland; the National Church of Iceland is subsidized by Icelanders through a church tax. However, the non-religious can choose to have their church tax donated to designated charities.

Of Iceland's religious minorities, Catholics are the largest group at about 4 percent, and there are about 1,000 Muslims estimated to call Iceland home, as well as about 100 Jews. There is not a single synagogue in Iceland, as the Jewish population has not requested one, but a rabbi has relocated from New York to Reykjavík with his wife and children in 2018. A mosque was approved by Reykjavík in 2014, and construction is ongoing as of 2022. The pagan Norse religion Ásatrúarfélagið has grown in membership in recent years to about 5,000.

ARTS

Music

Music plays an important role in Icelandic society. There's an emphasis on children learning to play instruments, with music schools around the country. It seems that everyone in Iceland is in at least one band. The earliest Icelandic music is called rímur, which is a sort of chanting style of singing that could include lyrics ranging from religious themes to descriptions of nature. Choirs are also very common in Iceland, and there are frequent performances in schools and churches that are usually well attended by the community.

As for modern music, Iceland boasts quite a few bands that have gained a following abroad. Of course, there's Björk, who put Iceland on the musical map back in the 1980s with her band, the Sugarcubes, and later her solo career. Icelanders tend to be quite proud of Björk, as both an artist and an environmentalist. Sigur Rós, who have been recording since 1994, have become an indie favorite. Of Monsters and Men, Kaleo, Ólafur Arnalds, Amiina, Samaris, and GusGus are taking the world by storm. Reykjavík has cool venues in which to check out local bands and DJs, and some great record shops to pick up the newest and latest Icelandic releases.

Literature

Iceland has a rich literary history. The sagas, considered the best-known examples of Icelandic literature, are stories in prose describing events that took place in Iceland in the 10th and 11th centuries, during the so-called Saga Age. Focused on history, especially genealogical and family history, the sagas reflect the conflicts that arose within the societies of the second and third generations of Icelandic settlers. The authors of the sagas are unknown; *Egil's Saga* is believed to have been written by Snorri Sturluson, a 13th-century descendant of the saga's hero, but this remains uncertain. Widely read in school, the sagas are celebrated as an important part of Iceland's history.

The nation's most celebrated author is Halldór Laxness, who won a Nobel Prize for Literature in 1951 for his cherished novel *Independent People*. His tales have been translated into several languages and center on themes near and dear to Icelanders—nature, love, travel, and adventure. Other authors who have been translated into English (and other languages) include Sjón, Arnaldur Indriðason, and Einar Már Guðmundsson.

Knitting

Icelanders have been knitting for centuries, and it remains a common hobby today. Wool from Icelandic sheep has been keeping Icelanders warm for generations, and a traditional, modern sweater design emerged in the 1950s or so in the form of the lopapeysa. A lopapeysa has a distinctive yoke design around the neck opening, and the sweater comes in a variety of colors, with the most common being brown, gray, black, and off-white. Icelanders knit with lopi yarn, which contains both hairs and fleece of Icelandic sheep. The yarn is not spun, making it more difficult to work with than spun yarn, but the texture and insulation are unmistakable.

Essentials

Transportation

GETTING THERE

Air

Keflavík International Airport (KEF; tel. 354/425-6000; www.kefairport.is), about 50 minutes west of Reykjavík, frequently gets kudos for being one of the best airports in Europe, and the plaudits are well deserved. Flying into Iceland is a pretty seamless experience. The country's main carrier, **Icelandair** (www.icelandair.com), serves more than 30 destinations in the United States, Canada, and Europe. Iceland's accessibility has been the country's main selling

Coronavirus in Iceland

At the time of writing in April 2022, Iceland had mostly stabilized from the effects of the coronavirus, but the situation is constantly evolving. As of February 2022, Icelandic authorities announced that facemasks would no longer be required to access indoor spaces and people would no longer have to quarantine. Authorities dropped all Covid restrictions: All tourists can enter Iceland without a negative Covid test, and tourists don't need to show that they have been vaccinated. Iceland is 100% open.

As of mid-April 2022, Iceland had roughly 185,000 reported cases of COVID-19 since testing began, and 110 deaths. The country was quick to enforce social distancing measures and mask mandates, and many companies had employees working from home during the height of the pandemic. Many travel-related businesses laid off staff, and restaurants were closed for a period of time. Given Iceland's strong social welfare system, unemployment benefits were quick to kick in and many businesses had access to loans to stay afloat. As of February 2022, about 85 percent of the population was vaccinated for COVID-19.

Now more than ever, Moon encourages its readers to be courteous and ethical in their travel. We ask travelers to be respectful to residents, and mindful of the evolving situation in their chosen destination when planning their trip.

BEFORE YOU GO

- Check local websites (listed below) for **local restrictions** and the **overall health status** of the destination and your point of origin. If you're traveling to or from an area that is currently a COVID-19 hotspot, you may want to reconsider your trip.
- If possible, take a **coronavirus test** with enough time to receive your results before your departure. Some destinations may require a negative test result before arrival, along with other tests and potentially a self-quarantine period, once you've arrived. Check local requirements and factor these into your plans.

point as a travel destination because it is just five hours from New York City and about three hours from London. Icelandair cleverly introduced an option years ago that allows North American travelers going on to Europe to stop over in Iceland for no extra cost. You can spend up to seven days exploring Iceland, and then continue on to your destination in Europe. The summer season is obviously the most expensive, with round-trip tickets that exceed $1,200 from North America. But Icelandair offers great deals during the winter months, when you can grab a round-trip ticket for around $700.

FROM NORTH AMERICA

In addition to Icelandair, travelers from North America have many options, including **Delta** from various cities in the United States, **United Airlines** from Newark, **Air Canada** from Toronto and Montreal, **PLAY Airlines** from Boston and Stewart Airport in New York, and **American Airlines** from Dallas.

FROM EUROPE

There are several direct flights to Iceland from Europe, and common flight routes include **British Airways** from London; **EasyJet** from London, Manchester, and Edinburgh; **Norwegian** from Oslo and London; **SAS** from Copenhagen and Oslo; **Wizz Air** from London, Vienna, Prague, and multiple

Previous: campsite at Álftavatn.

- Before you fly, check with your airline and the destination's health authority for updated **travel requirements.** Some airlines may be taking more steps than others to help you travel safely; check their websites for more information before buying your ticket, and consider a very early or very late flight, to limit exposure. Flights may be more infrequent, with increased cancellations.
- Check the website of any museums, restaurants and other venues you wish to patronize to confirm that they're open, if their hours have been adjusted, and to learn about any specific visitation requirements, such as **mandatory reservations** or **limited occupancy.**
- Pack **hand sanitizer,** a **thermometer,** and plenty of **face masks.** Consider packing **snacks, bottled water,** a **cooler,** or anything else you might need to limit the number of stops along your route, and to be prepared for possible closures and reduced services over the course of your travels.
- **Assess the risk** of entering crowded spaces, joining tours, and taking public transit.
- Expect **general disruptions.** Events may be postponed or cancelled, and some tours and venues may require reservations, enforce limits on the number of guests, be operating during different hours than the ones listed, or be closed entirely.

RESOURCES

- COVID-19 information website: **www.covid.is**
- Centers for Disease Control and Prevention website: **www.cdc.gov**
- Local news website in English: **www.grapevine.is**

cities in Poland; **Finnair** from Helsinki; and **Icelandair** from numerous cities in North America and Europe.

FROM AUSTRALIA AND NEW ZEALAND

There are no direct flights to Iceland from Australia or New Zealand; travelers will likely need to make a few connections. Common ones include first stopping in Singapore, Hong Kong, or Doha, Qatar, en route to one of the European hubs, where you can board a flight to Keflavík from there.

FROM SOUTH AFRICA

There are no direct flights to Iceland from South Africa; travelers should book a flight via one of the European travel hubs, such as London or Frankfurt, before connecting to their flight to Iceland. There are also common connections to Iceland from Cape Town and Johannesburg through Doha and Istanbul.

Boat

For those traveling from mainland Europe, a ferry can be a great option, especially if you want to bring a car, camper, or bicycle for the trip. **Smyril Line** (www.smyril-line.fo) is a Faroese company that runs the ferry *Norröna,* which goes to Iceland from Denmark, and the Faroe Islands. The ferry, which takes 19 hours from the Faroes and 36 hours from Denmark, drops you off in Seyðisfjörður, in East Iceland, which is convenient for those traveling with cars and who want to spend time in the countryside. But, if you want to stay in the south, where Reykjavík and Golden Circle attractions are, a ferry may not be the best option. The timetable tends to change frequently, so check the website for the latest information.

GETTING AROUND

Air

Iceland is surprisingly easy, if expensive, to get around by plane—if the weather is cooperating, that is. **Reykjavík City Airport** (tel. 354/569-4100; www.isavia.is) connects travelers to Akureyri, Egilsstaðir, Isafjörður, Vopnafjörður, Grímsey, and Þórshöfn. **Icelandair** (tel. 354/570-3000; www.icelandair.com) and **Eagle Air** (tel. 354/562-4200; www.eagleair.is) fly year-round.

Car

If you plan to stay in Reykjavík for most of your trip or want to do short day trips in the southern or western parts of the country, it's not necessary to rent a car; you can book tours and travel by bus. However, having access to a car gives you the ultimate freedom of seeing the island on your own schedule. But if you want a rental car and the freedom that comes with it, expect to pay dearly, especially in the summer months. Icelanders drive on the right side of the road.

CAR RENTAL

Car rental prices remind you that you are very much on an island with very little price competition. In short, it's wildly expensive to rent a car (depending on the model of the car and season, it can be $200 per day with insurance), and gas prices are sky high compared to many other counties (approximately $7.00 per gallon).

You can rent a car in advance or at the rental office at **Keflavík International Airport,** at **BSÍ bus station,** or within Reykjavík once you're settled. In the busy summer tourist season, it is recommended to **arrange your rental in advance** because some dealers sell out early.

Choosing the right car for your trip depends on what you want to see and where you plan to go. If you plan on staying close to Reykjavík and traveling on well-paved roads, such as the Ring Road, a **compact car** is the best and cheapest option. However, if you plan on going out to the countryside or to the highlands, don't try to get away with renting the cheap option. If you try to bring a compact car into a region that requires **four-wheel drive,** expect damage to the car at best, and being stranded and needing to be rescued at worst. Be smart and be prepared.

Car rental companies provide "full insurance" for each rental, which is the basic third-party insurance option. For an additional fee, drivers have access to "extra insurance" that includes a collision damage waiver. However, be aware that you will *not* be covered for damage caused by rocks, snow, wind, ice, and all the other elements that could damage a vehicle. If you have any damage to a car, you will be charged . . . *a lot.* Be sure to choose the right insurance for the region you plan to travel to. **Gravel insurance** is extra, and commonly purchased; if you're planning to travel on unpaved roads, it's recommended.

CAMPERVAN RENTAL

Traveling around Iceland by campervan is a popular option in season. This lets you explore at your own pace and frees you from worry over hotel reservations. However, there are important things to consider when traveling by campervan. Note that wild camping is strictly prohibited in Iceland and carries steep fines. Travelers must stay at **campsites,** where you will have access to facilities like toilets, showers, and cooking areas. Another important issue to consider is that traveling by campervan only makes sense during the summer months when campsites are open; many begin closing in early September. Additionally, campervans do not fare well in Iceland's windy winter conditions on icy roads. High winds can blow campervans off the road, leading to serious accidents; campervan companies that rent during the winter months are trying to take advantage of tourists. Here are a couple of reputable options:

- **Happy Campers** (Stapabraut 21, Keflavík 260; tel. 354/578-7860; www.happycampers.is; from 28,000ISK/day for two including insurance)

- **CampEasy** (Smiðjuvegur 72, Kópavogur; tel. 354/571-1310; www.campeasy.com; from 35,000ISK/day for two including insurance)

RULES OF THE ROAD

Always drive with **headlights** on (day and night). Do not drive off-road (expect heavy fines). Always wear your seat belt, and watch out for sheep and birds in the countryside.

Do not drink and drive. The law forbids any driving under the influence of alcohol, and police aggressively monitor drunk driving. There are also heavy fines.

Do not speed. Always remember that roads are unpredictable and car accidents involving foreign drivers are quite common. You can be traveling on a quiet, scenic paved road that suddenly turns into an unpaved, rough section, and lose control of the car quite easily. The maximum speed limit for the entire island is 90 kph (55 mph), but in towns and residential areas, it can be much less. Always respect the limit. If you do speed and are caught by a police officer, expect a huge fine and a stern talking to. Don't risk it.

Driving in Iceland can range from peaceful to harrowing, depending on the weather. To check road conditions, visit the **Icelandic Road and Coastal Administration** website (www.vegagerdin.is). If there is an advisory due to wind, rain, snow, or a volcanic eruption (it happens), stay off the road. Such advisories are to be taken seriously.

ROAD CONDITIONS

Road conditions in Iceland can change quite quickly, as the weather is unpredictable. As a rule, always check road conditions before you head out on a trip. The best way to get information about road conditions and the weather is to visit www.road.is for roads and www.vedur.is for weather.

The **Ring Road (Route 1)** is the most accessible and popular route around Iceland. It runs 1,332 kilometers (828 mi) and connects many of the country's most popular tourist attractions. The Ring Road is paved for most of its length, but there are still stretches in East Iceland with an unpaved gravel surface.

F roads are unpaved tracks that may only be driven in vehicles with four-wheel drive. Some F roads have river crossings, so trying to navigate them with a compact car is dangerous. In recent years, the Icelandic government has made a commitment to improving some gravel roads. You can check on road conditions at **www.road.is.**

GPS NAVIGATION

GPS coordinates are a popular way to navigate Iceland. You can input coordinates into navigational apps or GPS units to obtain directions. However, it's important to keep in mind that sometimes roads are closed, so do some research on the route you plan to take, and don't just rely on the shortest-distance option. You don't want to wind up stranded. Carry physical maps in addition to a GPS device.

Bus

The bus system in Iceland is surprisingly adequate, especially in Reykjavík.

BSÍ (Vatnsmýrarvegi 10; tel. 354/580-5400; www.bsi.is) is the main bus station in Reykjavík and serves as the first destination for many visitors to the city, as BSÍ is the initial stop on the **Fly Bus** (tel. 354/580-5400; www.flybus.is) from Keflavík International Airport. One-way tickets on the Fly Bus cost 3,499ISK. (For an extra fee, the Fly Bus can connect to several locations in downtown Reykjavík close to hotels and guesthouses.) BSÍ also serves as a main departure site for many day-tour bus trips, such as those to the Blue Lagoon and Golden Circle, offered by companies such as **Reykjavík Excursions** (tel. 354/580-5400; www.re.is).

Strætó (tel. 354/540-2700; www.straeto.is) operates the city bus system in Reykjavík, with bright yellow buses running on numbered routes. The routes are quite comprehensive, linking downtown Reykjavík to outlying neighborhoods. Tourists can pay exact change for one-way trips (490ISK). Strætó's blue long-distance buses depart from Mjódd station, traveling to several regions around the country.

Taxi

Outside of Reykjavík, taxis are not an option to get around the island. Towns and villages are small and taxis are nonexistent. For Reykjavík, the two things you need to know about taxis is that they are expensive, and you have to call ahead for one (for instance, a ride from the BSÍ bus station to Harpa takes about eight minutes and costs roughly 2,000ISK). **Hreyfill** (tel. 354/588-5522; www.hreyfill.is) and **BSR** (tel. 354/561-0000; www.taxireykjavik.is) are two popular taxi companies in the city. You can also reserve taxis with Hreyfill through an app. Taxis arrive 5-10 minutes after you call, and the price on the meter is inclusive—you don't tip in Iceland. Cab prices rival those in New York City: It's rare to spend less than 2,000ISK on a taxi ride, even for short distances. Rideshare apps like Uber and Lyft are not available in Iceland.

Cycling

Cycling in Iceland is a favorite pastime among locals and tourists. While seeing Iceland by bicycle can be exhilarating and budget friendly, the downside is that the weather is unpredictable, even in the summer. There are summers that are relatively dry and sunny, but realistically, you need to be prepared for rain, and lots of it. Some cyclists are lured by gorgeous landscape photos and the thrill of long summer days, but are challenged by keeping themselves dry and motivated. Also, bike theft is rampant on the island, so you must be vigilant in keeping your bicycle and gear under lock and key. The plus side, however, is that you get to see the country powered by your own two feet, and you have the freedom to control how long you stay at sites without being tied to a tour bus. There are numerous well-kept **bike paths** throughout the country, and brochures with trail information are available at tourist information offices. The best advice is to plan, plan, and plan some more for challenging roads and unpredictable weather.

Hitchhiking

Hitchhiking is common practice, and legal, in Iceland, as it's a safe country with lots of drivers. If you are attempting to hitch along busier routes such as along the Reykjanes Peninsula, you will likely have more luck; in more remote destinations, it can be hit or miss. It's not advisable to be dependent on hitching in the winter months, because roads are less frequently traveled and the weather can be punishing. If you do score a ride, make sure you offer some **cash for gas.** It's just good form.

Visas and Officialdom

PASSPORTS AND VISAS

Visitors to Iceland must have a valid passport that will not expire within three months of your scheduled departure. Tourists from the United States, Canada, South Africa, Australia, and New Zealand do not need a visa if they are traveling to Iceland for fewer than 90 days. If you want to stay longer, you need to apply for a residence permit at the Icelandic immigration office (www.utl.is). For Europeans, Iceland is part of the Schengen Agreement, which allows free travel between Iceland and European Economic Area (EEA) and European Union (EU) countries; visas are not necessary.

Icelandic Embassies and Consulates Abroad

Iceland has embassies in a number of countries, including:

- **Canada:** 360 Albert St., Suite 710, Ottawa, ON K1R 7X7; tel. 613/482-1944; www.iceland.is/ca

- **United Kingdom:** 2A Hans St, London SW1X 0JE; tel. 20/7259-3999; www.iceland.is/uk
- **United States:** 2900 K St. NW, Suite 509, Washington, DC 20007; tel. 202/265-6653; www.iceland.is/us

Foreign Embassies and Consulates in Iceland

If you have an emergency while traveling in Iceland and require assistance (for example, if you lose your passport), contact your embassy for help. Embassies in **Reykjavík** include:

- **Canada:** Túngata 14; tel. 354/575-6500; rkjvk@international.gc.ca
- **United Kingdom:** Laufásvegur 31; tel. 354/550-5100; info@britishembassy.is
- **United States:** Engjateigur 7; tel. 354/595-2200; reykjavikconsular@state.gov

Customs

Getting through customs in Iceland is quite easy compared to most other countries in Europe.

Travelers can import **duty-free** alcoholic beverages and tobacco products as follows: 1 liter of spirits, 1 liter of wine, and 1 carton or 250g of tobacco products; or 1 liter of spirits, 6 liters of beer, and 1 carton or 250g of tobacco products; or 1.5 liters of wine, 6 liters of beer, and 1 carton or 250g of tobacco products; or 3 liters wine and 1 carton or 250g of tobacco products. The minimum age for bringing alcoholic beverages into Iceland is 20 years; for tobacco, it's 18 years.

Iceland has a zero-tolerance policy on drugs, and all meat, raw-egg products, and unpasteurized dairy will be confiscated.

For additional information, visit the official **customs website** (www.tollur.is).

Recreation

Iceland truly is a nature buff's playground. There is much to do, and locals are thrilled to have you explore their treasured land—safely and responsibly. If you are heading out on a hike or a climb, report your whereabouts. Also, be sure to closely monitor weather conditions, bring all the water and gear you need with you, and be careful. Iceland's rescue team is often called upon to save unprepared tourists in completely avoidable situations. Have fun, but be safe.

HIKING

Hiking is by far the most popular outdoor activity on the island; its stretches of land beg to be explored. Hikers have their choice of terrain, whether they're looking for vast lava fields, steep mountains, or enormous glaciers. Hiking maps can be found in tourist shops around the country as well as in gas stations. Hikes can range from easy walks to very challenging. You should always be prepared before setting out for the day.

Do not underestimate the weather in Iceland—always dress appropriately for the activity of the day. The key is to be well prepared, safe, and smart. Monitor weather conditions, have all the proper equipment with you, and alert authorities about your plans at **www.safetravel.is.** In case something happens during your trip, the search and rescue teams will know where to look for you. While hiking is a beautiful way to explore the island, most emergency calls to the rescue service are due to ill-prepared tourists finding themselves in a predicament on a hiking expedition gone wrong. It cannot be overstated that you must respect Iceland's raw and sometimes treacherous nature.

Detailed maps are available at regional tourist information offices as well as online at the **Ferðafélag Íslands (Icelandic Touring Association)** (www.fi.is).

GLACIER WALKING

Walking on a glacier is an ideal way to get up close and personal with the actual ice in Iceland. There are numerous tours offered that provide guided glacier walks, ice climbing, and visiting ice caves. You should never attempt to walk on a glacier without a tour guide as it can be very dangerous. People have been known to fall through crevices. Some companies that offer tours include Icelandic Mountain Guides (https://www.mountainguides.is) and Reykjavik Excursions (www.re.is).

WILDLIFE WATCHING

It's possible to see wildlife in every region of Iceland and there are tours available to make it easier. You can watch whales, seals, dolphins, puffins, and even reindeer (only in the east of Iceland). These tours are family-friendly activities, and expert guides will explain everything about the species and their habitats. Please note that puffin-watching tours are only available in the summer.

SCUBA DIVING

Scuba diving in the Silfra fissure in Þingvellir National Park is a wonderful way to explore Iceland under the water. You will be fitted with a drysuit, provided with the proper gear and instructions, and will have an expert guide with you. There's even an opportunity for underwater photographs to be taken. The company Dive Iceland provides tours; you can see more details at www.dive.is.

FISHING

Fishing is how many Icelanders make their living, so who has fishing rights can be political. Your best bet is to sign up for a tour with a local operator who handles the necessary permit as well as bait and gear. A good place to start is through the tour operator **Iceland Fishing Guide** (www.icelandfishingguide.com), which offers fishing tours in Iceland's lakes, rivers, and streams. You have a chance at catching salmon, trout, and arctic char, depending on the tour location.

SWIMMING

Swimming is a big part of Icelandic culture. That may sound strange given the chilly temps compared to, say, Spain or Florida, but an Icelander's local swimming pool is part of his or her social scene. If you visit a pool, you will notice groups of Icelanders, friends and family, sitting in hot tubs, sunrooms, or in the children's pool with their little ones. They love the water and they love to socialize. Pools are heated, and many have extensive facilities that include a gym, sauna, and several hot tubs. There are more than 120 swimming pools in Iceland, and they are well used, no matter the weather. Even outdoor pools can be full when there is a light snowfall.

The part about Iceland's swimming culture that frazzles some tourists is the communal showering that takes place before and after your swim. In the gender-divided locker rooms, you will see Icelanders showering stark naked—that's right, sans bathing suit—and you're expected to do the same. You must thoroughly clean yourself before you join the pool. At larger pools, there are often attendants who make sure that visitors shower. Locals are used to shy visitors and find it amusing, but at the end of the day, it just doesn't matter. After a couple of visits to the pool, you get used to it.

Towels and lockers are available at the local pools, and some rent out bathing suits as well. Some pools have fitness centers as well as an area to purchase soft drinks.

Festivals and Events

There's always something going on in Iceland—and whether it's the Viking Festival in June celebrating the country's roots, or the huge Iceland Airwaves music festival in the autumn, there's something for everyone.

WINTER

WINTER LIGHTS FESTIVAL

Reykjavík; early Feb.

Held over four days, the Winter Lights Festival brightens up Reykjavík each winter with art exhibitions and light installations. The main event is an installation projected onto the famous Hallgrímskirkja church in downtown Reykavík.

SPRING

DESIGNMARCH (HönnunarMars)

Reykjavík; early Mar.

Typically held in early March over four days, DesignMarch showcases the newest and best Icelandic design in pop-up shops, lectures, and fun events around the city.

REYKJAVÍK BLUES FESTIVAL (Blúshátíð í Reykjavík)

Reykjavík; early Apr.

For a week in early April, blues music enthusiasts from around the world descend on Reykjavík for this annual festival that features international musicians and local artists.

REYKJAVÍK INTERNATIONAL LITERARY FESTIVAL

Reykjavík; Apr.

Every April, Reykjavík celebrates local and international authors during this five-day festival. The program includes discussions, readings, workshops, meet and greets, and lectures.

REYKJAVÍK ARTS FESTIVAL (Listahátíð í Reykjavík)

Reykjavík; late May-early June

For two weeks over late May and early June, Reykjavík is treated to exhibitions and outdoor installations of local and international artists.

VIKING FESTIVAL

Hafnarfjörður; mid-June

Just outside Reykjavík, the annual Viking Festival in mid-June has fun reenactments of fights with traditional dress and weaponry, as well as food, music, and a market. The week-long festival is great for kids.

SUMMER

REYKJAVÍK JAZZ FESTIVAL (Jazzhátíð Reykjavíkur)

Reykjavík; mid-Aug.

It may seem unexpected, but Icelanders have an affinity for jazz music, and they put on a great annual festival over five days in mid-August that features local and international musicians.

CULTURE NIGHT (Menningarnótt)

Reykjavík; end of Aug.

Held at the end of August, this daylong event is the biggest and most popular festival in Iceland, with more than 100,000 people participating. There's live music, food, and art to celebrate the end of the summer and Iceland's rich culture.

FALL

REYKJAVÍK INTERNATIONAL FILM FESTIVAL

Reykjavík; end of Sept.

Beginning at the end of September, this 11-day festival showcases short films, documentaries, and features from more than 40 countries.

ICELAND AIRWAVES

Reykjavík; late Oct.-early Nov.

The largest music festival of the year features more than 200 local and international artists over five days; in the past performers have included Kraftwerk, The Flaming Lips, and local band Of Monsters and Men.

Food

TYPICAL FARE

Descriptions of Icelandic food depends on who you ask. Certainly, fish and lamb take center stage. Typical fare can range from light to hearty. Local produce means what can survive outdoors (potatoes, rhubarb, moss) and what is grown in greenhouses (tomatoes, cucumbers, broccoli). Most of Iceland's food is imported, and it isn't cheap.

Local fish includes cod (fresh and salted), salmon, lobster, mussels, halibut, trout, and haddock. A classic Icelandic dish is whitefish cooked in a white sauce with potatoes and onions. A popular snack is hardfish, which is like a whitefish jerky, where the fish is dried and seasoned.

As for meat, lamb is the most prevalent, but there is plenty of beef, pork, and chicken in the Icelandic diet. Some Icelanders also indulge in horse and whale meat as well.

Hot dogs are wildly popular among Icelanders. Called **pylsur,** Icelandic hot dogs are done up in a traditional bun with chopped onions, mustard, ketchup, crispy fried onions, and pickled mayonnaise. They're delicious.

Dairy is an important part of Icelanders' diets, including milk, cheese, butter, and the yogurt-like soft cheese called **skyr,** which you should try. It's very tasty and chock-full of protein. Icelanders are also known to eat ice cream all year long, despite the weather. There are quite a few popular ice cream shops around Reykjavík, and the ice cream sections in supermarkets offer an astounding number of locally produced choices.

Once a year, Icelanders celebrate the traditional foods of the nation, which sustained their ancestors through the ages. The winter festival, called **Þorrablót,** features svið (singed lamb head), blood pudding, lamb intestines and stomach, ram's testicles, fermented shark, seal flippers, hardfish, and rye bread. The food that gets the most attention from foreigners is rotten shark or **hákarl,** which is meat from Greenland shark. The flesh is put through an interesting process: It's buried for at least two months and then is hung for another three or four months to cure. If you dare, hákarl is available in small containers for sale throughout Iceland. It's an experience you will not forget—if not the taste, then definitely the smell.

RESTAURANTS

Reykjavík is home to some excellent fine-dining establishments and casual eateries, but eating cheaply in Reykjavík, or on the island as a whole, is not easy. Hours tend to change depending on the season, but for the most part restaurants open their doors for lunch around 11:30am, and kitchens tend to close around 9pm.

Outside of Reykjavík and Akureyri, you will find a lot of fish and lamb restaurants that focus on local cuisine, but inside the two main cities, you have a lot to choose from. You will find sushi, tapas, Indian food, hamburger joints, noodle bars, kebab houses, and Italian restaurants, to name a few. International cuisine has been growing in popularity over the last 20 years, and new and interesting spots are always cropping up. If you have your heart set on a certain restaurant, it would be best to reserve ahead, but walk-ins are possible. **Tipping** is not expected in Iceland, but it is not considered an insult to tip.

DRINKING

The water in Iceland is pure and some of the tastiest in the world. Drinking from the tap is common and safe, and bottled water is frowned upon. Iceland is also a coffee-drinking nation. If you're a tea drinker, you will find some basic choices in coffee shops, but Icelanders are crazy about their coffee.

As for alcohol, given the expensive prices, beer is often the drink of choice when going out to a bar. And, believe it or not, beer is still relatively new to Iceland. A countrywide alcohol ban went into effect in 1915; the ban was relaxed in phases, with first wine and then strong liquors permitted, and beer eventually became legal to sell in 1989. Outside of bars, alcohol is available only at the government-run shops called **Vínbúðin.**

Accommodations

HOTELS

Iceland is not necessarily known for posh hotels, but there is a good mix of "upscale" accommodations, mid-level boutiques, and budget hotels. The "fanciest" options on the island are in Reykjavík, namely Reykjavík Edition and Hilton Canopy, which cater to guests who are willing to pay for top-notch service and amenities. Reykjavík also has mid-range boutique or family-run options if you are looking for something a bit more formal than a guesthouse.

Outside of Reykjavík, hotels tend to be of the local chain-hotel ilk in the form of **Fosshotels** (www.islandhotels.is), **Hótel Edda** (www.hoteledda.is), and **Icelandair Hótels** (www.icelandairhotels.is). They are clean, comfortable, and reliable options.

When they compare hotel prices to those in other European countries, some tourists feel that they don't get their money's worth. In fairness, Iceland is a more popular destination than it was 20 years ago, but it's still not meant to be a budget destination. In short, accommodations do cost a lot. Be prepared for shocking rates, especially in the summer months.

GUESTHOUSES

The most prevalent form of accommodation on the island is the guesthouse. Guesthouses range from comfortable bed-and-breakfasts that offer shared bathrooms and cooking facilities to more design-conscious options that are chic, modern, and fun. Some guesthouses in Reykjavík can still have "hotel-like" prices, as the competition for scoring a room in the high season has become almost a contact sport. Outside Reykjavík, however, guesthouses could be a good way to save a little money, depending on where you book. Always book a room in advance, as it's not recommended to leave where you will lay your head to chance.

HOSTELS

Hostels are another great option for the budget traveler, but as in guesthouses, beds tend to fill up, so make sure you book far in advance, especially in the summer. Some hostels in Reykjavík, like Kex Hostel and Loft Hostel, cater to young, music-conscious travelers, and beds are almost an afterthought. There is frequently live music in the lounge areas, and the bar is always packed with locals and tourists. Other hostel options cater to a more mature crowd looking to avoid the high hotel rates. Kex Hostel would be a good option for those travelers. Outside of Reykjavík, hostels are prevalent and it's key to book ahead.

SLEEPING BAG ACCOMMODATIONS

Some guesthouses and hostels around Iceland offer travelers sleeping bag accommodations, which can be great for the budget traveler. For a low price, guests can bring their sleeping bags and have access to shared bathroom facilities.

MOUNTAIN HUTS

Not to be confused with emergency huts, mountain huts are similar to cabin-style accommodation, with many providing a cozy, hostel-like atmosphere with bunk beds. Huts have running water, and there is usually a shared dining hall. As tourism in Iceland has increased, it has become necessary to book in advance to guarantee a place.

For more information, visit the website of **Icelandic Touring Association (Ferðafélag Íslands)** (www.fi.is), which runs several mountain huts around the country.

CAMPING

Camping can be a great option for some travelers, but be prepared. If you're going it alone with a tent, make sure you're ready for any type of weather—it can be unpredictable (even in summer), and you may be on the island during a good week, but maybe not.

There are campsites around the country that allow for tents as well as campers and RVs. Facilities vary; some campsites have top-notch cooking areas and steaming-hot showers, while others have adequate cooking facilities and just toilets.

Be advised that wild camping is strictly prohibited in Iceland, so travelers must stay in campsites. Those who break the law face steep fines.

Most campsites are open mid-May to mid-September. It's not necessary to book a site well in advance. To see a list of campsites, visit www.nat.is/camping/camping_sites.htm.

The main camping information centers in Iceland are:

- **Reykjavík:** info@visitreykjavik.is
- **Leifsstöð** (Keflavík International Airport): touristinfo@reykjanesbaer.is
- **Reykjanesbær** (Southwest Iceland): icelandreykjanes@reykjanesbaer.is
- **Borgarnes** (West Iceland): tourinfo@vesturland.is
- **Ísafjörður** (Westfjords): info@vestfirdir.is
- **Varmahlíð** (Northwest Iceland): upplysingar@skagafjordur.is
- **Akureyri** (North Iceland): tourinfo@est.is
- **Egilsstaðir** (East Iceland): info@east.is
- **Seyðisfjörður** (East Iceland): ferdamenning@sfk.is
- **Höfn** (Southeast Iceland): tourinfo@hornafjordur.is
- **Hveragerði** (South Iceland): tourinfo@hveragerdi.is

Health and Safety

VACCINATIONS

In March 2022, Iceland lifted all COVID restrictions. You do not need to show vaccination status or a negative COVID test prior to entering the country.

MEDICAL SERVICES

The Icelandic health-care system is top-notch, with hospitals in each large town and health clinics in smaller villages and hamlets. Most doctors, nurses, and emergency medical staff speak English. Non-EU citizens must pay for health services provided. If you are having a medical emergency, dial the number **112. Pharmacies** (called **apótek**) hold everything from prescription medication to aspirin. Some tourists from North America find it frustrating that cold medicine and aspirin cannot be bought in supermarkets, only at the pharmacy. Pharmacies are typically open 10am-9pm Monday-Friday, 10am-4pm Saturday, and are closed on Sunday and public holidays.

WEATHER

Weather is the number one safety concern in Iceland, trumping everything from violent crime to volcanic eruptions. The main danger is how fast weather can change. It could be a bright, sunny day when you head out on a trek in the highlands, but there could be a storm brewing that will bring high winds, rain, hail, and snow. And the storm could pass as quickly as it arrived. The joke among locals is that if you don't like the weather in Iceland, wait five minutes. The best defense against inclement weather is to closely monitor weather forecasts and obey advisories. You can check frequently updated forecasts at **www.vedur.is.** Icelanders deal with the weather by being flexible and never confirming plans far in advance. They learn to adapt after a lifetime of battling gale-force winds.

EMERGENCY HUTS

Iceland's emergency huts are strictly for emergencies. Don't even think of staying in one unless you are, in fact, experiencing an emergency. The huts are painted bright orange and are based in isolated areas. Inside the hut, you will find, water, food, bedding, and an emergency radio that will allow you to call for help. The huts can be located on maps, usually depicted as a red house. If you find yourself amid a storm, hunker down in an emergency hut and call for help by dialing the emergency number **112.**

CRIME

Crime is quite low in Iceland and is mostly limited to theft and vandalism; violent crime is rare. Be vigilant in protecting your possessions (especially bicycles) and trust your instincts. If you're out at night on Laugavegur in downtown Reykjavík on weekends, you might encounter loud and drunk locals or tourists. If you are a victim of a crime, contact the police by dialing the emergency number, **112;** all police officers are proficient in English.

Practical Details

WHAT TO PACK

How you pack depends on where you plan to go and what you're going to do on the island. If you're going for a "city-break" long weekend to Reykjavík, you can afford to pack light; however, if you plan on an extended stay that includes camping, packing light is not an option. Here are some suggestions and tips for your time in Iceland.

Clothing

The key to dressing warm and being comfortable in Iceland is **layers.** Depending on the weather, it can be a cotton T-shirt, fleece or sweater, parka or windbreaker, and perhaps a hat, scarf, and gloves. If it's summer and the sun is shining, it's common to see locals wearing a T-shirt in 15°C (60°F) weather. It's important to keep comfortable and add layers if the temperature warrants it. If you're out hiking, wearing **waterproof gear** along with proper hiking attire is key. Make sure fabrics are breathable and comfortable and underlayers are cotton.

Formal attire in Iceland is reserved for work or funerals; if you want to bring a nice outfit along for a "fancy" dinner, by all means, pack something, but you won't find stringent dress codes anywhere on this island. Lastly, a **bathing suit** is necessary. Chances are you'll want to take a dip in a pool or hot spring.

OUTERWEAR

Because the temperature varies so much depending on time of day, season, and where you are in the country, it's a good idea to bring a **hat, scarf,** and **gloves.** As for jackets, the best advice is to bring something waterproof; whether it's a **windbreaker** for summer or a **parka** for winter, you are likely to encounter rain at some point on your trip. If you need to go shopping for warmer layers in Iceland, expect to pay. Clothes are not cheap in Iceland.

FOOTWEAR

Again, if you are staying in Reykjavík for the duration of your trip, and don't plan to climb mountains, you don't need to invest in an expensive pair of hiking boots. That said, if you do plan to be outdoors quite a

Budgeting

Iceland is not a cheap place to visit. Don't be fooled by the news stories that declared Iceland cut prices to accommodate tourists after its economic crisis of 2008. That period was brief, and Iceland remains an expensive destination. Prices on accommodations, food, gas, and everyday necessities remain high, compared to many other countries. Here is a list showing prices of common items:

- **Milk (1 L):** 185ISK
- **Loaf of bread:** 440ISK
- **Dozen eggs:** 692ISK
- **Apples (1 kg):** 352ISK
- **Potatoes (1 kg):** 302ISK
- **Coke/Pepsi:** 336ISK
- **Meal for two:** 12,000ISK
- **Domestic beer:** 1,200ISK
- **Bottle of wine:** 2,500ISK
- **Pack of cigarettes:** 1,500ISK
- **Bus ticket (one-way):** 490ISK
- **Gasoline (1 L):** 241ISK
- **Average double hotel room:** 26,000ISK
- **Car rentals:** 21,000-52,000ISK per day

bit, **hiking boots** are a great idea. You will need a pair of shoes that can withstand rain, rocks, ice, mud, puddles, sand, and sometimes snow. It's recommended to buy boots in your home country because shoes can be expensive in Iceland, and it's not the best idea to break in a brand-new pair of boots if you plan to do a lot of walking and/or climbing. Comfort is key. **Socks** are also important to consider. You want socks that are breathable yet thick enough to keep you comfortable in your shoes/boots.

Camping Gear

If camping is in your plan, don't scrimp on the quality of the **tent** you bring. And, make no mistake, you should bring the tent with you, as quality tents are, you guessed it, expensive in Iceland. You will need something waterproof that can endure punishing winds. A **sleeping bag** is necessary for campers, but it's also great to have a sleeping bag for guesthouses and hostels, some of which offer sleeping bag accommodations at a much lower price. Be sure to call ahead to see if they're available. Because of the likelihood of encountering rain, a sleeping bag made from a synthetic material is the best option, and it should be able to withstand -9°C (15°F) temperatures in the summer and -18°C (0°F) in the winter. If you decide to camp, be sure to monitor weather conditions and be safe.

MONEY

Exchange Rates

The official currency of Iceland is the **króna** (abbreviated kr or ISK). The króna fluctuates often; at the time of writing, the exchange rate was 125ISK to US$1, 98ISK to CAD$1, 170ISK to GBP1, 142ISK to EUR1, 89ISK to AUD$1, 83ISK to NZD$1, and 828ISK to 100ZAR.

There are banknotes in the amounts of 500, 1,000, 5,000, and 10,000, and coins in the amounts of 1, 5, 10, 50, and 100 kronur. Coins are handy for having exact change for the local bus in Reykjavík.

Currency exchange is available at the airport and banks as well as tourist information offices. **ATMs** are available at all banks as well as supermarkets and other shops.

Banks

Banking hours are 9:15am-4pm Monday-Friday, and ATMs are available 24/7. There may be a limit on the amount of cash you can withdraw per your home bank's policy.

Credit Cards

Your best bet to get the most favorable exchange is to use your credit card. Cash overall is not a popular payment method; locals are known to use debit and credit cards for just about every transaction. Using plastic is so common in Iceland that many tourists will not need cash for anything; you can pay for parking, public toilets, and even campsite fees with a credit card. However, you may want to carry a little cash on you if you plan on **tipping** a guide for an excursion; guides will gladly accept any currency.

Visa and MasterCard are the two main credit cards accepted in Iceland. Please note that Iceland uses the chip and PIN system, which requires a 4-digit PIN for transactions, including at unmanned gas stations. If your card does not have a PIN, it's best to contact your home bank or credit card issuer before traveling to Iceland. ATMs are widely available.

OPENING HOURS

Most businesses in Iceland operate between 9am-6pm during weekdays and 10am-4pm on Saturdays. Many shops are closed on Sundays, with the exception of grocery stores and some shops that choose to have limited hours.

Public Holidays

Businesses in Iceland close on the following holidays:

- January 1: **New Year's Day**
- March or April: **Maundy Thursday**
- March or April: **Good Friday**
- March or April: **Easter Sunday**
- March or April: **Easter Monday**
- First Thursday after April 18: **First day of summer**
- May 1: **Labor Day**
- May or June: **Ascension Day**
- May or June: **Whitsun**
- May or June: **Whit Monday**
- June 17: **Icelandic National Day** (commemorates achieving independence from Denmark in 1944)
- First Monday in August: **Trading Day**
- December 24: **Christmas Eve**
- December 25: **Christmas Day**
- December 26: **Second day of Christmas**
- December 31: **New Year's Eve**

COMMUNICATIONS

Phones and Cell Phones

The country code for Iceland is **354.** There are no area codes; if you are calling from within the country, just dial the seven-digit phone number and you will connect.

Icelanders love their mobile phones, and for that reason pay phones became obsolete several years ago. You can purchase **international phone cards** at local shops (called **sjoppas**) as well as at post offices and gas stations. SIM cards are also available from providers **Vodafone** (www.vodafone.is) and **Siminn** (www.siminn.is) and can be purchased from phone retail shops, gas stations, and the airport.

Cell phone coverage in the countryside is surprisingly strong. You can buy phone credit refills for any amount, but 1,000ISK or 2,000ISK is recommended.

Most European mobile phones work on Iceland's network, but most North American phones use a different standard. You may need to contact your service provider to unlock your mobile phone for use abroad.

Internet Access

Iceland is wired, with Wi-Fi hot spots all over the country, even in the remote highlands. Hotels typically have free Wi-Fi, as do many coffeehouses.

Printed and Online News

Given its small population, it's refreshing to see Reykjavík is such a die-hard newspaper town. Locals have several Icelandic-language print publications and websites to choose from, but publishers haven't forgotten about English-language readers. The ***Reykjavík Grapevine*** (www.grapevine.is) is the unofficial guide to music, museum exhibitions, restaurant reviews, and just about every cultural event in the city. The website is updated daily, and the free print edition comes out every two weeks in the summer and monthly in the winter. ***Iceland Review*** (www.icelandreview.com) is the main English-language glossy magazine on the island. You will find in-depth features on travel, culture, and business issues as well as gorgeous photography.

RUV (www.ruv.is) is Iceland's national public-service broadcasting organization, which consists of one television channel and two radio stations. RUV's television programs feature news, dramas, and documentaries, as well as programming from foreign countries, including the United States, Denmark, and Sweden.

Shipping and Postal Service

It costs about 500ISK to mail a letter from Iceland to the United States. Business hours for post offices in Reykjavík are typically 9am-5pm Monday-Friday, but post offices in the countryside may have shorter hours. More information about post office services, locations, and hours can be found at www.postur.is/en.

MAPS AND TOURIST INFORMATION

Visit Iceland (www.visiticeland.com) is the main tourist information website for the country. The website has information on accommodations and activities for each region in Iceland.

To properly navigate Iceland, you need maps. That's a given. Lucky for you, they are available all over the island. You can pick up all-inclusive maps for the entire island as well as regional maps, road maps, and hiking maps at tourist information centers, bookstores, and gas stations. If you have the chance to purchase maps before your trip, do so, as they will likely be a lot cheaper in your home country. However, if you plan to stay in Reykjavík for the duration of your trip, it's not necessary to buy a map, because quite a few free maps do a nice job detailing downtown Reykjavík.

WEIGHTS AND MEASURES

Iceland uses the **metric system.** With regard to electricity, the standard voltage is **230 V** and the standard frequency is **50 Hz.** The power sockets that are used are type F, for plugs with two round pins. If you forget to bring an **adapter,** they can be purchased in most bookstores and tourist shops.

TIME ZONE

Iceland uses Greenwich mean time (GMT). However, the country does not observe daylight saving time, so Iceland is either four or five hours ahead of New York time, depending on the time of year.

As for the amount of daylight, what you've heard is true. The summers are full of long days, and darkness reigns supreme in the winter. To give you an idea of what that means, here are daylight hours for Reykjavík at different times of year:

- **January 1:** sunrise 11:20am, sunset 3:45pm
- **April 1:** sunrise 6:45am, sunset 8:20pm
- **July 1:** sunrise 3:05am, sunset midnight
- **October 1:** sunrise 7:30am, sunset 7pm

Travel Tips

TAX-FREE SHOPPING

As tourists encounter high prices for everything from accommodations to food, it only seems fair that you get a break when it comes to shopping.

A refund of local Value-Added Tax (VAT) is available to all visitors in Iceland. The refund will result in a reduction of up to 15 percent of the retail price, provided departure from Iceland is within three months after the date of purchase.

The fine print is that the refund does not apply to food or accommodations and the purchase must exceed 4,000ISK (VAT included) per store. Shops will provide you with a **tax-free form** (ask the store clerk for a "tax-free check"). Make sure you secure the forms and redeem the rebate at the cash-refund office at Keflavík airport before your flight. There, you will get an immediate cash refund.

You can also submit the receipts and paperwork by mail for a rebate on your credit card. This, of course, can take considerably longer.

TIPPING

Tipping is very new to Iceland. Workers in bars, restaurants, and hotels, as well as taxi drivers, earn a living wage and are not dependent on tips. In recent years, tip jars have cropped up in coffeehouses and bars, but it's just tourists who tend to tip.

ACCESS FOR TRAVELERS WITH DISABILITIES

Iceland has taken great strides in making as many tourist-related sites as wheelchair-accessible as possible. Visitors in wheelchairs will find that most museums, swimming pools, and restaurants provide access, as do transportation services. For instance, Keflavík International Airport and all domestic airlines can accommodate travelers in wheelchairs, and many buses come with automatic ramps to allow for easy boarding.

For more information on accessible travel, get in touch with the organization **Þekkingarmiðstöð Sjálfsbjargar** (tel. 354/550-0118; www.thekkingarmidstod.is). While the website is almost entirely in Icelandic only, information on traveling in Iceland has been translated into English (www.thekkingarmidstod.is/adgengi/accessible-tourism-in-iceland), and employees are happy to assist in English.

For information on services available to deaf travelers, contact the **Icelandic Association of the Deaf** (www.deaf.is), and for services for the sight-impaired, contact the **Icelandic Association of the Blind** (www.blind.is).

TRAVELING WITH CHILDREN

Children are the center of Icelandic society, and tourists traveling with children will feel right at home, whether in restaurants or museums or on child-appropriate tours. The island is a safe place for children, and many foreign travelers raise an eyebrow at how carefree parents can appear—whether it's a child walking around a shop, or an unaccompanied pram outside a coffeehouse. It's not irresponsible parenting, just a reflection on how safe Iceland is. While Iceland is safe, it needs to be said to always take care to watch out for the elements, whether it's high winds, a slippery surface, or cracks in a walking path.

As for attractions and restaurants, there are frequently **child rates** for museums and tours, and children's options on menus. Discounts can be as great as 50 percent for children under the age of 16.

WOMEN TRAVELING ALONE

Iceland is regularly ranked as being one of the best countries in the world in which to be a woman and a mother. Icelanders are proud to have elected the first woman president in the world as well as the first openly gay prime minister (a woman). However, Iceland is not a utopia. Women are subject to incidents of theft, intimidation, and physical violence. Always keep your wits about you, and if you are a victim of crime, contact the police at the emergency number 112.

LGBTQ TRAVELERS

Iceland is a leader in equality, and Reykjavík is one of the most gay-friendly cities in Europe. What many travelers find refreshing is that there is not just tolerance for gay, lesbian, bisexual, and transgendered individuals, but overwhelming love and acceptance of their fellow Icelanders. For instance, the gay pride festival, **Reykjavík Pride,** which takes place every August, attracts approximately 100,000 participants, for a country of just 320,000 people. As for laws, the LGBT community is protected from discrimination, gay marriage was legalized in 2010, and hate crimes are few and far between. For such a small population, it's hard to say there's a "gay scene," but there is one gay bar in Reykjavík, Kiki Queer Bar. More information can be found at the **Pink Iceland** website (www.pinkiceland.is).

TRAVELERS OF COLOR

Iceland is one of the least diverse countries in Europe, with immigrants accounting for around 11 percent of the population. That said, despite the country's homogeneity, Iceland is one of the safest countries on earth for its residents and tourists. There have been no reported acts of violence committed against tourists of color in Iceland in recent years, but if you feel that you have been a victim of a racially motivated crime or have been subject to discrimination, contact the police department at https://www.logreglan.is/english/. If it is an emergency, phone the emergency number 112.

For a Black perspective on living in Iceland, Jewells Chambers moved to Iceland from New York City in 2016 and runs the fun and informative blog All Things Iceland (www.allthingsiceland.com). She covers travel tips and life in Iceland through blog posts and videos.

Resources

Glossary

austur: east
bær: farm
bíll: car
bíó: movie theater
bjarg: rock, cliff
dalur: valley
ey: island
fjall: mountain
fjörður: fjord
fljót: river
flugvöllur: airport
foss: waterfall
gata: street
geysir: erupting hot spring
gistiheimilið: guesthouse
gríma: face mask
herbergi: room
hestur: horse
höfn: harbor
hradbanki: ATM
hraun: lava field
huldufólk: hidden people
Ísland: Iceland
jökull: glacier
kirkja: church
kort: map
laug: swimming pool
lopapeysa: Icelandic knitted sweater
lundi: puffin
norður: north
safn: museum
sími: telephone
stræti: street
strætó: bus
suður: south
sumar: summer
tjörn: pond
torg: town square
vatn: water
vedur: weather
vestur: west
vetur: winter

Icelandic Phrasebook

Icelandic is not the easiest language to understand. It's a North Germanic language that is related to Norwegian, Danish, and Swedish, but it has the added difficulty of declensions that the other languages lack. Icelandic nouns are declined in four cases, which stumps many people. Fortunately, just about everyone in Iceland speaks English.

The Icelandic alphabet has 32 letters, including letters not known in the English language, such as Ð and Þ. The letter Ð represents the sound "th" as in "this," while Þ represents "th" as in "thin."

PRONUNCIATION

Pronunciation can be very tricky, but Icelanders are thrilled when tourists give their language a shot. Be warned, though; if you attempt to speak an Icelandic phrase, your accent will tell them you're a foreigner, and they most likely will answer you in English.

Vowels

Some vowels in Icelandic have accent marks that modify the sound of each vowel. Vowels can come in long or short forms. In Icelandic, all vowels can be long or short. Vowels are long when they are in single-syllable words or when they form the penultimate syllable in two-syllable words.

A a like the "a" in "land"
Á á like "ow" in "cow"
E e like the "e" in "set"
É é like "ye" in "yet"
I i like "i" in "sit"
Í í like "ee" in "feet"
O o like the "o" in "not"
Ó ó like the "o" in "flow"
U u like the "u" in "put"
Ú ú like the "oo" in "soon"
Y y like the "i" in "sit"
Ý ý like the "ee" in "feet"
Æ æ like the "i" in "file"
Ö ö like the "ur" in "lure"

Consonants

Ð ð like "th" in "this"
J j like "y" in "year"
R r rolled, like Spanish "r"
Þ þ like "th" in "thin"

BASIC AND COURTEOUS EXPRESSIONS

Hello Halló
Good morning Góðan dag
Good evening Gott kvöld
How are you? Hvað segir þú?
Very well, thank you Mjog gott, takk fyrir
Good Allt gott
Not OK, bad Ekki gott
So-so Bara fint
OK Allt í lagí
And you? En þú?
Thank you Takk fyrir
Goodbye Bless
Nice to see you Gaman að sjá þig
See you later Sjáumst
Please Takk
Yes Já
No Nei
I don't know Ég veit ekki
Just a moment Augnablik
Excuse me Afsakið
What is your name? Hvað heiti þú?
Do you speak English? Talar þú ensku?
I don't speak Icelandic well. Ég tala ekki íslensku vel.
I don't understand. Ég skil ekki.
How do you say ... in Icelandic? Hvernig segir þú ... á íslensku?
My name is .... Ég heiti ....
What's your name? Hvað heitir þú?
Where is the bathroom? Hvar er salerni?

TERMS OF ADDRESS

I ég
you þú
he/him hann
she/her hún
we við
they þeir
girl stelpa
boy strakur
man maður
woman kona
wife eiginkona
husband eiginmaður
friend vinur
son sonur
daughter dóttir
brother bróðir
sister systir
father pabbi
mother mamma
grandfather afi
grandmother amma

FOOD

I'm hungry. Ég er svangur.
menu matseðil
May I have ...? Get ég fengið ...?
glass glas
fork gaffal
knife hnifur
spoon skeið

breakfast morgunmatur
lunch hádegisverður
dinner kvöldmatur
the check reikninginn
soda gos
coffee kaffi
tea te
water vatn
beer bjór
wine vín
white wine hvítvín
red wine rauðvín
milk mjólk
juice safi
cream rjómi
sugar sykur
egg egg
cheese ostur
yogurt jógúrt
almonds möndlur
cake kaka
bread brauð
butter smjör
salt salt
pepper pipar
garlic hvítlaukur
salad salat
vegetables grænmeti
carrot gulrót
corn korn
cucumber agúrka
lettuce kál
mushrooms sveppir
onion laukur
potato kartafla
spinach spinat
tomatoes tómatar
fruit ávextir
apple epli
orange appelsína
fish fiskur
meat kjöt
lamb lamb
beef nautakjöt
chicken kjúklingur
pork svínakjöt
bacon beikon
ham skinka

ACCOMMODATIONS

hotel hótel
guesthouse gistihús
Is there a room? Áttu laus herbergi?
May I see the room first? Má ég sjá herbergið fyrst?
What is the rate? Hvað kostar það?
Is there something cheaper? Ódýrara herbergi?
single room einsmanns herbergi
double room tveggjamanna herbergi
bathroom klósett
shower sturta
towels handklæði
soap sápa
toilet paper salernispappír
sheets rúmfötum
key lykill
heater hitari
manager framkvæmdastjóri

SHOPPING

money peningar
What is the exchange rate? Hvað er gengið á?
Do you accept credit cards? Tekur þú greiðslukort?
How much does it cost? Hvað kostar það?
expensive dýr
cheap ódýr
more meira
less minna
a little smá
too much of mikið

HEALTH

Help me! Hjálp!
I am ill. Ég er veikur.
I need a doctor. Ég þarf lækni.
hospital sjúkrahús
pharmacy apótek
pain verkir
fever hiti
headache höfuðverkur
stomachache magaverkur
burn brunablettur
cramp krampa
nausea ógleði

vomiting uppköst
antibiotic sýklalyf
pill pilla
aspirin aspirín
face mask gríma
vaccination bólusetning
ointment smyrsl
cotton bómull
condoms smokkur
toothbrush tannbursti
toothpaste tannkrem
dentist tannlæknir

TRANSPORTATION

Where is the ...? Hvar er ...?
How do I get to ...? Hvernig kemst ég til ...?
the bus station strætóstoppistöð
the bus stop strætóstopp
Where is the bus going? Hvert fer þessi strætó/rúta?
taxi leigubíll
boat bátur
airport flugvöllur
I'd like a ticket to ... Einn miða, aðra leiðina til ...
round-trip to ... Einn miða, báðar leiðir til ...
Stop here. Stoppaðu hér.
I want to rent a car. Get ég leigt bíl.
entrance inngangur
exit útgangur
to the; toward the til
right hægri
left vinstri
straight ahead beint áfram
past the ... framhjá ...
before the ... á undan ...
opposite the ... á móti ...
Watch for the ... Leita að ...
intersection gatnamót
street stræti
north; south norður; suður
east; west austur; vestur

STREET SIGNS

Stop Stans
One Way Einstefna
Yield Biðskylda
No Parking Engin Bílastæði
Speed Limit Hámarkshraði

AT THE GAS STATION

gas station bensínstöð
gasoline (petrol) bensín
diesel dísel
garage verkstæði
air loft
water vatn
oil change olíu skipti
tow truck dráttarbíll

VERBS

to buy að kaupa
to eat að borða
to climb að klifra
to do or make að gera
to go að fara
to love að elska
to want að vilja
to need að þurfa
to read að lesa
to write að skrifa
to stop að hætta
to arrive að koma
to stay að vera
to leave að fara
to look for að leita
to give að gefa
to carry að bera
to have að hafa

NUMBERS

zero núll
one einn
two tveir
three þrír
four fjörir
five fimm
six sex
seven sjö
eight átta
nine níu
10 tíu
11 ellefu
12 tólf
13 þrettán
14 fjórtán
15 fimmtán
16 sextán

17 sautján
18 átján
19 nítján
20 tuttugu
21 tuttugu og einn
30 þrjátíu
40 fjörutíu
50 fimmtíu
60 sextíu
70 sjötíu
80 áttatíu
90 níutíu
100 hundrað
101 hundrað og einn
200 tvö hundruð
500 fimm hundruð
1,000 þúsund
100,000 hundrað þúsund
1,000,000 milljón

TIME

What time is it? Hvað er klukkan?
It's one o'clock. Klukkan er eitt.
morning morgun
afternoon eftir hádegi
evening kvöld
night nótt
midnight miðnætti

DAYS AND MONTHS

Monday mánudagur
Tuesday þriðjudagur
Wednesday miðvikudagur
Thursday fimmtudagur
Friday föstudagur
Saturday laugardagur
Sunday sunnudagur
day dagur
today í dag
tomorrow á morgun
yesterday í gær
January janúar
February febrúar
March mars
April april
May maí
June júní
July júlí
August ágúst
September september
October október
November nóvember
December desember
early snemma
late seint
later seinna
before áður en

Suggested Reading

Guðmundsson, Einar Már. *Angels of the Universe.* 1997. This is a startling tale of a young man struggling with mental illness, set in Iceland in the 1960s. The book is disturbing at times, funny at others, and almost impossible to put down. It was made into a film in 2000, which was wildly popular in Iceland.

Helgason, Hallgrímur. *101 Reykjavík.* 2007. The protagonist, Hlynur, is a lazy, unemployed twentysomething who lives with his mother, watches a lot of pornography, and hangs out in bars in downtown Reykjavík. His life takes a turn when a former girlfriend announces she is pregnant and Hlynur becomes obsessed with his mother's lesbian lover. It's a fun, unexpected tale that was made into a popular movie in Iceland.

Indriðason, Arnaldur. *Jar City.* 2006. Arnaldur is Iceland's leading mystery author; he pens about one book a year. *Jar City* was the first of Arnaldur's books to feature detective Erlendur Sveinsson, who is a complicated man with a troubled relationship with his family and an obsession with solving Reykjavík's violent crimes. Other characters include his partner, Sigurður Óli, and a female colleague, Elínborg.

Kellogg, Robert. *The Sagas of Icelanders.* 2001. This huge volume includes 10 sagas and 7 shorter tales that give a wonderful overview of Iceland's history and literature. If you're looking for a short introduction, this isn't it. It's comprehensive and glorious.

Laxness, Halldór. *Independent People.* 1946. Laxness remains Iceland's sole recipient of the Nobel Prize for Literature for his novel *Independent People.* The tale follows the life of a Bjartur, a sheep farmer, as he grapples with life, loss, and the sacrifices he made to achieve independence. If you're going to read one Icelandic novel, this should be it.

Internet Resources

Discover North Iceland
www.northiceland.is

This is the regional tourism guide for North Iceland, which includes information on towns including Akureyri, Mývatn, and Húsavík. You will find events listings, accommodation information, and a large list of tour operators.

Icelandic Tourist Board
www.inspiredbyiceland.com

Iceland's tourist board provides a website with pages and pages of information for travelers. The site offers information on festivals, shopping, national parks, and outdoor activities like hiking, bird-watching, whale-watching, and catching the northern lights in the wintertime. There's also information on accommodations, tour operators, and maps.

Iceland Review
www.icelandreview.com

Iceland's main English-language magazine provides features on everything from culture to travel to politics. The website is worth checking out for in-depth articles as well as columns written by locals.

Reykjavík Grapevine
www.grapevine.is

Reykjavík's go-to English-language newspaper, which is published every two weeks in the summer and monthly in the winter, also maintains a website. You can bone up on local news as well as check out a listings section that details concerts, art exhibitions, and bars.

Visit East Iceland
www.east.is

Covering everywhere from Egilsstaðir to the Eastfjords, this tourism guide lists camping options, weather advisories, outdoor activities, and tour operators.

Visit South Iceland
www.south.is

Covering the south as well as the Reykjanes Peninsula, this tourism site offers detailed information on driving routes, maps, accommodation options, and tour operators. This region encompasses the Golden Circle as well as the Blue Lagoon.

Visit West Iceland
www.west.is

This is a regional tourism guide for the western section of the country, including Akranes, Borgarnes, Snæfellsnes, and the Westfjords. The site lists festivals and events, tour operators, and travel information for the region.

Index

A

B

C

D

E

F

G

H

I

JK

L

M

N

OP

R

S

T

V

WZ

List of Maps

Photo Credits

Title page photo: Björn Luðviksson;

page 4 © Supoj Taechapanyasin | Dreamstime.com; page 5 © Björn Luðviksson; page 6 © (top left) Jenna Gottlieb; (top right) Björn Luðviksson; (bottom) Saletomic | Dreamstime.com; page 7 © (top) Neurobite | Dreamstime.com; (bottom left) Bjorn Ludviksson; (bottom right) Svobodapavel | Dreamstime.com; page 8 © (top) Stacey Katz; page 9 © (top) Leonardospencer | Dreamstime.com; (bottom left) Jenna Gottlieb; (bottom right) Jenna Gottlieb; page 10 © Rndmst | Dreamstime.com; page 12 © (top) Checco | Dreamstime.com; (bottom) Jekaterina Sahmanova | Dreamstime.com; page 13 © (top) Björn Luðviksson; (middle) Alexeys | Dreamstime.com; (bottom) Jarcosa | Dreamstime.com; page 14 © Vitaliy Mateha | Dreamstime.com; page 15 © (top) Wasin Pummarin/123rf.com; (bottom) Mathiasrhode | Dreamstime.com; page 16 © Björn Luðviksson; Regardeauloin | Dreamstime.com; page 22 © Lance Anderson | Unsplash.com; Mpalis | Dreamstime.com; page 24 © (top) Oleksandr Korzhenko | Dreamstime.com; page 29 © Björn Luðviksson; page 30 © Hannamariah | Dreamstime.com; page 31 © (top left) Jenna Gottlieb; (top right) Michael Held | Unsplash.com; page 44 © (top) Takepicsforfun | Dreamstime.com; (left middle) Björn Luðviksson; (right middle) Bjorn Ludviksson; (bottom) Lilja Hauksdottir; page 49 © (top left) Bjorn Ludviksson; (top right) Björn Luðviksson; (bottom) Jenna Gottlieb; page 53 © (top left) Björn Luðviksson; (top right) Björn Luðviksson; (bottom) Bjorn Ludviksson; page 57 © (top left) Björn Luðviksson; (top right) Björn Luðviksson; (bottom) Marcin Kadziolka | Dreamstime.com; page 59 © Julia H Midland | Dreamstime.com; page 61 © (top) Bjorn Ludviksson; (bottom) Bjorn Ludviksson; page 67 © (top) Bjorn Ludviksson; (left middle) Bjorn Ludviksson; (right middle) Björn Luðviksson; (bottom) Bjorn Ludviksson; page 76 © Barbora Arnostova | Dreamstime.com; page 80 © (top) Alaskagm | Dreamstime.com; (bottom) Rudi1976 | Dreamstime.com; page 82 © Björn Luðviksson; page 83 © (top left) Björn Luðviksson; (top right) Laila Gebhard | Unsplash.com; page 93 © Ganna Stryzhekin | Dreamstime.com; page 101 © (top) Jenna Gottlieb; (bottom) Björn Luðviksson; page 103 © (top) Bjorn Ludviksson; (bottom) Fernando Silva | Unsplash.com; page 106 © Pitchathorn Chitnelawong | Dreamstime.com; page 108 © Bjorn Ludviksson; page 117 © (top) Stacey Katz; (bottom) Bjorn Ludviksson; page 122 © (top left) courtesy Meredith San Diego; (top right) Björn Luðviksson; (bottom) Sumos | Dreamstime.com; page 125 © (top) Bjorn Ludviksson; (left middle) Jenna Gottlieb; (right middle) Björn Luðviksson; (bottom) Björn Luðviksson; page 127 © Björn Luðviksson; page 129 © Stacey Katz; page 132 © Björn Luðviksson; page 133 © (top left) Mrallen | Dreamstime.com; (top right) Kavram | Dreamstime.com; page 139 © Björn Luðviksson; page 145 © (top left) Jenna Gottlieb; (top right) Bjorn Ludviksson; (bottom) Bjorn Ludviksson; page 148 © (top left) Bjorn Ludviksson; (top right) Jenna Gottlieb; (bottom) Bjorn Ludviksson; page 151 © (top) Maldesowhat | Dreamstime.com; (bottom) Oleksandr Korzhenko | Dreamstime.com; page 157 © Miroslav Liska | Dreamstime.com; page 159 © Björn Luðviksson; page 166 © (top) Björn Luðviksson; (bottom) Frédéric Maillard | Dreamstime.com; page 171 © (top left) Björn Luðviksson; (top right) Jenna Gottlieb; (bottom) Victorflowerfly | Dreamstime.com; page 174 © Stacey Katz; page 176 © Björn Luðviksson; page 177 © (top left) Rndmst | Dreamstime.com; (top right) Björn Luðviksson; page 179 © Shaiith | Dreamstime.com; page 183 © Santirf | Dreamstime.com; page 188 © Parys | Dreamstime.com; page 195 © (top left) Rudolft | Dreamstime.com; (top right) Lilja Hauksdottir; (bottom) Björn Luðviksson; page 199 © Deserttrends | Dreamstime.com; page 202 © (top left) Anna Pakutina | Dreamstime.com; (top right) Björn Luðviksson; (bottom left) Björn Luðviksson; (bottom right) Björn Luðviksson; page 212 © (top) Dalish | Dreamstime.com; (bottom) Jenna Gottlieb; page 216 © (top) Björn Luðviksson; (bottom) Lilja Hauksdottir; page 221 © (top) Björn Luðviksson; (bottom) Photopicturesproject | Dreamstime.com; page 225 © Björn Luðviksson; page 226 © minnystock | Dreamstime.com; page 228 © Zimu Liu | Dreamstime.com; page 229 © (top left) Fotograf9 | Dreamstime.com; (top right) Björn Luðviksson; page 240 © (top left) Yggdrasill33 | Dreamstime.com; (top right) Neurobite | Dreamstime.com; (bottom) Filip Fuxa | Dreamstime.com; page 245 © (top) Jenna Gottlieb; (bottom) Selenasoro | Dreamstime.com; page 254 © (top) Stacey Katz; (bottom) Oleksandr Korzhenko | Dreamstime.com; page 259 © (top) Lilja Hauksdottir; (left middle) Bjorn Ludviksson; (right middle) Jenna Gottlieb; (bottom) Shaiith | Dreamstime.com; page 261 © (top) Jenna Gottlieb; (bottom) Stacey Katz; page 264 © Bjorn Ludviksson; page 265 © (top left) Luciany | Dreamstime.com; (top right) Daniloforcellini | Dreamstime.com; page 270 © (top) Dmitry Naumov | Dreamstime.com; (left middle) Martinmolcan | Dreamstime.com; (right middle) Oleksandr Korzhenko | Dreamstime.

MAP SYMBOLS

- Highway
- Primary Road
- Secondary Road
- Unpaved Road
- Trail
- Ferry
- Railroad
- Pedestrian Walkway
- Stairs

- City/Town
- State Capital
- National Capital
- Highlight
- Point of Interest
- Accommodation
- Restaurant/Bar
- Other Location

- Information Center
- Parking Area
- Place of Worship
- Winery/Vineyard
- Trailhead
- Camping
- Train Station
- International Airport
- Regional Airport

- Park
- Golf Course
- Unique Feature
- Unique Feature Hydro
- Waterfall
- Mountain
- Ski Area
- Glacier

CONVERSION TABLES

°C = (°F - 32) / 1.8
°F = (°C x 1.8) + 32
1 inch = 2.54 centimeters (cm)
1 foot = 0.304 meters (m)
1 yard = 0.914 meters
1 mile = 1.6093 kilometers (km)
1 km = 0.6214 miles
1 fathom = 1.8288 m
1 chain = 20.1168 m
1 furlong = 201.168 m
1 acre = 0.4047 hectares
1 sq km = 100 hectares
1 sq mile = 2.59 square km
1 ounce = 28.35 grams
1 pound = 0.4536 kilograms
1 short ton = 0.90718 metric ton
1 short ton = 2,000 pounds
1 long ton = 1.016 metric tons
1 long ton = 2,240 pounds
1 metric ton = 1,000 kilograms
1 quart = 0.94635 liters
1 US gallon = 3.7854 liters
1 Imperial gallon = 4.5459 liters
1 nautical mile = 1.852 km

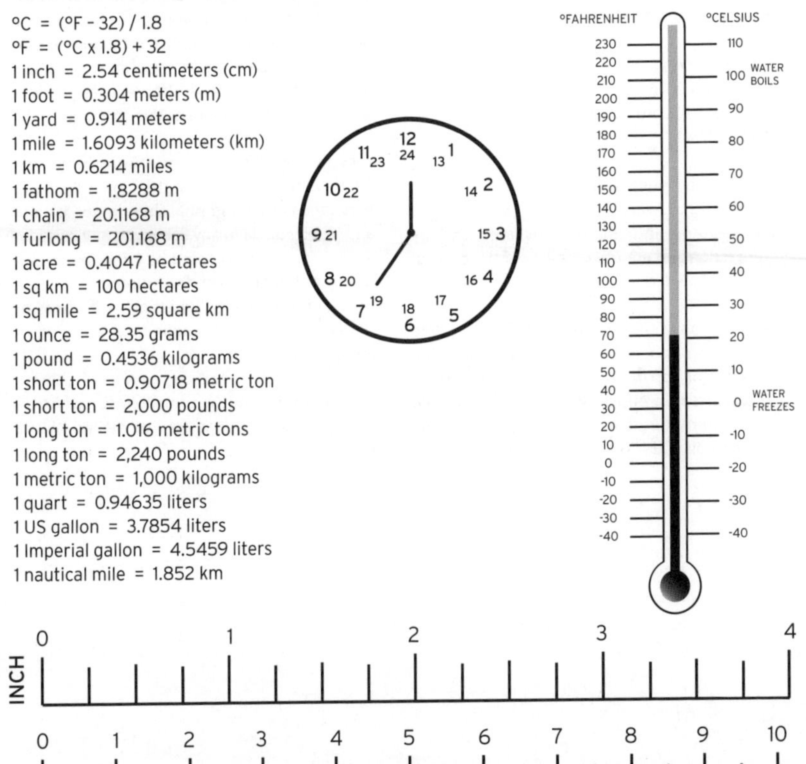

MOON ICELAND
Avalon Travel
Hachette Book Group
1700 Fourth Street
Berkeley, CA 94710, USA
www.moon.com

Editor: Megan Anderluh
Managing Editor: Hannah Brezack
Copy Editor: Jessica Gould
Graphics Coordinator: Ravina Schneider
Production Coordinator: Ravina Schneider
Cover Design: Toni Tajima
Interior Design: Domini Dragoone
Map Editor: Kat Bennett
Cartographers: John Culp, Lohnes + Wright, Brian Shotwell
Proofreader: Matthew Hoover
Indexer: Rachel Lyon

ISBN-13: 978-1-64049-706-1

Printing History
1st Edition —2016
4th Edition — February 2023
5 4 3 2

Front cover photo: Studlagil Canyon. Andrew Mayovskyy / Alamy Stock Photo
Back cover photo: Jökulsárlón Glacier Lagoon © Macsim | Dreamstime.com

Printed in Malaysia for Imago.